''STRANGERS'' OF THE ACADEMY

"STRANGERS"

OF THE ACADEMY

Asian Women Scholars
in Higher Education

Edited by

Guofang Li and *Gulbahar H. Beckett*

Foreword by
Shirley Geok-Lin Lim

STERLING, VIRGINIA

Sty/us

COPYRIGHT © 2006 BY
STYLUS PUBLISHING, LLC

Published by Stylus Publishing, LLC
22883 Quicksilver Drive
Sterling, Virginia 20166-2102

Library of Congress Cataloging-in-Publication Data
"Strangers" of the academy : Asian women scholars in
higher education / edited By Guofang Li and
Gulbahar H. Beckett ; foreword by Shirley Geok-Lin
Lim.—1st ed.
     p.   cm.
     ISBN 1-57922-120-3 (hardcover : alk. paper)—
     ISBN 1-57922-121-1 (pbk. : alk. paper)
     1. Asian American women college teachers—
United States.   2. Women scholars—United
States.   3. Discrimination in higher education—
United States.   I. Li, Guofang, 1972–
II. Beckett, Gulbahar, 1959–
LC2633.6.S84   2005
378.1'2'08995073—dc22   2004029617

ISBN: 1-57922-120-3 (cloth)
ISBN: 1-57922-121-1 (paper)

Printed in the United States of America

All first editions printed on acid free paper
that meets the American National Standards Institute
Z39–48 Standard.

First Edition, 2006

10 9 8 7 6 5 4 3 2 1

Dedicated to the loving memory of my mother, Chen Feng-Lan, a devoted mother and wife who remained invisible all her life.

GUOFANG LI

Dedicated to my master's thesis supervisor, Dr. Glenn Eastabrook, the first professor in Canada to teach me how to articulate critical issues like the ones included in this book effectively.

GULBAHAR H. BECKETT

CONTENTS

PART TWO: TEACHING, MENTORING, ADVISING, AND SECURING TENURE

PART THREE: GAINING VOICE, FORMING IDENTITY

ACKNOWLEDGMENTS

We sincerely thank the authors who contributed to this volume. Your excellent work has made this book possible. Many thanks to Shirley Geok-Lin Lim for the wonderful foreword and insightful feedback and comments on the chapters. Our appreciation also goes to our editor, John von Knorring, and the staff at Stylus Publishing, who have made the production of this book a pleasant experience. Many thanks also to Kelvin Beckett, Carol Frazier at the University of Cincinnati, and Chizuko Konishi at SUNY Buffalo for their editorial assistance. Our deepest appreciation goes to our family members for their love and support throughout the process.

IDENTITIES ASIAN, FEMALE, SCHOLAR

Critiques and Celebrations of the North American Academy

Shirley Geok-Lin Lim

"Strangers" of the Academy: Asian Women Scholars in Higher Education is a timely collection of essays that nonetheless displays the characteristic slipperiness of temporality in the subjects who narrate their identities and histories. Despite its clearly named focus on "Asian women scholars in higher education," many of the scholars and teachers whose professional stories are examined and interpreted here problematize or resist this naming. Their socialization in one original home culture and challenging resettlement in another very different society, their intellectual grounding in Western-based theories of self and other, autonomy and community, all bring into question and make impossible any easy or reductive notion of "Asian," "female," "scholarship," and even "education" in their understandings of their roles and identities in North American academe. Within the fascinating multiple layers of self-narrating and scholarly interpretations of "teacher stories" resides a core of ambivalence, contradiction, and paradox. For while many of these subjects begin as "strangers" in North American universities, their life stories trace their assimilation into these institutions and celebrate, albeit sometimes with and after struggle and painful adjustment, their increasing contributions to their adopted societies, whether in Canada, in the American South, or in the Midwest, in rural or in urban locations.

Hence, the chapters are concerned both with space—the movement of migrant Asian women into North American places of higher education, the contrast between first and second homeland territories—and with time—the inexorable compression of departures, arrivals, reorientations, personal transformation, and intellectual change and growth—bringing with them shifting relations and splits and reintegrated identities. Many of these essays may begin speaking as strangers in the academy but conclude by offering authoritative guidance to a twenty-first-century North American academe where education is multicultural and globalized, and faculty and students, now persuaded of the value of different perspectival epistemologies and of interdisciplinary methodologies, have come to value faculty from divergent backgrounds, including international, immigrant, and nonnative English-speaking women scholars.

The slipperiness in the subject of the "Asian woman scholar" is also evident in the slippages marked in these chapters, between Asian immigrant and Asian American, between foreign born and native born, between émigré and immigrant, between women of color and Asian women or Asian American women, between Asian women and Asian men, and so forth. The condition of immigration is first a condition of transit, of movement from an original home space to a new homeland, of giving up one society for another, of transformations. It is a condition of metamorphosis, with no prescribed time line; thus, these immigrant faculty and their experiences offer very complex materials for study, embedded as they are in multiple, declining, or emerging national, class, gender, and language structures. These are not the stories of butterflies emerging from chrysalides, a naturalized story of irresistible assimilation, the third world subject finding salvation in the new world. Instead, the chapters exhibit the strains in the ambitious attempt to encompass multiple, various, diverse, ever-changeful, vigilant, self-reflexive subjectivities and situations. On the one hand, many of these chapters speak of imaginations and intellects being reshaped by interlocutors and institutions and themselves reshaping their students, teachers, colleagues, and environment. On the other hand, for example, despite its title, the narratives in "Asian American Women in the Academy: Overcoming Stress and Overturning Denials in Advancement" concern Asian American women subjects rather than Asian immigrant women. In their recounting of two struggles for tenure, Loo and Ho locate ethnic difference and disciplinary bias as sources of discrimination, not second language or immigrant status, which form the major stressors in the texts by Asian immigrant women faculty.

In part 1 of the volume, "Asian Female Scholars in Context," Shirley Hune's opening mapping of the state of Asian Americans in U.S. higher education looks at a broader picture of faculty of color, teases out from these statistics the position of minority faculty women, then contrasts those figures with the different representations of Asian American men and women in

American higher education faculty. These contextual and imbricated employment figures, her chapter suggests, make the point that higher education policies bearing on diversity play across all racialized groups in the United States, even while, at the same time, it is important for the social scientist to take note of the particular consequences of such policies on distinct groups such as Asian Americans. Jaekyung Lee's analysis, based on a quantitative study of Asian American male and female students' career choices, offers this more particular approach, to nicely disrupt popular misconceptions about Asian American and women students; for example, his studies show that Asian American women students do better than their male non–Asian American counterparts in all science and engineering courses. The gender gap in achievement between male and female Asian American undergraduates in SME (science, mathematics, engineering) subjects is very narrow but becomes much more skewed in postgraduate work, pointing to the role of social forces in the different professional outcomes for Asian American women students. These two chapters demonstrate, as many others do, that the universal and the particular, the global and the local, the self and the other are always interrelated and form a holistic field and context of study.

The opening social-science-based approaches to the place of the Asian American woman scholar in U.S. higher education is well balanced in the volume's first section by Lin, Kubota, Motha, Wang, and Wong's chapter theorizing the concept of "lived experience" and the ways in which such experience may be mediated to offer valuable research resources for a "dialogic, public, political practice." Writing of their lived experiences collectively yet anonymously (using pen names for the subjects of their narratives), these scholars look for commonalities and patterns in their experiences through the critical apparatus of ideological critique, and finally propose for their discipline (second- and foreign-language education) an ethic of risk rather than an "ethic of control" that would valorize dialogic communication for "togetherness-in-difference." It is this kind of ideal—dialogic communication—that rules the spirit of the rest of the collection.

The next parts of the volume, "Teaching, Mentoring, Advising, and Securing Tenure" and "Gaining Voice, Forming Identity," are dominated by chapters by immigrant Chinese women faculty and by faculty in the field of second language and social science education. Inevitably there is some repetition in these chapters, but on the whole many of the chapters complement and supplement each other. Only a few chapters graph the bitterness of a struggle for academic legitimacy and respect, chiefly sited in the tenure process, but also existentially devolving around everyday moments of teacher-student interactions and acts of recognition or nonrecognition. Xiaoping Liang's interviews with three Chinese-speaking immigrant academics begin with the expected tales of alienation and discrimination, but soon it powerfully takes on, through Vygotsky's theory of the zone of proximate development (ZPD), the advantages of occupying an outsider-insider, marginal position and the ensuing discourse of direction, empowerment, and agency. To my mind, her analysis of these women's tactics—mediated, other-, and self-regulated strategies—offers useful insights for a successful institutional engagement for all women and junior faculty.

Such plangent notes of intellectual and professional striving are interwoven with close analyses of other equally important subjects, particularly that of the nature of relationships between student and faculty and between mentor and mentee. Samimy's, Guofang Li's, and Rong and Preissle's chapters develop and extend the extant literature on such relationships. Li takes on the conventional notion of the woman faculty of color serving as a role model to students of color to demonstrate that counterintuitive forces she terms "dysconscious racism" (citing King) act to de-legitimize her authority. "I had assumed," she wrote, "that Asian female doctoral students would be even more supportive and understanding of my achievement in becoming a professor in a Western institution as we share similar journeys." Her interpretation of their disrespect as operating out of a frame of race and gender biases inherent in the white and male hegemonic structure of the U.S. university is, as she notes, "one-sided and highly subjective"; yet in making her experience visible, Li is also able to insert a revised image of the Asian woman as oppressed by traditional patriarchal-dominant relations while at the same time emerging from these gender ideologies with a new "self and gender identity that is a hybrid . . . a sense of androgyny that is accompanied by our high level of occupational and educational attainment and personal fulfillment (citing Fong). The testimony of grievance together with the confident and brave voicing of a new empowered agency makes Li's chapter a compelling and frank study of a little-acknowledged phenomenon, the resistance not only of White but of minority students to minority women faculty.

Against this narrative of oppressive discriminatory relations, Rong and Preissle revise the conventional notion of mentoring to make the relation between mentor and student more equitable, so that reciprocity rather than charity, active exchange rather than unequal active-passive interchange, become the crux of the relationship. In their fascinating coauthored text, Rong and Preissle perform in writing the content of their thesis: that cross-cultural mentorship is "a dynamic reciprocal association" that does not merely provide "professional networking, counseling, guiding, instructing, modeling, and sponsorship," but at its highest level may produce "mutual cultural exploration," "foster equity," and result in collaborative, interdisciplinary, and even intergenerational research. The form of their chapter, structured in three voices, of Rong, Preissle, and "we," illustrates and illuminates their argument.

Reaching for philosophies that will enable them to cross and bridge social and cultural, epistemological and disciplinary borders, and apparent incommensurability, these faculty narrators present valuable criticisms and perspectives, revise institutional policies, and implement fresh pedagogical practices that contribute to the creation of new knowledge in higher education, both theoretical and practical. Yan Guo's chapter, for example, argues persuasively for the place of writing, not merely as a skill, but as a social practice, in professionalizing the Asian immigrant scholar; more significant is her expansion of the thesis, that nonnative English as a Second Language (ESL) scholars thus enjoy a unique privilege in their possession of not simply two languages and the educational systems that these languages structure, but also, in their experience of learning English itself as a second language, of a hybridity "between worlds," an intellectual locus now viewed as a valuable trait for new scholarship. Indeed, Pangsapa's celebration of the interdisciplinary department of women's studies as an institutional home for such transformative hybrid scholarship, for "activist politics and scholarly endeavors," is a useful reminder that the North American academy has spaces that welcome and encourage methodologies based on difference, where international, global, and "foreign" are folded into the broad content of women's histories, lives, and struggles for human rights.

The English language, spoken with or without an accent, and written in or against the grain of academic discourse, is a major thematic in these chapters; so also are the vocation and profession of the teacher/researcher. For many of these scholars, the two themes are not separate. Coming into actualization as a faculty person, the subject is also formed by the shaping forces of a second language, for, as Yan Guo notes, citing Ivanič, "Writing is an act of identity in which people align themselves with socio-culturally shaped possibilities for self-hood." If the sociocultural possibilities are perforce restrictive, nonetheless, the chapters by scholars such as Yan Guo, Guichun Zong, and others also make emphatic the rich potential in these possibilities: the mentors and collegial support, fellowships and employment prospects, processes for appeals and re-reviews, students who listen and praise, and entire apparatuses for revision, from revision of one's own writing to revision of the structures of higher education institutions themselves, all of which also have consequences for self-refashioning.

The volume does not carry the stories of the Asian immigrant women who have failed in academe; and there must, after all, be a few. Those discouraged, untenured, un- or underemployed. Those who abandoned dissertations and careers. Women who perhaps may never even have made it to university admission. Their self-reflections, to my mind, would have added a significant complexity to these interpretations of successfully emerged subjects. The collection also misses the points of view of a range of Asian women. With many Chinese immigrant faculty represented, the chapters include Korean, Thai, and South Asian subjects, but the sociocultural specificity of Chinese-mainland contexts in the volume must not be mistaken for the sum of Asian immigrant women experience. Nonetheless, despite these lacunae, *"Strangers" of the Academy* is an important pioneering publication. In taking the road less traveled, in Robert Frost's famous phrase, the subjects in these chapters have helped open for North American academe a new globalized world, one more dangerous after September 11, 2001, yet also more promising for the world's peoples, among whom North Americans are barely 5 percent. Asian American and Asian immigrant women faculty form hardly 2 percent of U.S. higher education faculty in all disciplines, and an even smaller percentage of faculty in teacher education and the humanities. Their contributions to their universities as practitioners of what Zong calls "global pedagogy" may thus be even more valuable for their scarcity.

These chapters, both when they critique and when they celebrate, serve as profound evidence of the kind of free inquiry and the valorization of the life of the mind that prevail in North American academes. It is this academic freedom that makes American universities the mighty engines of a civic society as well as the educational center for arts, sciences, professions, and business. In the multiversity, as these chapters testify, Asian American and Asian immigrant women scholars' unique contributions in teacher education, in language teaching, in the pedagogies of difference, and in other fields, are being recognized, albeit sometimes reluctantly and slowly. These chapters speak to the value—strategic, capitalistic, and humanist—that North American universities have placed on the stranger and the strange knowledge that the stranger carries with her identity. Their presence and scholarship are changing not just the face but the definition of higher education itself, calling into question any narrow, nationalistic mission and infusing the North American university with new curricula for a globalized knowledge base.

RECONSTRUCTING CULTURE AND IDENTITY IN THE ACADEMY

Asian Female Scholars Theorizing Their Experiences

Guofang Li and Gulbahar H. Beckett

This book project began over a coffee break at the American Educational Research Association in Seattle several years ago when we shared our own experiences and excitement as new faculty members trying to establish ourselves in the familiar yet strange academy. The academy was familiar to us because we were the apprentices of the academy for many years and we had learned the once unfamiliar discourses. Both of us were happy with our academic positions and were fortunate to have very supportive colleagues. Yet both of us felt we were "strangers" at times. After all, as Asian, foreign-born, and female faculty members, we were "newcomers" to the Western academy—we were "the traditional outsiders moving into the positions of tenure and/or administrative power" (Lim & Herrera-Sobek, 2000, p. 1). We both were faced with unfamiliar challenges such as gaining credibility as nonnative Teachers of English to Speakers of Other Languages (TESOL) professionals and as female scholars, and dealing with relations with students of Asian backgrounds. Sharing our personal and professional stories was an empowering experience—we understood better who we were as minority women and the path we had chosen. We believed that we were not alone. Realizing the power of sharing, we decided to edit a volume of works by Asian female scholars as a forum for our collective voice.

We wanted the academy to get acquainted with the Asian female "strangers" and to learn about these scholars' struggles and triumphs in their professional and personal lives. We also wanted a book for existing and aspiring minority faculty as a resource for their research, teaching, mentoring, and healing.

As we saw a need for a focused volume, we invited Asian female faculty members (and/or their mentors) to contribute and form such a forum. Although they come from a wide array of disciplines and backgrounds, many, like us, were not only "foreigners of one sort or another" (Kingston-Mann & Sieber, 2001) but also "outsiders within the academy" (Collins, 1986). These scholars combine research and personal narratives to explore the intersecting layers of relationships—language, culture, academic discourses, gender, class, age, generation, and race. Our objective in this volume is to highlight and celebrate Asian female scholars' struggles and triumphs when they try to "make it" in the academic environments that may differ from those in their countries of origin. By exploring their academic and personal experiences and theorizing them, we hope to contribute to the Asian women scholar's emerging effort to claim visibility and voice in the academy (Hune, 1999), as well as to the ongoing discussion on issues pertinent to the status of minority female scholars in higher education.

The Need to Tell Our Personal and Professional Stories

We feel there is an urgent need to tell our stories as Asian women because we have been living the outworn definitions of who we are in North America. Traditionally, Asian American women have been stereotyped as submissive, nonconfrontational, and dependent on Asian men. Living in the myth of the pleasing "model minority" images and in the shadow of Asian men, Asian females were rendered invisible in North American history (Fong, 1997; Hune, 1997). This invisible group, however, has had many triumphs in the past several decades. Unlike their predecessors who worked as lower-paid or unpaid laborers, Asian women have significantly increased their presence in a wide range of white-collar professions in North America in high-tech companies, the private sector, and in public administration. There is also a significant increase in their education levels and many have ventured into higher education as faculty members.

Although Asian female faculty members have made their way into higher education in the United States, they are underrepresented in the academy. Asian female faculty generally occupy the junior ranks and have one of the lowest tenure rates in the academy (Hune, 1999). In addition, they are also confronted with racial discrimination and stereotyping, as well as under-attention and disrespect for their research, teaching, and leadership. Despite these barriers, many Asian female faculty developed strategies to survive and thrive.

Since we are relative "newcomers" to the traditionally male-dominated academy, our trials and tribulations of surviving in the hierarchy remain un-examined. Our experiences living through the challenges of Western academic discourses are largely unknown. We believe by sharing our stories, we are able to reinvent "the bits and pieces of our experiences to create a coherent sense of meaning spanning past, present, and future" for Asian female scholars as a distinct cultural group in the Western academy (Florio-Ruane, 1997, p. 155). We hope that our stories are "educative" (McVee, in press) in the sense that they serve to redefine "who we are" in the academy and help negotiate better spaces for nurturing our new identities and growth in the years to come.

Reconstructing Culture and Identity and Reclaiming Voice: Outline of Chapters

The conceptual framework for this book consists of overarching themes that are foundational for understanding Asian female scholars in the Western academy. The chapters center on the personal, sociocultural, political, and academic issues encountered by Asian female scholars in higher education in cross-cultural contexts. First, like many women, Asian female scholars struggle with the double-edged sword of gender (the submissive who are eager to please) and the "model minority" (the educated and successful) stereotypes. In addition, they also experience barriers that are specific to their profession: (1) systematic gender and racial discrimination and marginalization within the hierarchy of higher education; (2) credibility issues as female and non-native English-speaking professionals; (3) difficulty in gaining tenure and promotion as minority faculty; (4) difficulty in building collegial relationships with White and fellow ethnic colleagues and students; (5) challenges in constructing positive cultural and professional identities; (6) complexity of multiple roles (e.g., minority researcher, professor, daughter, mother, and/or wife) that Asian female scholars must play within multiple value systems (e.g., Confucian/collectivism vs. individualism); and (7) challenges in developing strategies to overcome linguistic, cultural, and academic differences and thrive in the academy. These concerns permeate throughout the different "new stories of self" of the Asian female scholars who come from different cultural and linguistic backgrounds and who were trained in different disciplines and fields.

We have organized the chapters around four sections that reflect the varied aspects of our lived experiences as Asian female scholars in Western academe. These four sections are: (1) "Asian Female Scholars in Context"; (2) "Teaching, Mentoring, Advising, and Securing Tenure"; (3) "Gaining Voice, Forming Identity"; and (4) "Building Bridges, Building the Future." Together, the chapters within these themes portray the lived experiences, the trials and errors, and the struggles and triumphs of the Asian female scholars' journeys to success in the academy.

Part 1, "Asian Female Scholars in Context," comprises three chapters that contextualize and theorize Asian female scholars' lived experiences in a broader social and political milieu. Shirley Hune opens chapter 1 by situating Asian female scholars within the contested space between those who seek to preserve their place and privileges and those who want to create opportunities for women and minorities to attain equity within higher education. She addresses two important questions: How have Asian Pacific American (APA) women and men fared in academe since the 1980s? Have APA women overcome racial and gender disparities? Drawing on quantitative data, Hune demonstrates that APA women have made great strides in degree attainment at all levels, but APA men dominate as faculty and in tenured positions. Few APAs, especially women, are university presidents. Her analysis of qualitative studies shows that APA women experience greater barriers than APA men. The gendered, racialized, and sexualized spaces of academe contribute to their marginalization and devaluation and restrict their advancement in every sector. APA women remain outsiders and are far from being a "model minority." Hune argues that a cultural transformation of the climate, structure, and everyday practices of higher education is needed for APAs, but especially for APA women, to achieve their full potential.

Jaekyung Lee in chapter 2 draws upon national data from the 1993 Baccalaureate and Beyond Longitudinal Study and addresses two questions: Are Asian college male students different from their female counterparts in their academic and occupational paths after college education? If there is any gender gap in Asian American college students' educational and occupational trajectories, is it different from the patterns shown by other racial groups? While there was very little difference between the percentage of Asian male and female college graduates who go to graduate school, Asian males' representation in postsecondary faculty who specialize in science, mathematics, and engineering (SME) fields significantly increases, while Asian females' representation rate drops at the same time. Lee speculates that gender discrimination in the academic job market might be the most plausible explanation for the underrepresentation of Asian female faculty in higher education.

In chapter 3, Lin, Kubota, Motha, Wang, and Wong make deeper sense of their lived experiences by understanding and theorizing about the special ideological and institutional conditions underlying their experiences of marginalization and discrimination. This theorizing is, however, not meant to be merely private academic work, but a dialogic, public, political practice. Through engaging in this collective, dialogic writing project, they draw attention to the situation of women faculty of color in the field and contribute to the building of a wider community of scholars and researchers (consisting of both women and men, and both women of color and non-color) in which issues of marginalization and discrimination and issues of social justice and togetherness-in-difference can be continuously engaged as part of their dialogic, critical practice and political intervention.

Part 2, "Teaching, Mentoring, Advising, and Securing Tenure," consists of four chapters, each of which addresses the divergent issues pertinent to the everyday job requirements of Asian female professors. In chapter 4, Xiaoping Liang presents three Chinese-speaking women's personal narratives of their lived experiences of struggle and empowerment as nonnative English-speaking female academics in an English-speaking, male-dominant West Coast American university. In their narratives, the three scholars share their stories of the obstacles they encountered and strategies they used when professing in a language that is not yet perceived as their own, dealing with credibility and authority issues with native and nonnative English-speaking students, and constructing a nonnative English-speaking faculty identity in an English-speaking Western higher institution of education. These narratives also describe the three women's privilege of being nonnative English-speaking faculty and the positive attributes that their unique backgrounds and experiences enable them to bring and contribute to their students, their colleagues, their institution, and their profession.

Keiko Samimy takes a somewhat different slant in chapter 5 by describing how three non-Asian female faculty mentors, who became her role models at critical points in her early career, have helped her navigate as a university faculty at a major research university. She posits that these mentors were particularly instrumental not only in providing her with specific strategies and advice but also in helping her cope with the numerous linguistic, cultural, and academic challenges she encountered. As she further traveled the road of her career, however, she realized that she had to develop and nurture her own identity as an Asian female faculty that is quite different from that of her mentors. The challenges and pressures of playing multiple roles (e.g., mother and wife) equally well are also discussed in her story.

In chapter 6, Guofang Li reflects on the challenges of supervising and teaching fellow Asian students as a young female faculty member. While other minority scholars reflect on their interactions and struggles with the majority culture, in this chapter, Li focuses on within-race-and-gender interactions. She attempts to explore the interactions and relations between faculty and students of similar cultural backgrounds by reflecting on her own experience as a young Asian female scholar working with Asian female students in a North American university. Li's experiences illustrate the complex relationships of gender, race, ethnicity, and the inherited power relations that perpetuate the positioning of minority female faculty and students in academia.

Chalsa Loo and Hsiu-Zu Ho address the important issue of tenure and promotion for Asian female faculty in chapter 7. The chapter highlights two cases of Chinese American female faculty members in institutions of higher education who in the 1980s and early 1990s successfully overturned denials of promotion or tenure. It examines two Asian American women who independently coped with the stress of being denied tenure or a promotion partly by using some form(s) of sociopolitical mobilization. These included obtaining the support of organizations dedicated to the pursuit of equity and justice for Chinese Americans and/or women in higher education. In terms of active problem solving, the authors of this chapter describe specific methods of defense that were effective in overturning cases of denied advancement or retention that appeared bias-based. Through addressing issues of gender and racial identity, psychological stress, and sociopolitical mobilization, Loo and Ho provide Asian female faculty in institutions of higher education with strategies that may become critical to their retention in academia.

Part 3, "Gaining Voice, Forming Identity," looks at the positionality of Asian female faculty members either within the academy in general or in their specific fields of study. Nina Asher in her personal narrative interrogates the challenges and possibilities that she encountered as a South Asian, lesbian academic, who identifies herself as a postcolonialist, feminist scholar, in the U.S. academy. She traces her journey from the early days as a new, international graduate student in New York City to her current situatedness as an assistant professor of education working toward tenure at a Research 1 university in the Deep South, where race relations are construed mainly in terms of Black and White. In so doing, she discusses the intersecting issues of race-class-gender-culture-and-location as they relate to her identity and her research and teaching. Asher argues for personal and professional agency in terms of collaborating, seeking alliances, and arriving at a viable "third space" (citing Bhabha, 1994) from/in which to grow, teach, write, be. She maintains that the interstitial locations between different cultures and identities are useful and, indeed, critical in identifying new possibilities for personal and social transformation.

In chapter 9, Eunai Shrake presents her own personal and professional struggles with converging racial ("model minority") and gender ("lotus blossom") stereotypes throughout seven years of teaching at various college campuses. She was constrained to assume a mask (disguise) that corresponded to those simplified, stereotypical images and was unable to assert herself as a unique individual. Shrake views her masking as a form of subordination (colonization), while her efforts to unmask were an act of insubordination (decolonization). Her masking-unmasking experience encourages minority female professionals within and outside academia to actively and continuously engage in a decolonization process by resisting forces that attempt to marginalize and silence them.

Piya Pangsapa took a different route in chapter 10 by talking about her own experiences as a foreign Asian female scholar situated within a marginal but "legitimate" space of "women's studies" in a Western academic institution, and the implications such a positioning may have for the status, voice, and visibility of Asian female scholars in higher education in general. She raises an important question regarding the place and space of development for Asian female scholars: Are female Asian scholars better able to prosper, become enriched, and grow if they are situated in certain "safe" niches within the academy (such as in an interdisciplinary program like "women's studies")? Her experiences seem to suggest that being situated in a women's studies department and being in the company of other minority female scholars, without the presence of men, has provided a safe haven for her to freely pursue, explore, and share her research interests and to be able to "circumvent" the usual gender barriers.

In chapter 11, Yan Guo explores her autobiographical self by reflecting on her personal experience of learning to write in English for academic purposes. The chapter examines the process of how she, a successful and confident writer in China, became an incompetent writer at the beginning of graduate school in Canada, how she struggled to "appropriate voices" and eventually regained her confidence in writing in English. Guo demonstrates her struggles with the "self" that is an individual who tries to resolve the cultural, linguistic, and ideological conflicts between China and Canada, and with the "self" who celebrates the fluidity and hybridity of between-the-worlds identities.

In chapter 12, Beckett and Zhang address the identity politics of a natural science faculty of Asian origin. Because there is little that explores the issues encountered by minority female natural science faculty of Asian origin, this chapter bridges this gap through excerpts from a Chinese American medical professor's narrative of her journey from being a student in China to a Chinese American professor in the United States. The focal issues discussed in the chapter include how the Confucian theorem of modesty and moderation was useful in preparing Mei to be an extremely successful student and person in China, but became a hindrance for quick success in American society. The chapter discusses how Mei aced it all in China, entered a top university at age fifteen, and came to the United States as one of the few chosen elite, but her Confucian upbringing that socialized her to be modest and moderate hindered her from being able to passionately pursue her studies and career criticality.

Part 4, "Building Bridges, Building the Future" highlights how Asian female scholars transcend the cultural differences and barriers and develop transformative practices in their teaching-learning experiences. In chapter 13, Guichun Zong explores how her lived experiences have shaped her teaching pedagogy today and how she has reconciled her duality and marginality and used them as assets to advance teaching from a global perspective. Through discussing the impact of her border-crossing experiences on how she perceives herself, her identity, and how she teaches (her pedagogy), Zong highlights the inner strength that she has gained through the unique experiences of crossing cultural borders and teaching against the grain, and how they have helped empower some of her students in their pursuit of transformative pedagogy. Zong's experiences demonstrate that practicing global pedagogy in American universities required constant identity adjustments, border crossings, and cultural negotiations both on a personal and on a professional level.

In chapter 14, Xue Lan Rong and Judith Preissle present a unique, dynamic, reciprocal cross-cultural mentor-mentee relationship model through their creative collaborative autobiographical and autoethnographic narratives. Such a cross-cultural mentorship was developed through their three relationships—immigrant-host, student-teacher, and demographer-ethnographer. Based on their success stories, they argue that, without a strong desire to know about each other and to take risks to build a trusting and trusted relationship between two academics with different cultural backgrounds and history, no mentor relationship would have emerged. In order for the relationships to grow into long-term professional alliances, the collaboration must also be mutually beneficial and enrich the research experiences of both. Their productive experiences suggest that cross-cultural mentorship is necessary because most minority students still find themselves in situations where there are few, if any, faculty who are of the same culture or ethnicity in widely recognized graduate programs in major research universities.

In the last chapter, 15, Jing Lin reflects on how she consciously and unconsciously carved a life path that is underpinned by the pursuit of human equality and social justice. Catching the international wave of globalized economy, communication, and consciousness, Lin explores how she expands herself, dedicating herself to working for peace, environmental protection, and building cultural understanding and respect. She argues that it is essential to break down the notion of "deficit" and see her own unique background and experience as assets. Lin concludes that as Asian female scholars, we should not allow others, but ourselves, to define our identity.

Personal Experience as Research, and Research as Personal Experience

These chapters tell our stories in a "new" form of narrative that combines personal and professional experiences—"new stories of self" that reinvent culture, identity, and education (Florio-Ruane, 1997). Our lived experiences as minority women are seen and used as "a resource for apprehending social reality" within the larger political and ideological contexts of our lives (Vargas, 2002, p. 4). Our reflective, narrative writing about our lived experiences teaches us what we know and in what ways we know what we know (van Manen, 1990). In this sense, by writing about our lived experiences, our personal stories become multilayered texts for research. The contributing authors' reflections on their backgrounds; their stories of growing up in different cultures; their border-crossing experiences; and their multiple roles as mothers, wives, daughters, and professors are lived experiences that tell us who we were, who we are, and who we are becoming in the ever-changing social contexts of our lives. Through these multifaceted identity constructions, we negotiate our positionality and space within the academy as women and minorities, and we contribute to the diversity of the academy with our own personal meanings and ways of knowing.

In addition to looking at personal experiences as research texts, we also look at research as personal experiences. Neumann and Peterson (1997) posit that educational research is personal endeavors and experiences within and expressions of a researcher's life. They view research "as much a part of a researcher's life history as it is a part of her curriculum vitae" (p. 1). In line with their view of research as a personal and social phenomenon—an experience within a researcher's life, we asked the authors of this book to focus on the autobiographical antecedents of their work as female scholars—their growth as students, teachers, and pedagogues; their relationships with colleagues, mentors, and students; and their struggles and success as academics. These autobiographical accounts of their professional lives, together with their personal stories of self and the multiple theoretical frameworks applied to interpret these stories will no doubt shed light on how these Asian female scholars' personally derived intellectual endeavors have contributed to the reconstruction of scholarship and diversity in the academy. We hope readers find this insightful and enjoy reading it as much as we enjoyed editing it.

References

Bhabha, H. K. (1994). *The location of culture.* New York: Routledge.

Collins, P. H. (1986). Learning from the outside within: The sociological significance of Black feminist thought. *Social Problems, 33*(6), 14–32.

Florio-Ruane, S. (1997). To tell a new story: Reinventing narratives of culture, identity, and education. *Anthropology & Education Quarterly, 28*(2), 152–162.

Fong, Y. S. (1997). Asian-American women: An understudied minority. *Journal of Sociology and Social Welfare, 24*(1), 91–112.

Hune, S. (1997). Higher education as gendered space: Asian-American women and everyday inequities. In C. R. Ronai, B. A. Zsembik, & J. R. Feagin (Eds.), *Everyday sexism in the third millennium* (pp. 181–96). New York: Routledge.

Hune, S. (1999). *Asian Pacific American women in higher education: Claiming visibility and voice.* Washington, DC: Association of American Colleges and Universities.

Kingston-Mann, E., & Sieber, T. (2001). *Achieving against the odds: How academics become teachers of diverse students.* Philadelphia: Temple University Press.

Lim, S. G., & Herrera-Sobek, M. (Eds.). (2000). *Power, race and gender in academe: Strangers in the Tower?* New York: Modern Language Association of America.

McVee, M. (in press). Narrative and the exploration of culture in teachers' discussions of literacy, identity, self, and other. *Teaching and Teacher Education.*

Neumann, A., & Peterson, P. L. (1997). Researching lives: Women, scholarship, and autobiography in education. In A. Neumann & P. L. Peterson (Eds.), *Learning from our lives: Women, research, and autobiography in education* (pp. 1–17). New York: Teachers College Press.

van Manen, M. (1990). *Researching lived experience: Human science for an action sensitive pedagogy.* Albany, NY: SUNY Press.

Vargas, L. (Ed.). (2002). *Women faculty of color in the white classroom: Narratives on the pedagogical implications of teacher diversity.* New York: Peter Lang.

PART ONE

ASIAN FEMALE SCHOLARS IN CONTEXT

ASIAN PACIFIC AMERICAN WOMEN AND MEN IN HIGHER EDUCATION

The Contested Spaces of their Participation, Persistence, and Challenges as Students, Faculty, and Administrators

Shirley Hune

Institutions of higher education in the United States have been viewed as instruments of both social control and social change. As the former, colleges and universities are seen as political, economic, and cultural structures of power within the capitalist system. In this context, they help preserve the status quo by perpetuating existing hierarchies and reproducing gender, race, class, and other inequities. As the latter, higher education institutions provide opportunities for social mobility through their credentialing powers and their access to influential social networks (Carnoy & Levin, 1985; Tokarczyk & Fay, 1993). Those with a college education can increase their status and class position, broaden and deepen their social and cultural capital, and augment their earnings over a lifetime. If knowledge and degrees are power then disempowered groups like women and historically disadvantaged racial and ethnic groups can benefit by higher education.

The new social movements of the 1960s and 1970s in the United States sought dramatic changes to transform the nation into a more democratic, equitable, and inclusive society. Much attention has been placed upon higher education to open its doors and serve and employ a more diverse population. U.S. colleges and universities have been the focus of intense debate and policy formations and their efforts to diversify have been both praised and opposed. By the end of the 1980s, widespread reaction against affirmative action and related policies and practices to address inequities exposed the heightened resistance to higher education being made more accessible to historic outsiders. In the new millennium, U.S. colleges and universities remain highly contested and politicized spaces. Nonetheless, some changes have occurred.

General Trends in Higher Education

Of the many changes in U.S. higher education since the 1980s, three enrollment trends have caught the public's attention. One pronounced trend is the rise in total (undergraduate, graduate, and professional school) enrollment. More than three million additional students were enrolled between 1980 and 1981 and 2000 and 2001 (Harvey, 2003, pp. 19–21, 57–58). This nearly 27 percent increase over the two decades is a result of demographic changes—notably, new immigration, in conjunction with admission policies that seek a more diverse student body—and the recognition by the general populace that college degrees and professional preparation are critical for securing a middle-class standard of living that has eroded under recent global economic competitiveness.

A second trend is the increased presence of students of color. Whites continued to compose the vast majority of students (10.5 million compared to 4.3 million minorities) in 2000–2001, but students of color demonstrated a significant enrollment growth from 1980–81 to 2000–01. Over the two decades, minority students doubled their numbers and increased from 16 percent to 28 percent of total enrollment. African Americans, American Indians, Asian/Pacific Islander Americans (hereafter Asian Pacific Americans or APAs),[1] and Hispanics all made numerical gains, but Asian Pacific Americans and Hispanics had the largest percentage growth over the twenty years, 242 percent and 210 percent, respectively. In numbers, APA total enrollment grew from 286,000 to 978,000 from 1980–81 to 2000–01 and Hispanic total enrollment from 472,000 to 1,462,000 in the same period (Harvey, 2003, pp. 19–21, 57–58).

---

[1] Throughout this chapter, the data on Asian Pacific Americans include both Asians and Pacific Islanders. Where discussion pertains only to Asian Americans, the term Asian Americans is used.

That women have increased their participation in higher education at all levels and achieved parity with men is the third enrollment trend. There is a widening gender gap. Of total enrollment, women were 56 percent in 2000–01, compared to 51 percent in 1980–81. Women of color, in comparison, were 59 percent of total minority student enrollment in 2000–01, an increase from 55 percent of such enrollment in 1980–81. The minority gender gap is due in large part to the much higher number of African American women compared to African American men in colleges and universities (Harvey, 2003, pp. 19–21, 57–58).

An examination of employment trends in higher education uncovers similar and different tendencies for women and minorities. The number of minority faculty, like that of minority students, increased steadily over the 1980s and 1990s. Although they were 14.4 percent of total full-time faculty positions in 1999–2000, an increase from 9 percent in 1979–80 (Harvey, 2003, p. 89), minority faculty remains significantly underrepresented when considering their proportion in the U.S. population. Racial and ethnic minorities, including those who reported they were one race and those who stated they were mixed race, were about one-third of the total U.S. population in 2000 (U.S. Census Bureau, 2004).

Unlike the student body, where females now are the majority, a different gender gap exists at the faculty level. Women are increasing as faculty; however, men continue to dominate full-time faculty positions. In 1999–2000, women were 37.5 percent of total full-time faculty compared to 26 percent of total full-time faculty in 1979–80. Minority men were 66 percent of total minority full-time faculty positions in 1979–80 and 60 percent of these positions in 1999–2000. More women of color are joining the faculty, but minority male faculty still prevail (Harvey, 2003, pp. 43, 89).

Racial and Gender Disparities Considered

These general trends in higher education since the 1980s suggest a mixed outcome for women and men of color and White women as students and faculty. Inequities persist for groups different from European American males—long the dominant group in higher education—in spite of gains made by women and minorities. Critical race and gender theorists have addressed the persistence of social disparities. Racial theorists argue that the dominant order of Whiteness and maleness maintains spaces of difference between its members and "others" in order to ensure the continuation of their higher-ranked positions and privileges in society. The social construction of racial and ethnic groups deemed inferior to European Americans is the most prominent concept of difference (Lipsitz, 1998; Omi & Howard, 1994; Soja & Hooper, 1993).

Feminist scholars (Collins, 2000; Harding, 1991; Hune, 1997; Smith, 1987; Spain, 1992; Turner, 2002) incorporate gender as an organizing principle of hierarchy in society. They find that gender is embedded in multiple locations of education—epistemology, knowledge, theory, language, spatial arrangements, research methodologies, standpoint, and other aspects—to the disadvantage of women. Feminist scholars of color (Collins, 2000; Hune, 1997; Turner, 2002) argue that gender, race, and class are inseparable in understanding the experiences of minority women in higher education. The larger number of women in the post–civil rights era as students, faculty, and administrators does not mean that men, especially White men, do not continue to hold privileges (McIntosh, 1997). Small differences in the way women and men are treated accumulate over time into pronounced gender disparities that continue to advantage men in salary, rank, promotion, and prestige in professional positions (Valian, 1998). In the politics of difference how and where do APA women and men fit into the gendered and racialized spaces of higher education?

The purpose of this chapter is to assess the situation of Asian Pacific Americans in higher education and to consider their progress since the 1980s in the contested spaces of academe. Special attention is given to APA women. Using both quantitative data and qualitative studies, I consider how the participation, persistence, and challenges of APA women and men are similar to or different from one another and how APAs compare with other racial and ethnic groups. What is the status of APA women and men in higher education in the new millennium? Where are they in respect to the general trends outlined above? And how do APA women fare as women of color compared to their male counterparts and to other women as students, faculty, and administrators? But first, what is the popular perception of APAs in higher education?

Race, Gender, and the Social Construction of the "Model Minority"

Omi and Howard (1994) have expanded the notion of race as a social construction. They argue that racial formations in the United States are not fixed by the dominant order but are constantly negotiated and contested between the racialized groups and the dominant order. Beginning in the late

1960s as part of the social movements of the period, peoples of Asian descent in the United States rejected their being called "Orientals" by the dominant culture and began to identify themselves as "Asian Americans." Similar terms, such as Asian Pacific Americans and Asian Pacific Islander Americans are also used (Nomura, 2003). Such a category has become widely adopted, for example, by the U.S. government as a census classification (Nomura, 2003) and by higher education for data collection and the allocation of programs and services (Hune & Chan, 1997).

In this same period, Asian Americans, once viewed negatively by the dominant racial order as the "yellow peril," became touted as a "model minority," largely through journalistic and media representations of a small number of educationally successful students (Osajima, 1988; Suzuki, 1989). This racial (re)construction of Asian Americans cites their "over" representation in higher education, their professionalization, and their relatively high family incomes as evidence of how this visible racial group has achieved "success," and overcome past discrimination and present obstacles, if any. Cultural values related to respect for education, family cohesion, and authority in Asian societies, and a strong work ethic, are generally identified as explanations for the high educational presence and attainment of Asian Americans (Hune & Chan, 1997).

The "model minority" construct is not universally accepted, however. APA scholars have disputed the stereotyping of Asian Pacific Americans as such and provided empirical evidence to document their heterogeneity by ethnicity, education, class, and other characteristics. They point out the economic hardships experienced by many APA households, the inequities they face in the workplace, and the limitations of educational "success" for all Asian Pacific Americans (Hune, 2002; Hune & Chan, 1997, pp. 44–46; Lee, 1996; Osajima, 1993; Suzuki, 2002). Suzuki (2002) also argues that the older stereotype of Asian Americans as "perfidious foreigner" (pp. 24–25) has re-emerged in the 1990s. Their racial profiling as untrustworthy foreigners in the service of economic and political schemes of Asian states, such as in the case of Wen Ho Lee, the nuclear scientist who was falsely accused by the U.S. government of providing classified research documents to China and later acquitted, also affect how APAs are treated in higher education. These studies argue that such stereotyping, especially the "model minority" construct, contributes to APAs being bypassed in higher education as a population in need of services and advocacy to achieve equity. There is one exception. The National Science Foundation and other agencies recognize

Pacific Islanders, including Native Hawaiians, as an underrepresented group in their educational funding.

Does the "model minority" construct apply to APA women as well? Other researchers (Cho, 1997; Hune, 1997, 1998; Loo & Chun, 2002; Mau, 1990; Woo, 1989) have considered the circumstances of Asian Pacific American women in a range of educational situations. They find that the category of race alone and its impact fails to adequately appraise the participation and advancement of APA women in higher education. Their studies conclude that APA women endure spaces of difference that are gendered and sexualized, as well as racialized. Therefore, the challenges they face in securing their educational goals and aspirations are not identical to those experienced by APA men.

Data drawn from the National Center for Educational Statistics at the U.S. Department of Education and assembled by the American Council on Education covering the 1980s and 1990s allow for an examination of twenty years of APA higher education participation (Harvey, 2003). Limitations do exist in the data. Aggregating data on all APAs as individuals and groups homogenize findings and conceal complexities and differences between and within APA groups who differ widely by education, English language proficiency, family income, employment, and acculturation to mainstream American society as seen among the U.S. born, new immigrants, and refugees, and other characteristics. Therefore, an APA statistic may not resemble any real person or group. Moreover, the status and progress of specific APA groups are not discernible and differences by gender and by class between and within APA groups are obscured. Nonetheless, the data offer a unique opportunity to examine APA educational advancement since the 1980s and to evaluate whether APAs, and especially APA women, are indeed a "model minority" in higher education.

To situate the educational data in a larger context, the 2000 U.S. census reported a total population of 281.4 million for the nation; 51 percent were female and 4.5 percent were Asian and Pacific Islanders. More specifically, those who stated "Asian" on the census form, including those who reported they were one race and those who stated they were mixed race, made up 4.2 percent of the total U.S. population, or 11.9 million (Barnes & Bennett, 2002). Those who reported "Native Hawaiian" and "Other Pacific Islander," including those who identified themselves as one race and those who stated they were mixed race, made up .3 percent, or 874,000 of the total U.S. population (Grieco, 2001). What follows is an analysis of APA women and men at specific points in higher education as a pipeline and as a workplace.

Asian Pacific American Women and Men as Undergraduates

In 2000–01, APA undergraduates numbered 846,000, or 6 percent of total undergraduate enrollment, and 22 percent of total minority undergraduate enrollment (Harvey, 2003, p. 59). They accounted for 4.9 percent of total associate degrees in 2000–01, an increase from 2.1 percent in 1980–81. APA women and men were 57 percent and 43 percent, respectively, of total APA associate degrees in 2000–01, compared to 47 percent and 53 percent, respectively, of total APA associate degrees in 1980–81 (Harvey, 2003, p. 62). Of total bachelor's degrees awarded in 2000–01, APAs accounted for 6.3 percent, up from 2 percent in 1980–81. In 2000–01, APA women held 55 percent of total APA bachelor's degrees, an increase from 46 percent in 1980–81 (Harvey, 2003, p. 63). Both APA women and men are well represented as undergraduates given their proportion in the population, but the status of APA women is more complicated.

As noted, women are pursuing higher education at all levels and are the majority of total higher education enrollment. APA women increased their share of total APA associate and bachelor's degrees in this two-decade period, but lagged behind women in other racial and ethnic groups. In 1980–81, women undergraduates outnumbered men in each racial and ethnic group with the exception of APAs. APA women did not reach parity in undergraduate attainment with APA males until the mid-1990s (Harvey, 2003, pp. 62–63). By 2000–01, APA women were earning more than half of total APA associate and bachelor's degrees (table 1).

How do Asian Pacific American women and men compare with each

TABLE 1
Asian Pacific American Degrees Earned by Gender

	1980–1981		2000–2001	
	Male	*Female*	*Male*	*Female*
Associate Degrees	4,557	4,093	12,339	16,124
Bachelor's Degrees	10,107	8,687	35,865	43,037
Master's Degrees	3,773	2,509	11,349	12,934
First-Professional Degrees	991	465	4,518	4,743
Doctoral Degrees	281	171	741	641

Source. From *Minorities in higher education 20th annual status report* (pp. 62–66), by W. B. Harvey, 2003, Washington, DC: American Council on Education.

other and with all undergraduates in their choice of field of study? Business was the leading major for all male students at the bachelor's level in 1980–81 and remained so through 2000–01. The leading major for all women in 1980–81 was education, followed by business, but two decades later women overwhelmingly chose business, followed by education (Harvey, 2003, p. 77). In 1980–81, engineering was the most popular major for APA men, followed by business. In 2000–01, it was the reverse, with more APA males obtaining business degrees than engineering degrees. In 1980–81, APA women also selected business and then the health professions as their leading majors. In 2000–01, business was their overwhelming first choice, followed by the social sciences and the biological/life sciences (Harvey, 2003, p. 79).

APA women and men are like all students in their choice of business as their leading major. In a time of economic uncertainty, families are emphasizing practical endeavors, like business, which in their view will provide gainful employment. APA women's recent choices of the social sciences and biological/life sciences reflect their demographics, in part. More U.S.-born APAs are branching out to other majors, such as the social sciences, while immigrant APA households tend to give priority to science fields because they are seen as having a high value in U.S. society and offering greater financial security (Hune & Chan, 1997). APA female undergraduates are less likely than other women to choose traditional female-dominated fields, especially education, however.

Asian Pacific American Women and Men in Master's Studies

White women and women and men of color have increased their participation at the master's level. All women earned 50.5 percent of total master's degrees in 1980–81, compared to 58.5 percent of such degrees in 2000–01. Minorities were 18.5 percent of total master's degrees in 2000–01, an increase from 10.5 percent in 1980–81. Of total minority master's degrees awarded, women of color earned 56 percent and 65 percent in 1980–81 and 2000–01, respectively (Harvey, 2003, p. 64).

As part of the growth in minority participation, Asian Pacific Americans were 5.2 percent of total master's degrees in 2000–01, compared to 2.1 percent of such degrees in 1980–81. Here, too, APA women reveal their investment in education by increasing their share of total APA master's degrees. They earned 53 percent of total APA master's degrees in 2000–01, an increase from 40 percent in 1980–81 (Harvey, 2003, p. 64, table 1).

At the master's level, men chose business and women chose education as their leading major consistently over the twenty-year period (Harvey, 2003, p. 81). In the new millennium, APA women and men are alike in their first choice of major, but gender differences are evident in their other choices. Business followed by engineering was the key choice of APA males in 1980–81 and in 2000–01. However, in recent years, business has been their overwhelming choice. For APA women, business was their leading choice in 2000–01, followed by education and the health professions, in contrast to education, followed by business in 1980–81 (Harvey, 2003, p. 83). APA women are more like other women in choosing education among their top fields of study at the master's level in contrast to their undergraduate majors. More research is required to explain this shift.

Asian Pacific American Women and Men in First-Professional Studies

First-professional degrees include chiropractic, dentistry, law, medicine, optometry, osteopathic medicine, pharmacy, podiatry, theology, and veterinary medicine. Currently, the United States produces about twice as many first-professional degree recipients as doctoral recipients. In 2000–01, higher education awarded 79,707 first-professional degrees and 40,744 doctorates. That year, international students earned 2.6 percent of total first-professional degrees. Although the gender gap favors men overall—they were 53.8 percent of total first-professional degrees in 2000–01—there are differences by race and ethnicity (Harvey, 2003, p. 65).

The number of White male first-professional degree recipients declined from 1980–81 to 2000–01, but they continued to earn the largest number of such degrees, 32,717, or 41 percent of total first-professional degrees in 2000–01. Women and minorities made significant gains in this area. Women were 26.8 percent and 46.2 percent of total first-professional degrees in 1980–81 and 2000–01, respectively. The gains of White women are seen in their increase of total first-professional degrees from 24 percent in 1980–81 to 32 percent (25,881) in 2000–01. Of total first-professional degrees, minorities earned 23.9 percent in 2000–01, compared to 8.6 percent in 1980–81. Women of color earned 53 percent (10,143) of total minority first-professional degrees in 2000–01, up from 34 percent (2,092) of such degrees in 1980–81 (Harvey, 2003, p. 65).

Asian Pacific Americans, and specifically APA women, made the most dramatic increase among minority groups in first-professional degrees over the 1980s and 1990s. Of total first-professional degrees, APAs accounted for

2 percent (1,456) in 1980–81, but they were 11.6 percent (9,261) in 2000–01. Of total APA first-professional degrees, APA women grew from 32 percent (465) in 1980–81 to 51 percent (4,743) of such degrees in 2000–01, reaching parity with APA males (Harvey, 2003, p. 65, table 1).

Why the increased draw of women and men of color and White women to first-professional studies? They offer prestige, job security, and high earnings potential. Until very recently, these professions were largely the domains of White middle-class and upper-class males. Although they have been under great pressure to diversify, their educational preparation and training remain very much male defined and constructed (Hunter College Women's Studies Collective, 2005, chapter 10). For women, these fields offer new opportunities for professional development and advancement and for change in how females are treated in research and services. For students of color, professional degrees also offer ways to give back to their communities. Indeed, minority professionals are more likely to serve in racial and ethnic communities and to be in public service, in general, than their majority counterparts. Beyond diversifying first-professional studies, the preparation of women and people of color in these fields provides important services to underserved communities in the United States and to the nation, in general (Bowen & Bok, 1999).

Asian Pacific American Women and Men in Doctoral Studies

The percentage of doctorates granted by U.S. institutions of higher education has increased more than that of first-professional degrees since the 1980s. But as noted above, the current number of doctorates awarded is about half that of first-professional degrees. In contrast to their small representation among first-professional degree recipients, international students make up a significant share of total doctoral recipients. In 2000–01, they earned 11,601, or 28.5 percent, of total doctorates (Harvey, 2003, p. 66).

Men continue to dominate total doctorates awarded, but there are differences by race and ethnicity. Men earned 55.9 percent (22,769) of total doctoral degrees in 2000–01. Of domestic doctorates (those earned by U.S. citizens and residents) the number of White male doctorates has declined slightly since the 1980s. Nonetheless, they earned 52 percent (11,257) of total domestic doctorates held by Whites in 2000–01. White women increased their share of domestic doctorates held by Whites from 35 percent in 1980–81 to 48 percent in 2000–01 (Harvey, 2003, p. 66).

Women, in general, and minority women, specifically, demonstrated the largest percentage growth in doctorates from 1980–81 to 2000–01. Minority doctorates grew in their share of total domestic doctorates, from 7 percent to nearly 10.5 percent over these two decades. Minority women were responsible for most of these gains; they were 55 percent of total minority doctorates in 2000–01, an increase from 45 percent in 1980–81 (Harvey, 2003, p. 66).

The increase in Asian Pacific American doctoral recipients is significant, from 452 in 1980–81 to 1,382 in 2000–01, but the number is modest in light of total doctorates awarded and pales against APA first-professional degrees earned (table 1). APA men made up 741 or 3.3 percent of total doctorates and 54 percent of total APA doctorates in 2000–01. As doctorates, APA women were the only females to lag behind their male counterparts among the racial and ethnic groups. Nonetheless, they demonstrated significant gains from 171 doctorates in 1980–81 to 641 doctorates in 2000–01 (table 1), which increased their share of APA doctorates from 37 percent to 46 percent in the two-decade period (Harvey, 2003, p. 66).

In 2000–01, life sciences granted the largest number of doctorates, followed by the social sciences. Among APAs that year, the life sciences (430) was the leading Ph.D. choice, followed by engineering (256), physical sciences (198), social sciences (197), humanities (130), education (102), and other professional fields (69) (Harvey, 2003, p. 86). Choice of field by gender was not available.

The Spaces of Difference for Asian Pacific American Students

The quantitative data demonstrate that Asian Pacific Americans are well represented as students. Over the 1980s and 1990s, APAs have not only significantly increased their participation at all degree levels, they have also advanced and persevered in greater numbers in graduate and first-professional degrees. They are a powerful presence in U.S. colleges and universities. Clearly there is a measure of success here that both APA women and men can express about their achievements.

What is most distinctive is the growth in APA women in higher education at every level during this period. The data suggest that they are making a serious commitment to higher education. Numbers and rate of increase, however, provide an incomplete picture of APA academic success and level of satisfaction in academe. What do qualitative studies reveal about the higher education experiences of APA women and men?

Family encouragement plays an important role in APA educational attainment (Osajima, 1991; Zhou & Bankston, 1998). However, family support is a double-edged sword. Many students are resentful of unrealistic parental demands for straight "A" grades, for getting into medical school, and among recent immigrants, for them to become English proficient quickly to help the family negotiate daily life and to improve its economic status. Weighed down by family and community expectations and societal pressures to be a "model minority," some APA students drop out, experience personal problems, or perform poorly in academic studies. Others simply pursue a particular degree to please family members rather than to advance their own interests (Kiang, 1996; Osajima, 1991). Hence the less successful aspects of APA education are not reflected in statistical data.

Gender, race, and class are spaces of difference in higher education as elsewhere. They make difficult the efforts of APAs to belong and to carry out their aspirations, aspects critical for students to develop their full potential. APAs often report that their campus environment is unwelcoming and that they feel like "strangers" or "guests in someone else's house" (Turner, 1994). Interviews with Asian Pacific American students reveal the deep and hurtful ways that racism, both overt and subtle, in and outside of the classroom, serve to silence them, to track them into specific academic fields, and in other ways to restrict their "place" on U.S. campuses. Class plays a role as well. APAs who are first-generation college students, working class, or recent immigrants relate how class biases in accents, speech patterns, life experiences, dress, and so forth disrespect their intellect, research interests, and other contributions. APA students have consistently spoken out about their marginalization by faculty, staff, and administrators and of the lack of services available to them to address their academic and personal needs as they struggle to meet the demands of their parents and community to succeed, as well as the demands of U.S. society, including faculty, who expect them to be a "model minority" (Hune, 1998, 2002; Osajima, 1991, 1993; Suzuki, 2002). In short, like many students of color, APAs possess the intellect and motivation but experience structural and cultural barriers to doing their best (Tierney, Campbell, & Sanchez, 2004).

The educational lag that Asian Pacific American women experience in reaching parity with their male counterparts compared to women in other racial and ethnic groups cannot be explained solely by the different treatment of females and males from infancy in Asian cultures, whereby males historically have been privileged and remain so and females are called upon to set lesser goals for themselves. For in the midst of this lag, APA women demonstrate significant growth in higher education. The increased numbers of APA female students at all levels suggest they have made a decided choice to be academic strivers. In many cases, they are encouraged in their pursuits by supportive parents. Often, this support comes with the mixed message that a college education is a good thing for women to have to support themselves and their families, but that excessive schooling might cause a woman to become too independent and jeopardize her marriage and motherhood opportunities, which are considered to be more acceptable roles for females (Hune, 1998).

Studies on the "chilly climate" for women in higher education (Hall & Sandler, 1982, 1984; Sandler & Hall, 1986) pertain to APAs as well and shed light on their lack of parity. In one study of APA female students' experiences, they expressed the multiple impediments they face in the intersection of gender, race, and class (Hune, 1998). For example, they report being rendered invisible, discounted, ignored, or silenced in everyday interactions in and outside of the classroom that reward masculine and Eurocentric ways of thinking, being, and doing as normative. APA female students contend with having their scholarly abilities, research interests, and career commitments questioned. Rarely do faculty and counselors encourage them to pursue graduate studies. As graduate students, many feel unsupported in advisement and guidance through doctoral programs and academic careers (Hune, 1998). When APA graduate women serve as teaching assistants, they find that as women of color they are treated as less competent. Hence students are more likely to challenge their expertise and authority, which further contributes to an inhospitable climate (Hune, 1998; Hwang, 2000).

APA female students also oppose being sexualized as "exotics" instead of being considered serious students. Like other women on campus, too often APA women experience some form of sexual harassment from students and faculty, in spite of institutional efforts to educate the higher education community about appropriate behavior (Cho, 1997; Hune, 1998; Kelley & Parsons, 2000). Through incorporating students' voices and perspectives, we find that higher education is politicized space for Asian Pacific American students, but more so for APA women. As students of color in spite of their increased presence and gains, APAs do not have the benefits of those who are fully integrated in academe (Tierney, Campbell, & Sanchez, 2004).

Asian Pacific American Women and Men as Faculty

Among doctorates, academe is one career choice. Other choices include the private sector, especially industry; self-employment; and the public sector.

Increasingly, White women and women of color are choosing the academy, and this is reflected in their significant growth as faculty since 1979–80. However, in contrast to student patterns where females are the majority of total enrollment, men, in general, and White men, specifically, predominate as faculty, holding 62.5 percent and 85.6 percent, respectively, of all full-time faculty positions in 1999–2000. Nonetheless, faculty of color persisted. They increased their share of total full-time faculty positions from about 9 percent to 14.4 percent, more than doubling their number over the twenty years (Harvey, 2003, pp. 43–45, 89).

Faculty diversity (or lack of it) varies by rank. In 1999–2000, White men and men of color held the majority of faculty positions with respect to their female counterparts as assistant, associate, and full professors. However, when broken out by race and ethnicity, there are differences. For example, African American and American Indian faculty women exceeded their male counterparts at the assistant professor level that year. It is only as instructors and lecturers that women were in the majority, with some variation by race and ethnicity. Specifically, more White women and African American women served as instructors and lecturers than their male counterparts, while APA women were close to parity with APA males in these positions in 1999–2000 (Harvey, 2003, pp. 90–91, table 2).

Asian Pacific American faculty grew from 2.9 percent to 6 percent of total full-time faculty from 1979–80 to 1999–2000. APA female faculty growth was larger than that of APA males in this period. APA women accounted for 30 percent of total APA faculty in 1999–2000, compared to 19 percent in 1979–80. APAs were 4.4 percent of total instructor and lecturer positions, 7.6 percent of total assistant professors, 6.1 percent of total associate professors, and 5.5 percent of total full professors in 1999–2000 (Harvey,

TABLE 2
Asian Pacific American Faculty by Rank and Gender

	1980–1981		1999–2000	
	Male	*Female*	*Male*	*Female*
Full Professor	3,507	252	7,519	1,267
Associate Professor	2,749	513	5,865	1,887
Assistant Professor	3,390	959	6,199	3,519
Instructor and Lecturer	1,087	724	2,047	2,052

Source. From *Minorities in higher education 20th annual status report* (pp. 90–91), by W. B. Harvey, 2003, Washington, DC: American Council on Education.

2003, pp. 89–91). APA women were 36 percent, 24 percent, and 14 percent of total APA assistant, associate, and full professor positions, respectively, in 1999–2000. They are concentrated at the junior faculty level and much less likely than APA males to be at the tenure rank of associate professor and above (table 2).

Asian Pacific American Women and Men as Administrators

White men continue to hold the majority of administrative positions in higher education, but women and minorities made gains in recent years. Of total full-time administrators, women increased their share from 32.5 percent in 1983–84 to 47.6 percent in 1999–2000. Minorities were 14.6 percent of total full-time administrators in 1999–2000, compared to 10.3 percent in 1983–84. Asian Pacific Americans made up 2.1 percent of total full-time administrators in 1999–2000, an increase of 1 percent from 1983–84. APA women held 48 percent of total APA full-time administrator positions in 1999–2000, a gain from 36 percent in 1983–84 (Harvey, 2003, p. 93). Hence women, in general, and APA women, specifically, are near parity with their male counterparts as total full-time administrators.

How do women fare at the highest levels of administration? There are nearly 3,200 colleges and universities in the United States today. Of the many administrative positions, that of president or chief executive officer is the highest. White men dominate the president's office. Women were 15 percent of total presidencies in 1993, growing to 21.5 percent in 2003. The percentage of presidencies held by minorities increased from 12 to 13 percent from 1993 to 2003. Asian Pacific American presidents were less than 1 percent (24) of total president positions in 1993 and 1 percent (33) of total president positions in 2003. Of the 33 APA presidents in 2003, 5 were APA women, an increase from 1 in 1993. Three led two-year institutions and 2 headed four-year institutions (Harvey, 2003, pp. 94–96). APAs, in general, and APA women, specifically, are very much underrepresented as college and university presidents.

The Spaces of Difference for Asian Pacific American Faculty and Administrators

The data on APA faculty are problematic because they combine U.S. citizens and residents of APA descent with Asian international students who stayed and found employment in academe. The quantitative data suggest that APAs are increasing their presence and moving up the faculty and administrative ranks, but they are not yet a "model minority" in higher education as a workplace. Is it just a matter of time until APAs will hold more positions as faculty and administrators and at their highest levels? Qualitative studies reveal in greater detail the challenges that APA faculty and administrators experience in the Eurocentric culture of academe.

It would be expected that higher education institutions that espouse diversifying their faculty would proactively seek out newly minted or soon-to-be doctorates of color for academic positions. One study of highly qualified doctorates of color, which included Asian Americans, indicates that this has not been the case. New doctorates of color were not being pursued for faculty positions, and the public perception of bidding wars over them was very much exaggerated (Smith, Wolf, & Busenberg, 1996). Hence the practice of faculty searches and hires does not necessarily follow the rhetoric of increasing faculty diversity.

Further, although many campuses have increased their efforts to mentor junior faculty, faculty of color continue to be disappointed by the limited support extended to them by their departments and institutions. This is especially critical for faculty of color such as the vast majority of Asian Pacific Americans, who are first-generation academics and lack knowledge about the "rules of the game" to survive and thrive. APA faculty, especially women, report being treated, at times, as invisible or just marginalized, and at other times, being made hypervisible, paraded out for diversity events and being responsible for diversity matters and students of color in their department and across the campus (Hune, 1998). Many faculty of color continue to be "the only one" in their department, which carries responsibilities and burdens not assumed by majority faculty. In their multiple spaces of interaction, such as the classroom, department meetings, and scholarly presentations, faculty of color find their perspectives, competence, expertise, and authority questioned by students, faculty, and administrators, all of which contributes to the inhospitable environment in academe (Johnsrud, 1993).

Many APA faculty have demonstrated great courage in contesting unequal treatment at their institutions. Those whose scholarly areas are in the relatively new interdisciplinary fields of Asian American and Pacific Islander American studies and feminist studies, which are not yet fully accepted as legitimate areas of inquiry, face additional scrutiny about their teaching, research, theoretical approaches, methodologies, and publication records. Like other faculty of color, APAs often find resistance in being appointed, and especially for APA women, in gaining tenure and promotion. The experiences of APA faculty who have proactively and successfully fought their departments and institutions in tenure and promotion cases reveal that their efforts have not been without high personal costs of anger, despair, anxiety, and a loss of any belief in a meritocratic system, causing some to leave academe (Cho, 1997; Loo & Chun, 2002; Nakanishi, 1993).

Women faculty face other hardships that most male faculty do not. In the gendered spaces of academe, APA women contend with racialized sexual harassment, resistance to feminist research and practices, high demands for them to serve students, and a general sense that they and their values are less worthy (Hune, 1998). Moreover, family-friendly institutions are still an ideal, not a reality. So-called "neutral" practices, especially the tenure clock, and gaps in one's curriculum vitae disadvantage women more than men (Williams, 2003). APA women, like all women, generally assume more household, child care, and elder care responsibilities than their male counterparts. Women with babies experience work and family conflict that contribute to many of them dropping out of academe, choosing a less competitive career track, or working part-time. Tenured women are less likely to be married than their male counterparts, and those who are have fewer children, if any (Mason & Goulden, 2002). APA women also experience role conflict in meeting demands to serve their communities in conjunction with family and professional responsibilities (Hune, 1998).

The dearth of Asian Pacific Americans as university and college presidents is another indicator of difficulties they face in advancement. Many APAs seek administrative positions but assert that they are not being identified, mentored, or recruited for them. They cite cultural biases, including questions about their leadership styles; perceived language limitations, such as speaking with an accent; notions that APAs are better suited as technicians or researchers rather than as leaders; and other forms of subtle discrimination that serve as barriers to their gaining high-level administrative positions (Hune & Chan, 1997). Further, the discourse on APA values, communication skills, and leadership styles being too different from those held by the dominant culture for APAs to perform well in administrative positions does not fully explain why U.S.-born and raised APAs are not better represented in administration (Hune, 1998).

Racialized stereotypes about APA women as demure, exotic, or "dragon ladies" when assertive diminish their opportunities as academic leaders and administrators. They report that biases about their appearance, such as being youthful looking, and often their smaller stature, as well as their communication styles, which are often gendered like politeness and consensus building in interactions, are misread as meaning they are less competent. Highly capable APA women, on the other hand, find that their authority is often undermined when they demonstrate strong leadership. Consequently, APA female administrators are punished whether they fit or do not fit male-defined and Eurocentric notions of leadership and racialized, gendered, and sexualized stereotypes of appropriate roles and places for them (Hune, 1998).

Qualitative studies suggest that the spaces of difference are broader and the hurdles are higher for APAs to achieve as faculty and administrators than as students, and especially for APA women. Woo (2000) concludes that there is a glass ceiling for APAs in the workplace of higher education and elsewhere.

Conclusions

Asian Pacific American participation and persistence in higher education is a mixed picture. There is both good news and bad news. The good news is that the numbers tell a very positive story. APA student participation is high in proportion to their population and has increased over time. Also, APAs have persisted through to advanced degrees, into faculty positions, and administration. APA women are to be lauded for the even greater strides that they have made in comparison to APA males at all levels. APA women and men can take great pride in their achievements and in their efforts to oppose resistance to their advancement in academe. How does one measure "success?" One set of bad news is that APAs are not as well represented at the doctoral level, as full-time faculty, and especially in administration at the highest levels. But reliance on aggregated statistical data gives only a partial view of APA experiences in higher education. For example, there is a lack of information about specific APA groups. If institutions and agencies provided disaggregated data by APA group and by gender, we would have a more precise picture of APA educational attainment. But most important, the perspectives and voices of Asian Pacific Americans in qualitative studies shed a different light on their everyday interactions and experiences in academe and contest the notion that their increased presence on U.S. campuses can be deemed "successful." From the viewpoint of APAs themselves, and especially APA women, they are not a "model minority."

U.S. universities and colleges have become more diverse, but the culture of academe has changed very little in response to the new demographics. Higher education is contested and politicized space. There is more bad news here. Its institutions remain uncomfortable with difference, especially with efforts to change student and faculty recruitment, curriculum, and disciplines. APAs have earned a place in academe, but they do not yet feel at home in it. Here the research literature has given much attention to the racialized space of academe, to class dynamics, and to the difficulties of racial and ethnic minorities in gaining access and equal treatment. APAs may participate in higher education at many levels, but they are not fully integrated in all its components, such as the classroom, the campus, research, publications, and decision making. APAs want to feel fully welcomed and included in their departments and institutions, but they remain outsiders.

Feminist scholarship has sought to explain how women are disadvantaged in academe and how women of color are further disadvantaged by both racialized and gendered spaces of difference. APA women also suffer from the masculine hegemony of higher education, which is less welcoming of women's ways of being, knowing, doing, and leading. Stereotypes of APA women also devalue them as faculty and administrators (Hune, 1998). Therefore, the barriers that Asian Pacific American women encounter are not the same as those of APA men and are more difficult to overcome without institutional change.

Diversity is of compelling interest to excellence in higher education (Hunter College Women's Studies Collective, 2005, chapter 10). A diverse academy is critical for creating a culturally pluralistic learning and work environment for all participants to achieve fully (Tierney, Campbell, & Sanchez, 2004). APAs contribute new and different theoretic perspectives, knowledge, research interests, curriculum, and ways of being, thinking, and doing in higher education. They also serve as mentors and role models and make significant contributions to their academic fields and to society. APA women seek to be successful and to actively participate in dissolving spaces of difference, creating spaces of empowerment, appreciating different worldviews and intellectual interests, and in sharing decision-making powers.

Creating opportunities for Asian Pacific American women is not about having them work harder in place to be successful. Notions of competency and authority are culturally based and socially constructed. If higher education institutions are to be agents of social change they must engage in a cultural transformation of their climates, structures, and everyday practices to provide the kind of welcome, support, and integration at all levels to allow APAs, and specifically APA women, to achieve their full potential.

References

Barnes, J. S., & Bennett, C. E. (2002). *The Asian population: 2000. Census 2000 Brief.* Washington, DC: U.S. Census Bureau, U.S. Department of Commerce.

Bowen, W. G., & Bok, D. (1999). *The shape of the river: Long-term consequences of considering race in college and university admissions.* Princeton, NJ: Princeton University Press.

Carnoy, M., & Levin, H. M. (1985). *Schooling and work in the democratic state.* Stanford, CA: Stanford University Press.

Cho, S. K. (1997). Converging stereotypes in racialized sexual harassment: Where the model minority meets Suzie Wong. In A. K. Wing (Ed.), *Critical race feminism: A reader* (pp. 203–220). New York: New York University Press.

Collins, P. H. (2000). *Black feminist thought: Knowledge, consciousness, and the politics of empowerment* (2nd ed.). New York: Routledge.

Grieco, E. M. (2001). *The native Hawaiian and other Pacific Islander population: 2000. Census 2000 Brief.* Washington, DC: U.S. Census Bureau, U.S. Department of Commerce.

Hall, R. M., & Sandler, B. R. (1982). *The classroom climate: A chilly one for women?* Washington, DC: Association of American Colleges.

Hall, R. M., & Sandler, B. R. (1984). *Out of the classroom: A chilly campus climate for women?* Washington, DC: Association of American Colleges.

Harding, S. (1991). *Whose science? Whose knowledge? Thinking from women's lives.* Ithaca, NY: Cornell University Press.

Harvey, W. B. (2003). *Minorities in higher education 20th annual status report.* Washington, DC: American Council on Education.

Hune, S. (1997). Higher education as gendered space: Asian-American women and everyday inequities. In C. R. Ronai, B. A. Zsembik, & J. R. Feagin (Eds.), *Everyday sexism in the third millennium* (pp. 181–196). New York: Routledge.

Hune, S. (1998). *Asian Pacific American women in higher education: Claiming visibility & voice.* Washington, DC: Association of American Colleges and Universities.

Hune, S. (2002). Demographics and diversity of Asian American college students. In M. K. McEwen, C. M. Kodama, A. N. Alvarez, S. Lee, & C. T. H. Liang (Eds.), *Working with Asian American college students* (pp. 11–20). San Francisco: Jossey-Bass.

Hune, S., & Chan, K. S. (1997). Asian Pacific American demographic and educational trends. In D. J. Carter & R. Wilson (Eds.), *Minorities in higher education 15th annual status report* (pp. 39–67, 103–107). Washington, DC: American Council on Education.

Hunter College Women's Studies Collective (2005). *Women's realities, women's choices: An introduction to women's studies* (3rd ed.). New York: Oxford University Press.

Hwang, S. M. (2000). At the limits of my feminism: Race, gender, class, and the execution of a feminist pedagogy. In S. G. Lim, & M. Herrera-Sober (Eds.), *Power, race, and gender in academe: Strangers in the tower?* (pp. 154–170). New York: The Modern Language Association.

Johnsrud, L. K. (1993). Women and minority faculty experiences: Defining and responding to diverse realities. In J. Gainen & R. Boice (Eds.), *Building a diverse faculty* (pp. 3–16). San Francisco: Jossey-Bass.

Kelley, M. L., & Parsons, B. (2000). Sexual harassment in the 1990s. *The Journal of Higher Education, 71*(5), 548–68.

Kiang, P. N. (1996). Persistence stories and survival strategies of Cambodian Americans in college. *Journal of Narrative and Life History, 6*(1), 39–64.

Lee, S. J. (1996). *Unraveling the model minority stereotype.* New York: Teachers College Press.

Lipsitz, G. (1998). *The possessive investment in whiteness.* Philadelphia: Temple University Press.

Loo, C. M., & Chun, M. (2002). Academic adversity and faculty warriors: Prevailing amidst trauma. In L. Jacobsa, J. Cintrón, & C. E. Canton (Eds.), *The politics of survival in academia: Narratives of inequity, resilience, and success* (pp. 95–123). Lanham, MD: Rowman & Littlefield.

Mason, M. A., & Goulden, M. (2002). Do babies matter? The effect of family formation on the lifelong careers of academic men and women. *Academe, 88*(6), 21–27.

Mau, R. (1990). Barriers to higher education for Asian/Pacific American females. *The Urban Review, 22*(3), 183–197.

McIntosh, P. (1997). White privilege and male privilege: A personal account of coming to see correspondences through work in women's studies. In R. Delgado & J. Stefancie (Eds.), *Critical white studies* (pp. 291–299). Philadelphia: Temple University Press.

Nakanishi, D. (1993). Asian Pacific Americans in higher education: Faculty and administrative representation and tenure. In J. Gainen & R. Boice (Eds.), *Building a diverse faculty* (pp. 51–59). San Francisco: Jossey-Bass.

Nomura, G. M. (2003). Introduction: On our terms: Definitions and context. In S. Hune & G. M. Nomura (Eds.), *Asian/Pacific islander American women: A historical anthology* (pp. 16–22). New York: New York University Press.

Omi, M., & Howard, W. (1994). *Racial formation in the United States* (2nd ed.). New York: Routledge.

Osajima, K. (1988). Asian Americans as the model minority: An analysis of the popular press image in the 1960's and 1980's. In G. Okihiro, S. Hune, A. Hansen, & J. Liu (Eds.), *Reflections on shattered windows* (pp. 165–174). Pullman: Washington State University Press.

Osajima, K. (1991). Breaking the silence: Race and the educational experiences of Asian American college students. In M. Foster (Ed.), *Readings on equal education* (pp. 115–134). New York: AMS Press.

Osajima, K. (1993). Hidden injuries of race. In L. A. Revilla, G. M. Nomura, S. Wong, & S. Hune (Eds.), *Bearing dreams, shaping visions* (pp. 81–91). Pullman: Washington State University Press.

Sandler, B. R., & Hall, R. M. (1986). *The campus climate revisited: Chilly for women faculty, administrators, and graduate students.* Washington, DC: Association of American Colleges.

Smith, D. E. (1987). *The everyday world as problematic.* Boston: Northeastern University Press.

Smith, D. G., Wolf, L. E., & Busenberg, B. (1996). *Achieving faculty diversity: Debunking the myths.* Washington, DC: Association of American College and Universities.

Soja, E., & Hooper, B. (1993). The spaces that difference makes. In M. Keith & S. Pile (Eds.), *Place and the politics of identity* (pp. 183–205). London: Routledge.

Spain, D. (1992). *Gendered spaces.* Chapel Hill: University of North Carolina.

Suzuki, B. H. (1989) (November/December). Asian Americans as the "model minority": Outdoing whites? Or media hype? *Change,* pp. 13–19.

Suzuki, B. H. (2002). Revisiting the model minority stereotype: Implications for student affairs practice and higher education. In M. K. McEwen, C. M. Kodama, A. N. Alvarez, S. Lee, & C. T. H. Liang (Eds.), *Working with Asian American college students* (pp. 21–32). San Francisco: Jossey-Bass.

Tierney, W. G., Campbell, C. D., & Sanchez, G. J. (2004). *The road ahead: Improving diversity in graduate education.* Los Angeles: Center for Higher Education Policy Analysis, Rossier School of Education, University of Southern California.

Tokarczyk, M. M., & Fay, E. A. (1993). Introduction. In M. M. Tokarczyk & E. A. Fay (Eds.), *Working-class women in the academy* (pp. 3–24). Amherst: The University of Massachusetts Press.

Turner, C. S. V. (1994). Guests in someone else's house: Students of color. *The Review of Higher Education, 17*(4), 355–370.

Turner, C. S. V. (2002). Women of color in academe: Living with multiple marginality. *Journal of Higher Education, 73*(1), 74–93.

U.S. Census Bureau. (2004). *Fact sheet. United States: Highlights from the census 2000: Demographic profiles.* Retrieved on May 20, 2004, from www.census.gov.

Valian, V. (1998). *Why so slow? The advancement of women.* Cambridge, MA: The MIT Press.

Williams, J. (2003, Monday, April 14). The subtle side of discrimination. *Chronicle of Higher Education,* p. 1.

Woo, D. (1989). The gap between striving and achieving: The case of Asian-American women. In Asian American Women United of California (Ed.), *Making waves* (pp. 185–194). Boston: Beacon.

Woo, D. (2000). *Glass ceilings and Asian Americans: The new face of workplace barriers.* Walnut Creek, CA: AltaMira Press.

Zhou, M., & Bankston III, C. L. (1998). *Growing up American: How Vietnamese children adapt to life in the United States.* New York: Russell Sage Foundation.

2

ASIAN AMERICAN GENDER GAP IN SCIENCE AND TECHNOLOGY

Tracking Male versus Female College Students' Paths toward Academic Careers

Jaekyung Lee

It is well known that Asian Americans are extraordinary educational achievers with higher levels of educational attainment and achievement than other racial groups (Flynn, 1991; Kao, 1995; Sue & Okazaki, 1990). While this phenomenon is often generalized to all Asian Americans regardless of their gender and attributed to home-related factors (e.g., child-rearing and socialization practices), very little is known about an Asian American gender gap that may arise from social stereotyping and institutional discrimination as well as differential parental expectations and family support for boys versus girls at home. Clearly, there is a gender gap across the board in traditionally male fields such as science and technology, where male and female students tend to show markedly different levels of academic interest, engagement, and achievement while in school, and ultimately different occupational choices after graduation. Asian Americans may not be free from such a pervasive gender gap problem, despite their relatively greater participation and accomplishment in science and technology.

Research assistance for this publication was provided by Maggie Stoutenburg and Reva M. Fish in the Department of Counseling, School and Educational Psychology of the University at Buffalo.

Two major questions are addressed in this chapter: Are Asian male college students different from their female counterparts in their academic paths toward careers in traditionally male-dominated science, math, and engineering (SME) fields? If there is any gender gap in Asian American college students' educational and occupational trajectories, is it different from the patterns shown by other racial and ethnic groups? In light of these questions, I will review previous research and then present the findings of my own original research.

Factors Influencing Gender Gap in SME Fields

The gender gap in math and science, and the newer gap in technology (i.e., computer science and engineering) have received much attention over the last decade (Meyers, 2003). In 1991, the American Association of University Women (AAUW) released the results of its national survey of gender-related inequalities in the nation's schools (AAUW, 1991). While the survey emphasizes the importance of students' perceived ability in math and science and self-esteem for both boys and girls, it also revealed that girls' relatively lower self-esteem, and its association with poor representation in math and science, dampened their career aspirations. In 1998, the AAUW conducted a follow-up study and found that although the overall gender gap in math and science has narrowed, a gap remains in the level of courses taken; there is a particularly large gap in physics and computer science (AAUW, 1998).

Previous national surveys of college students reported gender differences across race and ethnicity in characteristics of college students including their undergraduate major, grade-point average (GPA), and educational aspirations (Clune, Nuñez, Choy, & Carroll, 2001). With respect to their undergraduate experiences, women were more likely than men to major in certain fields, most notably education (18% vs. 6%) and health professions (10% vs. 4%). Men, in contrast, were more likely than women to major in business and management (26% vs. 19%) and engineering (12% vs. 2%). Women graduated with higher GPAs than men: 61 percent of women had GPAs of 3.0 or higher, compared with 49 percent of men.

What are the key factors that contribute to these uneven gender differences? Previous research has shown them to be sex-stereotyping of subjects, courses, and careers. Subjects and courses were often classified as masculine or feminine according to whether they have been taken by a majority of one sex over the other (Harvey, 1984; Schweigardt, Worrell, & Hale, 2001; Stables & Stables, 1995; Whitehead, 1996; Williams, 1994). Traditionally masculine subject areas included math, science, and engineering, while traditionally feminine subject areas included writing and literature, languages, and social sciences (Schweigardt, Worrell, & Hale, 2001).

This gender difference in course-taking patterns was found to be related to perception of ability in the subject. In a study of high school students, boys chose advanced math classes more than girls, and females' choices were affected by their perceptions of lack of ability in the subject (Pedro, Wolleat, Fennema, & Becker, 1981). Further, studies also reported gender differences among high school students in their perceived efficacy for sex-stereotypical occupations: Female students reported greater self-efficacy for occupations such as social worker, teacher, nurse, or secretary (Lapan & Jingeleski, 1992). The differences in occupational preferences between males and females are also related to a gender-segregated labor market (Gaskell, 1984). Even when girls enter traditionally male-dominated professional fields such as medicine and law, they tend to enter female-oriented, less prestigious areas such as pediatrics and family law (Meyers, 2003). In technology-oriented fields, females tend to enter office-type jobs where they are directed by the technology while males enter fields such as engineering in which they direct the technology.

Are there any earlier gender differences in the level of academic ability and achievement in K–12 math and science, the subjects that are critical for success in SME fields in higher education and the job market? National Assessment of Educational Progress (NAEP) showed that there were few gender differences in average math and science achievement (Coley, 2001). Data from the National Education Longitudinal Survey (NELS) also showed no gender differences in math achievement on average. However, significant male advantages were found in the high end of math achievement (Fan, Chen, & Matsumoto, 1997; Hedges & Nowell, 1995). The observed gender differences for higher-achieving high school students raised concerns about the gender imbalance in the flow of new students into science and engineering careers because these students are likely to purse careers in SME (Fan, Chen, & Matsumoto, 1997).

According to a study, few females serve on faculty despite Title IX's discrimination ban; science and engineering faculties remain overwhelmingly White and male across the nation, including the top fifty universities in the United States (Nelson, 2003). The study found that the percentages of women among full professors in those disciplines ranges from 3 percent to 15 percent. While there is little overt discrimination, the study said that the cycle of male dominance tends to perpetuate itself. The lack of female faculty undermines efforts to attract girls to science and engineering, and particularly into the classroom on the college level—largely due to a lack of role models.

Racial and Ethnic Differences in Gender Inequalities

Is there evidence of significant interaction between gender and race factors in terms of participation and performance in SME fields? In other words, does the gender gap in SME fields vary among different racial and ethnic groups? While prior research clearly suggests a gender gap in SME fields, the status of female performance may vary significantly among different racial and ethnic groups. It is necessary to see how race/ethnicity factors interact with gender factors to affect inequalities in SME fields. The literature review suggests mixed findings, depending on the type of outcomes measured, the nature of samples selected, and the stage of one's education and career examined.

As far as math and science achievement of students as measured by standardized test scores is concerned, one argues that "there are more similarities than variations in gender differences among racial and ethnic groups" (Coley, 2001). Despite the prevailing gender gap in math and science, Asian females still perform better than other minority groups' males who outperform their female counterparts in math and science. At the same time, a gender gap also exists for all racial groups in terms of their academic participation and choice, but the status of females tends to vary among racial groups. Hsia (1988) reported that the proportion of Asian American female college students who major in math, physical science, or engineering is comparable to males of all other ethnic groups.

A national survey of college students reported racial differences in their undergraduate and graduate experiences. Consistent with historical trends, persistence rates for students pursuing a bachelor's degree tended to be higher for Asian/Pacific Islander students than for Hispanic and Black, non-Hispanic students (Horn & Maw, 1995). Asians also tended to pursue professional degrees after college graduation more than any other racial group (Clune et al., 2001). However, there was very little difference in the percentage of Asian male and female college graduates who go to graduate school. At the same time, similar proportions of Asian men and women were employed following graduation. This provides some evidence of overall gender equality among Asian college graduates in their educational opportunities and outcomes in the United States. Nevertheless, studies also show that Asian Pacific

American women are underrepresented in higher education in doctoral studies, as faculty, and at higher levels of academic administration (Hune, 1998).

Previous studies demonstrated that Asian Americans are more likely to have professional and technical occupations than their White counterparts. While Asian Americans achieve a better occupational status through higher education, some studies suggest the influence of Asian Americans' status in society on educational attainment and choice of careers. Sue and Okazaki (1990) argue that the educational attainments of Asian Americans are highly influenced by the opportunities present for upward mobility. They suggest that, in certain career activities including leadership, entertainment, sports, politics, and so forth, many Asian Americans perceive limitations in their career choices or upward mobility because of English language skills or social discrimination. According to this view, Asian Americans tend to choose majors in college that require quantitative skills (e.g., math and computer science) as opposed to fields requiring more cultural knowledge and English proficiency (e.g., social sciences and humanities), and they also tend to pursue professional and technical occupations in which they have a greater chance of upward mobility.

Although this view of cultural and language barriers may be truer for recent immigrants, it hardly explains why similar patterns of educational and occupational choices persist among the third generation and afterward. Hsia (1988) suggested that the overrepresentation of Asian Americans in certain occupations, such as science and engineering, has always been found primarily in the foreign born, and that the high occupational profile of Chinese and Japanese Americans did not persist in the American environment among those born and educated in the United States. However, Flynn (1991) refuted the argument by showing that native-born Chinese and Japanese are not different from their foreign-born counterparts in terms of occupational achievement.

There is also a view of possible gender differences among immigrant Asian Americans in their motivation and acculturation (Brandon, 1991). This view suggests that since Asian Americans emigrate from countries in which females' status is relatively more inferior than in the United States, the contrast of opportunities may serve as a potent motivator for Asian American immigrant girls. It also suggests that the socialization of Asian American females may allow them to adopt traditional American male sex roles and that Asian American males might acculturate less easily or quickly to American culture than Asian American women. While it remains unclear how such cultural and language factors might affect Asian female representation and

performance in SME fields, the currently available data does not render statistical differentiation of Asian American females by their generation status
and primary language for possible investigation of the role of culture and
language.

Data and Methods

This analysis draws upon national data from the 1993 Baccalaureate and Beyond Longitudinal Study (B&B:1993/1997, www.nces.ed.gov/surveys),
which includes about eleven thousand students who completed their bachelor's degree in the 1992–93 academic year. The analysis also used follow-up
surveys of the same students conducted in 1994 and 1997 to trace changes
in employment and graduate school enrollment. In addition to the student
interview data, B&B:93/94 collected postsecondary transcripts covering the
undergraduate period. These transcripts provide information on academic
engagement and achievement at the undergraduate level.

First, students in the B&B sample were classified by gender for the comparison of their undergraduate and graduate major, courses taken, and grades
in SME fields. The original sample consisted of males (40.5%), females
(49.3%), and missing (10.2%). Those cases missing gender were dropped
from the analysis. Second, comparisons were made by students' race and ethnicity within each gender group. The original sample contained five mutually exclusive groups: American Indian/Alaska Native (0.5%), Asian or
Pacific Islander (4.4%), Black, non-Hispanic (5.4%), Hispanic (4.5%),
White, non-Hispanic (74.1%), plus missing or unknown category (11.1%).
American Indian/Alaska Native was excluded from the analysis because of
the group's small sample size. Pacific Islanders were included in the same
category as Asians, following the survey's classification of race and ethnicity.
Although this study focused on overall distinguishable patterns of Asians relative to other racial groups and thus did not attempt to further break down
the Asian/Pacific Islander group, their diversity is acknowledged. In the analytical sample, the Asian/Pacific Islanders group consisted of multiple ethnic
subgroups: Chinese (25%), Filipino (12.5%), Hawaiian (2.5%), Japanese
(15%), Korean (10%), Vietnamese (7.5%), Asian Indian (15%), and other
Asian or Pacific Islanders (12.5%).

Further, this analysis draws upon national data from the 1998–99 National Study of Postsecondary Faculty (NSOPF:99), which included 960
degree-granting postsecondary institutions and an initial sample of faculty
and instructional staff from those institutions. Approximately 28,600 faculty

and instructional staff were sent a questionnaire. Subsequently, a subsample of 19,813 faculty and instructional staff was drawn for additional survey follow-up. Approximately 18,000 faculty and instructional staff questionnaires were completed for a weighted response rate of 83 percent. NSOPF gathered information regarding the backgrounds, responsibilities, workloads, salaries, benefits, attitudes, and future plans of both full- and part-time faculty.

First, faculty in the B&B sample were classified by gender for the comparison of their teaching and/or research in SME fields. The NSOPF data sample consisted of more males (58.8%) than females (41.2%). Second, comparison was also made among racial/ethnic groups. The sample consisted of American Indian/Alaska Native (0.8%), Asian or Pacific Islander (5.1%), Black, non-Hispanic (5.0%), Hispanic (3.5%), White, and non-Hispanic (85.6%). The American Indian/Alaska Native group was not included in the analysis because of its small sample size. The sample represents different ranks of faculty: professor (20.3%), associate professor (15.2%), assistant professor (15.1%), instructor/lecturer (34.6%), and others (14.8%).

Results

Undergraduate Major, Courses, and Grades in SME Fields

More Asian males and females choose an undergraduate major in science, math, or engineering than their Black, Hispanic, and White counterparts (see figure 1). Particularly, Asian females significantly exceed females in other racial groups in terms of their representation in those SME fields of major: 1.8 times greater than Blacks and 2.7 times greater than Hispanics or Whites. However, there is still a significant gender gap in these fields across racial groups, and Asians are not an exception to this pattern. Asian males chose SME fields 1.7 times more than their female counterparts. This Asian gender gap is relatively larger than the Black gender gap, but smaller than Hispanic and White gender gaps.

These racial differences in undergraduate major are reflected in course-taking patterns. The average number of total course credits in math, science, and engineering by race and gender are shown in figure 2. Asian males take more course credits in math, science, and engineering than Black, Hispanic, or White males (the Asian advantage relative to other racial groups is in the range of 1.3 to 1.5 in ratio). The same is true of Asian females (1.2 to 1.7 in ratio). Therefore, the effect of being Asian on course-taking patterns exists regardless of gender, and it is consistent with the expectation based on previ-

FIGURE 1

Percentages of College Graduates by Race and Gender Whose Undergraduate Major Was in Science, Math, or Engineering Fields

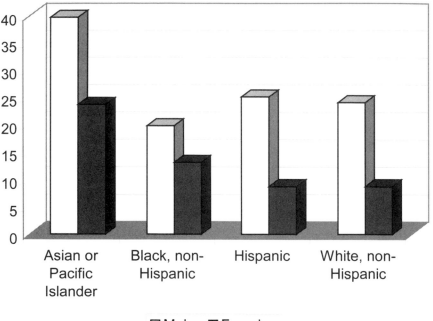

☐ Males ■ Females

Data Sources. Baccalaureate and Beyond Longitudinal Study (B&B) 1993/1994. This variable in the survey identifies a respondent's undergraduate major field of study.

ous studies. However, there were significant differences between Asian males and females; Asian males take 1.5 times more course credits in math, science, and engineering than their female counterparts. The other racial groups show significant gender gaps, although the degree of the gap varies from group to group: about 1.3 for Blacks and 1.7 for Whites and Hispanics. It is worth noting that Asian females still lag behind Asian males, although the Asian females' level of academic engagement in the fields of math, science, and engineering is highly comparable to other racial groups' males.

Asian male students have higher academic achievement in SME fields than their Black, Hispanic, and White male counterparts. The same is true of Asian females who outperformed the females of other racial groups in SME courses. Nevertheless, female students tended to perform better than males in

FIGURE 2

Average Number of Credits for Science, Math, or Engineering Undergraduate Courses Taken by College Graduates by Race and Gender

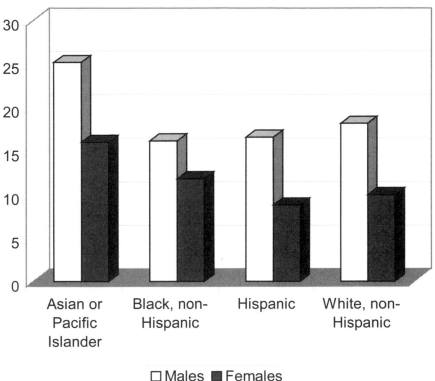

□ Males ■ Females

Data Sources. Baccalaureate and Beyond Longitudinal Study (B&B) 1993/1994. This variable in the undergraduate transcript identifies total number of course credits taken at the sample school.

most cases; the only exception was Asian Americans in mathematics. Figures 3 and 4 show the average grade point averages (GPA) by race and gender in science and engineering fields and in math, respectively. Among students who took courses in science and engineering, Asian students also tended to attain significantly better grades, on average, than the other racial groups except for Whites. Asian students also performed significantly better than all other racial groups including Whites in mathematics. Both male and female Asian students' GPAs were above 2.5 and their differences were not statistically significant. In contrast, female Blacks and Hispanics had higher GPAs than their

FIGURE 3
Grade Point Average by Race and Gender in Undergraduate Science and Engineering Courses

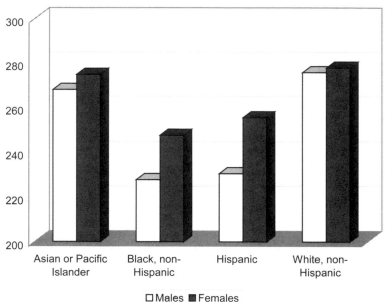

□ Males ■ Females

Data Sources. Baccalaureate and Beyond Longitudinal Study (B&B) 1993/1994. This variable in the undergraduate transcript identifies grade point averages (GPA) of all science and engineering courses as multiplied by 100.

male counterparts in math, science, and engineering. Female Whites performed better than males in math but not in science and engineering. The tendency to higher academic achievement of females in SME fields may be attributable to their selectivity; there is underrepresentation of females compared with their male counterparts, and those females who choose the SME fields are likely to be a more selective group, having a higher motivation and ability for learning those subjects than normal expectations.

Graduate Major and Faculty Career in SME Fields

Does the gender gap in undergraduate education persist through graduate education? Very similar patterns of gender and racial gaps are observed in students' choices of math, science, and engineering for graduate majors (see figure 5). Both male and female Asians major in those fields more than their

FIGURE 4
Grade Point Average by Race and Gender in Undergraduate Math Courses

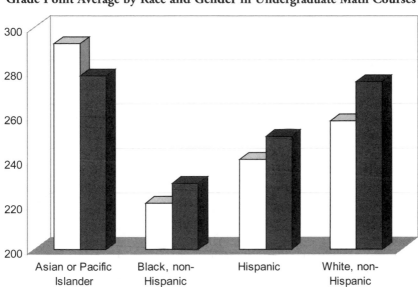

□ Males ■ Females

Data Sources. Baccalaureate and Beyond Longitudinal Study (B&B) 1993/1994. This variable in the undergraduate transcript identifies grade point averages (GPA) of all math courses as multiplied by 100.

Black, Hispanic, or White counterparts. The gender gap for Asians is 1.7, which is about the same as the Black gap (1.5) but smaller than the Hispanic gap (2.3) and the White gap (2.3). Female Asian students' representation is comparable to that of other racial groups' males and their predominance in these fields continues throughout graduate school.

Students who have a graduate level education may seek more professional and technical careers than those who have only an undergraduate level education. While graduate students' actual choice of occupation depends on their personal aptitude and circumstances, their choice of academic jobs at colleges and universities is of particular interest, because those females who choose a teaching and research career as a faculty member can serve directly as a role model for the next generation who would consider the SME fields as their career choice. Figure 6 shows the representation of

FIGURE 5
Percentages of Graduate Students by Race/Ethnicity and Gender Whose Graduate Major Was in Science, Math, or Engineering Fields

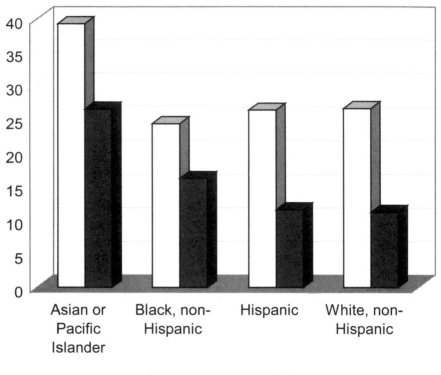

□ Males ■ Females

Data Sources. Baccalaureate and Beyond Longitudinal Study (B&B) 1993/1997. This variable in the survey identifies a respondent's graduate major field of study.

different racial and gender groups in SME fields among the postsecondary education faculty population who picked university teaching or research as their career. Gender differences are still evident across racial groups. Both Asian males and females still exceed their counterparts from other racial groups.

Gender Gap in Asian American Path from Learning to Teaching in SME Fields

The Baccalaureate and Beyond Longitudinal Study (B&B) provides information concerning education and work experiences after completion of

FIGURE 6

Percentages of Postsecondary Faculty by Race/Ethnicity and Gender Whose Principal Teaching or Research Field Is in Science, Math, or Engineering

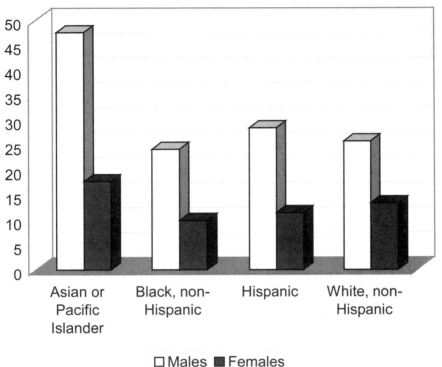

☐ Males ■ Females

Data Sources. 1998–99 National Study of Postsecondary Faculty (NSOPF:99). This variable in the survey identifies the general program area of a respondent's principal field of teaching. If no field of teaching was specified, this variable reflects the field of research.

bachelor's degrees. It should be noted that the B&B survey did not provide longitudinal information on the employment of graduate students as college or university faculty in SME fields. On the other hand, the National Study of Postsecondary Faculty (NSOPF) provides cross-sectional survey information of the faculty status in SME fields. Despite the lack of direct linkages between the two databases, they both include nationally representative samples of college students and faculty respectively, and linking the results of two surveys can give us some insight into college students' trajectories from undergraduate education to graduate education, and then to teaching and/or research careers in academia.

Figure 7 combines the results of the previous analyses as shown in figure 1, figure 5, and figure 6. As the NSOPF data includes all faculty and instructors across rank, there exists a significant time gap between the B&B cohort group, some of whom may have just gotten a graduate degree to join higher education faculty, and the NSOPF sample, most of whom must have become a faculty member much earlier. Nevertheless, when the analysis of the teaching/research field in figure 7 was restricted to the category of assistant

FIGURE 7
Different Racial and Gender Groups' Trajectories of Major and Specialization in Science, Math, and Engineering (SME) Fields.

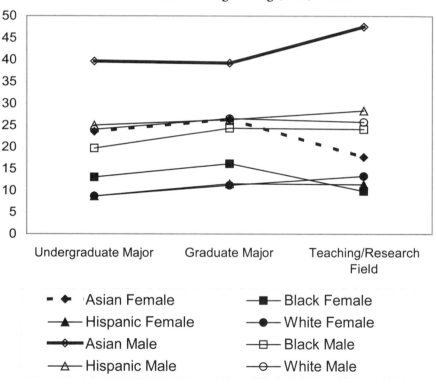

Data Sources: Baccalaureate and Beyond Longitudinal Study (B&B) 1993/1997; 1998–99 National Study of Postsecondary Faculty (NSOPF:99). This line graph shows each group's representation at the three stages: undergraduate major (Percent Undergraduate Students' Major in SME Fields), graduate major (Percent Graduate Students' Major in SME Fields), and teaching/research field (Percent Postsecondary Faculty's Teaching/Research in SME Fields).

professors, very similar patterns were found for junior faculty who had entered academia recently.

When the rates of choosing SME fields are compared among those eight groups as classified by race/ethnicity and gender in figure 7, it appears that there are three distinct clusters. First, Asian males surpass all other groups, and they stand out with as high as a 40–50 percent range. Second, White, Black, and Hispanic males and Asian females form the second tier in the range of 20s. Finally, White, Black, and Hispanic females cluster around the 10 percent range. Figure 7 shows that all race and gender groups maintain their representation in SME fields from undergraduate education to graduate education level, so that their gaps hardly change over the course of postsecondary education. Moreover, most groups also continue their initial trajectory of educational specialization once they get into academia. The notable exception is found among Asians at their critical transition from the stage of learning as an undergraduate or graduate student to the stage of teaching and research as a faculty member at the university. Asian males' representation in postsecondary faculty who specialize in SME fields significantly increases, while Asian females' representation rate drops at the same time.

Discussion

It is evident that a gender gap prevails in traditionally male-dominated SME fields. The gap appears to grow throughout the period of K–12 education, particularly during adolescent years, and it results in unequal choices of academic majors in SME fields during college education. Previous research identified the number of advanced mathematics and science courses taken in high school as the strongest direct influence on choice of a quantitative undergraduate major. Unequal representation of female students in SME fields persists into graduate school education and has an even greater impact on their choice of a teaching and research career in academia.

While prior research generally indicated strong gender inequality and female underrepresentation throughout the pipeline of education in SME fields, a study indicated that the problem of no critical mass of women faculty is not only directly attributable to an insufficient supply of female Ph.D.s but is also exacerbated by the underutilization of women Ph.D.s for faculty positions (Nelson, 2003). In some instances, the percentage of female students far outweighs the proportion of professors of the same gender. The study also showed, with the same kind of utilization data for racial/ethnic groups, that underrepresented minority Ph.D.s in science and engineering are generally placed into faculty positions less often. However, the study did not address the questions of how gender and race factors interact to affect inequalities, and how the inequalities evolve from undergraduate to graduate school level toward an academic career. Moreover, the literature did not pay attention to Asians viewed as a model minority group nor explain why female Asians, who outperform even males of other racial groups, still lag behind their male counterparts in SME fields.

This research attempts to fill the void by tracking diverging career paths among different racial and gender groups of college students toward their academic majors and specializations in SME fields. Given the study's focus on Asian Americans, its finding on the widening gap between Asian males and females in their representation in SME fields for postsecondary teaching/research career raises many questions that need further investigation and explanation. What are the barriers in one's transition from the role of learning as a graduate student to the role of teaching as a faculty? Is this widening gender gap unique to SME fields? As figure 7 shows, it is only Black and Asian females who dropped their representation from graduate major to faculty teaching/research. Is this change in gender gap due simply to females' different career interests and opportunities (e.g., jobs in the government or industry) or more closely related to their different qualifications for university teaching/research jobs (e.g., fewer Ph.D.s or weaker graduate GPAs/research records)? Or is it attributable to any systematic gender discrimination in academic job placement and promotion in the colleges and universities?

There is no evidence that Asian female students do not prefer academic jobs in higher education, particularly teaching and doing research as faculty members. There is also no evidence that Asian females do not perform as well as their male counterparts in graduate school. According to the literature, female students often do not obtain the highest level of achievement because of their low confidence and not their ability level, and confidence plays a large role in the persistence students possess when faced with a challenge. The challenge may come from the stereotype that girls do not perform well in mathematics-related fields (Manning, 1998; Steele, 1999). Encountering these negative stereotype threats may generate anxiety and fear for some students, particularly those who are highly motivated academically and who identify strongly with their chosen school and field of study. However, those female students who chose SME fields and successfully entered graduate school may already have overcome such stereotype threats. Finally, gender discrimination in academic job placement and promotion might be another plausible explanation. Indeed, many universities have been slow in hiring and promoting more women since thirty years ago, when the federal government banned gender discrimination in all academic programs that receive federal aid. However, this simple explanation is challenged by different patterns of gender gap among racial and ethnic groups as shown in figure 7.

Further research is needed to examine the interaction of psychological, cultural, and institutional factors that result in different career paths in SME fields for male versus female college students of different racial and ethnic backgrounds. I would suggest that subsequent research pay attention to the simultaneous influences of multiple forces on Asian females in SME fields, particularly "double-edged stereotype threats" and "lack of role models." Asian females in SME fields are likely to face dual, conflicting stereotype threats: a negative stereotype of females as low achievers in SME fields on one hand, but a positive stereotype of Asians as high achievers in SME fields on the other hand. Asian female students are likely to struggle hard to cope with the negative stereotyped image of females and to live up to the positive stereotype of Asians while in school. However, they are less likely to find professors of the same gender and race in their department who may serve as role models. There is no critical mass of Asian female faculty in SME fields; for example, only 1.1 percent of chemical engineering faculty at the top U.S. engineering schools are Asian females, whereas 11.3 percent are Asian males (Nelson, 2003). The combination of those factors, the double-edged stereotype threats, and the lack of female Asian faculty as mentors and role models in SME fields could set "glass ceiling" barriers for Asian female students who otherwise may stay and survive in academia.

Longitudinal research may be designed to empirically test the above or other related hypotheses, explaining why Asian female students pick SME fields for undergraduate and graduate education, but their choice of major does not translate into careers in academia. This line of research may help us become more aware of the unique problem with the Asian female group in SME fields that has been obscured because of the aggregate racial statistics reinforcing a widely held group image of high performance and over-representation in SME fields. This research may have implications for other minority female groups as well, to improve their opportunities and reduce barriers throughout the pipeline of postsecondary education and academic career in SME fields.

References

American Association of University Women. (1991). *Shortchanging girls, shortchanging America*. Washington, DC: Author.

American Association of University Women. (1998). *Gender gaps: Where schools still fail our children.* Washington, DC: Author.

Baccalaureate and Beyond Longitudinal Study (B&B:1993/1997). Retrieved November 1, 2004, from www.nces.ed.gov/surveys.

Brandon, P. R. (1991). Gender differences in young Asian Americans' educational attainments. *Sex Roles, 25,* 45–61.

Clune, M. S., Nuñez, A., Choy, S. P., & Carroll, C. D. (2001). *Competing choices: Men's and women's paths after earning a bachelor's degree* (NCES 2001-154). Washington, DC: U.S. Department of Education, National Center for Education Statistics.

Coley, R. (2001). *Differences in the gender gap: Comparisons across racial/ethnic groups in education and work.* Princeton, NJ: Educational Testing Service, Policy Information Center.

Fan, X., Chen, M., & Matsumoto, A. R. (1997). Gender differences in mathematics achievement: Findings from the National Education Longitudinal Study of 1988. *The Journal of Experimental Education, 65,* 229–242.

Flynn, J. R. (1991). *Asian Americans: Achievement beyond IQ.* Hillsdale, NJ: Erlbaum.

Gaskell, J. (1984). Gender and course choice: The orientation of male and female students. *Journal of Education, 166*(1), 89–102.

Harvey, T. J. (1984). Gender differences in subject preference and perception of subject importance among third-year secondary school pupils in single-sex and mixed comprehensive schools. *Educational Studies, 10,* 243–253.

Hedges, L. V., & Nowell, A. (1995). Sex differences in mental test scores, variability, and numbers of high scoring individuals. *Science, 269*(5220), 41–45.

Horn, L., & Maw, C. (1995). *Minority undergraduate participation in postsecondary education* (NCES 95-166). Washington, DC: U.S. Department of Education, National Center for Education Statistics.

Hsia, J. (1988). *Asian Americans in higher education and work.* Hillsdale, NJ: Erlbaum.

Hune, S. (1998). *Asian Pacific American women in higher education: Claiming visibility and voice.* Washington, DC: Association of American Colleges and Universities.

Kao, G. (1995). Asian Americans as model minorities? A look at their academic performance. *American Journal of Education, 103,* 121–159.

Lapan, R. T., & Jingeleski, J. (1992). Circumscribing vocational aspirations in junior high school. *Journal of Counseling Psychology, 39,* 81–90.

Manning, M. L. (1998). Gender differences in young adolescents' mathematics and science achievement. *Childhood Education, 74*(3), 168–171.

Meyers, M. (2003). *The high school experiences of female engineering majors.* Unpublished research paper.

National Study of Postsecondary Faculty (NSOPE:99). Retrieved November 1, 2004, from www.nces.ed.gov/surveys.

Nelson, D. J. (2003). The standing of women in academia. *Chemical Engineering Progress, 99*(9), 38S–41S. Retrieved October 27, 2004, from http://cheminfo.chem.ou.edu/faculty/djn/diversity/Pubs/CEP03Aug/p38S–41S.html

Pedro, J. D., Wolleat, P., Fennema, E., & Becker, A. D. (1981). Election of high school mathematics by females and males: Attributions and attitudes. *American Educational Research Journal, 18*, 207–218.

Schweigardt, W. J., Worrell, F. C., & Hale, R. J. (2001). Gender differences in the motivation for and selection of courses in a summer program for academically talented students. *Gifted Child Quarterly, 45*(4), 283–292.

Stables, A., & Stables, S. (1995). Gender differences in students' approaches to A-level subjects: A study of first-year A-level students in a tertiary college. *Educational Research, 37*, 39–51.

Steele, C. (1999). Thin ice: "Stereotype threat" and black college students. *Atlantic Monthly, 284*(2), 44–54.

Sue, S., & Okazaki, S. (1990). Asian-American educational achievement: A phenomenon in search of an explanation. *American Psychologist, 45*(8), 913–920.

Whitehead, J. M. (1996). Sex stereotypes, gender identity, and subject choice at A-level. *Educational Research, 38*, 147–160.

Williams, J. E. (1994). Gender differences in high school students' efficacy-expectation/performance discrepancies across four subject matter domains. *Psychology in the Schools, 31*, 232–237.

3

THEORIZING EXPERIENCES OF ASIAN WOMEN FACULTY IN SECOND- AND FOREIGN-LANGUAGE TEACHER EDUCATION

Angel Lin, Ryuko Kubota, Su Motha,
Wendy Wang, and Shelley Wong

This collective writing project originated from the participation of a number of us in the colloquium on Gender in TESOL at the 2003 TESOL (Teachers of English to Speakers of Other Languages) conference. While we have witnessed a recent growing interest in researching gender issues in second- and foreign-language education (e.g., Pavlenko, Blackledge, & Teutsch-Dwyer, 2001; Sunderland, Cowley, Rahim, Leontza-kou, & Shattuck, 2002), there has been little research on the systematic marginalization of Asian women faculty working in the second- and foreign-language education fields. The dearth of research in this area stands in contrast to the amount of research published on the systematic marginalization of women in higher education (e.g., Bagilhole, 2002; Halvorsen, 2002; Hornig, 2003; Jackson, 2002; Luke, 2001; Morley & Walsh, 1995, 1996; Walsh, 2002) and marks a significant absence of serious public attention to the mar-

---

Parts of this chapter have been taken from Lin, Grant, Kubota, Motha, Tinker-Sachs, Vandrick, and Wong's article in *TESOL Quarterly*, Autumn Issue, 2004.

ginalization of Asian women faculty in second- and foreign-language education. However, our sharing of experiences reveals consistent patterns of marginalization across different institutional contexts that require feminist theorizing to attend to issues not only of gender but also of race and social class. Additionally, in the fields of second- and foreign-language education, issues of Nonnative English Speaking Professionals (NNESP) and speakers of World Englishes must be addressed. Discursive practices of gender, class, and race must be connected to histories of conquest, slavery, and colonialism. We feel a strong need to make deeper sense of our lived experiences by understanding and theorizing the special ideological and institutional conditions underlying our lived experiences of marginalization and discrimination. This theorizing is, however, not meant to be merely private academic work, but a dialogic, public, political practice. While it starts as textual practice (i.e., in the act of producing a textual product—a paper), it is not meant to end there. As Stuart Hall (1992) puts it:

> I come back to the critical distinction between intellectual work and academic work: they overlap . . . but they are not the same thing. . . . I come back to theory and politics, the politics of theory. Not theory as the will to truth, but theory as a set of contested, localized, conjunctual knowledges, which have to be debated in a dialogical way. But also as a practice which always thinks about its intervention in a world in which it would make some difference, in which it would have some effect. (p. 286)

Through engaging in this collective, dialogic writing project, we hope to both draw attention to the situation of Asian women faculty in second- and foreign-language education and contribute to the building of a wider community of second- and foreign-language education scholars and researchers (consisting of both women and men, and both Asian and other racial/ethnic groups) in which issues of marginalization and discrimination, of social justice and togetherness-in-difference (Ang, 2001) can be continuously engaged with as part of our dialogic, critical practice and political intervention. As feminist standpoint theorist Nancy Hartsock (1983) says:

> Women's lives, like men's, are structured by social relations which manifest the experiences of the dominant gender and class. The ability to go beneath the surface of appearances to reveal the real but concealed social relations requires both theoretical and political activity. Feminist theorists must demand that feminist theorizing be grounded in women's material activity

and must as well be part of the political struggle necessary to develop areas of social life modeled on this activity. (p. 304)

We are therefore going to ground our theorizing in our lived experiences. We first wrote our narratives of lived experiences and then electronically circulated them and responded to the emerging themes in one another's writings. In the second section of this chapter we shall share excerpts of our narratives, and in the third section we shall summarize some emerging patterns and issues, and analyze the ideological and institutional conditions underlying patterns of marginalization. In the final section we shall propose directions in which second- and foreign-language education as a discipline needs to be re-visioned and reshaped.

Our Lived Experiences in Different Contexts

Due to limited space, we provide only key excerpts from our narratives, hoping to give the reader a feel of our experiences in the different institutional contexts that we work in (we are from diverse racial/ethnic backgrounds: Chinese American, Chinese, Japanese, and Sri Lankan Australian. Pen names are used for anonymity).

The Paradox of (Hypo)critical Pedagogy: Anne's Story

Gender and racial discrimination persists in higher education. Various faculty of color have recently exposed issues of gender and race in their personal narratives, focusing mainly on their challenges in the classroom (Jacobs, Cintrón, & Canton, 2002; Mabokela & Green, 2001; TuSmith & Reddy, 2002; Vargas, 2002). As a woman second-language teacher-educator of color and nonnative speaker of English, I share similar challenges. Yet my experiences have also been influenced by same-gender politics or relationships with white[1] women colleagues. While it is important to take a nonessentialist approach to gender and race by viewing them as relational rather than categorical, allowing multiple positionalities and experiences (Ng, 1995), it is equally important to acknowledge hegemony that perpetuates racial, gender, and linguistic domination and subordination.

In my department, I am often positioned as an illegitimate faculty member. I have had the following disturbing experiences in working with some

---

[1] We have deliberately used small letter "w" for the word "white" in this article as we want, as a colonial move, to alter the convention of capitalizing whiteness and white people.

of the white women colleagues and administrators: being excluded from communication related to important decisions about the program that I work in, forced to do a large amount of work beyond my assigned duties, treated as if I were a teaching assistant by being deprived of decision-making power, blamed for students' complaints about the program for which I am not primarily responsible, deprived of opportunities to work with graduate students interested in my specialty area, expected to do student-teacher supervision rather than teaching a graduate course, and given the lowest salary at my rank. Worse yet, I was insulted by having my cultural and linguistic heritage devalued in the following comments from a senior white female administrator: "I want you to do ESL [English as a Second Language] (teacher education); XXX [my native language] isn't important" [even though I was originally hired to create a foreign-language teacher education program for that language]. The same woman criticized me as being "sulky" and flippantly advised me to say "Fuck you [*sic*]" to another white woman colleague who had mistreated me; she said this would improve the situation for me.

The above experiences reveal that racial minority women faculty's experiences of oppression are not always caused by male domination but sometimes by same-gender politics in which some white women seek power to maintain the center stage for themselves. These women usually project such public images as being progressive, promoting ethics and social justice with regard to race, class, and gender, endorsing postmodernism, and advocating for diversity. However, what they say they believe in does not match the ways they have treated me. What is promoted here can be called *(hypo)critical pedagogy*—a pedagogy and educational vision that appears to be critical but is hypocritical because of a mismatch between the vision and everyday practice. One way to understand such a paradox is to situate it in colonialism.

Collins (1998) argues that whites who advocate for minorities and social justice resemble what Memmi (1965) called "colonizers who refuse," that is, colonizers with a progressive stance who resist and challenge the power and privilege bestowed on them by the colonial system. Collins draws a parallel between colonizers who refuse and postmodern scholars who appropriate the notion of the decentering of power, which originally aimed to challenge the centers of power—e.g., whites, men, middle class—and to shift power from the center to the margins. However, colonizers, whether they refuse or accept their power and privilege, still benefit from the colonial system and can afford to resist injustice and oppression in the abstract without giving up their privileges. In Collins's (1998) words, "groups already privileged under hierarchical power relations suffer little from embracing the language of decentering denuded of any actions to decenter actual hierarchical power relations in academia or elsewhere. Ironically, their privilege may actually increase" (p. 137). The power of white women colleagues would not be threatened by their act of theorizing the decentering of power because they are not actually giving up their privilege; rather, such theorization only gives them more power in academe.

What would happen, however, if colonizers refuse to encounter voices of the colonized who attempt to move to the center? Collins (1998) states:

> Despite their good intentions, when colonizers who refuse come into contact with *actual* colonized people who speak out, as compared to either *ideas* about colonized people or natives who remain silenced, colonizers realize that their interests and those of the colonized are fundamentally opposed. If colonialism were abolished and colonized people were to gain power, little privilege would remain within new social relations for former colonizers, even those who refuse. (pp. 130–131)

This suggests that as long as women faculty of color remain silent and show respect for white women colleagues who refuse, these colleagues can maintain their status and continue to serve as power brokers, advocating for minority colleagues. Yet they keep minority faculty from obtaining equal opportunities to make important decisions, have leadership roles, or teach advanced courses, because these opportunities would threaten their status in power. When they face oppositional voices of women faculty of color, they cease to play the motherly role and instead protect their power by preventing minority faculty from having access to information, resources, and opportunities.

The paradox of (hypo)critical pedagogy seems to lie in some white women colleagues' struggle to maintain their status in the racial hierarchy of power while claiming as their own the role of advocate for the marginalized and promoter of a postmodern decenterization of power. How can women faculty of color cope with this hypocrisy? How can they have a diplomatic relationship with white women faculty who refuse?

Salary Inequity and Denial of Tenure: Bertha's Story

Within the field of education there are hierarchies of knowledge related to power, gendered roles, and salary differentials. Preschool teachers and childcare providers, who are primarily women, receive low pay and are at the bottom of the hierarchy. You will find as you move from elementary schools to high schools and on to tertiary education and graduate schools that the field of teaching goes from being overwhelmingly female in the care of infants and toddlers to a teaching staff at the university and graduate level that is largely composed of men. Women are paid less than men not only because there are differences in pay between teaching young children and teaching undergraduate and graduate students, but also at the same rank, in the same department, women are paid less than men.

Inequality in pay between men and women is due to many reasons that reinforce and reproduce each other. In a market economy, women as a commodity are valued less. The initial salary offered to women is lower. We are not socialized to negotiate salaries and are so used to being outsiders that we consistently underestimate our own value. Because child care is seen as our responsibility as women, each time we leave the workplace to have a child, our salaries go down. In my own case, after finally finishing my dissertation and taking care of my baby and being a care provider for an older family member in her nineties, I returned to teaching as an adjunct professor. Although I had been paid a higher salary previously, I began again, new to the area, as a part-time instructor. I taught at three different universities and made less than $9,000 that year with no benefits. This barely covered my child-care expenses. When I got a tenure-track position at University X I was so happy to have a full-time "real" job that I didn't negotiate my salary and took what was offered me. Younger white male professors were hired at higher salaries even though they did not have as many years of teaching experience and some had not completed their dissertations. Not only were they paid higher salaries, but they were given release time to do research and were mentored in numerous ways to avoid certain labor-intensive teaching assignments (for example, clinical assignments and supervising student teachers) and assigned to less time-consuming, more prestigious committees. It is assumed that men should get paid more to support their families, but when we as women are the sole support for our families we are not given the same consideration.

University X had been a segregated university until the 1960s. Justice Thurgood Marshall, the first African American to be appointed to the U.S. Supreme Court, applied to and was denied entrance to University X's law school in the 1940s. In the entire history of my former department at University X, only two African Americans and one Hispanic have been granted tenure. To this day, my former department has *never* granted tenure to an African American woman. The year I was denied tenure, in the entire College of Education there were only three tenured African American professors out of 123 faculty members. In my department at the time I was denied tenure, the last five men who had gone up for associate professor with tenure or full professor had all been promoted while the last five women to do the same had all been denied or withdrew from the process.

The number of my publications was equivalent to that of a white male who had been promoted the year before. But even though I was supported by my department (19 for, 2 opposed) and my college (5 to 0), the vote on the University Promotion and Tenure Committee was four against, one for, with two abstentions. While my teaching and service were deemed sufficient, the quality of my scholarship was questioned. The university committee wanted to know why I had not published in linguistic journals (they had never heard of the journals in which I had published, which included top-tiered journals). They considered my work to be "too applied." In addition, they pointed out that letters from external reviewers came from institutions that were not deemed top-ten research institutions (although the reviewers are all prominent figures in second- and foreign-language education) and they didn't understand why the letters came from a number of different departments (i.e., English, education, communication, and linguistics) rather than a single department.

University X is a "Research 1" institution and its College of Education is viewed as being too "practical" and insufficiently research oriented. Within the College of Education, my department—which was involved in teacher education—was at the bottom of the hierarchy. We had heavier advising workloads, taught more classes, and were paid less than those in other departments. There were more women in our department than in the other departments. The departments at the top of the college hierarchy focused on educational policies and administration (which are still largely the domains of men). The educational psychology model of large-scale quantitative research is viewed as "real research." Classroom research was not as valued as much as research on human development in out-of-school settings, which were viewed as more "naturalistic."

My work in collaboration with teachers in school districts and as a teacher-researcher on my own teacher education courses was also not seen as "real" research. There are differing standards concerning what constitutes a "line of research." If a CV lists twenty articles with "discourse processing" or "input-output" in the titles it is viewed as a "consistent" line of research, but when my CV listed twenty articles with "critical," "multicultural," or "minority" in the title, it was viewed as "repetitive" and "fluff" and "an insufficiently serious and robust research agenda." In the field of Second

Language Acquisition, "physics-envy" (Lantolf, 1996) values certain terminology related to machinery and technology as being scientific and objective. Mechanistic, computer metaphors in educational research are valued over interpretive, feminist, and critical race epistemologies. For example, the "input-output" computer metaphor is viewed as a more "scientific" model than the metaphor of "participation" to account for how someone learns a second or foreign language.

Tenure rates in higher education for women and minorities are lower than those for white males. According to an article published in 1997, the year I was denied tenure, the 1993 annual report of the American Council on Education's Office of Minorities in Higher Education stated that the tenure rate for white men in tenure-track positions was 78 percent, compared with 52 percent for Asian American women. Women in all categories fared worse than men:

TABLE 1
Tenure Rates in Tenure Track Positions in 1993

White men	78%	White women	61%
African American Men	63%	African American Women	58%
Hispanic Men	66%	Hispanic Women	57%
Asian American Men	67%	Asian American Women	52%
American Indian Men	72%	American Indian Women	49%

Source: From "Who Makes the Cut?" by D. Goldberg, July 27, 1997, *Washington Post Education Review*, p. 4.

However, when I filed an appeal, the university appeals committee had no record of the disparity between men and women either in my department, college, or at the university level because the official tenure rates for University X did not include the women and minorities who voluntarily withdrew from the process. Candidates often leave an institution before a tenure decision is made if they are told or suspect that it is unlikely that they will be granted tenure. Withdrawing from the process is not counted as being denied tenure.

Renegotiating Legitimacy, Authenticity, and Authority in English to Speakers of Other Languages (ESOL) Education: Catherine's Story

As Amin (1999) has observed, in the field of TESOL much attention has been given to the "race, ethnicity, culture, and gender of the learners, but far less attention has been given to how these variables in the teacher may impact on the classroom" (p. 93). Even in critical writing addressing inequality issues in the ESL classroom, as Amin points out, teachers in the position of power are often referred to as white. If unequal power is embedded in the classroom relationship between white teachers and students of color, what does it mean to be a nonwhite teacher in a predominately white teacher education classroom? If language is power, what does it mean to be a TESOL professional positioned as a nonnative English speaker? The notion of native and nonnative speakers of English, as Pennycook (1999) argues, is "interwoven with issues of race and ethnicity, as one's nativeness as a speaker of English is often assumed to correlate with the paleness of one's skin" (p. 333). If nativeness is equated with whiteness and thus awarded "authenticity" and "authority," what does it mean to be a double minority, that is, a nonnative English speaker and a visible minority faculty member, in the predominantly white TESOL field?

From an English as a Foreign Language (EFL) learner in China to an ESL teacher in Canada, and now an ESOL teacher educator in the United States, I have lived a life unimagined in the world of tradition. It has been an incredible journey in which I have been subject to continuous negotiation of social positionings. My experience as an Asian female TESOL faculty member reflects the larger sociopolitical context that can be illustrated in the following incidents:

> When I came to the States five years ago, a typical conversation often began with the question, "Where do you come from?" Being a Chinese Canadian, I replied that I came from Canada. This response often triggered further inquiry. "Where do you *really* come from?" Obviously, the authenticity of my Canadianness was being questioned. To feed people's obsession with authenticity, I once responded that I came from China. For someone who knew that I was a professor of TESOL, such a response was received with bewilderment. My peripheral origin and my profession did not seem to match. The authority of my knowledge base was then under scrutiny.

> *   *   *

> Another question that I have to deal with is "What do you do?" My honest answer is often received with a look of disbelief and a moment of silence followed with "Uh!" The worst case occurred when I crossed the Ambassador Bridge between Windsor and Detroit. I was stopped for a routine check. In response to the immigration officer's question, "What do you do

in the States?" I replied, "I am a professor." The look on his face told me that he didn't believe me. "What do you teach?" he asked. "I teach English." Afraid that I might confuse him if I used the term "TESOL," I deliberately left it out. The next thing I knew I was being escorted into the immigration office for a thorough check; the officer even tore up my trunk in search of evidence for my dubious claim. The next time I crossed the border, in response to the same routine question, I calmly replied, "I am a professor of Chinese." I was let go immediately.

These two incidents, appearing to be innocent but not uncommon, are reflective of some dominant perceptions and stereotypes of nonnative English speakers and visible minority professionals. These stereotypes pervade the society we live in. In both cases, I was imagined otherwise, and was obliged to assume a subjective position socially constructed for me. The persistent social tendency to define nonwhites as Other, as foreign, questions my right to belong. When Canadianness is perceived to equate with whiteness, it puts hyphenated Canadians of color in an ambiguous and dislocated position, making us feel less "authentic," and hence "less Canadian." The second incident is yet another reminder that in this race-, class-, and gender-conscious society, there is a tendency to assume that immigrants, particularly visible minority women, are at the bottom of the social ladder. To claim that I was a professor, particularly a professor of English, went beyond the American dream. This incident also raises the issue of ownership of English. The color of my skin and the English language were perceived to be mutually exclusive. To claim to teach a language other than my own was to be questioned.

These daily incidents provide a glimpse of the struggles that I have in my professional life as a nonnative English speaker and an Asian female faculty member in a Master's in Teaching English as a Second Language (MA TESOL) program where I work with five other TESOL colleagues, all Caucasian. Although English has been my professional language all these years, the biodevelopmental definition of the native speaker does not speak to my relationship with English, positioning me as an unauthentic English speaker, and hence an unauthentic ESL teacher (Amin, 1999). Like many people new to the profession, particularly nonnative English-speaking TESOL professionals of color, I have spent an incredible amount of time and energy establishing myself as a legitimate professor in the eyes of both my students and my colleagues. "Prove yourself" seems to be written everywhere no matter where I turn. Echoing the minority teachers' experiences reported by Amin

(1999), Liu (1999), and Thomas (1999), my credibility, knowledge, and authority are easily questioned. Challenges to my credibility come from native English-speaking graduate students as well as from international students who have come to the United States with an expectation to be taught by " 'American' teachers."

As a TESOL professional, I would like to characterize my teaching approach as one that encourages mutual engagement and inquiry. For example, following the principle of building a classroom learning community, I often ask graduate students to bring in questions and take turns to lead class discussions, an approach that is democratic in nature. It was my hope that this approach would give students the opportunity to pose their own questions and have them answered through mediated discussions. Many of my students did enjoy student-led class discussions, as they indicated in the course evaluation; some students, however, made comments as follows: "The teacher needs to teach the class, not the students." Although such comments are subject to different interpretations, they are no doubt a challenge to my credibility as a teacher. Being positioned to prove myself makes it difficult, if not impossible, to consider certain pedagogical strategies. When observing my colleagues, I truly admire the comfort they enjoy when they say "I don't know" in response to students' questions, a strategy commonly used by many professors. As I struggle for recognition and credibility, I too, like Amin (1999), avoid showing my humanity in the classroom. While I believe that the "I-don't-know" strategy can create an open and conducive learning environment and even improve the teacher-student relationship because it humanizes the teacher, I am less inclined to use it because of the way I am positioned. This creates an unjustified challenge, suggesting that as a double minority faculty member I have to be twice as good as others to be considered competent.

I have to admit that I am fortunate to be working with colleagues who embrace what Brutt-Griffler and Samimy (1999) call a "difference" approach, recognizing the positive elements that nonnative English-speaking teachers bring to the TESOL profession. This has provided the space I need to negotiate legitimacy, authenticity, and authority on terms that give me the confidence to claim expertise in certain areas without undue challenge. To this end, the "difference" discourse at my workplace is empowering; however, since I am being constructed within the context of the native and nonnative dichotomy, my knowledge and expertise tend to be marginalized. I remain constructed as Other, often assigned to teach courses that my Caucasian colleagues feel less inclined to teach. In spite of the good intention underlying the "difference" discourse, I am aware that the legitimacy and authority that I have negotiated within the existing discourse at my workplace prescribes only limited roles for me to play, and thus continues the native and nonnative divide initiated by the "dominant" discourse that legitimizes inequalities between native and nonnative English-speaking TESOL professionals (Braine, 1999; Brutt-Griffler & Samimy, 1999). Reflecting on my experience as a nonnative English speaker and an Asian female faculty member, I feel an imperative need for a critical discourse, one that can break down the divides of nativeness-nonnativeness, superiority-inferiority, and Self-Other (Braine, 1999; Brutt-Griffler & Samimy, 1999; Canagarajah, 1999; Lin, Wang, Akamatsu, & Riazi, 2002; Pennycook, 1999); one in which dealing with tensions surrounding legitimacy, authenticity, and authority is no longer perceived to be my personal issue; and one that encourages renegotiation of legitimacy, authenticity, and authority on terms that are liberating for all TESOL professionals.

"A Second-Class TESOL Professional": Denise's Story

Ever since the very moment of my appointment in my university I have been constituted as "a local classroom person" and assigned to do the labor-intensive work of student practicum supervision and school placement coordination.

I learned later that, at the time my institution hired me, they had two positions open. One position was to replace a local (i.e., nonwhite, nonnative English) Chinese woman faculty member who was leaving academia to return as the principal of a secondary school. The other position was for someone to teach second language acquisition (SLA) and second- and foreign-language education research methods.

Although I had extensive training in research methodology, including both qualitative, ethnographic methods and sophisticated statistics and measurement theories and techniques (e.g., path analysis and LISREL [linear structural relations], factor analysis, and other types of inferential statistical analyses), my employer seemed to ignore all my research training (which was given on my CV) and focused on me as a "local classroom person" because my thesis research was a sociocultural and discourse analytic study of local classrooms. I later learned from the Caucasian colleague from the United States who filled the other position that when he was hired, he was told that they needed a local person to teach the classroom modules and needed him to teach the SLA and research methods modules.

So, from the very beginning of my career as a faculty member I was both constituted and pigeonholed as a "local classroom person," which has had the consequence of giving my superiors a rationale for assigning me to the labor-intensive, administrative-heavy workload that senior Caucasian faculty members choose not to have. Another useful rationale is found in the argument that they need someone who speaks the local language (and preferably a woman—isn't a woman traditionally most suitable for a public relations job?) to liaise with the schools in soliciting practicum places for our students. Whenever we counterargued that the local school personnel do speak English, our superiors would argue that it would be better to have a local person who is "more familiar" with the school system when liaising with school personnel. This argument assumes that the expatriate senior faculty members, first, do not need to learn at least a little of the local language of the students and teachers, and second, do not need to acquaint themselves with the local educational issues and schooling system. One wonders in what ways they can fully benefit our preservice and in-service student teachers if they take it for granted that it is OK for them to remain unfamiliar with both the local educational issues and the local linguistic and cultural milieu of our student-teachers and their future students.

Another instance also speaks to their pigeonholing me as a classroom person (though I have great respect for classroom research). Two years ago I was deputy program leader of our undergraduate TESL program. However, one day I was told by my program leader, a Chinese male colleague, that they would like to have another of my colleagues (who did not have a Ph.D. but was a British Caucasian and native English speaker) to become the deputy program leader to boost the public profile of our TESL program in the local communities. His exact words were: "It'd be better to have a native English-speaker as our deputy program leader—it will increase the prestige of the program, as local students and parents look up to foreign, native-English speaking experts." I was asked to give up the deputy program leadership and take up the heavy administrative, coordinator work of the practicum module *again* (after many years of having done it previously). I protested in an e-mail message to my Chinese male colleague, saying that what he proposed would only reproduce the society's denigration of local English staff. He replied that he wouldn't enter into such a nonfruitful argument with me, and said all he cared about was the good of the program.

I held nothing personal against my British colleague or my Chinese male colleague. Both of them had been and are still good friends of mine. I fully understood that this is what my Chinese male colleague truly believes: A British name on our undergraduate program will boost our public image.

However, what I agonized about was that all my years of intensive research to develop expertise in the local educational issues had only earned me a "second-class" status in the second- and foreign-language education profession. I still think that my male Chinese colleague was "well intentioned" (i.e., working "for the good of the program"), but he had let the ideology of native-speakerism speak and exercise its power through him (Gee, 1996), and he was totally unaware (or refused to be aware?) of the injustice to me by reproducing this colonial ideology.

Silencing Discourses: Frances's Story

Beyond instances of blatant discrimination within academia, certain discursive practices, controlling images, and stereotypes work quietly but relentlessly to stifle minority voices, including those of Asian women. As a doctoral student teaching a diversity class for master's-level teacher candidates, I frequently muted myself for fear of solidifying an angry, unreasonable, or pushy woman-of-color stereotype. For instance, in one assignment in a diversity class, I tried to problematize the notion of privilege by asking students to write their own version of Peggy MacIntosh's (1997) "White Privilege: Unpacking the Invisible Knapsack," about any facet of their own identities in which they held privilege. Wayne, a white, able-bodied, Christian, heterosexual male refused, denying that he had privilege. He embraced meritocratic ideologies that coupled the work ethic with race, and he implied that I had been hired on the basis of my skin color and regardless of my qualifications. I was terrified that if I showed anger or impatience, I would alienate him, and in retrospect I realize that I invested a great deal of energy in constructing myself counter to the angry minority identity that he had disparaged. I sought the advice of the other faculty teaching the cohort (all white), who were caring and supportive, but whose overwhelming focus was reaching Wayne:

> "If your intention is transformation, you need to be careful that he doesn't turn off because then he'll never hear what you have to say."

> "What's more important to you, Wayne doing the assignment or Wayne understanding the notion of privilege?"

Within the context of teaching for diversity, I notice another example of discursive practices that surface repeatedly and disturbingly and play a silencing or marginalizing function. That is, the language commonly used in the literature on teaching for diversity constructs discussions of race and ethnicity as *dangerous* for dominant groups. We need to problematize the discourses of "risk," "safety," and "vulnerability" that surround discussions about "diversity." I hear constant reminders about the comfort levels and "safety" of students from dominant groups, about the "risk" and "vulnerability" implied in talking about oppression. These warnings privilege the interests of dominant groups over social justice. Classroom discussions about race don't make students from dominant groups unsafe! They do not increase the likelihood of their being unfairly jailed, attacked in hate crimes, forced into internment camps, or denied employment or housing! Yet, these are the consequences for minority children when discrimination is not deconstructed and challenged. Using the language of safety and vulnerability in discussions of diversity, the same language that is used to challenge discrimination, minimizes the experience of discrimination and redirects our focus from subjugated groups back to dominant groups. I do not discount the importance of creating appropriate spaces in which members of all groups, including dominant groups, can safely deconstruct their biases. I simply suggest that concerns for safety must not disrupt work against oppression.

Similarly, language practices that amount to subtle censorship circulate around me. Senior faculty, anonymous manuscript reviewers, and others have advised me to depoliticize my language, cautioning me against, for instance, the words "oppression," "ideology," "subjugate," "feminist," "critical," and "political." This advice ignores the fact that my interest in the relationship between social power and the various dimensions of difference is rooted in my lived experience as an Asian woman, so that encouraging me to deny or suppress this lens equates to a deprecation of my experiences.

As an educator for diversity and social justice, I believe that we cannot begin to respond to the needs of minority children in our schools without addressing the challenges facing minority candidates in teacher education and, furthermore, minority teacher educators. During my doctoral work, the sole Asian faculty member in my department was unjustly denied tenure and left the institution. Not unrelated, during the time that I was doing my doctoral work, the number of minority Ph.D. students graduating from the College of Education at my institution decreased from 32 percent in 1999 to 28 percent in 2002 and then 17 percent in 2003. At the same time, in the public school system in the county in which the campus is located, minority enrollment in the student population has risen from 86 percent in 1999 to 92 percent in 2004. In the neighboring county whose public school system is the largest employer of my institution's graduates, minority enrollment has increased from 44 percent in 1999 to 56 percent in 2004.

Recently in my diversity class, a student I had assumed was biracial self-identified as white, adding: "My mother tried not to indoctrinate me with all that Chinese stuff, and I think she did a good job." The comment made me wonder about the ways in which silencing discourses shape the complex connections among students' cultural identity development in public schools, teacher socialization within teacher education classes and public schools, and the often hostile environment that Asian women encounter within academic contexts.

Emerging Patterns of Systematic Marginalization

It is important to note that gender and racial categories should be seen as relational and not categorical, and do not invariably prescribe a particular type of social experience for members of those categories (whose membership can sometimes be negotiated) (Ng, 1995). Thus we will refrain from taking an essentializing approach to our experiences. And yet, although our narratives show a diverse range of experiences, some clear, common patterns of systematic marginalization and silencing emerge, indicating that these lived experiences of marginalization are not isolated, random, individual happenings. It is a theoretical analysis of these often masked structures that we shall turn to below.

Gendered and Racialized Task/Labor Segregation

Almost all of our lived experiences point to a common pattern of gendered and racialized task and labor segregation; namely, Asian women faculty are often assigned to labor-intensive administrative and teaching duties (e.g., Denise was consistently asked to do the heavy administrative work of liaising with schools for students' teaching practicum, Bertha was asked to do all the paperwork and revise all the syllabi for an accreditation review, Anne was consistently excluded from communications related to important program decisions and was given a large amount of work beyond her assigned responsibilities). Two decades ago feminist standpoint theorists had already pointed out gendered labor segregation in modern academia. For instance, Dorothy Smith (1974, 1987) argues that "women's work" relieves men of the need to take care of the everyday, practical chores of the local places where they exist, freeing men to immerse themselves in the world of abstract concepts and theories. Moreover, the more successfully women perform their work, the more invisible the work becomes to men. This is precisely what Denise experienced, for instance. Without her heavy administrative work to secure places for students' practicum every year, her department's second- and foreign-language education program would not have been viable. The male faculty can enjoy the benefits of her labor and they can focus on teaching privileged "theoretical" courses and writing research papers, or take up leadership roles in the department. Anne was likewise excluded and exploited by her senior colleagues, and this time they were white female faculty. We therefore want to extend the model of the feminist standpoint theorists to point out that this segregation of labor is very often not only gendered but also *racialized*. We can draw a parallel between task segregation in modern academia and the well-documented racialized task/labor segregation in the nineteenth-century United States (Liu, 2000). We argue that such an invisible internal colonial model is also in operation in today's academia, especially in the second- and foreign-language education discipline, where a pecking order of tasks seems to exist. It is to an analysis of the epistemological and political consequences of this task hierarchy and task segregation that we turn in the next section.

The Great Theory-Practice Divide

As an "applied" discipline, second- and foreign-language education has borrowed extensively from the theories and research methodologies of other, "pure" disciplines such as Chomskyan linguistics, psychology, and cognitive science. While recent years have seen the discipline's top journals become more receptive to research in postpositivist, sociocultural, or critical paradigms, mainstream second- and foreign-language education theoretical and research canons still follow the parent disciplines, which are modern academic disciplines established in the tradition of Enlightenment rationality and philosophy. Modern disciplines born of the Enlightenment tradition subscribe to specific sets of ontological and epistemological assumptions. Under Enlightenment assumptions, the ideal agent of knowledge, the ideal scientist, is a transhistorical, unitary, individual, and a disembodied mind, whose scientific endeavors are not supposed to be in any significant ways shaped or constituted by their historical, social, cultural, and institutional contexts and locations. The contents of their discoveries, the theories and findings, likewise are eligible to lay claims to the status of transhistorical, universal truths. (See Harding, 1996, for a summary of feminist standpoint critiques of Enlightenment epistemology.) In practice, mainstream second- and foreign-language education research largely follows the paradigm of positivism and physicalism. The chief concern under this paradigm is to *opera-*

tionalize and *quantify* (i.e., define and measure in numerals) human and social phenomena (e.g., language learning and teaching) in terms of "variables," and to *verify* hypotheses about the relationships (e.g., causal or correlational) among different variables. (See Taylor, 1985, for a theoretical alternative to physicalism and positivism in understanding human actions.)

It is not a trivial point to note that the Enlightenment philosophers were typically males who theorized and philosophized in a historical period when they occupied privileged social and economic positions with slaves and servants attending to their everyday practical needs, thus freeing them to do their theoretical work. Today we can see the shadows of parallel structures of gendered and racialized divisions of labor in academic disciplines and in second- and foreign-language education, a discipline that models itself on its parent disciplines. In the second- and foreign-language education field, those who teach future professors and researchers are at the top, those who teach future ESL/EFL teachers come next, and those who teach ESL or EFL are at the bottom. Furthermore, ESL/EFL teachers are disproportionately part-time, adjunct, or temporary, and it is typically females (among whom there are many women of color) who fill up these bottom ranks.

Feminist standpoint theorists have pointed out the unfortunate epistemological consequences of such gendered segregation of labor. They hold that movements for social liberation advance the growth of knowledge. As summarized by Harding (1996):

> [Feminist standpoint theorists] explicitly call for women of color, working-class women, and lesbians to be present among the women whose experiences generate inquiry. They all discuss the limitations of sciences emerging only from white, western, homophobic, academic feminism. (p. 311)

In our lived experiences, we note that it is precisely this gendered and racialized theory-practice divide in our discipline that has contributed to the inadequate generation of theories of practical knowledge that are relevant to the work of frontline practitioners in second- and foreign-language education. The experiences and activities of the majority of frontline education workers (typically female classroom teachers) do not have a chance to enter the ranks of prestigious mainstream theories and research, as frequently they are not given the institutional resources, time, and opportunities to theorize their experiences and share and publish them in the discipline's prestigious journals. And when they actually get to the point of engaging in research, their research agendas and projects are often denigrated as "soft, ethnographic" work that does not qualify for "scientific" status.

Apart from the silencing effect of this kind of derision and the negative epistemological consequences of devaluing teachers' knowledge embedded in teachers' practice, there are also grave political consequences of this gendered and racialized theory-practice divide. As the knowledge generated by the experiences and activities of female researchers and teachers, of women of color, of different social classes and sexualities, does not have a chance to enter the discipline's knowledge base and cannot contribute to the content of the discipline's curriculums, students coming from these dominated groups are consistently denied the kinds of knowledge and theories that speak to and value their own lived experiences as minorities in society. For instance, Bertha was silenced when her research on multiculturalism and minority issues was denigrated by her superiors as "repetitive." This kind of systematic, institutional suppression of research and teaching on minority and diversity issues has dangerous implications not only for the education of minority students but also for the education of white students. As Patricia Williams (1991) points out with respect to the discipline of sociology, the consequences of such suppression are grave:

> The result will be students who are cultured to hate; yet who still think of themselves as very, very good people; who will be deeply offended, and personally hurt, if anyone tries to tell them otherwise. I think this sort of teaching, rampant throughout the education system, is why racism and sexism remain so routine, so habitually dismissed, as to be largely invisible. (p. 87)

This brings us to a discussion of a recurrent theme in our lived experiences: We are often seen as "angry" Asian women who make our white colleagues and students "uncomfortable." It is to an analysis of this issue that we turn in the next section.

Relations with White Faculty and Students: Problematizing the "Angry," "Sulky" Image of Women Faculty of Color

In "The Uses of Anger: Women Responding to Racism" Audre Lorde (1984) writes:

> Every woman has a well-stocked arsenal of anger potentially useful against those oppressions, personal and institutional, which brought that anger into being. Focused with precision it can become a powerful source of energy serving progress and change. (p. 127)

Frances's experience of being advised by her well-intentioned colleagues on how to avoid gaining the image of a "angry woman of color" tells us how difficult it is for a woman of color to voice her protest of marginalization without being seen as stereotypically "angry" and indulging in "incessantly narrating her suffering." Anne has also been told by her white female colleagues that she is "sulky." Anger, and indignation, are understandable responses to unfair treatment in many cultures. However, when women faculty of color express anger it is often seen as evidence of their emotional instability, lack of reason, or their inability to enjoy themselves and engage in fruitful argument. Invoking the unsmiling "angry Asian woman" or "angry woman of color" stereotype is a discursive ploy that serves to silence and subordinate the voices of women of color. For instance, when Denise protested to her male superior against unfair work arrangements (and gave a well-grounded reason: His act would only reproduce the society's denigration of local Chinese English staff as second class to "native English speakers"), she was accused of starting a "nonfruitful argument." The implication was that she was not willing to sacrifice for the good of the program. Thus, women of color are frequently expected to sacrifice for the "larger good," and when they protest against being treated unfairly, they are frequently accused of being unreasonable or emotional and thus pushed to the margins and silenced.

However, we are also painfully aware of the possible consequences of our expressions of anger and of the potential negative effect of anger on communication between people located in very different positions. Answering anger with anger will only ensure the breakdown of communication. For instance, there is a tendency among some colleagues to conclude that women faculty of color have unfairly taken their jobs (with the implicit assumption that these jobs originally belonged to, or should belong to them) and they, our colleagues, are victims of an unfair affirmative action policy at universities. For instance, after a conference presentation relating to race, a white woman approached one of us and expressed anger that a faculty position she had applied for had been given to a woman of color. The white woman believed that her application had not been seriously considered because she was white.

This brings us to the issue of how to communicate an ethic of togetherness-in-difference (Ang, 2001). Can there still be any common ethical grounds for discussing issues of social justice, diversity, and mutual respect when everybody claims to be a victim based on her own lived experiences in a radical relativist version of postmodernist discourse?

Toward a Communicative Ethic of Togetherness-in-Difference: From Second- and Foreign-Language Education to Teaching English for Dialogic Communication in a Globalized World

How can we achieve such a "constraint-free understanding" between differently positioned subjects, between, for instance, colleagues who feel that affirmative action is unfair and colleagues of color who think that it is just a small step in redressing the huge ethnic/racial and gender imbalances found in institutions of higher education, especially in light of the increasingly diversified ethnic/racial and gender makeup of student populations? We have not yet found a perfect solution to this problem, but we believe that between the dichotic poles of Enlightenment transhistorical rationality and radical relativist forms of postmodernism, there should be middle-road alternatives that can serve as common ethical grounds for interposition and intercultural communication and understanding pertaining to issues of social justice, minority and diversity, and mutual respect for and recognition of difference.

A Communicative Ethic of Risk

Sharon Welch (2000) gives us some hope in her proposal of a communicative ethic of risk in an attempt to overcome the limitations of both Enlightenment universality and postmodernist fragmentation. Drawing on Foucault, she argues that dialogue across difference should be achieved not by searching for objective consensus but by "recognizing the differences by which we ourselves are constituted and . . . by actively seeking to be partially constituted by work with different groups" (p. 151). We would add that the dialogue must continue even though there is no guarantee of successful communication at any point in time. A communicative ethic of risk demands a commitment to take the risk involved in any communicative act across different social positions even though it might mean making one uncomfortable (e.g., by challenging one to rethink one's deep-rooted, taken-for-granted beliefs and one's implication in social injustice). Welch points out that our society operates on "an ethic of control," which seeks to protect people from any risk or discomfort resulting from uncertainty or ambivalence when they interact with others who are different from them. Frances made an insightful analysis of this in her story by pointing out that trying to make students "safely uncomfortable" might work against encouraging them to become aware of issues of privilege and power.

A professor from another institution once said: "We *must* talk about this [issues of diversity and social justice]. I *want* my students to be uncomfortable." To which another educator replied: "Safely uncomfortable." The problem is that adding "safely" to "uncomfortable" runs the danger of not only mitigating the point, but nullifying it.

A communicative ethic of risk challenges us to enter into an often unsafe, uncomfortable dialogue, to open ourselves up to different ideas and values of *others*, to make ourselves vulnerable by becoming open to the dialogic process of mutual challenge and mutual transformation. It is only through such a risky, dialogic communicative process that we can expand our knowledge, transcend our location- and privilege-induced blind spots, and become enriched both culturally and ethically. Welch (2000) points to the deep satisfaction and liberation one gains when one says *no* to the ethic of control and when one refuses to hold on to privilege or to allow privilege to become one's sole identity, blinding one to social injustice. And we add that middle-class women of color likewise need to listen to working-class women (of color), and straight women of color need to listen to lesbian women (of color). Under the communicative ethic of risk, no one is exempt from the obligation to constantly engage in dialogic communication with *others* to discover and transcend the blind spots inherent in our respective locations. But this must go beyond mere words; otherwise, it will degenerate into *(hypo)critical pedagogy*, as illustrated in Anne's story; for the communicative ethic is also an ethic of *accountability* and *respect*. It demands a commitment to accountability and a willingness to give up privilege when one realizes that one's privilege perpetuates social injustice:

> Accountability entails recognition of wrongdoing and imbalances of power and leads to self-critical attempts to use power justly. Respect is not primarily sympathy for the other, but acknowledgement of the equality, dignity, and independence of others. (Welch, 2000, p. 15)

Policies and Practices

We call for comparative analysis of the connections between the different sociopolitical contexts (Wiley, 1999) in which Asian women—and indeed all scholars of color—practice, and the policies that support their continued oppression. The many overlapping dimensions of difference mean that entrance to the academy and subsequent selection for tenure and promotion is a complex and lifelong struggle. While women of color seem to be recruited into entry-level academic positions in higher numbers, certain specific policies (awaiting further research and comparative analysis) surrounding these recruitment practices seem to encourage their long-term failure. We therefore advocate the following policy-based strategies.

Educational and administrative leadership should be vigilant in its support of individual minority women's research agendas by instituting policies that ensure that they are granted at least as much release time and graduate student support as their male and white counterparts. Minority women's advising, teaching, and practicum supervision loads should be monitored by leadership, and they should be protected from serving on large numbers of committees. Scholars of color are often not privy to information considered "common knowledge" by dominant groups. (Bertha, for instance, was not provided with the same informal guidance about the academic publishing process and context as her white male peers.) Minority scholars therefore need special support to redress discriminatory and exclusionary practices, whether these be conscious or unintentional. They need thoughtful and supportive senior colleagues who are committed to their success and help them negotiate the gap in cultural capital as well as guide them toward appropriate publishing; "equal pay for equal work" should be a reality. Most of us have been paid less than our white and male counterparts; similarly, most of us have heavier workloads than other members of our departments. In addition to the sexual harassment workshops that are raising the consciousness of academicians, universities need workshops to address other forms of discrimination, including harassment on the basis of religion, sexual orientation, race, immigration status, and language minority status. Hiring and retention policies should ensure that more than one person of color is recruited within each department, because the pressure of being "singular" marks scholars of color and subjects them to higher scrutiny. Within each institution, the development of policy should be revisited to critically examine the processes whereby policies become accepted practices and are adopted by those in the next tier of leadership.

Re-visioning Second- and Foreign-Language Education's Disciplinary Goals

The second- and foreign-language education discipline likewise needs to be re-visioned and reshaped in our increasingly globalized world of diversity. Instead of taking as our disciplinary goal the finding and gaining of *certain* (as opposed to situated, uncertain) knowledge of the most effective technology (as if there exists a universally effective technology) to teach language, a more urgent task would be that of finding situated, dialogic ways of teaching and learning language (or literacies in the field of literacy education) for relatively "constraint-free" understanding and communication among people coming from very different locations (geographical and/or social) and with very different sociocultural experiences (see Lin & Luk, 2004; Wong, in press). In the case of English-language teaching, the traditional technicalized concerns of the discipline need to be expanded by equally important concerns about how to value linguistic and cultural diversity and promote social justice in the (often hegemonic) spread of English in different parts of the world.

In embarking on this collective, dialogic writing project, we were not aiming at "narrating our suffering," nor were we "invested in rewards" (Velez, 2000, p. 325). We have gained a sense of community in engaging in this dialogic writing, and in this community we have drawn strength for healing and transformation. We are not alone in this world. What gives meaning to this job and profession of ours as we continue to work as women faculty of color in the second- and foreign-language education and literacy education disciplines? It is the hope that our work will contribute to a world in which there is greater intercultural understanding, greater social justice, and less marginalization and discrimination because of various ideological and institutional structures, and a world in which minority children and students of different racial/ethnic, social, gender, and sexuality backgrounds can have their identities and experiences valued and their potential affirmed and developed in their education.

References

Amin, N. (1999). Minority women teachers of ESL: Negotiating white English. In G. Braine (Ed.), *Non-native educators in English language teaching* (pp. 93–104). Mahwah, NJ: Erlbaum.

Ang, I. (2001). *On not speaking Chinese: Living between Asia and the West.* London: Routledge.

Bagilhole, B. (2002). Against all odds: Women academics' research opportunities. In G. Howe & A. Tauchert (Eds.), *Gender, teaching and research in higher education* (pp. 46–56). Hampshire, England: Ashgate.

Braine, G. (Ed.). (1999). *Non-native educators in English language teaching.* Mahwah, NJ: Erlbaum.

Brutt-Griffler, J., & Samimy, K. (1999). Revisiting the colonial in the postcolonial: Critical praxis for nonnative English-speaking teachers in a TESOL program. *TESOL Quarterly, 33,* 413–431.

Canagarajah, S. (1999). Interrogating the "Native Speaker Fallacy": Non-linguistic roots, non-pedagogical results. In G. Baine (Ed.), *Non-native educators in English language teaching* (pp. 77–92). Mahwah, NJ: Erlbaum.

Collins, P. H. (1998). *Fighting words: Black women & the search for justice.* Minneapolis: University of Minnesota Press.

Gee, J. (1996). *Social linguistics and literacies: Ideology in discourses.* London: Falmer Press.

Goldberg, D. (1997, July 27). Who makes the cut? *Washington Post Education Review*, p. 4.

Hall, S. (1992). Cultural studies and its theoretical legacies. In L. Grossberg, C. Nelson, & P. A. Treichler (Eds.), *Cultural studies* (pp. 277–294). New York: Routledge.

Halvorsen, E. (2002). Gender audit. In G. Howe & A. Tauchert (Eds.), *Gender, teaching and research in higher education* (pp. 9–19). Hampshire, UK: Ashgate.

Harding, S. (1996). Feminism, science, and the anti-Enlightenment critiques. In A. Gary & M. Pearsall (Eds.), *Women, knowledge, and reality: Explorations in feminist philosophy* (pp. 298–320). New York: Routledge.

Hartsock, N. (1983). The feminist standpoint: Developing the ground for a specifically feminist historical materialism. In S. Harding & M. Hintikka (Eds.), *Discovering reality: Feminist perspectives on epistemology, metaphysics, methodology, and philosophy of science* (pp. 283–310). Dordrecht, Netherlands: D. Reidel.

Hornig, L. S. (Ed.). (2003). *Equal rites, unequal outcomes: Women in American research universities.* New York: Kluwer Academic.

Jackson, S. (2002). Transcending boundaries: Women, research and teaching in the academy. In G. Howe & A. Tauchert (Eds.), *Gender, teaching and research in higher education* (pp. 20–32). Hampshire, England: Ashgate.

Jacobs, L., Cintrón, J., & Canton, C. E. (Eds.). (2002). *The politics of survival in Academia: Narratives of inequity, resilience, and success.* Oxford, UK: Rowman & Littlefield.

Lantolf, J. P. (1996). SLA theory building: Letting all the flowers bloom. *Language Learning, 46*(4), 713–749.

Lin, A., & Luk, J. (2004). Local creativity in the face of global domination: Insights of Bakhtin for teaching English for dialogic communication. In J. K. Hall, G. Vitanova, & L. Marchenkova (Eds.), *Contributions of Mikhail Bakhtin to understanding second and foreign language learning.* Mahwah, NJ: Erlbaum.

Lin, A., Wang, W., Akamatsu, A., & Riazi, M. (2002). Appropriating English, expanding identities, and re-visioning the field: From TESOL to teaching English for globalized communication (TEGCOM). *Journal of Language, Identify, and Education, 1,* 295–316.

Liu, J. (1999). From their own perspectives: The impact of non-native ESL professionals on their students. In G. Braine (Ed.), *Non-native educators in English language teaching* (pp. 159–176). Mahwah, NJ: Erlbaum.

Liu, J. (2000). Towards an understanding of the internal colonial model. In D. Brydon (Ed.), *Postcolonialism: Critical concepts in literary and cultural studies* (Vol. 4, pp. 1347–1364). London: Routledge.

Lorde, A. (1984). *Sister outsider: Essays and speeches.* Freedom, CA: Crossing Press.

Luke, C. (2001). *Globalization and women in academia.* Mahwah, NJ: Erlbaum.

Mabokela, R. O., & Green, A. L. (Eds.). (2001). *Sisters of the academy: Emergent black women scholars in higher education.* Sterling, VA: Stylus Publishing.

McIntosh, P. (1997). White privilege: Unpacking the invisible knapsack. In B. Schneider (Ed.), *Race: An anthology in the first person* (pp. 120–26). New York: Crown.

Memmi, A. (1965). *The colonizer and the colonized.* Boston: Beacon.

Morley, L., & Walsh, V. (Eds.). (1995). *Feminist academics: Creative agents for change.* London: Taylor & Francis.

Morley, L., & Walsh, V. (Eds.). (1996). *Breaking boundaries: Women in higher education.* London: Taylor & Francis.

Ng, R. (1995). Teaching against the grain: Contradictions and possibilities. In R. Ng, P. Staton, & J. Scane (Eds.), *Anti-racism, feminism, and critical approaches to education* (pp. 129–155). Westport, CT: Bergin & Garvey.

Pavlenko, A., Blackledge, A., & Teutsch-Dwyer, M. (2001). *Multilingualism, second language learning and gender.* Berlin: Mouton de Gruyter.

Pennycook, A. (1999). Introduction: Critical approaches to TESOL. *TESOL Quarterly, 33,* 329–348.

Smith, D. (1974). Women's perspective as a radical critique of sociology. *Sociological Inquiry, 44,* 7–13.

Smith, D. (1987). *The everyday world as problematic: A feminist sociology.* Boston: Northeastern University Press.

Sunderland, J., Cowley, M., Rahim, F., Leontzakou, C., & Shattuck, J. (2002). From representation to discursive practices: Gender in the foreign language textbook revisited. In J. Sunderland & L. Litosseliti (Eds.), *Gender, identity and discourse analysis* (pp. 223–255). Amsterdam/Philadelphia: John Benjamins.

Taylor, C. (1985). *Human agency and language.* Cambridge, UK: Cambridge University Press.

Thomas, J. (1999). Voice from the periphery: Non-native teachers and issues of credibility. In G. Baine (Ed.), *Non-native educators in English language teaching* (pp. 5–14). Mahwah, NJ: Erlbaum.

TuSmith, B., & Reddy, M. T. (Eds.). (2002). *Race in the college classroom: Pedagogy and politics.* Piscataway, NJ: Rutgers University Press.

Vargas, L. (Ed.). (2002). *Women faculty of color in the white college classroom: Narratives on the pedagogical implications of teacher diversity.* New York: Peter Lang.

Velez, D. L. (2000). Anger, resentment, and the place of mind in academia. In The Social Justice Group at the Centre for Advanced Feminist Studies, University of Minnesota (Ed.), *Is academic feminism dead? Theory in practice* (pp. 311–326). New York: New York University Press.

Walsh, V. (2002). Equal opportunities without "equality": Redeeming the irredeemable. In G. Howe & A. Tauchert (Eds.), *Gender, teaching and research in higher education* (pp. 33–45). Hampshire, UK: Ashgate.

Welch, S. D. (2000). *A feminist ethic of risk*. Minneapolis, MN: Fortress Press.

Wiley, T. G. (1999). Comparative historical analysis of U.S. language policy and language planning: Extending the foundations. In K. A. Davis & T. Huebner (Eds.), *Sociopolitical perspectives on language policy and planning in the U.S.A.* (pp. 18–37). Amsterdam: John Benjamins.

Williams, P. J. (1991). *The alchemy of race and rights: Diary of a law professor*. Cambridge, MA: Harvard University Press.

Wong, S. (in press). *Dialogic approaches to teaching English to speakers of other languages: Where the gingko tree grows*. Mahwah, NJ: Erlbaum.

PART TWO

TEACHING, MENTORING, ADVISING, AND SECURING TENURE

4

PROFESSING IN A NONNATIVE TONGUE

Narrative Construction of Realities and Opportunities

Xiaoping Liang

While there has been a growing interest in researching racial and gender marginalization of minority women faculty in White-male-dominated U.S. higher institutions (e.g., Benjamin, 1997; Mabokela & Green, 2002; Vargas, 2002), little has been done to explore the linguistic peripheralization of immigrant female scholars at a junior rank who profess in a nonnative tongue in university classrooms with diverse student bodies. This chapter documents the linguistic challenges experienced by three Asian women academicians (Nina, Terry, and Sue are pseudonyms) in their journey to become competent instructors in English as their second language, the strategies they used to overcome their linguistic disadvantages, and the professional satisfaction they gained during their struggle.

Nina, Terry, and Sue were all born in Asia and grew up speaking Chinese.[1] They started learning English as a required subject in junior high schools, came to the United States as adults to pursue graduate studies in different disciplines, and obtained their master's and doctoral degrees at dif-

[1] The author is deeply indebted to Nina, Terry, and Sue for their generosity in agreeing to participate in this project when they felt they did not have enough time for their own research, and in granting their permission to share their lived experiences of struggle and empowerment as nonnative English-speaking new faculty members. A debt of gratitude is also owed to Sara Smith, whose valuable comments and suggestions contribute to the chapter in important ways.

ferent U.S. higher institutions of learning. Nina and Sue specialized in education; Terry focused on a field in social sciences. At the time of the study, they had stayed in the United States for thirteen, nine, and twelve years respectively and were tenure-track assistant professors in different departments at a U.S. university that had a diverse student population. The faculty population was less diverse. Although Nina, Terry, and Sue were not the only minority faculty in their departments, they were nevertheless among the few second-language-speaking female professors who became acquainted with the American educational culture after they had received their baccalaureate degrees in their homeland.

The study lasted three months from February to May in 2004. Twenty-five hours of reflexive conversations in Chinese with the three immigrant women faculty was a major source of data. In this chapter, English translations of their retrospective first-person narratives will be used as legitimate sources of data (Lyons & LaBoskey, 2002; Pavlenko & Lantolf, 2000) to apprehend the complexities of an often messy and unpredictable teaching practice in a sociocultural context. These personal testimonies play a powerful role in these junior women academicians' discursive construction of self and realities. Throughout the chapter, the singular first-person pronoun "I" will be reserved for Nina, Terry, and Sue to tell their stories of struggle and empowerment that might otherwise not be told. At the end of each narrative, the speaker's pseudonym will be provided to give individual voice to each woman scholar.

As second-language-speaking junior faculty, Nina, Terry, and Sue had both positive and negative teaching experiences in their first few years. This chapter will start with some challenging instances of rejection they encountered and end on a positive note with some fulfilling moments of acceptance. Specifically, the first section excerpts these women academics' reflexive accounts to tease out the reality of their classroom lives and their ongoing battles with linguistic, gender, racial, and cultural issues. The second section uses the Russian cultural-historical psychologist Vygotsky's (1978, 1987) sociocultural theory lens to reflect on their strategic approaches to taking action and progressing in the academy. In light of Vygotsky's concept of mediation, the third section theorizes the three immigrant female faculty's journey of loss and recovery to suggest a pedagogy of mediated co-construction of opportunities.

Narrative Construction of Realities

This section describes teaching as a minefield (Luthra, 2002) of student resistance and negative attitudes for Nina, Terry, and Sue in their first few years

in the academy. It captures these women faculty's internalized peripheralization of linguistic self and their socioculturally marginalized professional identity.

Teaching as a Minefield of Student Resistance

Like Thomas (1999), Nina, Terry, and Sue felt that their initial credibility
(or lack of it) seemed to be related to their language and accent. Since they
did not speak like White American professors, students a priori questioned
their credibility as course instructors and challenged their authority to teach
in their fields of specialization. The episodes below reveal what would otherwise be the private realities of these second-language-speaking immigrant
faculty.

> An American student seemed to have a hostile attitude toward me. She
> often talked to others when I was speaking. When I asked her why she was
> not paying attention, she answered, "I don't understand you." I told her
> that she could ask me or raise her hand whenever she had difficulty under-
> standing me so that I could explain in a different way. Or she could come
> to my office and I could explain to her in detail. But she never did. (Nina)

> I had a student who really had a bad attitude toward me. He always sat in
> the front row and sought every opportunity to challenge me. He liked to
> take over and be in control. There was once, for a multiple-choice question
> in a test that was worth 0.5 points, he chose A while the answer was B. He
> argued that B was also a correct answer according to the textbook. When
> I explained why B was incorrect, he pointed at the book and said to me,
> "Read the textbook." He really meant that I didn't understand the text
> because of my English and that was the reason why the multiple-choice
> questions were not clear. Every class, he would find some fault in me. . . .
> It really made me dread to stand in front of him. I would stand on the side
> worrying about what fault he would find in me next. . . . It might have
> something to do with the fact that I am a junior faculty and that I am a
> second language speaker. Otherwise, he wouldn't have told me to read the
> textbook. (Sue)

> This semester, I have a student who . . . seems very reluctant to come to
> class. We started a project in the computer lab on Wednesday. Today, she
> had problems with the project. I suggested that she try one thing, but it
> didn't work. We could always try another way if this one doesn't work. But
> she just said to me accusingly, "I followed your instruction. Why didn't it
> work?" A lot of work we do in this course is new technology. It's really
> trial and error. I didn't say that I knew everything. I am also trying things

out. She often speaks with an accusing tone every time something goes wrong. I have worked hard to accommodate her needs. She's still like that. I just don't understand why. I don't know whether it's because I'm not a native English-speaking American professor. (Sue)

In addition to face-to-face oral encounters, Nina, Terry, and Sue also had to deal with student resistance in writing. In the following excerpts, Nina shared her experiences of student challenges to her English competence in course and instructor evaluations.

They will not tell me that I have made errors, but will wait till the end of the course and write negative comments on the evaluation form. For example, "I sometimes cannot understand what she says." I know that I have an accent. I try to improve it, but it's not that easy. (Nina)

I speak English with an accent. For example, I sometimes pronounce students' names incorrectly because I have never seen many of them before. Some students will correct me if I say their names wrong. Some will not but will feel uncomfortable. . . . In a midterm survey of my teaching, a student wrote, "Do not call names. Just pass out the signing sheet. Your name-calling is not correct sometimes." (Nina)

Apart from language and accent, student resistance and negative attitudes also seem to point in the direction of the Asian immigrant women academicians' sharing of their cultural capital (Bourdieu, 1977, 1986), such as "cultural awareness" and "information about the school system" (Swartz, 1997, p. 75). Nina, Terry, and Sue had rich learning and working experiences in different contexts that they sometimes drew on in their teaching. However, they felt that their cultural capital was at times not appreciated by students. This sentiment is evidenced in the following narrative account.

There was a graduate student who had a very negative attitude. When I used examples from my working experiences in another state or in China to illustrate a research or a pedagogical issue, she said, "How come . . . you always use examples from elsewhere? How can you not use local examples if you teach here?" She was also very opposed to comparative studies in education that had a focus on international perspectives. She seemed very cross when I pointed out the weaknesses in American math education. She accused my comparison of math education in the U.S. with that in China as like comparing an orange with an apple. She just seemed narrow minded and unable to tolerate the discussion on the weaknesses in U.S. education. (Nina)

It is possible that what this student was unable to tolerate was not simply criticism of weaknesses in American education, but, at a deeper level, the different perspectives and viewpoints of a person who was perceived as an other, culturally and linguistically.

Professional Identity Peripheralized

In her discussion of nonnative English-speaking teachers and issues of credibility, Thomas (1999) stated that English-as-a-second-or-other-language instructors "are not merely 'strangers in academia' . . . we are sometimes strangers on the periphery" (p. 5). The feeling of being on the periphery was echoed in Nina's, Terry's, and Sue's reflexive conversations. The excerpts reported above show that these female faculty were figuratively as well as literally peripheralized by their negative teaching experiences. These negative experiences seemed to have infected Nina's, Terry's, and Sue's perceptions of their own language capacity. When asked about the source of student resistance and negative attitudes, they at times look to their own perceived incompetence in English for an explanation. The following narratives portray their sense of peripheralized professional identity.

> Sometimes I make grammatical errors because I put English words in Chinese syntactic structures. Other times, there are new big vocabularies in my field that I need to learn. I pronounce them according to the International Phonetic Alphabets in English-Chinese dictionaries, but my pronunciation turns out to be different from how Americans would pronounce. I have to learn by listening to how Americans say those words. (Nina)

> I have a big vocabulary for reading but a small vocabulary for speaking. . . . I can't express some of the things I want to say. For instance, during my lectures, an idea that I have never talked about would come into my mind. I am not prepared and would need to talk as I think. I would be nervous and worry about not being able to express the idea clearly. My speech would be worse under such circumstances because I am nervous. I would not find appropriate words to fully express my meaning. . . . I feel limited by my English when I want to lead discussion to a deeper level. I wish my English was better. (Terry)

> I have language anxiety when making a public speech. Having to speak to an audience in a second language makes it even worse because I am not

certain whether my English is correct or not. Sometimes, students sit there having no reactions whatsoever. When I have no idea whether students understand or not, I get nervous. (Sue)

I'm nervous when speaking English. I am in a different mode in English than in Chinese. Every time, every moment I speak English, I need to be very attentive and feel mentally stressed and not relaxed. I want to speak appropriately without making errors. That becomes a filter, a barrier in my mind. (Sue)

The first-person narratives above evidence Nina, Terry, and Sue's struggle to construct a pedagogical context that would allow them to restructure a new professional identity as expert instructors professing in a nonnative tongue in U.S. university classrooms. Although they were well qualified to teach and had high confidence in their content and research knowledge, they did not seem to have the same level of confidence in their English. In their own words,

I have confidence in the content of my class. It's just that I'm not as accurate as I'd like to be in English pronunciation and grammar. (Nina)

I am a very confident person. I have some confidence in my English, but I don't feel very confident. It's a conflicting feeling. (Terry)

I wouldn't hesitate that much if I were to write student assignment comments in Chinese. I would just write what I think. In English, I really need to work hard on how to express what I really mean appropriately in this culture. (Sue)

This conflicting sense of alternating confidence and functioning levels appeared to have made Nina, Terry, and Sue feel fragmented much of the time. Their feeling of fragmentation was not entirely metaphorical as "there were indeed two 'selves' who needed to communicate" (Verity, 2000, p. 191) in these immigrant women faculty: the confident Chinese-speaking self at home and the not-so-confident English-speaking self in the classroom. The following testimony clearly depicts the dual nature of their private and public selves in two languages (Watkins-Goffman, 2001), and, perhaps, their subconscious regret in needing to speak their first language.

My English is not very stable. Sometimes, I am very fluent in speech. Sometimes, I just stumble, forget what words to use, or have wrong pronunciation. . . . I think it has something to do with speaking Chinese at home. My English is usually better on Wednesday than on Monday. After a whole weekend of Chinese, my tongue doesn't seem very flexible on Monday. I don't speak that much Chinese on Tuesday. On Wednesday, my English sounds better. (Terry)

Sociocultural Context of Peripheralization

In her book on the pedagogical challenges faced by women faculty of color in the White classroom, Vargas (2002) discussed the issue of how classroom social life and teacher-student interactions were shaped by social distinctions, and presented the argument that the challenges women faculty of color deal with were "not a personal technical deficiency but a socio-political problem" (p. 1). Although Nina, Terry, and Sue had a high consciousness of being nonnative English-speaking faculty, they did not accept their linguistic disadvantage as the sole or, indeed, the major reason for their negative teaching experiences. In their narratives below, they pointed to institutionalized racial and gender inequalities as a crucial source of their professional peripheralization.

> I truly feel that to teach in this educational context, you would be at an advantageous position if you were male and/or White. I think it's also true in this society. I don't think that the student would treat me like that in class if I were White. (Sue)

> I find that most of [the] students who challenged me were White. . . . I had a student who really had a bad attitude toward me. He always sat in the front row and sought every opportunity to challenge me. He liked to take over and be in control. (Sue)

It needs to be pointed out that although much of the resistance and negative attitudes of students that Nina, Terry, and Sue encountered were launched by male students, many were also generated by female students. The following two excerpts describe their experiences of negative attitudes from female students.

> I think it was a combination of a number of factors: I was a junior minority faculty who spoke English with an accent. She was very disrespectful. She never said she did that because I was Chinese, but you could sense that from the questions she asked. (Nina)

> Most of my students are female. They seem to be more respectful to and more receptive of male professors. Female students put down female professors. It really shouldn't have happened. (Sue)

It also needs to be noted that not all student challenges were directed to Nina, Terry, and Sue by White students. These immigrant Asian women faculty also experienced student challenges from minority students, including those from Asia, although the Asian students they had did not tend to initiate face-to-face verbal confrontations in public.

> I had an Asian student who looked as if she just couldn't be bothered with my class, but she never challenged me openly. I couldn't tell whether she learned anything from the class because she never communicated. I didn't know what she was thinking in class. (Sue)

Nina's, Terry's, and Sue's retrospective reflections indicate that these second-language-speaking junior faculty's first few years of teaching in U.S. university classrooms were like a minefield of student resistance and negative attitudes toward their professional credential and authority. These women scholars felt belittled by their negative teaching experiences and by their internalized English-speaking self on the periphery. At a more fundamental level, they felt peripheralized by the racial and gender inequalities in the institution and in the society at large.

Mediational Strategies to Survive and Thrive

This section analyzes the strategies Nina, Terry, and Sue employed to survive and thrive as junior immigrant female faculty in the academy. The analysis draws on a sociocultural theory conceived by Vygotsky and his followers, especially the concept of mediation as the basis of higher psychological processes.

In his search for the social origin of human psychological functioning, Vygotsky (for example, 1978) distinguished two levels of psychological processes: the lower-level processes (that is, direct, natural, unmediated functions) and the higher-level processes (that is, indirect, cultural, mediated functions). The natural and unmediated functions are "totally and directly determined by stimulation from the environment," while the cultural and mediated functions are characterized by "self-generated stimulation" (p. 39). That is to say, in higher-level psychological processes, the individual actively modifies the stimulus situation through the creation and use of mediating cultural artifacts such as signs and tools. In his view, the mediated aspect of psychological operations is an essential feature of higher mental processes and "at this higher stage of development behavior remains mediated" (p. 45).

Vygotsky (1978) regarded social interaction as the origin of higher psychological processes, and language as the tool or mediational means for both the interpsychological (transactions between people) and the intrapsychological (mental processes within the individual's mind). He wrote:

> Language arises initially as a means of communication between the child and the people in his environment. Only subsequently, upon conversation to internal speech, does it come to organize the child's thought, that is, become an internal mental function. . . . internal speech and reflective thought arise from the interactions between the child and persons in her environment, these interactions provide the source of development of a child's voluntary behavior. (pp. 89–90)

In his discussion of the mediational function of teaching/instruction, Vygotsky (1978, 1987) proposed the concept of the zone of proximal development (ZPD). He differentiated two levels of mental development: the actual developmental level and the potential developmental level. The actual developmental level describes what the child can do independently whereas the potential developmental level describes what the child can do with assistance. Vygotsky defined the distance between the actual and the potential developmental levels as the zone of proximal development. He argued that teaching/instruction creates "the content of the concept of the zone of proximal development" (1987, p. 220) in which school-age children can perform functions that they have not mastered independently "under guidance, in groups, and in collaboration with one another" (1978, p. 87). "With collaboration, direction, or some kind of help the child is always able to do more and solve more difficult tasks than he can independently" (1987, p. 209).

Following Vygotsky, Lantolf (2000) considered mediation as the key ingredient of sociocultural theory that views humans as using symbolic tools to mediate and regulate our relationships with others and with ourselves and to change the nature of these relationships. He saw the site where mediation and regulation develop as the ZPD. Applying the mediation concept to second language learning and teaching, Lantolf wrote:

> to be an advanced speaker/user of a language means to be able to control one's psychological and social activity through the language . . . for interpersonal (social interaction) and intrapersonal (thinking) purposes. In both

circumstances, individuals move through stages in which they are controlled first by the objects in their environment, then by others in this environment, and finally they gain control over their own social and cognitive activities. These stages are usually referred to in sociocultural theory as object-, other-, and self-regulation. (p. 6)

This study proposes to extend Vygotsky's model to the situation faced by new faculty members, especially those who come from a different culture and language background. In the case of Nina, Terry, and Sue, instead of being disempowered by their peripheral status, they turned outward (object-and-other-regulation) as well as inward (self-regulation) for assistance. Teaching became a ZPD for them in which they looked for and used various strategies to overcome the challenges to their credibility and authority and to mediate their relationships with their students and with themselves.

Object-Regulated Strategies

The narratives in this section exhibit the object-regulated strategies Nina, Terry, and Sue used in their mediational practice. The symbolic artifacts that they used to establish a mediated relationship with their students included the Internet, graphics, logic, examples, exercises, activities, and other material objects in their teaching environments.

> I post relevant materials on the Web site to make them available for students at all times, including syllabus, assignment requirements, assignment samples, teaching notes, guidelines, worksheets, handouts, rubrics, et cetera. Students responded positively toward my use of [the] Web site for teaching. One class actually asked me to burn a CD for them at the end of the semester. Apparently, they found the materials in my Web site useful. (Sue)

> I turn my classes into hybrid courses. I prepare a chapter summary for each class and post it online with my lecture notes and the overhead transparencies that I use in class. Students can have access to course materials at any time. Once a month, I deliver a lecture and hold class discussion online. Students do not need to come to campus. They get online and enter virtual class. I post my questions online and students post their answers there. (Nina)

> I use graphics a lot. I draw them on the board. They help students with understanding. . . . I use graphics to help students understand the concepts I teach. . . . Graphics can be used to explain a phenomenon; they can also

be used to help with calculation. Some graphics help with understanding of theories that don't require calculation. (Terry)

When I prepare for class, I focus on how to explain logics clearly. You need to be extremely clear about these logics yourself before you can make them clear to students. . . . For example, I would show students how to solve a problem step by step. I would ask them how we should start. Students would give me some suggestions. I would explain which suggestions are feasible and which ones are not and why not. I would then write down the feasible suggestions. Then I would ask students to think of the next step. So, step by step until we solve the problem . . . Students like this teaching method. . . . It's easy for them to learn this way. You can explain a difficult problem very clearly. When students have learned to solve a difficult problem, they naturally feel happy. They naturally think that your teaching is very clear. (Terry)

I use examples or exercises to help students understand concepts. To only verbally introduce and discuss concepts requires a higher linguistic ability. When I first started teaching, I relied little on my verbal explanation because the more I spoke, the more errors I would make. That would confuse students. Using examples and exercises help students understand what I say, students wouldn't be misled by my possible use of wrong words. (Terry)

Other-Regulated Strategies

As novices in the academy, Nina, Terry, and Sue sought external mediation from their department chairs and colleagues to bounce their questions and ideas off them and to develop their expertise in teaching. Throughout their retrospective conversations, this emerged as a favorite other-regulated strategy.

I sometimes asked people in my department how to communicate with students effectively. They told me to speak more slowly so that I could speak more accurately. (Nina)

I asked for advice from several colleagues in the department when I first started teaching here. . . . They told me that the most important thing in teaching was consistency—that I should make my goals and requirements clear to students, and that I should relate exams to my requirements. That way, students would not have objections even if I taught them difficult stuff. They gave me advice on how to survive and avoid negative opinions from students. (Terry)

My department chair was my mentor when I first started teaching here. . . . I phoned her, asked if I could speak with her, and then dashed into her office every time I came across a problem. She listened to me, gave me many suggestions, and backed me up. . . . I really felt fortunate to have her as my mentor. She played a major role in my adjustment to this educational environment. . . . My colleagues are also very helpful. I often discuss practical classroom issues with them. (Sue)

My department chair and colleagues have been very helpful. Whenever I ask them a question, they are willing to answer to their best knowledge. They are nice to junior faculty. They are not like, "I had a hard time being a junior faculty, now it's your turn." They have been very supportive of me. (Sue)

Nina, Terry, and Sue also turned to students in their effort to develop a mediated relationship with them. They developed a teaching style that directed students' attention to their own learning. They worked on shifting the responsibility of learning to students by raising their interest in the subject and the course and by getting them to participate in class actively. Below are a few examples of their other-regulated strategies that engaged students.

I paired up students or assigned them to work on an activity in small groups. Once they have a task to complete and other students to work with, those male students who like to be in control would focus less on me. (Sue)

I try to raise students' interest in the subject by asking them questions during my lectures and making them curious about the answers. As they think hard about how to solve a problem, they become interested in the problem itself, and gradually in the subject and the course. . . . When I prepare my lessons, I think about what I need to cover. When I actually deliver a lesson, I turn each point into a question. . . . All my questions are connected, each question being at a deeper level than the previous one. . . . After students get the answer to a question, I then ask another question about the next point. Thus, step-by-step, I cover the lesson with questions. I give students much time to think on their own after each question. I keep their curiosity that way. . . . Students can always learn content knowledge from books. They don't have to come to my class. To get students interested in the subject is more important. (Terry)

I ask students a lot of questions in class. . . . In my explanation, I stop often to ask students questions to get them [to] think why we get such a result, and whether we would always get such a result. Thinking is the most important. Students may forget about the content they learn. But once they've learned to think, they will always benefit from it. . . . Through thinking continuously, students will understand better what they learn. (Terry)

I try to activate students' enthusiasm in learning. I ask many questions to challenge students. Students who are active in learning will take the challenge and try to find answers to those questions. Student participation plays a major role in my teaching. (Terry)

I invite questions from students at every step and shall only continue explaining the next step when there are no questions. At the beginning of a semester, very few students ask questions. Towards the end, many students do. . . . Asking questions is a very good way of learning. If students have questions, it's evidence that they're following my teaching; it's evidence of their active thinking. I especially encourage students to ask questions. (Terry)

Self-Regulated Strategies

In describing how hard second-language-speaking instructors work to establish their credibility as professionals, Thomas (1999) cited a colleague's words: "I sometimes feel that I have to do twice as well to be accepted" (p. 5). This seemed to be Nina's, Terry's, and Sue's experience also. They reported having invested a significant amount of time and energy preparing for classes. Below are some of the self-regulated strategies they exploited in their lesson planning to compensate for their linguistic disadvantages.

Using Different Teaching Approaches and Methods

Before each class, I work seriously on the lesson plan to incorporate different approaches in my teaching. For example, I may lecture on a new concept first. I would then lead students to do an activity so that they can understand the concept through experiential learning. Then I would provide students with questions for them to discuss in what way this concept would help their future students learn. (Nina)

I use three approaches to teach every concept: graphical, numerical, and verbal. I would use one approach and let students use the other two approaches to solve the problems by themselves. . . . If students find it difficult to get the idea through one method, I would use another method. (Terry)

Modeling What They Preach

> I can't just stress the need for them to help their students of different abilities and learning styles. I need to model it in my own class. Students in my classes have different abilities and learn at different paces. Some students learn fast and finish an activity quickly. In my lesson planning, I think about different ways of pairing up students and design additional activities for groups that finish early. (Sue)

> A student came up to me at the end of a semester and said, "You proofread very carefully and I didn't find a single error in the handouts you gave us in class." I was really surprised because I didn't think that students would pay attention to little details. Ever since then, I became even more careful when preparing my handouts. I would phone friends if I'm not sure about certain things. I was really careful to avoid making any mistakes. . . . If you require students to proofread their assignments, you would need to set up a good example for them. (Sue)

Adjusting Teaching Based on Student Needs

> Most students here are commuters and work on part-time jobs to support themselves. I didn't take this into consideration when I first designed course assignments. I told the class that they had to find time to do their collaborative work. But collaborative projects didn't work in the first two years and the quality was not satisfactory. Now, I take into consideration students' work and lifestyle when designing course assignments. I give students class time to work on their projects. Students are more willing to do group projects and consider collaboration beneficial. (Sue)

In the narrative of her development of professional satisfaction, Verity (2000) took professional identity to be "a zone of historically situated activity vulnerable to external conditions and influences which may require strategic maintenance, rather than a fixed state of being" (p. 180). The retrospective accounts in this section describe Nina, Terry, and Sue's mediational practice of strategically maintaining not only external but also internal conditions and influences. In their processes of mediation, they employed symbolic and material tools to gain object-regulation, collaborated with their colleagues and students to obtain other-regulation, and worked hard in their second language to achieve self-regulation.

Mediated Co-Construction of Opportunities

This section makes further use of Nina's, Terry's, and Sue's reflexive narratives to report on their reconstructed professional identity and mediated relationships with students. Drawing on Vygotsky's (1978, 1987) sociocultural theory of mediation, it theorizes Nina's, Terry's, and Sue's journey of peripheralization and reconstruction to suggest a pedagogy of mediated co-construction of opportunities.

Second Language Speaking as a Privilege

To reconstruct their own definition of second-language-speaking faculty, Nina, Terry, and Sue exploited mediational strategies of object-regulation, other-regulation, and self-regulation. In so doing, they turned their linguistic disadvantage and their experiences with it into a resource for their own teaching and for their students' learning.

In her description of Black, tenured, female faculty's success in the ivory tower, Alfred (2001) emphasized the role of positive self-definition in their management of White-dominated cultures. The Black women scholars in her study "define their marginality as a positive attribute. To them, it's a privilege to be marginal" (p. 59) because their marginality allowed them to "watch, observe, and learn the behaviors of the dominant group while preserving their own cultural identity and self-definition" (p. 61). As a second-language-speaking teacher-educator in a U.S. university, Kubota (2002) also regarded marginality as an asset that could and should be appropriated and turned into "a tool for advocating racial, ethnic, and linguistic diversity" (p. 303). Exploring how minority immigrant women teachers negotiated with nativism and the native-English-speaker construct, Amin (2001) took nonnative identities to be a source of empowerment based on the finding that her participants were more effective in the classroom when building their pedagogy on their nonnative identities rather than following the native speaker norm.

For Nina, Terry, and Sue, being nonnative English speakers appeared to be a disadvantage and a privilege simultaneously. It was an obstacle but also an asset when it was transformed into a resource. The following excerpts highlight their privileges and strengths of being nonnative English-speaking faculty.

> There are international students in my class who have language difficulties. I remember the difficulties I had when I first came here. So I can totally understand their difficulties. . . . When I was a student, I paid much attention to learning strategies. I give students suggestions on how to study based on my own experience as an international student. . . . I had a student from Japan whose English was weak. He wrote me via e-mail that he

didn't understand why he did poorly on tests since he came to class just the same as other students and did all the work. I gave him a long reply, advising him to pay attention to his studying strategies. I made a few suggestions on how to study based on my own experience as an international student. . . . I told students in class that I would be happy to share my learning strategies with them. Some students came to my office and some wrote me e-mails asking for advice on learning strategies. I would share my experience with them and encourage them to try. . . . My native English-speaking American colleagues don't have such experiences and may not be able to give such advice on studying strategies. (Terry)

I'm probably stronger than English-speaking faculty in some areas. . . . For example, I am sensitive to student reactions in class and adjust my teaching accordingly. . . . My English is not particularly strong. I'm more patient [with] students because of that. . . . You would be more ready to tolerate others' weaknesses if you yourself have weaknesses. My English might make students confused. I should be more patient to clarify any confusion students might have. Even if there is only a slight possibility of confusion, I have the responsibility to clarify it. (Terry)

I know the level of students really well and have adjusted my teaching to this level. I was once a student here. I found everything easy when I first started. Then at a certain point, I just got stuck. Everything became difficult and I couldn't understand anything. I still remember the difficulties I had then. So I would try ways to help students not to get stuck with the same problems I had. (Terry)

This university has a diverse student population. Many students' first language is not English. I have gone through and survived the learning processes that many nonnative English-speaking students are going through. I understand their struggle with language when working on course assignments and can see from their perspective and standpoint. Although I don't have the linguistic intuition of a native English-speaker and can't use the language as freely as I would like to, I have my own strength in communicating with students. . . . I am more sympathetic of students' difficulties and know what resources to refer them to for help. I often used supportive resources when I was a graduate student. (Sue)

Through mediational practice, Nina, Terry, and Sue seemed to have regained confidence in their reconstructed professional identities. The narratives below depict their determination to make use of the positive attributes that their unique backgrounds and experiences have given them to make contributions to their students, their colleagues, their institutions, and their profession.

> I've had education in both Chinese and American universities, and have worked with different age levels in China as well as in different states in the U.S. I have insights of different perspectives and views from various pedagogical contexts. This is a strength that many native English-speaking American faculty probably don't have. . . . In this state, the student body is so linguistically and culturally diverse. Teachers would need to be prepared so that they will know how to help these students learn. Teachers need to know that different cultures have different ways of, for example, doing math, and their ways are not the only ones. So they would not consider an immigrant child wrong when she or he uses a different way and would not insist on the child following their ways. They need to have an open mind and learn to value these different ways, instead of having a linear view and seeing from only one angle. (Nina)

> I have an outsider as well as an insider position. . . . I have insights of different perspectives and views. . . . That's the kind of instructor I want to be. I want to bring my students to see different perspectives. I developed a new course on case studies in education that serves that purpose. The course includes analysis of very different cases of education in the United States, China, Japan, Germany, Russia, et cetera, and debates on the issue of effective teaching methods. The purpose is for students not to have a narrow mind but to have a global perspective. (Nina)

> My experiences in China and in the States are helpful in my current teaching. I can compare the U.S. economic system with that of China and talk about the problems in each. Take ownership for example: China has a different ownership compared to the States. I would talk about different characteristics and results of different ownerships and do some comparison. . . . Take for another example environment. There are environmental problems in China such as pollution. . . . It's related to China's administrative system. . . . The United States and other developed countries started protecting the environment since the seventies. They have a lot of experiences. But China doesn't have much experience yet in this regard. (Terry)

Teaching as a Mediational Space

In their mediational practice, Nina, Terry, and Sue turned teaching from a minefield of student resistance into the ZPD that "functions . . . as a mediational space" (Verity, 2000, p. 184), in which they worked collaboratively with their students and colleagues to construct opportunities for professional growth in a new educational culture. During their continual mediational processes, they developed a style of teaching that drew on student responses, shared instructional goals with students, and shifted learning responsibility to them. They developed a sensitivity to students' different learning abilities and needs, and an ability to engage students in the classroom learning environment.

The self-testimonies above document Nina's, Terry's, and Sue's journey through stages of loss to stages of recovery (Pavlenko & Lantolf, 2000). The stages of loss are characterized by their negative experiences of student challenges to their linguistic capacity for content delivery and the interactive exchange of thoughts and, thereby, their requisite expertise to teach the courses they were teaching. The stages of recovery are marked by their positive experiences of professional satisfaction and, along with it, a new sense of professional identity. The following narratives illustrate these immigrant women scholars' mediated relationships with their students.

> I've had pretty good reviews so far. My teaching evaluation was close to the department and college means, sometimes a little above and sometimes a little below. Students' comments were mostly positive. Some students voluntarily wrote letters to the department, saying nice things about my teaching. I didn't even solicit them. (Sue)

> Students became more and more interested in my class. I could see their reactions in class. Their facial expressions tell me that they are with me. When they first started the class, they weren't reactive at all. There wasn't any expression on their faces. Gradually, they became more participatory and active. They would frown, shake their heads, nod, or smile. When they get their volunteered answers correct, their eyes would shine. . . . When they found the content interesting and they felt that they could learn something from me, they became more and more interested. I enjoy this experience. (Terry)

> Some students wanted to continue keeping in touch with me and receiving my advice. A Japanese American student came to see me several times after graduation. She didn't know what to do when she first started student teaching. I gave her some suggestions and a few activity ideas. She was very grateful. Later, she found a full-time job. Recently, she wrote me an e-mail asking about how she could start in a master's program. She also expressed an interest in pursuing Ph.D. studies. These students trust me and admire

me. If I have helped a student succeed in education, it's a kind of reward, isn't it? (Nina)

Conclusion

This chapter has presented three Chinese-speaking women's personal narratives of their lived experiences of struggle and empowerment as nonnative English-speaking female academics in a U.S. university. The narratives are contextualized within the theoretical framework of sociocultural theory, especially as it relates to the concept of mediation in the ZPD (Vygotsky, 1978, 1987). In their narratives, the three immigrant women scholars shared their stories of obstacles they encountered and mediational strategies they used when professing in a language that was not yet perceived to be their own, when dealing with credibility and authority issues with native and nonnative English-speaking students, and when constructing nonnative English-speaking faculty identities in an English-speaking U.S. institution of higher education.

By turning outward (object- and other-regulation) as well as inward (self-regulation), the three female faculty created collaborative dialogues with their students and colleagues, which are considered a key form of mediated teaching and learning. In their mediational practice, they turned teaching from a minefield of student resistance into a mediational space, in which they worked jointly with their students, colleagues, and department chairs to "co-construct contexts in which expertise emerges as a feature of the group" (Lantolf, 2000, p. 17). In these co-constructed pedagogical contexts, the scope of the ZPD includes more than just expert/novice interaction between instructors and students, or between senior faculty and junior faculty. The ZPD in these co-constructed contexts includes mediated co-construction of opportunities for professional development and identity (re)construction on the part of the nonnative English-speaking immigrant female faculty and meaningful active learning on the part of their students.

References

Alfred, M. V. (2001). Success in the ivory tower: Lessons from Black tenured female faculty at a major research university. In R. O. Mabokela & A. L. Green (Eds.), *Sisters of the academy: Emergent black women scholars in higher education* (pp. 57–79). Sterling, VA: Stylus Publishing.

Amin, N. (2001). Nativism, the native speaker construct, and minority immigrant women teachers of English as a second language. *CATESOL Journal, 13*(1), 89–107.

Benjamin, L. (Ed.). (1997). *Black women in the academy: Promises and perils.* Gainesville: University Press of Florida.

Bourdieu, P. (1977). The economics of linguistic exchanges. *Social Science Information, 16,* 645–668.

Bourdieu, P. (1986). The forms of capital. In J. G. Richardson (Ed.), *Handbook of theory and research for the sociology of education* (pp. 241–258). New York: Greenwood Press.

Kubota, R. (2002). Marginality as an asset: Toward a counter-hegemonic pedagogy for diversity. In L. Vargas (Ed.), *Women faculty of color in the white classroom: Narratives on the pedagogical implications of teacher diversity* (pp. 293–307). New York: Peter Lang.

Lantolf, J. P. (Ed.). (2000). *Sociocultural theory and second language learning.* New York: Oxford University Press.

Luthra, R. (2002). Negotiating the minefield: Practicing transformative pedagogy as a teacher of color in a classroom climate of suspicion. In L. Vargas (Ed.), *Women faculty of color in the white classroom: Narratives on the pedagogical implications of teacher diversity* (pp. 109–124). New York: Peter Lang.

Lyons, N., & LaBoskey, V. K. (Eds.). (2002). *Narrative inquiry in practice: Advancing the knowledge of teaching.* New York: Teachers College Press.

Mabokela, R. O., & Green, A. L. (Eds.). (2002). *Sisters of the academy: Emergent black women scholars in higher education.* Sterling, VA: Stylus Publishing.

Pavlenko, A., & Lantolf, J. P. (2000). Second language learning as participation and the (re)construction of selves. In J. P. Lantolf (Ed.), *Sociocultural theory and second language learning* (pp. 155–177). New York: Oxford University Press.

Swartz, D. (1997). *Culture and power: The sociology of Pierre Bourdieu.* Chicago: University of Chicago Press.

Thomas, J. (1999). Voices from the periphery: Non-native teachers and issues of credibility. In G. Braine (Ed.), *Non-native educators in English language teaching* (pp. 5–14). Mahwah, NJ: Erlbaum.

Vargas, L. (Ed.). (2002). *Women faculty of color in the white classroom: Narratives on the pedagogical implications of teacher diversity.* New York: Peter Lang.

Verity, D. P. (2000). Side affects: The strategic development of professional satisfaction. In J. P. Lantolf (Ed.), *Sociocultural theory and second language learning* (pp. 179–197). New York: Oxford University Press.

Vygotsky, L. S. (1978). *Mind in society: The development of higher psychological processes.* Cambridge, MA: Harvard University Press.

Vygotsky, L. S. (1987). *The collected works of L. S. Vygotsky: Vol. 4. Thinking and speaking.* New York: Plenum Press.

Watkins-Goffman, L. (2001). *Lives in two languages: An exploration of identity and culture.* Ann Arbor: University of Michigan Press.

5

MULTIPLE MENTORS IN MY CAREER AS A UNIVERSITY FACULTY

Keiko Komiya Samimy

U nderstanding the socialization process in the academic community is critical for junior faculty members for their survival. Socialization can be defined as a "life-long process that helps to determine a person's ability to fulfill the requirements for membership in a variety of life groups . . . work, school, clubs, family" (Van Maanen, 1984, p. 213), or as a means of reproducing the cultural capital of society (Bourdieu, 1986), or as a "ritualized process that involves the transmission of the organizational culture" (Tierney & Bensimon, 1996, p. 37). In this socialization process in the academic community, having mentors is extremely crucial since it provides us with "ample informal networks of academic, administrative, and political information; collegiality and positive social contact; intellectual exchanges, and other valuable opportunities" (Rong, 2002, p. 138).Yet, existing literature (Tierney & Bensimon, 1996; Vargas, 2002) clearly suggests that women of color are faced with many challenges such as lack of mentors and a chilly climate (Vargas, 2002).

Statistics from the American Council on Education (1995) indicate that only 12.9 percent are faculty of color out of 538,023 full-time undergraduate faculty teaching positions in higher education (as cited in Vargas, 2002). Out of that, there were 12,988 African American women; 7,287 Asian American/ Pacific Island women; and 5,078 Latinas and Native American women (Wilds & Wilson, 1998, p. 102, as cited in Vargas, 2002). Furthermore, the tenure rate for women professors of color is at the lowest (54%) and only 2.1 percent of all full professors are women of color (Wilds & Wilson, 1998, pp. 41–43, as cited in Vargas, 2002). This dismal representation of women of color in the academic community may be explained by a number of inter-related factors, according to Tierney and Rhoads (1993), which include: (1) inadequate anticipatory socialization, (2) weak mentoring as faculty, (3) fewer networking opportunities, (4) divergent priorities, that is, lack of guid-ance as to what is recognized as important for academic success, and (5) addi-tional demands (e.g., childbirth, child care, serving on campus committees).

How and where do we find our mentors who can help us with our ques-tions regarding our tenure and promotion, publication, or getting external grants, just to name a few? According to Tierney and Bensimon (1996), ju-nior faculty can seek mentors across race, ethnicity, and gender both formally and informally. In the following narrative, I will share my experience as a university faculty as to how I was inspired and helped by three mentors as I tried to achieve my own professional identity as a female faculty in a large midwestern research university.

How It All Started

Becoming a university professor was not something I had even imagined as a child who was born and raised in a small town in the northern part of Japan. As a child, I liked to play school; being a teacher in particular was my favorite role. As far as I could remember, being an English teacher at a local middle school or high school was the extent of my career goal. So, how did I end up being a university professor in America?

In retrospect, there were three role models and/or mentors who officially or unofficially helped me to navigate my career as a university professor at a major research university where I currently teach. They were particularly instrumental not only in providing me with specific strategies and advice but also in simply being role models in academia at critical junctures of my ca-reer. While none of these mentors were Asian female faculty, what I learned from them was quite helpful at different times and places. As I further trav-eled the road of my career, however, I realized that I had to develop and nurture my own identity as an Asian female faculty that was different from that of my mentors. Pressures of playing multiple roles equally well as a uni-versity faculty, mother, and wife, were continuous challenges, particularly when I was faced with the process of tenure and promotion from assistant professor to associate professor. In the following, I will discuss my own experiences with three mentors by drawing on the concept of socialization in an academic community at different stages of my career.

Finding Mentors

According to Tierney and Bensimon (1996), socialization in the academic community can be a two-stage process. Stage one is called "anticipatory socialization," which takes place "before an individual sets foot on campus" (p. 37). That is, she is socialized as a graduate student or as faculty at other institutions (Tierney & Rhoads, 1993). Stage two is called "organizational socialization," which has two phases. The first phase is called "initial entry," which takes place prior to one's employment at the university or shortly thereafter. Job interviews or orientation for new faculty members are examples of this first phase. The second phase is called "role continuance," which occurs throughout the tenure and promotion process, and it can be either formal or informal. In other words, the tenure promotion process is formal; however, conversations with senior colleagues on the subject, for example, could be an informal socializing experience. And if the second phase is successful, ideally speaking, a new faculty member has "a set of internalized role specifications, a sense of satisfaction with work, and a high degree of job involvement and commitment. She or he is carried along within the structure of the career to later stages, which may involve the maturing, more independent professional in sponsoring, socialization, or other organizational leadership roles and generative activities" (Clark & Corcoran, 1986, p. 24). In my case, the first two mentorings occurred during the anticipatory socialization process and the third mentoring occurred during the organizational socialization process.

First Mentor in My Anticipatory Socialization Process: Charles A. Curran, Professor of Clinical Psychology at Loyola University of Chicago

Professional socialization opportunities in graduate school are an extremely important factor for successful professional academic careers for women (Clark & Corcoran, 1986). Yet, research thus far has revealed that generally minority women have fewer opportunities for professional socialization opportunities in graduate school in comparison to majority women. That is, in comparison to majority women, minority women were reported to have fewer opportunities in apprenticeship, mentoring, and support networks in the department they belong to (Turner & Thompson, 1993).

In retrospect, my first anticipatory socialization process in the academic community began when I met Professor Curran. At that time, I was completing my senior year majoring in English at a small women's Catholic college in a midwestern town. My original plan was to become an English teacher in the local middle school or high school in Japan upon my graduation. When I met Professor Curran, he was looking for a research assistant who could help him with his work in a less commonly taught language such as Japanese. I had no idea what his research was about, but was delighted with the opportunity to teach my language and culture and I felt naively confident about my teaching abilities. Only later, I learned that Professor Curran is the originator of the Counseling-Learning (C-L) and Community Language Learning (CLL) approach, and he had done extensive research in other foreign languages by applying his ideas. As a foreign student who was in the midst of a painful acculturation process and often felt marginalized and silenced, Professor Curran's invitation to teach Japanese truly revitalized my forgotten cultural and linguistic capital (Bourdieu, 1986). While my teaching was shaky sometimes because of my lack of metalinguistic awareness in Japanese, after teaching a year, Professor Curran offered me the position to work for him as a research assistant at Loyola University in Chicago. This had opened up a wonderful opportunity for me to pursue an M.A. in clinical psychology and to be involved in Professor Curran's research in C-L and CLL (Curran, 1976, 1977). Personally, the fundamental philosophy of Counseling-Learning, which asserts that "learning is persons" and that learning involves not only a person's intellect but his or her whole person, was very convincing and encouraging. Having studied under Carl Rogers who originated the client-centered therapy, I could see how Professor Curran's learner-centered approach is a key pedagogical framework in his approach to teaching. When I joined Professor Curran's graduate research seminar in Chicago, the group had already established a very supportive atmosphere and I felt welcome as their Japanese language expert, that my cultural and linguistic capital was valued. In addition, I had numerous opportunities to travel nationally and internationally with Professor Curran to attend workshops and conferences. While my knowledge in C-L and CLL was very limited, Professor Curran always encouraged me to present my role as a Japanese language expert in his research, which reinforced my cultural and linguistic capital (Bourdieu, 1986). Under Professor Curran's apprenticeship, not only was I given a firsthand opportunity to learn what it means to be a professor in an American university, but also I began to regard myself as an emerging researcher.

Unfortunately, after a few years, my apprenticeship with Professor Curran came to a stop because of his sudden death. However, the legacy that I received from him became tremendous assets, or cultural capital (Bourdieu, 1986), throughout my tenure as a doctorate student at a major midwestern university in Illinois. It helped me to get my teaching assistantship in the Japanese program where I was nominated for outstanding TA for four consecutive years, it guided me to select my doctorate dissertation topic early in my doctoral program, and I was able to publish an article based on it (Samimy, 1989). Professor Curran's mentoring helped me socialize into academia because it gave me: (1) experience in publication and conference presentations prior to my doctoral program, (2) understanding of the politics of the academic community (hierarchical relationships among faulty members and/ or faculty and graduate students), and (3) made me aware of my unique cultural capital and of how I could contribute to the academic community.

In summary, my first anticipatory socialization process had significant impact on who I am today not only as an academician but also as a person in general because I was greatly influenced by Professor Curran's ideas and what he stood for as a scholar. In other words, for a meaningful socialization process to occur, our individual forces such as our cultural values, prior experiences with socialization, personalities, individual support system, and level of commitment (Lindsay, 1988) must be in concert with our mentors' to some degree.

My Second Anticipatory Socialization and First Phase of Organizational Socialization: Having a Spouse as a Mentor

When I was hired as a tenure-track assistant professor in foreign- and second-language education at a large midwestern university, I had some knowledge of being an assistant professor in a major research university since my husband has been a faculty member in the engineering department for several years. Having a senior member in the same academic community at home was very handy and helpful to consult with numerous issues related to my job. My husband was a role model who helped me to navigate my career in a significant way, particularly in my initial years of my career. In preparation for my job interview, for example, I was able to brainstorm with my husband as to what kind of questions I needed to ask the chairman of the department. The questions involved salary, teaching load, advising load, requirements for tenure and promotion, and research grants, just to name a few. Having these questions beforehand made me feel much more in control of the job interview when one often feels very vulnerable. As a part of anticipatory socialization, Tierney and Bensimon (1996) suggest assigning two individuals who can help a new faculty member with formal and informal tasks, because "The search committee may have been adjourned, thinking their task is completed; the departmental chair may not feel that he or she should yet be involved, and the deal will be too busy" (p. 130). My husband fit the role of the individual who could help me with the informal tasks.

In addition to being an informal mentor during my anticipatory socialization process, my husband was instrumental during the initial stages of my organizational socialization, that is, after I was employed as an assistant professor. Going through a tenure promotion process is an extremely anxiety-provoking period for junior faculty members. Gaining prior knowledge about it from my spouse had eased the overwhelming fear toward this monster called "tenure and promotion." What helped me to plan strategically was to have some understanding of (1) the time line, when formal evaluations occur (e.g., fourth year and sixth year) and what kind of feedback I could expect to receive; (2) how I should prepare my dossier, what criteria are used to evaluate a candidate's dossier (e.g., quality, number, balance among scholarship, teaching, and service); and (3) the voting process in the department, college, and university.

Since my husband went through his tenure and promotion process a few years ahead of me and "knew the ropes," he was able to give me some valuable pointers. In addition, the fact that my husband, who is not a native speaker of English, passed his tenure and promotion without any difficulties meant a great deal to me and gave me hope to pursue mine. Only later in my career, however, did I realize that we lived in totally different departmental cultures, and what worked well for him did not necessarily work for me. In other words, being a nonnative speaker of English in the engineering department was not an issue since the majority of the faculty members are nonnative speakers. Hence issues such as power struggles between native- and nonnative-speaker professionals, marginalization and/or discrimination of nonnative-speaker professionals seemed to be nonexistent in his department. Nonetheless, having informal opportunities to ask questions about tenure-promotion, publication, conference presentations, writing grant proposals, and departmental politics was very helpful in reducing my anxiety about surviving in a "chilly, foreign" land.

The Second Phase of Organizational Socialization: Mentor in My Department

I was very fortunate to have a senior female faculty member who was extremely successful in our field of foreign- and second-language education as my role model and mentor. She was instrumental in both the initial entry stage and the role continuance stage of the organizational socialization process, to use Tierney and Rhoads's (1993) terminology. During my initial entry stage, having a mentor of the same sex made it easier for me to approach her with my questions and concerns. In addition, the fact that my mentor was the chair of the search committee when I applied for the position made my entry to the academic community less scary and overwhelming.

Clark and Corcoran (1986) underscore the significance of early stages of socialization in the academic community for "developing commitment to work, for stimulating motivation, and for internalizing occupationally relevant attitudes and behaviors that sustain productivity and continued achievement throughout the career" (p. 24). In fact, the year I was hired, the college organized a retreat for new faculty members, and my mentor was invited as one of the speakers to give us advice based on her experience. While I don't remember everything she said, I do remember that the title of her presentation was something to do with the "Ten Commandments" for surviving in academia and how seriously I took her ten commandments and tried to put them into practice. In fact, what I learned from her at the orientation has had a long-lasting impact on me throughout my career.

While there are some theoretical discussions on significant roles that mentors play in the academic socialization process (Clark & Corcoran, 1986; Menges & Exum, 1983; Tierney & Bensimon, 1996; Turner & Thompson, 1993; Vargas, 2002), how mentoring actually happens is not well documented. In the following section, I would like to share how my mentor was instrumental in my role continuance stage, particularly in areas of teaching and research.

For teaching, my mentor was generous in sharing her syllabi and teaching materials with me, which saved my time and energy tremendously. In addition, she came to my conference presentations and/or asked her friends from other institutions to come when she was not able to do so. Based on her observations of my presentations, my mentor wrote a letter of support with regard to my teaching skills for my tenure-promotion evaluation.

As with Professor Curran, my mentor was able to help me channel my linguistic and cultural capitals into my research. Utilizing my knowledge of Japanese language and culture, we were able to collaborate in writing research grant proposals, a journal article, a book chapter, and doing conference presentations. In our collaborative work, I felt that both of us contributed equally by bringing our unique resources; hence, I did not experience any feeling of exploitation. The highlight of our collaboration was when we wrote a grant proposal to teach Japanese to a group of engineering students, and my mentor, my husband, his colleagues, and I flew together by the university airplane to the National Science Foundation headquarters in Washington, D.C. Although we did not receive the grant, the experience was very exciting and empowering to me, to say the least.

To summarize, I was extremely fortunate to have three excellent mentors readily available to me at both the anticipatory and organization socialization processes. The three mentors officially or unofficially helped me navigate my professional career, providing me with much needed knowledge and coping strategies in the academic community. While what I learned from each of them was invaluable in my socialization process in the academic community, the birth of my daughter almost forced me to take a different path from the roads that my mentors have taken in their careers. In other words, being a mother, full-time university faculty, and wife was not the path that any of my mentors chose to take. This was the time when I felt most challenged and lonely in my career.

Managing Multiple Roles and Renegotiation of My Identity

One year before I became associate professor, my daughter was born. Perhaps this was the most stressful time in my career since I was trying to juggle three roles: mother, assistant professor going up for tenure and promotion, and wife. Clearly, this was "role overload" (Clark & Corcoran, 1986) and I felt extremely stressed out and resentful. Unfortunately, my resentment was directed toward my husband, despite the fact that he was such a good mentor to me prior to our daughter's birth. It appeared to me his being a father and husband did not seem to affect his career involvement and commitment to the extent that my multiple roles affected my professional career a great deal (Clark & Corcoran, 1986). In other words, my time and energy were spread so thin I did not get a sense of fulfillment or accomplishment in any of my roles, and I always felt alone in my struggles. Lack of support for childbirth and child care is still omnipresent since the academic community is based on male chauvinism. Even after affirmative action and women's entry to the academy, the "structured absence" or "sexless professorial body" (Tierney & Bensimon, 1996) makes the lives of female faculty with children extremely difficult. The year I gave birth to my daughter, I had one quarter off, but I had to make it up during my off-duty quarter, which did not give me sufficient time to recover from childbirth nor to make necessary arrangements, such as finding a reliable caretaker for my newborn baby on the days when I had to be on campus. Even after a caretaker was hired, when my daughter became ill, I ended up staying home; actually I wanted to stay home with her so that I could take care of her.

Acculturation of becoming parents who are both academicians taught my husband and me some invaluable lessons. Lesson 1: Never schedule our classes on the same day so that in case of an emergency because of our daughter's illness, for example, one of us is available. Lesson 2: Never schedule our conference presentations during the same week. This may sound unbelievable, but we have actually scheduled to be out of town in the same week thinking (hoping) that the other one was going to be in town to take care of our daughter. Lesson 3: Do not take work home unless it is absolutely necessary especially when a child is still small and needs a lot of attention. This was extremely difficult for me since I was used to doing some work at home before my daughter was born. However, I found that doing my work at home and taking care of my daughter was counterproductive and frustrating. I also learned that when a mother is feeling stressed out and resentful, no one in the family is happy. Consequently, I had to learn (and am still learning) to use my time as efficiently as possible by reorganizing my priorities as well as by delegating responsibilities. Lesson 4: Do not try to be a perfectionist in everything. While I was not consciously trying to be a perfectionist, I must admit that I was trying very hard to do at least a better than adequate job in all three roles. Being a mom, for example, I always told myself that my daughter came first, before my career, and that I should demonstrate that credo whenever I could. Hence, when my daughter was in the first or second grade, I used to actively volunteer to be a classroom helper or to be involved in other school-related activities. On her birthday, for example, I used to make homemade cookies or brownies with special decorations for her to take to the class rather than sending store-bought ones. In retrospect, I was overcompensating for the lack of time I was able to spend time with my daughter by doing what a stay-at-home mom might typically do for her children.

Being a wife was another challenge for me. While the three mentors helped my socialization in the academic community immensely, having my mother in Japan as a role model for being a mother and a wife, in fact, increased my stress level. Since my mother was the only role model I knew as a Japanese wife and mother, I tried to emulate what she used to do for my father and me. She was a superb housekeeper, always preparing wonderful meals for the family and keeping our house clean and comfortable. She really spoiled us in many ways. If my memory serves me correctly, my father never cooked a meal for himself nor did he know how to do the laundry, which was not unusual at that time in our society. To me, trying to emulate her as a mother and wife while pursuing my career, however, was an impossible dream. Yes, I was able to manage it to some extent but I did not feel happy nor fulfilled. When I came to this realization, I knew that I had to reorganize my priorities and renegotiate my identities.

Renegotiating My Identity

When I began my career as a university professor, being successful meant to me to secure large research grants, publish many articles in prestigious journals, and present my research findings at national and international conferences. However, after my daughter's birth and my promotion to associate professor, my priorities in life changed. Instead of trying to be a super mom, researcher, and wife, I became much more realistic with regard to my goals and ambitions. I decided that my family came first, and then my career. I wanted to live my life with joy and satisfaction rather than constantly feeling unhappy and resentful. As a mother of two and as a researcher, Sasaki (2003) shares a similar sentiment in her autobiographical article, "A Scholar on the Periphery: Standing Firm, Walking Slowly," in which she maintains "to avoid every possible situation where my life as a mother (and often as a wife) would conflict with my life as a researcher. I learned that being torn between my family and my work is the last thing I want to do" (p. 212). I could not have agreed with her more.

Furthermore, I came to the important realization that I had to stop my futile efforts to be a Japanese mother and wife. I used to feel resentful because I felt that I was pressured to play the prescribed roles by the people around me and society in general. However, it became clear to me later that I was the one who was boxing myself into those roles and making myself miserable. After having lived in America longer than in my home country, my cultural and linguistic identities have become much more complex and multidimensional than they used to be; hence, I could no longer fit into the stereotypical image of Japanese mother and wife. More important, my perceived beneficiaries (my daughter and husband) perhaps did not even care whether or not I was trying to be a Japanese mom (wife), as long as I was happy with who I am.

Implications: Where Do We Go from Here?

I must confess that up until recently, I have not read much about the socialization of women faculty and faculty of color. However, the more I learned about the dilemma that women and faculty of color face, the more keenly I realized how atypical my socialization processes with my mentors had been. In other words, I was extremely fortunate to have three mentors who were readily available and willing to help me succeed. The existing literature repeatedly highlights how underrepresented women and people of color are in the academic community because of the lack of adequate socialization, whether it is during the anticipatory socialization process or the organizational process. While informal mentoring can happen and is extremely valuable, someone, particularly a senior faculty member, should be designated to junior faculty, and in particular to women faculty of color, as a formal mentor to provide "structured, systematic feedback to an individual on an ongoing basis" (Tierney & Bensimon, 1996, p. 131). In fact, embedding the role of mentor in the evaluation of senior faculty, as Tierney and Bensimon suggest, is an excellent idea so that senior faculty will "accept responsibility for overall success of the collective" (p. 133). In addition, Tierney and Bensimon (1996) make excellent suggestions, which include:

- Think of orientation (for junior faculty) as dialogistic rather than a session at which information is conveyed.
- Establish ongoing forums for new faculty to seek advice and discuss their needs.
- Create environments that honor collaboration rather than individualism.
- Ensure that one individual who is aware of the structure of faculty development is assigned to each tenure-track faculty member.
- Designate an individual to be in charge of mentoring.
- Understand that underrepresented groups may be called on frequently to serve as role models, so take care not to overburden them with extraneous assignments.
- Develop seminars and workshops for senior faculty to help them understand how they might need to change their professional behavior as the composition of the faculty evolves.
- Establish an office on campus to orient faculty of color and facilitate their professional development. Such an office can also assist departments in creating strategies to recruit and retain faculty of color and to assess departmental climates for faculty of color periodically. (pp. 133–135)

Finally, childbirth and child care pose an enormous challenge for female faculty. Presently, the lack of paid maternity leave policies places female faculty with a newborn in a very vulnerable position, because the availability of options to them is often left to the discretion of department chairs (Tierney & Bensimon, 1996) or because they must decide whether to stop the tenure clock for one year or switch teaching quarters. As a process of academic socialization, female faculty, in particular junior faculty, need to discuss with their department chairs the options they have with regard to maternity leave and its impact on their tenure-promotion process.

In summary, there are numerous cultural barriers that female faculty of color have to overcome. As mentioned above, the academic community is still based on male chauvinism, and we, female faculty of color who have made tenure and promotion, need to become catalysts to create "women-affirming cultures" (Tierney & Bensimon, 1996, p. 94) in colleges and universities for incoming junior female faculty of color by becoming sensitive to the personal lives of women, especially if we are in an administrative position such as department chair, or by advocating an equity-oriented institutional ethos, and by actively recruiting female faculty of color (Tierney & Bensimon, 1996).

References

Bourdieu, P. (1986). *The forms of capital*. In J. G. Richardson (Ed.), *Handbook of theory and research for the sociology of education* (pp. 241–258). New York: Greenwood Press.

Clark, S., & Corcoran, M. (1986). Perspectives on the professional socialization of women faculty. *Journal of Higher Education, 57*(1), 21–43.

Curran, C. A. (1976). *Counseling-learning in second languages*. Apple River, IL: Apple River Press.

Curran, C. A. (1977). *Counseling-learning: A whole-person model for education*. East Dubuque, IL: Counseling-Learning Publications.

Lindsay, B. (1988). Public and higher education policies influencing African-American women. *Higher Education, 17*, 563–80.

Menges, R. J., & Exum, W. H. (1983). Barriers to the progress of women and minority faculty. *Journal of Higher Education, 54*(2), 123–44.

Rong, X. L. (2002). Teaching with differences and for differences: Reflections of a Chinese American teacher educator. In L. Vargas (Ed.), *Women faculty of color in the white classroom: Narratives on the pedagogical implications of teacher diversity* (pp. 125–144). New York: Peter Lang.

Samimy, K. K. (1989). A comparative study of teaching Japanese in the Audio-Lingual method and the Counseling-Learning approach. *Modern Language Journal, 73*(2), 169–177.

Sasaki, M. (2003). A scholar on the periphery: Standing firm, walking slowly. In C. P. Casanave & S. Vandrick (Eds.), *Writing for scholarly publication* (pp. 211–221). Mahwah, NJ: Erlbaum.

Tierney, W. G., & Bensimon, E. M. (1996). *Promotion and tenure: Community and socialization in academe.* Albany, NY: SUNY Press.

Tierney, W. G., & Rhoads, R. A. (1993). *Enhancing promotion, tenure and beyond.* Washington, DC: ERIC Clearinghouse on Higher Education.

Turner, C. S., & Thompson, J. R. (1993). Socializing women doctoral students: Minority and major experiences. *Review of Higher Education, 16*(3), 355–370.

Van Maanen, J. (1984). Doing new things in old ways. The chains of socialization. In J. L. Bess (Ed.), *College and university organization: Insights from the behavioral sciences* (pp. 211–224). New York: New York University Press.

Vargas, L. (Ed.). (2002). *Women faculty of color in the white classroom: Narratives on the pedagogical implications of teacher diversity.* New York: Peter Lang.

6

NAVIGATING MULTIPLE ROLES AND MULTIPLE DISCOURSES

A Young Asian Female Scholar's Reflection on Within-Race-and-Gender Interactions

Guofang Li

ecent statistics from the U. S. Department of Education indicate an increase in the number of minority professors (including African American, Latino, and Asian female faculties) in higher education (14% in 1999). There is also a significant increase in the number of minority students in higher education. The proportion of Asian/Pacific Islander students rose from 2 percent to 6 percent, and the Hispanic proportion rose from 4 percent to 10 percent during 1976 and 2000 (U.S. Department of Education, 2002). The increased diversity among the faculty as well as the students' populations suggest that there is a change in the traditional White-and/or male-dominated teaching structure, and more and more students are receiving instruction and supervision from minority (female) professors.

With the increasing diversity in higher education in recent years, a body of literature and research has emerged that addresses the lived experiences of minority female scholars (Braine, 1999; Kingston-Mann & Sieber, 2001; Lim & Herrera-Sobek, 2000; Vargas, 2002). Many minority female scholars' personal narratives indicate that these groups of newcomers in academia face many challenges and barriers in their career advancement. Unlike their White female counterparts, many minority female scholars face triple disadvantages in terms of language, race, and gender, and are socialized into different discourses. Thus far, research on minority female scholars has generally focused on cross-cultural (White vs. non-White) and/or cross-gender (male vs. female) studies (Braine, 1999; Kingston-Mann & Sieber, 2001; Vargas, 2002). Very few studies have explored minority female faculty's experiences working with minority students who come from similar backgrounds.

While other minority scholars reflect on their interactions and struggles with the majority culture, in this chapter, I focus on within-race-and-gender interactions. That is, I will attempt to explore the interactions and relations between faculty and students of similar cultural backgrounds by reflecting on my own experience as a young Asian female scholar working with Asian female students in a North American university. I hope to illustrate the complex relationships of gender, race, ethnicity, and the inherited power relations that perpetuate the positioning of minority female faculty and students in academia. First I will narrate my own journey of becoming an academic in North America and my own experiences working with Asian students as a teacher, professor, and supervisor. I will then present a contextualized understanding of my experiences within larger sociocultural and sociopolitical contexts.

My Journey to Becoming an Academic

I was born and raised in a remote, rural village of about one hundred people in central China in the 1970s. My parents were farmers and in a traditional sense, were "illiterate" as they never had formal schooling. My father taught himself how to read and write Chinese and he was elected to become a government leader of the local commune, a position he held for over thirty years. As a child growing up in rural China, I witnessed the symbolic historical change of women's status in China. My grandmother had bound feet and worked mostly at home doing domestic chores while my grandfather worked in the fields of local feudal landlords to earn a living as a *Chang Gong*, that is, a long-term laborer. My parents spent their teens in the Communist era. Unlike my grandparents who married by parental arrangement, they broke their respective arranged engagements and married each other by their own choice. Under the Communist slogan that women "were able to hold half the sky," my mother (and all the other mothers of her generation) who no longer had bound feet not only had to work in the fields to earn points for the family but also had to do all the housework. Even though my mother and the other women worked as hard as the men in the commune fields, they were given many fewer points than the men because they were women.

As a child when I helped with commune chores, I was given fewer points than the boys because I was a girl. I learned early that boys were more valuable than girls as most families did not want girl babies. My neighbors, for example, were very ashamed of themselves and their daughters because they could not give birth to a son.

In the late 1970s, China reformed its commune system and started to divide the land to rent it to individual families. During this time, elementary education was compulsory in rural China. Many rural parents sent their sons to school and kept their daughters at home. Those who sent their daughters to school usually withdrew them to work in the fields. In 1978 when I was one year short of school admission age, I followed my older playmates (who were boys) and registered myself in school. My father was not happy that I sent myself to school, but he realized that I did not have children to play with, and he did not object to my going to school one year earlier. He thought that if I could not learn anything the first year, I could repeat grade one the next year when I was at the right age. To his surprise, I passed first grade without any difficulty.

By the time I was in the third grade, all the girls from my village were forced by their parents to quit school to work on the farm and at home. My father did not ask me to quit school because being a government official had made him realize the importance of education. Instead, he encouraged me to study hard so that one day I could go to college and have a government-paid job in the city. In 1983, I became the only girl in my village to finish elementary school and to attend middle school.

In 1989, I passed the highly competitive college entrance examination with very high scores. However, I did not get admitted to the higher-ranking university of my dreams because my college applications were not filled out properly due to my ignorance of the admission process. I was very sad and disappointed at the university I was admitted to because it was not the university I wanted. I cried for two days, but my parents were thrilled at the fact that I passed the college entrance examination and made it to the university. To them, going to any college was good enough for a farm girl.

I had no choice but to attend the university that accepted me. When I completed my undergraduate education with honors in 1993, I decided to pursue a graduate degree at a prestigious school, Wuhan University. Since no one in my extended family had a graduate degree, none of them believed that I could make it. My parents and my brothers thought that since I was from a lower-ranking university than the university I applied to, I would not have the ability to pass the exams. They told me that I was too ambitious.

My aunts and uncles believed that I should not pursue a graduate degree because a university degree was enough for a woman, and I did not need any more education. Against all the odds, I passed the entrance examination and was admitted to the graduate program at Wuhan University with good standing. Three years later, I decided to pursue a Ph.D. degree overseas. When I announced my decision to my family, my parents were very proud, but my aunts and uncles were worried that too much education might hinder my prospects for marriage, as a woman with too much education would be too intimidating for a man.

In 1996, I started my Ph.D. program in curriculum studies in Canada. Like many international students coming from the East to the West and becoming a racial minority in Canada, I experienced initial culture shock and an identity crisis (Li, 2002). I was, however, very fortunate to have been associated with a group of exceptional scholars—my doctoral dissertation committee that mentored me in Western academic discourses. I learned about critical theories, feminist theories, Western popular pedagogies, and the culture of academic publishing. I felt overwhelmingly empowered by the knowledge I gained from my studies. When I completed my Ph.D., I felt I was ready for any challenges I would face as an academic.

I was wrong. My training in my doctoral program did prepare me for the academic part of being a faculty member in terms of teaching and research. It did not prepare me for the sociocultural challenges I encountered as a young Asian female faculty member. Like many other minority scholars, my initial fear of becoming a faculty member was about my interactions with mainstream students and peers and how they would perceive me as an authority (Braine, 1999). Although I did experience some resistance and disrespect from some of my older White students (both male and female), I encountered much stronger resistance from my Asian students. It was the resistance from students of my own cultural background and gender that prompted me to rethink of my own positionality in Western academia and my own identity as a minority female scholar.

My Experiences as an English as a Second Language (ESL) Instructor

I began my teaching career in Canada as a part-time instructor in 1999. During 1999–2000, I taught four different courses with three different student populations. One was an undergraduate course on ESL theories and methods; one was an advanced Chinese literature course with undergraduate Chinese students from mainland China, Hong Kong, and Taiwan; and the other two were advanced ESL reading and writing courses for the affiliated English Language Institute at my university. My students for the reading and writing courses were mostly Chinese-speaking precollege students. Like many other minority faculty members, my levels of success in the different courses I taught were quite different (Kutoba, 2002; Rong, 2002). I received positive acceptance and evaluation from the students in my Chinese literature class and from the White students in my ESL theories and methods class. They regarded me as knowledgeable and dynamic as an instructor. However, I received negative acceptance from the Asian students in my ESL reading and writing classes.

I was the first nonnative speaker to be hired by the English Language Institute to teach English as a Second Language. My first week at the Institute caused a stir among the teachers as well as the students. I later learned after I left the Institute for a postdoctoral position at another university that the teachers initially thought I was hired because I had connections with the director of the Institute (not because of my ability to teach). The ESL students had curiosity, surprise, and sometimes distrust written all over their faces. I was constantly followed by a group of Asian (mostly Chinese) students, and I soon realized that they treated me very differently and had less respect for me as an instructor than for my colleagues. For example, when I was having conferences with students at our library about their projects, many students gathered and watched. Some even laughed and finished my sentences when I was conversing with my students. I never observed similar behavior toward any other faculty members, and I was shocked and outraged by the disrespect they exhibited to me. The ESL students also challenged my grading practices claiming that I graded them differently in order to please my White employers and colleagues. And some expressed preference for a native English-speaking teacher.

My fellow students' distrust of my teaching also influenced how the administrators treated me as a professional. Our academic coordinator constantly observed my classes to make sure I was doing all right. She meticulously pointed out every single error I made in my speech during class including some common speech errors any native English speaker would make. I welcomed her observations and saw them as opportunities for improvement, but felt uncomfortable because I was more scrutinized than my White native-speaking colleagues. It was not until later at a faculty meeting when I shared my observations of the challenges Asian students faced in learning the English language and offered my suggestions that the academic coordinator saw my bilingual and bicultural backgrounds as assets and offered me a small grant to do research with Asian students at the Institute.

Becoming a Graduate Supervisor

After completing my postdoctoral research in 2001, I accepted a tenure-track position in second language education at the Graduate School of Education, State University of New York at Buffalo—a Research 1 university. In our master's programs, half of the student population are U.S. nationals and half are international students from Asian countries, mainly Korea, Japan, Taiwan, and China. In our doctoral programs, although there are a few U.S. nationals, the majority of them are international, female students from Asia. I teach both master's and doctoral courses and supervise doctoral students. Several doctoral students work for me as graduate assistants to support my research activities.

I was the first Asian faculty to be hired at the Graduate School of Education (after me, five more female and male Asian faculty were hired). My presence (along with that of two other African American faculties) no doubt has changed the predominantly White face of the school. I was also the youngest faculty member. When new students first met me, their first reaction was "Gosh, Dr. Li, I did not know you were so young! You look like a student!"

Being a young minority professor in English as a Second Language education definitely has had an impact on how I was perceived by my students, especially international students. I have enjoyed a high level of success with my master's students. My interactions with them suggest that most of them respect me and treat me as their role model. Many students wrote to tell me how much they enjoyed my class and how well I could understand their cultural backgrounds. I assumed that Asian female doctoral students would be even more supportive and understanding of my achievement in becoming a professor in a Western institution as we shared similar journeys. However, to my surprise, I encountered tremendous difficulty with my doctoral students who worked for me as graduate assistants. Jenkins (2000) suggests that interactions in academia are characterized by a status differential between teacher and student, with a higher status accorded to the teacher; such a status is preserved by politeness strategies in communication. Use of different politeness strategies can create positive or negative relations. In my interactions with my doctoral graduate assistants, I experienced a reversal of the status differential between teacher and student, and such a role reversal has resulted in a breakdown in our communication and, thus, in negative relations.

My first two graduate assistants were Korean women who were older than me. They both treated me as if I were a student. The first assistant, whom I call E. K., always wanted my work to fit into her schedule, and I had to make an effort to make an appointment with her to discuss our work. When her task was assigned (e.g., I asked her to input data in the NUDIST program), she would do minimal work, and went on vacation whenever she decided, and gave the work back to me and told me to finish it myself.

My second Korean graduate assistant, S. K., treated me in the same way. She would come into my office at any time without knocking on the door. When she talked to me, she assumed an authoritarian voice. Whenever I asked her to do some work, she always negotiated with me the time she wanted to work. Finally, when she informed me that she could not work on most workdays and did not wish to be contacted on weekends, I told her there would be no more negotiations and she had to finish her work by a certain time so that I could get on with my research plans. Surprised at my reaction, she challenged me and asked me, "How long do you think you are going to be a professor?" Her bluntness to me was a sharp contrast to the kind of respect she exhibited to my White, particularly male, colleagues. Later, when she was assigned to work with one of my senior female colleagues, she never negotiated or complained about her work time with the professor. Another male colleague of mine told me that S. K. showed so much respect to him that it made him feel uncomfortable, "Every time S. K. sees me, she bows to me so many times and even walks backwards. It's embarrassing when she does that for so long in the hallway!"

My third doctoral assistant was a Chinese woman, H. X., also older than me. During the first week of her Ph.D. program, H. X., along with another of my Chinese advisees, rejected my suggestions for selecting courses to take and for participating in a research study conducted by another graduate student. Like the two Korean students, H. X. never knocked on my door even when I was having a meeting with students or faculty members. She talked to me as if I were a student, and sometimes, with her arms crossed, she raised her voice to me if she was unhappy about the work assigned. When I set up work hours with her, she expected me to give her less work, and informed me that she did not like to work on Fridays. Like the other two graduate assistants, she always negotiated work time and it was a constant struggle to get her to complete the assignments. Without consulting or informing me, she decided herself when to take time off for vacation. Before she finished her term as a graduate assistant, I was conducting an important research project that needed her help. H. X. took off without any notice, faked a doctor's note, and then informed me that she would not come back to work. As a result, my project was seriously delayed.

My graduate assistants' aggravating attitudes toward me suggest that they violated the implicit rule that required them to make contributions congruent with their status as student (Bardovi-Harlig & Hartford, 1990). When I went to my senior professors for explanations and help to deal with these situations, they regarded it as an age issue: "You look too young, Guofang." Some jokingly suggested that I dye my hair gray. But is it only an age issue? Reflecting on my relationships with my graduate assistants, I believed that there were more profound issues than age. My interpretation was that my image as a young Asian female faculty member was streamlined into different sociohistorical discourses in which my female Asian graduate assistants projected their understandings of our mutual positionalities and respective roles in Western academia. In the following, I illustrate how these projections work using my own experiences.

Multiple Roles and Multiple Discourses: A Contextualized Understanding of My Experiences

Reflecting on my experiences teaching and supervising these students, I realized that my image as a young Asian female scholar is constantly projected by my graduate assistants into different discourses that undergird Western academia. By discourse, I mean "a set of historically grounded statements that exhibit regularities in presuppositions, thematic choices, values, etc.; that delimit what can be said about something, by whom, when and where, and how; and that are underwritten by some institutional authority" (McKay & Wong, 1996, p. 579). These discourses, as McKay and Wong suggest, do not operate in isolation, but interact and sometimes overlap each other. Within these discourses, we enact different social identities, make sense of our experiences, and recognize how different value systems interact (Gee, 1996). In the following, I illustrate my experiences within these intertwining discourses that include discourse of race and gender in higher education, native speaker/nonnative speaker discourses, and last, the discourse of dual cultural frames in gender roles.

Discourses of Race and Gender in Higher Education

Women (both White and non-White) have been historically marginalized in higher education. In 1995, 75.5 percent of full professors, 63.1 percent of associate professors, and 47.5 percent of assistant professors in universities were White males; 14.3 percent of full professors, 24.7 percent of associate professors, and 36.0 percent of assistant professors were White female. Only 0.4 percent of full professors, 1 percent of associate professors, and 2.1 percent of assistant professors were Asian female. In 1999, 50 percent of college faculty were White males; 35 percent were White females; and only 5 percent were Asian Pacific Islanders (U.S. Department of Education, 2002). These demographics demonstrate that Western academia has been a White (male)-dominated system in which the norms, power, and legitimacy manifest the privilege of definitions enjoyed by Whites (males) (Bassett, 1992; Contreras, 1998; Ortiz, 1998; Vargas, 2002). Such White privilege is "an unusual container where social reality is constructed to perpetuate the dominance structures that are deemed normal" (Contreras, 1998, p. 143). Bassett (1992) points out that inherent in this White (male) system is that White (men) have the birthright to be innately superior, and anyone who does not belong to this system is innately inferior. Thus, such a system consistently denies and devalues the experiences of women and minority groups.

Academia becomes a highly contested terrain with "sites of racial, gender, and class conflicts" (Contreras, 1998, p. 143). Researchers have identified that the White (male) hegemony and the resulting stereotypes of the female as problematic have an adverse impact on women of color in higher education (Bassett, 1992; Statham, 1996). The adverse impact, however, does not come from White male dominance over women and minority groups alone. Bassett (1992) suggests that women and people from various ethnic and racial groups may inadvertently support the White male system. The emerging issue of same-gender politics illustrated in chapter 3 in this volume is an example that sometimes even White females can fall into "the trap of attacking other women and minority females so that they themselves will one up on the status with white males" (Bassett, 1992, p. 15).

Students (White and non-White) can also be powerful supporters of the White (male) hegemony. The autobiographic narratives of female professors of color in White college classrooms in Vargas's (2002) edited volume suggest White students are part of the entrenched hierarchical social distinctions within the White (male) system, and their resistance to the presence of women professors of color inadvertently supports the status quo and enforces the traditional hierarchy in academia.

Instead of becoming allies of minority female professors in the highly contested terrain of higher education, many minority students tacitly accept the dominant White norms and privileges (Hwang, 2000; King, 1991; Thomas, 1999). King calls this kind of uncritical habit of mind "dysconscious racism" with which students justify inequity by accepting the existing status quo. In her personal narrative, Hwang described that she faced strong resistance and hostility from minority students because her young Asian appearance did not measure up to the cast image of "professor as a middle-aged white male" (p. 154). Similarly, my experiences with my female doctoral assistants suggest that they dysconsciously devalued my legitimate power and authority as a professor because I was not a member of the White (male) group. I was deemed inferior and, therefore, deserved less respect than my White male and female colleagues.

Discourses of Native/Nonnative English-Speaking Professionals in Second-Language Education

In addition to my struggles with the discourses of gender and race at the periphery of the White (male) system, I believe my students' attitude toward me also has to do with my identity and positionality as a nonnative English speaker in English as a Second Language education. English as a Second Language education has traditionally been a field dominated by native English-speaking professionals. The referent of the ESL classrooms (and ESL teacher training programs) is the White native speaker who is regarded as the only truly valid and reliable source of language data (Amin, 1999; Ferguson, 1992). Under such a climate, foreign-born, nonnative-speaking professionals are marginalized in the field and are often regarded as "unnecessary by-products of the M.A. and Ph.D. programs in applied linguistics and TESOL in North America" (Braine, 1999, p. xiii):

> Almost from their arrival, many of them [nonnative speakers] discovered that their credentials are questioned, their accents are misunderstood, and that they are marginalized in the profession. (p. xiii)

The nonnative speaker label is often associated with ineptitude, less competent, inferior, and ineffective; and on the contrary, the native speaker label is often the synonym of "the ideal teacher of English" who held authority on the language (Canagarajah, 1999; Phillipson, 1992). Researchers such as Canagarajah and Phillipson have interrogated the "native speaker fallacy," and argued that nonnative-speaking professionals can bring invaluable benefits to their teaching—experiences that native speakers would never be able to attain as monolinguals. Despite these arguments, the personal narratives in several edited volumes (e.g., Braine, 1999; Vargas, 2002) suggest that the "native speaker as the ideal English teacher" fallacy is still prevalent in the field of second language education within the institutions and among the professionals and nonnative students. Similar to the race and gender inequity in the larger discourse in higher education (as discussed in the previous section), nonnative-speaking professionals faced discriminatory treatment in many crucial aspects such as hiring practices and representation in professional organizations (Thomas, 1999).

Such discriminatory practices have further reinforced the marginalization of nonnative-speaking professionals and the negative stereotypes they face in the field. Researchers revealed that male and female nonnative students often challenge the credibility of minority teachers and professors, and show a decided preference for White teachers over non-White teachers (Amin, 1999; Braine, 1999; Thomas, 1999). My students at the English Language Institute, for example, shared similar stereotypes of the authentic English teacher, judged me based on my race and ethnicity, and showed less respect to me as an instructor. For my doctoral students, even though I have as strong a publication record and scholarly qualifications as my White (male) colleagues do, they undermined my authority as a professor and challenged my role as their supervisor.

In observing nonnative students' resistance to nonnative-speaking professionals' authority and credibility, Thomas (1999) believed that we must situate it in the larger discourses in society as we "usually learn to value what we see valued and to undermine what we see undermined" (p. 8). Supporting Thomas's view, Amin (1999) further points out that (nonnative) students are cognizant of the message that the larger society is giving them about who is important and who is not, and that their response to their minority female teachers "is forged in the structural context of a society in which we communicate the message that important people are White, Anglo, and male" (p. 103).

I will also add that the (nonnative) students' response is not forged in the context of North American society alone, it is also a legacy of internationalization and postcolonial discourses. Critical linguists such as Phillipson (1992), Pennycook (1994), and Skutnabb-Kangas (1998) have documented that the spread of English in the world has created unequal power relationships between English-speaking European nations (e.g., the United States and the United Kingdom) and other regions of the world, especially the third world nations. Such linguistic imperialism has promoted the superiority of English and its native speakers, and the inferiority of indigenous languages and their speakers. Students who come from countries with such ideologies may unconsciously reproduce them in the host societies, especially in their perceived superior countries such as the United States. For example, some Japanese ideology legitimates the superiority of native speakers of English and the White race, and such ideology may have contributed to Japanese students' attitudes toward a Japanese woman faculty in that she is less legitimate as a professor than White faculty on the same campus (Kutoba, 1998, 2002). For my Asian students who undermined my authority and treated me in disrespectful ways while doing the opposite to my White colleagues, such ideologies may also be at play.

Discourses of Dual Cultural References to Gender Roles

In addition to the aforementioned discourses, I speculate that my difficulty with Asian female graduate assistants may also be related to the expectations of gender roles that both students and I brought from our home countries. As immigrant minorities, we have dual cultural references in gender relations in host and home countries. The ideologies in these two countries influence our understanding and perceptions of our particular positionality and identity within different contexts.

In many Asian countries, such as China, Japan, and Korea, the traditional expectations for women and men tend to reinforce

> traditionally "feminine" characteristics—submissiveness, passiveness, affiliation, altruism, adaptiveness, and timidness—and to discourage the so-called "masculine" traits of independence, assertiveness, and competitiveness. (Fong, 1997, p. 94)

In modern Japan, for example, traditional gender relations are still prevalent. Although women are provided with increased options outside the home, they have not occupied positions of significance in policy making and business, and their existence and voices have been pretty much ignored by men in formal arenas (Iwao, 1993; Rosenberger, 2001). In China, both the Nationalists and the Communists promised women status as equal citizens to Chinese men, but gender inequality was primarily reconstituted in a new form (Rofel, 1994). As evidenced in my own experiences and those of my mother and grandmother, China's reform did not change the superior status of men or their privilege over women. Yu (1987) described similar situations for women in Korea:

> Sexism and paternalism remain very much alive. Women toil at home and work, but they are treated as second class citizens in almost every realm of society. In terms of status and role, tradition remains strong. (p. 25)

In Korea, gender relations are also influenced by U.S. neocolonial domination and its recent anticolonial nationalist movement. The former, according to Choi (1998), reproduces already familiar gendered and sexualized relations between the two countries (e.g., devaluing Korean women and privileging White women). The latter idealizes the self-sacrificing woman dedicated to nationalist husbands and sons. Such patriarchal ideologies force women to comply with male-centered imaginings:

> The boundaries are drawn and the terms set by a male elite, so that women, though always indispensable participants in political struggles, are relegated to the status of voiceless auxiliaries. (Kim & Choi, 1998, p. 4)

If students came to North America with these ideologies, they may respond to women minority professors with disapproval as they are outside the norms set by men. Many women minority professors, like me, may have developed a new sense of self and gender identity that is a hybrid of both masculinity and femininity—a sense of androgyny that is accompanied by our high level of occupational and educational attainment and personal fulfillment (Fong, 1997). Students who scrutinized us from a traditional gender lens may consider us less deserving of respect because we are outside their familiar gender boundaries.

In summary, many factors may play a role in minority students' resistance to minority female scholars. In understanding their positioning, it is necessary to situate their response within larger institutional, cultural, and transnational contexts.

Conclusion

In conclusion, I want to emphasize that my reflections on and interpretation of my own experiences are specific to the particular contexts in which I was situated, and they cannot be generalized across contexts. My experiences with the particular students I encountered could be unique to our specific situations in that particular sociohistorical time of our lives. I also want to emphasize that not all Asian female students are disrespectful to their fellow Asian female professors. Furthermore, since I did not have the students' input on their perspectives, this reflection is inevitably one-sided and highly subjective. Nevertheless, I believe my stories are important to share, and I hope by sharing, I can contribute to our collective understanding of Asian female scholars' struggles on their journey to navigate the multiple roles and multiple discourses in Western academia.

In what ways can my stories inform us about overcoming the kinds of resistance young minority scholars face when interacting with students of similar cultural backgrounds? I believe that we have the social responsibility not only to assist minority female students in accessing higher education but, more important, to affect their own sense of social and political responsibilities as "junior" minority female scholars. I propose two steps to impose such an impact.

First, I believe that many students may come to graduate programs with limited knowledge and understanding of gender and racial inequalities in their host and home societies, in institutions such as universities, and in a particular field, such as TESOL. We need to educate them and equip them with cognitive knowledge of how power operates in these public arenas and how such power structures may have an impact on their everyday lives. Providing graduate courses in gender and race studies or incorporating critical theories into existing courses would help students gain such cognitive knowledge.

Second, I propose that both minority female professors and students need to work toward "reciprocal empowerment" that aims to "foster mutual attention, mutual empathy, mutual engagement, and mutual responsiveness" (Darling & Mulvaney, 2003, p. 3). Achieving such reciprocal empowerment requires both minority female professors and students to interact in ways that increase connection and enhance personal power for each, and both need to support themselves as minority women while supporting others. Avis (1991) suggests such an empowerment is a holistic process that involves our comprehensive integration of

> 1) a political understanding of the oppression of women, including its embeddedness in the culture, its maintenance in family relationships and its internalization with women; with 2) a high degree of respect for women, their strengths, and their self wisdom; and 3) an understanding of change at individual, family, and larger system level. (p. 199)

References

Amin, N. (1999). Minority women teachers of ESL: Negotiating white English. In G. Braine (Ed.), *Non-native educators in English language teaching* (pp. 93–104). Mahwah, NJ: Erlbaum.

Avis, J. M. (1991). Power politics in therapy with women. In T. J. Goodrich (Ed.), *Women and power: Perspectives for family therapy* (pp. 183–200). New York: Norton.

Bardovi-Harlig, K., & Hartford, B. S. (1990). Congruence in native and nonnative conversations: Status balance in the academic advising session. *Language Learning, 40,* 467–501.

Bassett, P. (1992). Resolving pink and brown conflicts resulting from the white male system. In L. B. Welch (Ed.), *Perspectives on minority women in higher education* (pp. 13–22). New York: Praeger.

Braine, G. (Ed.). (1999). *Non-native educators in English language teaching.* Mahwah, NJ: Erlbaum.

Canagarajah, A. S. (1999). Interrogating the "native speaker fallacy": Non-linguistic roots, non-pedagogical results. In G. Braine (Ed.), *Non-native educators in English language teaching* (pp. 77–92). Mahwah, NJ: Erlbaum.

Choi, C. (1998). Nationalism and construction of gender in Korea. In E. H. Kim & C. Choi (Eds.), *Dangerous women: Gender and Korean nationalism* (pp. 10–32). New York: Routledge.

Contreras, A. R. (1998). Leading from the margins in the Ivory Tower. In L. A. Valverde & L. A. Casenell Jr. (Eds.), *The multicultural campus: Strategies for transforming higher education* (pp. 137–168). Walnut Creek, CA: AltaMira Press.

Darling, P. S. E., & Mulvaney, B. M. (2003). *Women, power, and ethnicity: Working toward reciprocal empowerment.* New York: Haworth Press.

Ferguson, C. A. (1992). Foreword. In B. B. Kachru (Ed.), *The other tongue: English across cultures* (pp. xiii–xvii). Urbana: University of Illinois Press.

Fong, Y. S. (1997). Asian-American women: An understudied minority. *Journal of Sociology and Social Welfare, 24*(1), 91–112.

Gee, J. P. (1996). *Social linguistics and literacies: Ideology in Discourses.* London: Taylor & Francis.

Hwang, S. M. (2000). At the limits of my feminism: Race, gender, class, and the execution of a feminist pedagogy. In S. G. Lim & M. Herrera-Sobek (Eds.), *Power, race and gender in academe: Strangers in the tower?* (pp. 154–170). New York: Modern Language Association of America.

Iwao, S. (1993). *The Japanese woman.* New York: Free Press.

Jenkins, S. (2000). Cultural and linguistic miscues: A case study of international teaching assistant and academic faculty miscommunication. *International Journal of Intercultural Relations, 24,* 477–501.

Kim, E. H., & Choi, C. (1998). Introduction. In E. H. Kim & C. Choi (Eds.), *Dangerous women: Gender and Korean nationalism* (pp. 1–9). New York: Routledge.

King, J. E. (1991). Dysconscious racism: Ideology, identity, and the miseducation of teachers. *Journal of Negro Education, 60*(2), 133–146.

Kingston-Mann, E., & Sieber, T. (2001). *Achieving against the odds: How academics become teachers of diverse students.* Philadelphia: Temple University Press.

Kutoba, R. (1998). Ideologies of English in Japan. *World Englishes, 17,* 295–306.

Kutoba, R. (2002). Marginalization as an asset: Toward a counter-hegemonic pedagogy for diversity. In L. Vargas (Ed.), *Women faculty of color in the white classroom: Narratives on the pedagogical implications of teacher diversity* (pp. 293–308). New York: Peter Lang.

Li, G. (2002). *"East is east, west is west"? Home literacy, culture, and schooling.* New York: Peter Lang.

Lim, G. S., & Herrera-Sobek, M. (Eds.). (2000). *Power, race and gender in academe: Strangers in the tower?* New York: Modern Language Association of America.

McKay, S., & Wong, S. (1996). Multiple discourse, multiple identities: Investment and agency in second-language learning among Chinese adolescent immigrant students. *Harvard Educational Review, 66*(3), 577–608.

Ortiz, F. I. (1998). Career patterns of people of color in academia. In L. A. Valverde & L. A. Casenell Jr. (Eds.), *The multicultural campus: Strategies for transforming higher education* (pp. 121–136). Walnut Creek, CA: AltaMira Press.

Pennycook, A. (1994). *The cultural politics of English as an international language.* London: Longman.

Phillipson, R. (1992). *Linguistic imperialism.* Oxford, UK: Oxford University Press.

Rofel, L. (1994). Liberation nostalgia and a yearning for modernity. In C. K. Gilmartin, G. Hershatter, L. Rofel, & T. White (Eds.), *Engendering China: Women, culture and the state* (pp. 226–250). Cambridge, MA: Harvard University Press.

Rong, X. L. (2002). Teaching with differences and for differences: Reflections of a Chinese American teacher educator. In L. Vargas (Ed.), *Women faculty of color in the white classroom: Narratives on the pedagogical implications of teacher diversity* (pp. 125–144). New York: Peter Lang.

Rosenberger, N. (2001). *Gambling with virtue: Japanese women and the search for self in a changing nation.* Honolulu: University of Hawai'i Press.

Skutnabb-Kangas, T. (1998). Human rights and language wrongs—a future for diversity? *Language Sciences, 20,* 5–28.

Statham, A. (1996). *The rise of marginal voices: Gender balance in the workplace.* New York: University Press of America.

Thomas, J. (1999). Voices from the periphery: Non-native teachers and issues of credibility. In G. Braine (Ed.), *Non-native educators in English language teaching* (pp. 5–10). Mahwah, NJ: Erlbaum.

U.S. Department of Education. (2002). *Digest of education statistics.* Washington, DC: Office of Educational Research and Improvement.

Vargas, L. (Ed.). (2002). *Women faculty of color in the white classroom: Narratives on the pedagogical implications of teacher diversity.* New York: Peter Lang.

Yu, E. (1987). Women in traditional and modern Korea. In E. Yu & E. H. Philips (Eds.), *Korean women in transition: At home and abroad* (pp. 16–29). Los Angeles: California State University.

7

ASIAN AMERICAN WOMEN IN THE ACADEMY

Overcoming Stress and Overturning
Denials in Advancement

Chalsa M. Loo and Hsiu-Zu Ho

I dentity development involves asking and answering questions like "Who am I?" "What do I want to do with my life?" and "What do I believe in?" These questions must be answered in such a way as to secure a stable and consistent identity, which is essential to finding a meaningful place in society (Carter, 1995). Many Asian American women who are faculty in the academy develop strong identities as academic faculty members (professors) and as professional members of their discipline. In Confucian philosophy, the scholar was a highly respected member of society, and we believe that many Chinese American professors experience a sense of pride in their professorial identity.

We propose that when Asian American women faculty are denied promotion or tenure, assaults on their employment retention can shake the foundations of their sense of identity. Problems in the retention of faculty of color in institutions of higher education have been thought to be because of racial and ethnic bias in tenure and promotion practices and/or isolation from the departments' informal networks (Turner, Myers, & Creswell,

Parts of this chapter have been taken from Loo and Chun's (2002) chapter "Academic Adversity and Faculty Warriors: Prevailing amidst Trauma. In Jacobs, L., Cintrón, J. & Canton, C. (Eds.). *The Politics of Survival in Academia* (pp. 95–124). These portions have been reprinted with permission from Rowman & Littlefield.

1999). Should the Asian American woman who is denied a promotion or tenure attribute the denial to racial or gender bias, this may further strengthen the identification with and awareness of the various roles associated with being female or Asian American. Thus one's group membership (gender and ethnicity) may become a critical aspect of one's psychosocial identity (Carter, 1995), particularly after encountering obstacles to advancement that could be attributed to bias against women or against Asian American women.

We also assume that denials of tenure and promotion generate psychological stress particularly among those toward whom race or gender bias may be directed. Stress has been defined as a "reaction to the environment in which there is either (a) the threat of a net loss of resources, (b) the net loss of resources, or (c) the lack of resource gain following investment of resources." (Hobfoll, 1988). Loss of tenure or denied promotion represents a threat of loss of job, threat to financial security, loss of financial gain, and loss of future gain and resources following years of investment of time and professional energy. We propose that such stress is expressed and experienced in a variety of ways, dependent on the nature and level of the perceived threat to one's self-esteem or self-worth, the amount of emotional support or sociopolitical mobilization that the woman has at her disposal or is able to generate, and the woman's coping skills.

Stress models propose that individuals respond to stress with coping behaviors that seek to minimize loss and maximize gain. In regard to responses to racial oppression or bias, Duckitt (1992) describes two types of responses: (a) in-group inferiority and negative social identity, and (b) rebellion or mobilization of the subordinate group to change the intergroup power relationship. Sociopolitical mobilization by those being treated as inferior serves to challenge the advantage of Whites and the doctrine of racial superiority (Duckitt, 1992). Loo (1993, 1998), for instance, provides two examples of political activism and sociopolitical mobilization in response to racial oppression or bias: (a) the formation of the American Citizens for Justice (ACJ), a pan–Asian American activist group that demanded a retrial of Ebens and Nitz, who in 1982 in Detroit, bludgeoned Vincent Chin to death in a race hate crime; (b) the redress and reparations movement, which culminated in the Civil Liberties Act of 1988—a legislative act that provided Japanese American internees of World War II with an apology and financial remuneration for having been denied their civil rights after the Pearl Harbor attack.

Among various approaches to coping with stress, seeking social support and active problem solving are but two forms. This chapter examines two Asian American women who independently coped with the stress of being denied tenure or a promotion partly by using some form(s) of sociopolitical mobilization. These included obtaining the support of organizations dedicated to the pursuit of equity and justice for Chinese Americans and/or for women in higher education. In terms of active problem solving, the authors of this chapter describe specific methods of defense that were effective in overturning cases of denied advancement or retention that appeared bias-based. Our hope for this chapter is to provide Asian female faculty in institutions of higher education with strategies that may become critical to their retention in academia.

The present chapter highlights two cases of Chinese American female faculty members in institutions of higher education who, in the 1980s and early 1990s, successfully overturned denials of promotion or tenure. Each of the two cases that are presented includes a summary of the personnel case, a review of the various strategies employed to overturn the promotion denials, and the changes their professional lives have taken fifteen years later. Each case addresses issues of gender and racial identity, psychological stress, and sociopolitical mobilization.

Promotional Steps within Academia

Before reviewing these two cases, we include a brief description of the academic structure and promotional procedures. There are several promotional steps in the academic arena. While the structure and procedures vary across institutions, generally, a professor begins at the assistant professor level and is evaluated every two years (via routine merit reviews) for step advances within this level (i.e., assistant professor I, II, III . . .). The biggest hurdle for academicians is the tenure promotion which, when attained, ensures the faculty member a permanent position with that university. In most institutions the rank acquired after tenure is the associate professor level. After tenure, the process of evaluation continues. The merit reviews at the associate professor level typically occur every two years and can continue for another two or three reviews until one comes up for review for promotion to full professor. Thereafter, merit reviews continue typically every three years, and there are various steps within the full professor rank. The promotions to associate professor and full professor and special steps within full professor require reviews that include external evaluations from experts in one's own field. Throughout one's academic career as a professor, accelerations are possible, which means a faculty member can be advanced to a higher step level at a quicker rate than normal. The structure detailed here is specific to a large state university in the United States.

Teaching, research, and service are generally the three areas upon which promotion and tenure are based, with the more prestigious research institutions generally having higher academic standards for research and publication as well as placing higher priority on research productivity relative to teaching and service. The phrase "publish or perish" refers to the expectation that if a professor fails to publish a body of original research, she or he can expect to be denied tenure, which equates to losing one's job.

A professor's career, determined by merit reviews and promotions, lies in the evaluations by faculty of higher rank. While departments, even *within* an institution, may differ in their voting structure, many have adopted a hierarchical voting structure in which only those with a higher professorial rank may vote on lower-ranking faculty. That is, full professors determine the academic fate for associate professors, and both full and associate professors determine the academic fate of assistant professors. Higher in the academia hierarchy are other reviewing agencies including deans, the vice president or vice-chancellor, the presidents or chancellors—who in many institutions have the power to consider appeals and overturn a lower decision. In promotion cases (i.e., not in routine merit reviews), an *ad hoc* committee, made up of faculty members from other departments, composes an additional reviewing agency.

The Case of Danielle: Monumental Struggle for a Measly Merit Increase

The Initial Confidence

Danielle, the only ethnic minority, tenured faculty member in a department of psychology, was denied a merit increase for the period of 1978–1980. Going into the merit review for a step increase within the associate professor level, Danielle was confident about her research and publication accomplishments. In the two-year period covered by the review, she had been awarded a large, three-year research grant from the National Institute of Mental Health. She had given ten presentations at professional conferences over those two years. She had published two articles in professional peer-reviewed journals. The American Psychological Association had awarded her a fellow status for having made "significant contributions to the profession of psychology" during her career. Finally, the department and university had approved her request for a one-year-and-one-quarter leave of absence, as her research grant bought out her salary for that period. Danielle had a strong sense of identity as a productive scholar, an academic psychologist, and (having already been tenured), she had a strong sense of identity as a permanent member of the academic faculty.

Sense of Identity Shattered

Despite the aforementioned achievements, by a mixed vote, the tenured faculty in her department denied her a merit increase. "My original sense of security was shaken, and my original sense of identity was being questioned," she remarked. Three different chairpersons served during the *seven* years it took Danielle to prevail in a battle for what is normally a routine merit review for a step increase within the associate professor level. In this chapter, these three chairpersons will be referred to as Chair A, Chair B, and Chair C.

Danielle's identities as a worthy scholar, contributory member of the university, valued member of the department, and social science researcher were challenged. The review committee stated that Danielle's work was of questionable value to the field of social sciences. The committee criticized Danielle for limited service to her university and department, stating that Danielle "had irregular attendance at department meetings" and "less than expected conscientiousness in supervising students in individual study."

The review committee neglected to consider the fact that the department had approved a leave for Danielle to conduct research off campus in another city. She therefore could not be expected to regularly attend department meetings, nor could she be expected to provide service to the university or to university students during the time she was on approved leave. The more evidence Danielle uncovered that suggested that the full professors had been biased in their evaluation of her, the more Danielle felt estranged from others in the department, which had previously been a core part of her identity.

Mobilization: Individual and Sociopolitical

Danielle mobilized. She presented data to refute unfounded claims by the review committee. She secured an attorney and the assistance of the campus ombudsperson. She requested a detailed summary of her confidential personnel file. As there was no statute of limitations on appeals, Danielle did not appeal the personnel decision until a new administrator was hired and was one whom she believed would be fair-minded and just.

Danielle filed an administrative appeal citing sections of the Academic

Personnel Manual that her department had violated in its review of her work. First, the department had failed to evaluate all the work that she had submitted for review. Danielle had previously brought this matter to Chair A's attention, but he had refused to investigate her claim. Danielle then submitted evidence from the department's administrative analyst demonstrating that two articles and one awarded grant proposal, which had been submitted for this review, had never been reviewed for this promotion.

The department had also violated another section of the personnel manual by failing to establish the role of the candidate in any joint authorship. Danielle had coauthored a chapter with a historian. She suspected that when the review committee stated that Danielle's work was of questionable value to the field of social sciences, reviewers had mistaken the historical portion of the chapter, which was written by a historian, to have been written by Danielle.

To rebut the department's claim of "limited service to her university and department," Danielle offered contrary evidence—letters from other faculty on campus that attested to the valuable contributions Danielle had made to university-wide committees during that two-year time span. She pointed to disparate treatment based on race and gender. A White male professor, who had performed *no* service for the department, had not been penalized for nonservice when he had come up for a merit review promotion.

Danielle also asserted that she had carried two students in independent study when she was not required to take on any teaching responsibilities. Only one student had remarked that Danielle was not always available when the student had wanted to meet with her. Danielle argued that elevating the opinion of one student to the importance given in Chair A's letter was not reasonable, especially as the university does not expect a faculty to be available to students when on authorized research leave.

To the complaint that she "had irregular attendance at department meetings," Danielle provided evidence that when she was *not* on authorized leave, she had attended *all* department meetings. Being punished for not attending department meetings while on authorized leave was "entirely unreasonable" she remarked. Danielle also mobilized parties outside the department who could enlighten the department about their errors in judgment, or at a minimum, question those in judgment. In response to Danielle's request to academic personnel for information, the coordinator of academic personnel wrote to the department:

> The Privilege and Tenure Committee assumes that if a [department] has demonstrated their support of a faculty member's grant by giving them a

leave, that they cannot expect that faculty member to serve the department during that time. If, in fact it is felt that a faculty member is not carrying his/her weight in the department, then the department should not have granted a leave in the first place.

A Pattern of Discrimination Revealed

After reviewing Danielle's appeal and attached documents, the vice-chancellor concluded that the department had made procedural errors. He ordered the department to conduct a re-review. In the meantime, Danielle read through her confidential personnel file and discovered what she and her attorney perceived to be a pattern of discrimination beginning from her first hire (see Loo & Chun, 2002). Danielle collected data on publications, research grant awards, the number of citations to publications in the Social Science Citation Index (the most objective reflection of the quality of scholarly research), length of employment, and the current step for all faculty in the department. Danielle's number of publications and grant awards were comparable to those of White males who had been *accelerated* above her. The number of citations to her work in the Social Science Citation Index far exceeded those of two male professors who had been promoted above her, and was comparable to a faculty member who had been promoted *three years* ahead of her. She argued that by the most widely used academic index of scholarly work, she had been underpromoted and underpaid.

The First Re-Review

The department completed the first of what would become three re-reviews, and voted unanimously against granting Danielle a merit increase. The department gave two reasons for the denial. First, it argued that Danielle "could some time later request an accelerated merit increase or promotion when the research carried out under the current grant proposal produces its findings and she publishes them in a book or journals." "This was ridiculous," remarked Danielle, "I had demonstrated my scholarly worth for the two years in review. There was *no* reasonable justification for delaying me a merit increase with no guarantee of future remedy."

Sociopolitical Mobilization: Civil Rights Organizations

The review committee claimed that new ground had not been broken by Danielle's research grant proposal. This, Danielle noted, was a criteria that had never been applied to the promotion of White faculty for a merit increase. Danielle sought the consultation of Chinese for Affirmative Action

(CAA), a civil rights organization. Henry Der, the director of CAA, wrote to the university, arguing that Danielle's research *was* groundbreaking. Moreover, he questioned whether the department had unfairly penalized her because of her research in an ethnic minority community and her involvement in university affairs that promote ethnic minority participation. Related to this point, the dean of social sciences had previously asked Danielle to serve on the division's affirmative action committee, which was charged with the responsibility of increasing the number of ethnic minority faculty on campus. Chair A had threatened Danielle that harm would come to her if she served on that committee. Disregarding Chair A's threat, Danielle accepted the dean's appointment, never believing the threat to be real.

Academic and Sociopolitical Mobilization

Danielle's attorney brought the case to the attention of a member of the board of regents as well as to an assistant to the speaker of the state assembly. He wrote: "Her fight revolves around both the unfair treatment accorded her and the granting of merit increases and in the insensitive perceptions of Asian Americans. She has been denied merit increases with qualifications much greater than White males who have received such increases."

Danielle broadened the academic mobilization to outside scholars from universities equal to or superior to her university in prestige. The director of a nationally known research institution wrote to the vice-chancellor, referring to the department's actions as "strange and unbelievable . . . by most standards I would regard Danielle as having achieved distinction, national recognition and scholarly accomplishment that year. . . . She deserves very real congratulations." Letters such as these lay the groundwork for suspicion regarding the appropriateness and fairness of criteria used to judge Danielle, building a strong case for bias in the reviews.

Questions about Inappropriate Criteria

Another White male (Chair B) replaced Chair A. Hoping for a more reasonable person in command, Danielle met with Chair B to provide him with the comparative data that she had compiled. She requested that the department accelerate her in order to rectify past under-promotions. "I felt this was a reasonable method by which the department could accomplish some 'damage control,'" she stated. Danielle had also been offered a job elsewhere. She informed Chair B of the offer, anticipating that the outside offer might further validate her academic worth.

Chair B stated that he personally felt that Danielle was a valuable colleague. However, he cautioned that he needed to consult other senior faculty before proceeding to recommend an acceleration. After consulting the senior faculty, Chair B stated that he could not recommend an acceleration because of "the feelings" of some faculty. He further advised Danielle that she should respond positively to a solid offer from elsewhere. When Danielle reported this shocking development to her attorney, her attorney suggested that she ask Chair B to put his remarks in writing. She did, not expecting that Chair B would comply. To Danielle's surprise, Chair B did comply. Danielle's attorney used this document as evidence that the department was biased, as here stated:

> The Chair's remark that while Professor X has been "very valuable to the department and campus in teaching and service" but that it would be "good for you to respond to a solid offer from elsewhere because some . . . faculty have feelings impairing full colleagueship" violates personnel policies. "Feelings," as emotional reactions and subjective sentiments should have no place in an informed and objective judgment of qualifications and performance" [*Academic Personnel Manual*–160 (1a)]. By not restricting its judgment to criteria indicated in the APM—teaching, research, and service—the department had violated the Faculty Code of Conduct . . . which states that "it is unacceptable conduct to evaluate the professional competence of faculty members by criteria not directly reflective of professional performance" or to discriminate against a faculty member for reasons of race, religion, sex, or ethnic origin or for other arbitrary or personal reasons.

Danielle's attorney concluded in his letter to the vice-chancellor: "Under the circumstances, I seriously question whether the Psychology Department can be objective and non-biased in judging Danielle's performance" (Loo & Chun, 2002, p. 103).

The professor in charge of preparing Danielle's review had interviewed Danielle prior to making his recommendation. In this interview, he had asked Danielle how long she planned to remain at the university and whether she would accept another job offer. After the department denied her a merit increase, Danielle consulted the coordinator of academic personnel about whether the probability of remaining at the university is proper criteria for promotion, which Danielle believed it was not. The coordinator wrote to the department chair, citing the policies: "The policy for merit increases does not address future intentions to commitment . . . [only] demonstrated evidence of what a faculty member has done in the last two years is applicable for merit increases."

Work-Related Stress

The level of distress that Danielle experienced made it increasingly difficult for her to continue teaching there. Before the following quarter began, she consulted her attorney who believed she had a legitimate worker compensation claim. He advised her to see a worker compensation attorney who concurred and filed a worker compensation distress claim on her behalf.

In response, three university administrators sent letters to Danielle alleging that she had breached her contract by not continuing to teach there. Countering this line of attack, Danielle's attorney wrote to the vice-chancellor stating that if such a contract existed, it was the *university* who failed in its responsibilities to Danielle and had breached the implied covenant of good faith and fair dealing. Danielle's attorney maintained that the university's treatment deprived Danielle of her rights under state and federal laws. The university's failure to properly process and review her grievances was sufficient alone to conclude that a breach had occurred. The university, through errors it made in the process of review, had caused the very situation it was now claiming to constitute a breach of contract. By alleging breaches of contract as well, the university was only aggravating Danielle's condition.

The Second Re-Review

The second re-review vote was taken. This time, the majority of the faculty voted in the affirmative.

> Finally, the merit increase that I was due was recommended, seven years later, but the victory was bittersweet. The summary contained inaccurate statements, prejudicial omissions, discriminatory criteria, and biased tone, terminology, and biased weighting of evidence. Those faculty who refused to alter their vote admitted to imposing a more rigorous standard than the psychology profession itself uses for acceptance of an original article for publication. They also ignored the evaluations of external reviewers who were experts in my field. (Loo & Chun, 2002, p. 104)

Throughout this struggle, Danielle had challenged, in writing, every false or biased statement made by the department or members of the department. Seven years following the denied merit increase, Danielle received retroactive pay and a retroactive merit increase within the associate professor rank. Her worker compensation case was found compensable. The university made a monetary settlement for the worker compensation claim.

Cumulative Psychological Stress: Shattered Assumptions

Danielle's battle for a measly merit increase began four years following the denial. It ended three years later. Danielle experienced intrusive thoughts, avoidance, and anger. "There were four years of *hiding* my hurt and anger, which, after filing the administrative appeal, were followed by three years of *feeling* my hurt and anger." There was the shock that the outcome would contradict one's expectations and basic beliefs.

> [The denial], especially after I was already tenured, was very unexpected and markedly distressing. I was tenured, but tenure does not protect you from being unfairly attacked. My belief in a meritocracy, fairness, and justice had been shattered. I just couldn't believe it. It is difficult to not think of their criticism as a reflection of your worth. To respond by feeling depressed is very realistic. To respond by feeling anger is also realistic. When your record for the period under consideration is extremely strong, it is unreasonable to be denied a normal promotion. But I came to realize, in retrospect, that racial and gender bias is *not* reasonable. Prejudice is blind to reality. Sexism and racism are blind to fact.
>
> The emotional distress can affect everything you do—your relationships, your priorities, enjoyment of activities that normally would bring you pleasure, perception of yourself, and perception of others. You find yourself reliving in your mind the negative statements made to you or about you and your work, even when you don't want to think about these distressing events. You find yourself avoiding reminders of the stress—the workplace, the persons in that workplace, and you feel estranged or detached from others. You may have difficulty sleeping, difficulty concentrating, become more easily irritable, or hypervigilant.

Searching for Bruce Lee

Work-related stress can significantly impair one's relationship with significant others. The need for emotional support can be very great. "The stress tests the limits of how one partner provides or does not provide emotional support to the other," Danielle explained. "Relationships can be destroyed by work-related distress." Danielle needed her partner to express anger about how her department had treated her. She needed Bruce Lee—someone who could fight the enemy! Instead, her partner's response was low key, restrained, unemotional. His responses? "I would have left that job years earlier," and "For me to express anger would be artificial." Dissatisfied with this form of "emotional support," Danielle left the relationship.

Warrior, Not Victim

To successfully cope with work-related distress requires summoning one's energies toward the goal of winning a battle. Danielle advises Asian women to think like a warrior and not a victim, and to reframe intrusive thinking wherever possible. Feeling victimized will only limit one's ability to function effectively.

> The tendency we have is to interpret others' actions as an attack on your integrity—until you realize that the process of rectifying the situation is really a test of *their* integrity. That realization was an emotional turning point for me, one that I do believe was God-inspired.

Additive Stresses

As a minority woman in an Ivory Tower, unfair treatment in the form of unwarranted denials of merit increases or tenure can function as *additive* stress to ongoing, preexisting stress.

> As an Asian woman in a White male workplace, even before the promotion or tenure denial, you may already have a sense of estrangement and detachment. A promotion or tenure denial is likely to intensify any pre-existing sense of estrangement, alienation, and detachment from others [in the department].

Cultural Beliefs in a Meritocracy

From a cultural perspective, Asians are often taught that rewards come from working hard—they maintain a strong belief in a meritocracy. For those who hold such beliefs, the unexpected denial of promotion or tenure can be a shattering experience. Dale Minami, an attorney who has represented many Asian Americans in academic battles, made this observation:

> The academic institution is not immune from political considerations in tenure decision . . . among my Asian American clients in these situations; I have noticed a common attitude. Invariably, they believe in the merit system: If you work hard, you will be duly rewarded. When faced with an adverse decision based on something other than merit, they have difficulty accepting that reality. All too often, they never understand that politics and racism may have as much to do with a particular decision as merit. (Minami, 1990, p. 85)

Denigration of Danielle's work was not inconsistent with some of the preexisting treatment she experienced in the department. At times, Danielle felt she was being treated like a secretary, servant, waitress, or as if she were invisible. At a luncheon buffet for the psychology faculty, one of the male faculty asked Danielle if she was going to serve them. When the department wanted to have a dinner at the Chinese restaurant downtown, they asked Danielle to make the reservation and preorder the dishes. At department meetings, when Danielle would contribute a suggestion or idea, she was treated as "invisible." Yet, when a male made the identical point five minutes later, his ideas were roundly acknowledged and praised.

Discrepant Treatment

Danielle noticed a discrepancy between the department's treatment of her and its treatment of male faculty.

> If I had been a White male and had received a job offer from another university, my value to the other faculty would have been enhanced. Instead, a minority woman who considers a job offer elsewhere is considered an "unfaithful wife or servant." In regard to research leave, "I felt that I was being punished for not being on campus despite the fact that the department chair and university had approved my leave to be off-campus to conduct research. It would have been acceptable to be a *male* on leave with a research grant, but it was *unacceptable* to be an Asian American *woman* on leave with a research grant.

Fifteen Years Later

Altered Sense of Identity: "Let Them Give Up Their Right Arm"

After winning her merit increase and prevailing on the worker compensation claim, Danielle decided not to return to that university. She had experienced a change in her sense of identity. Her values and beliefs changed. What she wanted to do with her life changed.

> Your values change as a result of this experience, the people you once respected, you don't feel that sense of respect or collegueship any longer. You've won your case, but for me, I lost any desire to return to that department or university. I remember Chair A once telling me that people would give their right arm to be a faculty member in that department. After what I went through, my attitude was: "Let them give up their right arm!" I needed to save my spirit and keep both arms. I chose to leave.

Chair C tried to persuade Danielle to return to the university, but her view of that department as a hostile workplace remained unchanged. She left that university, spent an uneventful year at another university, then took a position at a third university, only to find its politics to be not much different from the first.

Today, living in another state, Danielle has established an independent practice as a clinical psychologist. She also holds a part-time position as a clinical research psychologist, specializing in post-traumatic stress disorder (PTSD), a mental disorder involving anxiety because of a clearly defined external cause(s). Among her clientele in her private practice are a substantial number of worker compensation patients whom she evaluates and treats. While it was not her initial intention to practice in the worker compensation field, referrals from physicians and attorneys attest to the effectiveness with which she has been able to relate to and assist patients who suffer from work-related injuries and distress. While many clinical psychologists resist dealing with worker compensation patients, partly because of its adversarial nature, Danielle believes that her prior experiences have made her better skilled at professionally assisting patients who are adversely affected by events at their workplace. Regarding her field of research specialty, Danielle noted: "The constellation of PTSD symptoms—involving reliving, avoidance, and physiological arousal—are often found among victims of trauma and some of these symptoms may be evidenced in persons suffering from work-related injuries or distress."

While "fighting the good fight" was distressing, apparently the skills acquired and lessons learned seem to have contributed to Danielle's developing a fuller understanding of the experiences of work-related stress and injuries, as well as being comfortable with its adversarial nature. In regard to identity and beliefs, Danielle developed a stronger respect for civil rights organizations that provide sociopolitical mobilization for victims of bias and discrimination. She admits to lasting admiration for those individuals who stood up for her in her struggle for justice. And, in terms of identity and support, she concludes: "It is great if you have Bruce Lee in your life, in times of trouble. But if not, become your own Bruce Lee!"

The Case of Julia: Presumed Academic Discipline Bias

Tenure Denied

Julia was an Asian American woman, employed at a top-tiered public research university, the only ethnic minority faculty member in her department. Sensing something amiss when Julia learned of her tenure denial, her four-year-old son asked, "What's wrong, Mommy?" Julia simply replied, "They just didn't play fair." Her son's desire to protect and comfort his mother was reflected in his statements to her the next day: "Mommy, I don't know if you should go to school if they don't like you. Mommy, they just don't know you. Well, if you have to go to school, Mommy, then just play with the people who are nice to you." After further thought, the toddler blurted, "Mommy, you tell me who's bad to you, and I'll go kick 'em."

While her son attributed his mother's plight to lack of familiarity by her peers, Julia saw no justification for the denial of her tenure. Searching for explanations, she recognized that she "was not part of the departmental network"; her office, physically separated from nearly all other departmental colleagues, was located in another building, making her psychologically separated from the rest of the department. She noted that the departmental program she was hired for had since been formally eliminated. Also of significance, the written criticisms underlying her tenure denial appeared to be a reflection of the larger historical division between the two subdisciplines of psychology. Julia was a differential psychologist in a department with virtually all other faculty members being experimental psychologists. Finally, she wondered about gender and racial discrimination:

> I could not really know why my departmental colleagues voted the way they did—what was in each of their heads when they voted. A few of my supporters suggested that the motive may have been the new directions of the department in which I did not fit. Whether I had been "Mommy-tracked" or stereotyped as an Asian "number-cruncher," I couldn't know. I did not have evidence of overt gender or racial discrimination, so I could only fight on the basis of the written criticisms that were provided.

Fighting within the System: Request for Re-Review

Julia argued that the department failed to conduct a fair and procedurally proper review. She requested a reconsideration on grounds of "bias within the profession—that one group of specialists within her field devalued the work of another group of specialists due to historical longstanding philosophical, theoretical, and methodological differences." Julia argued that the denial of her tenure had nothing to do with her accomplishments but everything to do with the fact that the evaluation of her "promotion to tenure was not based on criteria appropriate to the field to which I was hired." She argued that procedures of the university's Academic Personnel Manual had not been followed in her tenure review (Loo & Chun, 2002, pp. 105–106):

One, the strengths for which I was hired are now evaluated as weaknesses.

Two, my research was evaluated from the viewpoint of experimental psychology rather than from the viewpoint of my field (differential psychology) wherein APM [Academic Personnel Manual] 210-1 specifies that "promotion to tenure positions should be based on consideration of comparable work in the candidate's own field or in closely related fields," there is considerable evidence that this was not followed in my case.

Three, despite positive external reviews, departmental criticisms reflected the experimentalist bias.

Four, my primary research focus and its implications for method and theory in my field were virtually ignored, and

Five, after the letters were received, an important safeguard procedure was violated.

She framed her arguments academically, using citations to scholarly works to inform the campus reviewing agencies about the historical bias within her field of psychology. Julia cited points made in presidential and keynote addresses to the American Psychological Association (APA) on the two disciplines of psychology.

Her eight-page request to the administration for a tenure reconsideration concluded by stating:

> I believe that I am being denied tenure because the orientation of my research differs from that of my departmental colleagues and because criteria to evaluate the merits of my scholarship were drawn from a very different sub-discipline within psychology. . . . I respectfully submit that, had I been given a fair and appropriate evaluation, my overall research record and trajectory and the external reviews all suggest that my case would have been seen as tenurable. I therefore ask that you undertake another review of my case. I appreciate your efforts to afford me fair consideration.

The Re-Review

A reconsideration was granted by the administration. A re-review was conducted in the next academic year. The re-review began with a new department review, in which a new set of external letters from experts in the field was solicited. As they did in the first review, the external letters in the second solicitation attested to the high quality of Julia's work. Again, there was a small group of support for her tenure within her department. Yet, on the second vote, the majority vote against her case increased slightly. Responding to the department's recommendation of tenure denial in the second review, Julia again argued that the external experts, who were more familiar with her line of work, should have been given greater weight. She noted:

> A serious discrepancy exists between the departmental majority opinion and the opinion of the external reviewers, a discrepancy that grew even larger this year with further external letters solicited. . . . I believe that the judgments of experts within my specialty should be given more weight than appears to have been the case.

She expressed several problems in the department's re-review of her tenure case. She expressed concern that her case would not be treated with fairness because the original parties who were biased initially were being asked to change their opinion, and cited research from her colleagues' own experimental research to show that impressions once formed are difficult to change.

> "While a re-review may correct procedural errors, it does not, however, provide a new jury to examine the case with a clean slate. It may be particularly difficult to change the mindset of some departmental colleagues when the candidate's specialty is unique to the department, the academic philosophies, methods, and goals of the candidate's sub-discipline differ significantly from those of her departmental colleagues and when traditionalists of the two sub-disciplines have historically tended to strongly devalue each other's work, and when the departmental program in which the candidate was hired has formally been eliminated and the recruitment strategy in the department has changed. (Loo & Chun, 2002, p. 15)

Julia reiterated the point that a re-review does not guarantee fairness. In fact, it can provide the department with an opportunity to "clean up" its procedural errors, thus giving the faculty of color fewer flaws to cite in arguing that bias or discrimination occurred. Even though certain procedural errors were corrected, Julia continued to point to the inappropriate criteria used in both reviews that had not been corrected.

Her response also pointed to pertinent teaching evaluations missing from the department's evaluation. "The chair's letter includes ratings for all my undergraduate courses except the course of my area of expertise in which I received the highest ratings." She argued that its absence added to the lack of fairness in the review.

Sociopolitical Mobilization

Julia had the strong support of a few departmental colleagues who, as part of the safeguard procedures of the review process, wrote a separate departmental "minority" letter in support of Julia that accompanied the departmental letter (which represented the departmental "majority" view). One of Julia's strongest departmental supporters also coordinated a group (comprised of both departmental and other campus colleagues who were strongly in favor of the case) to meet with the chancellor. A small subset of this group (some of them social scientists keenly aware of such subdiscipline biases) also met with the vice-chancellor to discuss the case.

At a national conference, a legislative aid who knew of Danielle's successful effort to overturn a negative merit review decision advised Danielle of Julia's tenure denial. Networking was new to Julia. "I didn't even know what the term 'networking' meant. All I knew about networks were neuronal networks in the brain." Making her case known to strangers was uncomfortable for Julia. Aware of incidents of student rallies that took place at other campuses in support of minority faculty who were denied tenure, she was wary of such attention. But the discussions with Danielle of their "shared experiences" were extremely helpful to Julia. Following Danielle's advice, Julia sought the help of Chinese for Affirmative Action and Executive Director Henry Der.

Der's letter to the university in support of Julia praised her record, noted the apparent flaws in the review, and reminded the university of its commitment to ethnic diversity.

It appears from our examination of the record that the department by its own admission was ill-equipped to evaluate the quality of Julia's work . . . after soliciting an unusually large number of letters from experts in her subfield, departmental critics ignored the overwhelmingly positive assessment of [her] work. . . . Given [Julia's] outstanding record and the questionable practices in the tenure review process, CAA is puzzled and bothered that the Department of Psychology has voted twice to deny her tenure. CAA takes notice that [Julia] is the only ethnic minority professor and one of very few females in the department. . . . In response to President Z's call to all Chancellors to reaffirm the University's commitment to achieving racial and ethnic diversity on each campus . . . you have the opportunity to fulfill the commitment to faculty ethnic diversity. [Julia] deserves to be granted tenure not because she is an Asian American but because she has been an outstanding Asian American professor with a strong record of publication, research, and excellence in teaching. (Loo & Chun, 2002, pp. 107–108)

Julia also sought the help of her local chapter of the American Association of University Women (AAUW) where she was a member. In its letter to the university, the local AAUW chapter pointed out:

At the national level the AAUW has through its Legal Advocacy Fund supported faculty women who have been discriminated against. We recognize that biases (whether academic, gender or racial) in academia are often hidden under the guise of "insufficient scholarship." Since such biases may take place in subtle forms, we urge that steps be taken to insure that fine scholars are retained.

From the materials that we have available, we observe that Dr. [Julia] is an active and productive scholar, an excellent teacher, and is highly regarded by scholars in her specialty. . . . We also note the importance of her role model as a "career mom." From the materials made available to us, it seems likely that academic biases may have played a role in her department review. . . . With respect to Dr. [Julia's] case, we have the following concerns:

1. Given that psychology is a field that is well represented by female scholars, why are there only three tenured women in a department with 21 tenured faculty members?
2. Why has Developmental Psychology, a subfield that typically has a higher female than male faculty ratio, been formally eliminated from her department? Has the elimination of this subfield (to which Dr. [Julia] was hired) played a part in the evaluation made by her departmental colleagues?
3. Is [Julia's] scholarship being properly evaluated along the criteria of her specialty within psychology?
4. Why is Dr. [Julia] the only ethnic minority scholar in her department?

The letter added:

Because Dr. [Julia] in a number of ways is representative of the diversity to which the academic community has made commitment, it is disturbing that her "diversity" may be the very source of her tenure struggle. We therefore ask that you undertake a careful examination of Dr. [Julia's] case.

Beating the Bullies

Given past cases, Julia recognized that the chances of subsequent reviewing agencies overriding the department's negative tenure recommendation were not likely. Nevertheless, despite the outcome of her first review, her belief in meritocracy was still strong. Two years following the initial departmental review, the long-awaited news came in the form of a letter from the chancellor—Julia was finally awarded tenure. When told of his Mom's victory, her son responded: "Mommy, mommy, you won! I'm so proud of you. You *won* at a game where the bullies treated you bad!"

This experience taught Julia "much about systems, about how they work and don't work, about the importance of networking, about being aware of important networks, about being political, and about subtle as well as overt discrimination." Whether the case *really* was about academic discipline bias, Julia will never know.

Cumulative Psychological Stress and Coping Strategies

The denial of tenure that resulted from the first review came to Julia in the form of a letter. "I received a letter from the chancellor stating that I'd been given a "terminal appointment" of one year. I felt that I had a terminal disease. I had one year in which to live or die."

Julia had felt hopeful during that first year of her tenure battle. She believed that all of her detailed written responses rebutting the department's inaccurate statements and criticisms would be grounds for subsequent campus reviewing agencies to overturn the department's recommendation of tenure denial. She believed they would "right the wrong." Accordingly, the resulting denial of tenure was a "huge disappointment." The "terminal illness" triggered the "emotional impact of anxiety, anger, and depression" over the potential "loss of my career and professional identity."

In addition to the regular demands of her professional and family responsibilities, it was stressful to have to check up on all the procedures and safeguards and insist that they be followed. Julia perceived this role as compounding her level of stress.

> I'm trying to fight my case based on the merits, but I'm also having to spend a lot of time and energy in finding out the procedures, and then having to convince my department of the rights that I am entitled to. I feel that I'm having to be my own jailhouse lawyer.

The approval of a re-review by the administration gave Julia hope, and she geared up for another series of rebuttals and responses in the following year.

During the two years of constant stress and anxiety, I was obsessed with the fight over my tenure. I felt the need to rebut each and every inaccurate statement made in the departmental letter. On the positive side—I had the strong support of a number of departmental and campus colleagues and a nurturing spouse and son. . . . I was tenacious. Fortunately, I believed in myself. The glowing comments from the external letters contributed to my feelings of self worth. On the negative side, it was a tremendous strain on my family life, and professionally, there was continuous pressure to publish. I took every opportunity provided in the university safeguard procedures to provide written responses to evaluations provided during the process. All the hundreds of pages that my request for reconsideration, responses to departmental recommendations, responses to external reviews, responses to requests for further information by subsequent reviewing agencies, etc., all summed up to what now seems like a huge volume of wasted time and energy—I can't add those documents to my vita. But on the other hand, that volume was my coping strategy, the only way I knew how to fight the "bullies."

Julia also spoke of the differences in her family members' reactions.

My husband was extremely angry with the department and attributed malicious intent on their part. I tried to cerebrally cope with the situation as an "honest mistake" and my son just wanted to beat up the "bullies." At times, it was very difficult when the level of our responses were so different. After patiently reading pages after pages of rebuttals, my husband would be frustrated with what appeared to him as a naive or "Pollyanna" belief on my part that meritocracy would prevail.

Gender and Ethnic Biases and Identity

When Julia initially learned of her tenure denial, her strong culturally influenced belief in meritocracy was shattered. She had always performed well in school: "No one could question the interpretation of an 'A' or a 4.0 in high school or college, but in academia, the judgment of what counted as scholarly work could be arbitrary. What some may praise as 'breadth' in scholarship, others could criticize as 'lack of focus.'" The department had managed to turn external reviewers' positive acknowledgment of her "quantitative sophistication" and statistical expertise into a negative criticism of being "merely methodological" and "being driven by the availability of data and methods" rather than by theory. They criticized her for being more of an empiricist than a theorist. Julia wondered if this represented denigration based on an Asian stereotype—the "number cruncher."

With respect to gender bias, fewer than 15 percent of the tenured faculty members in her department were women, a ratio far below that of the availability pool in her discipline. Julia noted that the eventually disbanded area in which she was hired comprised three faculty women. Julia also was the first woman faculty in the department to allow her "biological clock" to run alongside her "tenure clock." Her pregnancy during her assistant professor years may have caused some to question her career goals. Being both female and an ethnic minority (a "double whammy") typically decreases the chances of fitting in and being part of the departmental network.

In Julia's case awareness of these racial and ethnic biases led to a stronger identification with her Asian American and gender identity.

> Prior to all this, I really hadn't thought of myself as an ethnic minority scholar, an Asian or Asian American scholar, or as a female scholar. I was simply a scholar. But during the tenure crisis, I began to [be] more aware of the type of biases that ethnic minority and female faculty face. For the first time in my career, I became aware of the existence of (and attended national meetings of) Asian Pacific Americans in Higher Education. I found I came to identify myself as an Asian American scholar and could relate to the barriers in academia that other Asian American scholars faced.

Fifteen Years Later

Following the tenure promotion, as a constructive coping strategy, Julia adopted the general attitude that, given their academic bias, her colleagues made an "honest mistake" and that she was willing to let the past rest and move on to a productive future. She requested an office in the main psychology building and moved in to join the rest of her colleagues. During a subsequent merit review, Julia again found herself having to spend time rebutting criticisms regarding her work. Furthermore, when she requested a parental leave during her second pregnancy, she found herself having to question why she was asked to take on a list of additional tasks when a male faculty member who had been previously granted a parental leave was not required to take on any additional tasks.

Disappointed with the negative energy and the effort it took to, once again, defend herself, this time for a routine merit review, Julia decided that she could not face further rounds of re-reviews. Instead, she sought out other related departments for her interdisciplinary work and subsequently left the psychology department, with the support of campus administrators who helped to facilitate her move to another department.

In her new department, Julia noted a different sense of membership right away, even during her first department meeting. She discovered that the new department had an egalitarian voting structure; namely, each faculty member, irrespective of rank, could vote on everyone's personnel reviews, which contrasted to the hierarchical voting structure of the previous department (where only those faculty members of a higher rank could vote on those of lower rank). The new department appeared to be a good fit for Julia. There was a breadth of academic diversity—her new department included a diversity of disciplinary, theoretical, philosophical, and methodological approaches, which suited Julia well.

Since her move to her new department, Julia received departmental support for each of her reviews and has been promoted to the rank of full professor. She collaborates with a number of colleagues in her new department on various research projects and enjoys a multidisciplinary approach to her research. She has been active in both her campus and community, particularly on issues concerning women and ethnic minorities. She has served as the chair of her campus's committee on the status of women for over seven years, being a "watchdog" on campus women's issues, and has regularly conducted "tenure workshops" for junior faculty women. Although her experience during the tenure battle was extremely difficult, Julia reflects that her experience "has made her a stronger person, more sensitive to the needs and struggles of individuals and groups." She has gained a sense of duty to help others overcome their struggles, whether in academia or other domains.

Discussion and Conclusion

This chapter addresses certain commonalities and differences in two cases of Asian American women who faced adverse actions in their academic advancement as faculty in prestigious universities in the United States. In addition to similar outcomes (advancement and prevailing in overturning negative decisions in their respective departments), common themes include the use of similar strategies to fight for their just advancement. Specifically, the two women (a) repeatedly used written rebuttals of all criticisms made of their work or performance, (b) relied heavily on citing violations of university procedures or policies to argue that the decision to deny was flawed, and (c) used and benefited from the written letters of outside reviewers or scholars who knew their work and organizations dedicated to the civil rights of Chinese Americans or women in higher education, whose representatives pointed to the value of their work and/or addressed critical flaws in the opinions or actions of the university.

In the case of both Danielle and Julia, awareness of either subtle or overt ethnic and/or gender biases probably strengthened each woman's identification with being Asian American or female. Their need for, and use of, socialpolitical mobilization approaches to fight for justice in their advancement in academia is noteworthy. For both women, after encountering obstacles to their personnel advancement that were attributed to gender and ethnic bias, their ethnic and group membership appears to have become more central to their identities and subsequent life directions.

For both women, the first departmental re-review resulted in departmental votes in which the number of faculty opposing their advancement *increased*, despite greater attention to procedures and policies, and despite stronger objective evidence for advancement. A departmental backlash to being instructed by the vice-chancellor to conduct a re-review might account for this increase in negative votes. Faculty may react with defensiveness or resentment when told by an administrator that they had erred (at least procedurally) in their initial review. For Danielle, by the second re-review, or third review, it may have appeared that the department realized that "this case was not going away," but instead the stakes appeared to get higher with each succeeding denial. In fact, it seemed likely that the candidate with the administrators' support was going to keep on requesting re-reviews until they got it "right."

In both cases, there appeared to be a strong research record. Yet, there appears to be a common theme that, at the time they were denied advancement, both women were engaged, even partially, in research that deviated from what their department might consider "mainstream." Turner, Myers, and Creswell (1999) described the devaluation of "minority" research or denigration of their research interests because their research area is not "traditional" as one barrier to retention for faculty of color. Julia's area of specialty was clearly not in the mainstream of her department's interest and appeared to have been devalued by the experimentalists in her original department. In Danielle's case, while her previous research had been primarily conducted on mainstream populations, the large research grant, awarded at the time of her merit review, studied an Asian American community. Danielle believed that members of her department did not consider such a topic to constitute "psychology."

In addition to differences in research orientation, other perceived differences such as culture (values, beliefs, communication styles, etc.), gender, political ideologies, and religious beliefs tend to further isolate the minority scholar from informal networks. This isolation from the department's informal network is pointed to as one of the primary barriers to the retention of faculty of color (Turner, Myers, & Creswell, 1999). The solution is not for minority scholars to change their values, beliefs, research orientation, and personalities to conform to that of their mainstream colleagues, but clearly for the majority to embrace the breadth and enrichment of education that diversity provides.

Also on the issue of retention, there is another common theme. Neither Danielle nor Julia remained in her university or department despite their "victories." By choice, Danielle eventually left academia. Julia moved to a different department in the same institution. Both women warriors "fought the good fight," then ultimately attempted to move to a less adversarial life, either in another department in academia or outside of academia altogether.

Both women drew from their "battle" experiences to contribute, a decade and a half later, to something they may otherwise have not pursued. For Danielle, it was a clinical practice inclusive of patients in need of evaluation and treatment for worker compensation injuries and/or distress, and research on post-traumatic stress disorder. For Julia, it was the work to improve the circumstances of campus women, ranging from conducting tenure workshops to helping to develop family-friendly policies for the university.

Both cases speak to the common theme of psychological distress experienced by "academic warriors," regardless of the rank of promotion or length of time required to resolve their cases. In coping with stress, both women used an active problem-solving approach.

Despite the many commonalities, differences exist. One difference lay with attribution. Julia used a coping strategy of fighting a battle that she attributed to a subdiscipline bias, a type of "honest mistake." The alternative of malicious intent may have been too personal and too painful to face. For Danielle, on the other hand, it was very clear in her mind that she was battling bias driven by race and gender discrimination. She perceived "nothing honest" about the department's "mistake," and interpreted it as clearly malicious.

Both women spoke of emotional support as it was or was not expressed by partners, spouses, or family members. Both commented on the importance of social-emotional support in coping with the high level of stress and multiple obstacles they faced. For Danielle, who felt she received functional but not emotional support from her partner, the relationship could not survive. Her need for "Bruce Lee" could not be met. Julia, on the other hand, had a spouse who readily expressed anger at her department and a "Bruce Lee" son who was ready to "kick" the bullies. Julia's family remained intact.

Finally, both women used some forms of social-political mobilization and pointed to the importance of support in the larger community of Asian Americans and/or women, and the critical role that organizations like Chinese for Affirmative Action or the AAUW can play for minority women facing advancement obstacles.

In the search for changes in institutional culture and policy that promote a safe and nurturing environment for all minority women faculty, we identify specific barriers that are particularly relevant for ethnic minority female faculty members. One barrier is ethnic, racial, cultural, and/or gender bias toward either the minority woman or her "nontraditional" research, which can express itself in the minority woman's experiences of having difficulty gaining access to informal networks within her department, lack of mentors, or tendencies to be excessively assigned a high load of administrative and university service responsibilities.

Recognizing these barriers we recommend (1) increased recruitment of minority faculty; (2) sensitivity to where minority faculty physically reside, namely, that the office be a central location that promotes social interaction; (3) establishment of a faculty mentoring program; (4) increased breadth in academic diversity; (5) establishment of/adherence to procedural safeguards; (6) establishment of equitable practices so that minority faculty are not disproportionately overrepresented in the teaching of large service courses; and (7) identifying and changing review policies. While the barriers identified are not unique to faculty of color, they are likely to be more common among ethnic minority or women faculty. If indeed we are committed to building multicultural institutions of higher learning, these problems that relate to faculty of color must be addressed.

In conclusion, it is not our purpose to celebrate the two cases presented, although victory over adversity is worthy of it. As stated by Loo and Chun (2002), "On the contrary, it is a tragic instance that this chapter had to be written at all, for no one but the victim can fully understand what both of these "faculty warriors" experienced or the lasting impact their experiences had on their lives" (p. 122). While both these women remarked the pain experienced to conjure up the memories and reflect on the past events, their stories provide a context in which to understand the battles that minority women may face. We present these two cases of Asian female faculty warriors to provide details of specific strategies that were employed as well as to share the psychological stresses that these warriors experienced in their battles for equity in hopes of providing support to those who now or in the future find themselves facing that glass ceiling of the academy.

References

Carter, R. T. (1995). *The influence of race and racial identity in psychotherapy.* New York: Wiley.

Duckitt, J. (1992). *The social psychology of prejudice.* New York: Praeger.

Hobfoll, S. E. (1988). *The ecology of stress.* New York: Hemisphere Publishing.

Loo, C. (1993). An integrative-sequential model of treatment for post-traumatic stress disorder: A case study of the Japanese American internment and redress. *Clinical Psychology Review, 13,* 89–117.

Loo, C. (1998*). Chinese Americans: Mental health and quality of life in the inner city.* Thousand Oaks, CA: Sage.

Loo, C. M., & Chun, M. (2002). Academic adversity and faculty warriors: Prevailing amidst trauma. In Jacobs, L., Cintrón, J., & Canton, C. (Eds.), *The politics of survival in Academia* (pp. 95–124). Lanham, MD: Rowman & Littlefield.

Minami, D. (1990). Guerrilla war at UCLA: Political and legal dimensions of the tenure battle. *Amerasia Journal, 16*(1), 81–158.

Turner, C. S. V., Myers, S. L., & Creswell, J. W. (1999). Exploring underrepresentation: The case of faculty of color in the Midwest. *Journal of Higher Education, 70*(1), 27–59.

PART THREE

GAINING VOICE, FORMING IDENTITY

8

BROWN IN BLACK AND WHITE

On Being a South Asian Woman Academic

Nina Asher

A ll these grammar corrections! How come when you grew up else- where your English is so good?!" The student—a young, White woman enrolled in the required multicultural education class I taught—scowled and blurted this out indignantly. She was taking in my feedback on her assignment; in addition to addressing substantive issues, I had also asked her to pay attention to grammar. Then, as she perceived her peers' shocked and embarrassed countenances, she blushed a bright, tomato red. Of course, I, too, registered the inappropriateness of this questioning of my authority—the student had presumed to challenge my feedback, *not* be- cause she disagreed with the *substance* of it but rather because, in her eyes, I, although her teacher, was from "elsewhere." It seemed that she was unable to accept that someone who was not "American" could correct her English. In the few seconds in which all of this played out, I found myself noting the unexamined "othering" inherent in the question, recognizing its inappropri- ateness, feeling angry about the racism implied by it, and then returning from my own emotional responses (*not* reaction) into the "outer" space of the classroom, to acknowledge to myself that the student was speaking out defensively in response to my feedback on her assignment. Somewhere in all of this, I must have drawn the proverbial deep breath, and then I said: "I will answer the question. But first let us talk about where this question is coming from."

This, from my perspective and experience, is the work of multicultural teacher education today. Let me elaborate by sharing my own inner dialogue between my personal and professional selves. There is Nina, *the person*—who spent the first three decades of her life in Bombay, India, and New York City and is now teaching in the Deep South. There is Nina *the teacher-educator*—who knows that teaching multiculturalism entails the demanding work of "unpacking" and deconstructing prejudice and defensiveness bit by bit. So, here is a fragment of my inner dialogue—the issues with which I struggle each time I experience the painful shock of prejudice, as in the above episode.

> *Nina, the person*: Dammit! I did not struggle to put myself through Teachers College, Columbia, to put up with such disgusting comments.
>
> *Nina the teacher-educator*: Well, at least now I know that my teaching is making a difference—at the very least by disrupting the assumption of what is "normal" on the part of students who may see themselves as part of the established norm. Besides, I know that I must not take such remarks personally. They really are to do with the other person's issues and fears related to race and difference.
>
> *Nina, the person*: Yes, 'tis true. But *why!* does the onus always have to be on us women of color to be the *patient*, "multicultural" teacher education people? bell hooks and Audre Lorde, wish you were here, holding my hand.
>
> *Nina the teacher-educator*: Well, yes, this is sad. But there is the occasional non-person-of-color who teaches these required courses on multicultural education. And, of course, when it comes to issues of gender, sexuality, and even class—that is when one defines "multiculturalism" *outside* the box of race and culture—one finds a number of White colleagues across the country. But, to return to the episode at hand, no one compelled me to apply for a position teaching in Louisiana.
>
> *Nina, the person*: Crossing borders always helps me learn . . . I guess, then, I am learning. And, come to think of it, as I have discussed elsewhere (Asher & Crocco, 2001), even as a teaching assistant/instructor, during my time as a graduate student in New York City—that mecca of multiplicities and hybridities—the few times that my authority was challenged, it was by White students.
>
> *Nina the teacher-educator*: At least, over time, I have acquired some wherewithal to deal with such shocks. And, as I wrote a couple of years ago (Asher, 2003b) it is good that, in the process, I have not become numbed to the pain. Because, if I were "unable to feel the pain, unable to make it conscious," then, of course, I would be "unable to engage the possibility of transformation" (p. 242).

The episode I open this personal essay with occurred right at the end of my first year as an assistant professor at Louisiana State University, the very first time I had taught the required, undergraduate, multicultural education course. I was conscious then of *both* having weathered such shocks before *and* that, over the summer, I would be reflecting particularly on my first year as a faculty member in the Deep South. Even as I left the Northeast for the Deep South, I had fully expected that old learnings would gain new meanings and dimensions with this latest crossing of borders. Indeed, I have found that this self-reflexive process has enabled me to grow personally, as a teacher, and a scholar.

In the rest of this personal narrative, I interrogate the challenges and possibilities I encounter as a South Asian woman in the U.S. academy. I reflect critically on my own evolution as an academic woman who identifies herself as a postcolonialist, feminist scholar. I trace my journey from the early days as a new, international, graduate student in New York City to my current situatedness as an assistant professor of education working toward tenure at a Research 1 university in the Deep South. In so doing, I discuss the intersecting issues of race-class-gender-culture-and-location as they relate to me and the work (research and teaching) I do. My essay, drawing as it does on my particular experiences, is embedded in and speaks to my theoretical engagement with critical, postcolonial, and feminist scholarship. In particular, I am conscious of my own interstitial location as a South Asian immigrant woman teaching currently in the Deep South, where race relations are construed mainly in terms of Black and White. Furthermore, as a scholar who writes in the area of Asian American education, I am aware of the relative dearth, even today, of literature on South Asian Americans as compared to, say, Chinese or Japanese Americans. The concluding section discusses the implications for personal and professional agency in terms of collaborating, seeking alliances, and arriving at a viable "third space" (Bhabha, 1994) from/ in which to grow, teach, write, be. Specifically, I argue that the interstitial locations between different cultures and identities are useful and, indeed, critical in identifying new possibilities for personal and social transformation. Self-reflexively, I am aware that the development of my own scholarship and teaching is informed, at least in part, by my own negotiation of multiple identifications and cultures in particular locations. For instance, my interrogation of my current locatedness, as a South Asian, lesbian academic in the Deep South, informs my work not only in postcolonial and feminist theory in education, but also in Asian American education and multicultural education pedagogy (see Asher, 2003a, 2003b, in press).

I note here that I feel conscious of the artificiality of separating my personal and professional journeys—after all, they are necessarily intertwined. However, I have decided to create different sections to highlight specific issues and implications in these domains of my life as a South Asian woman academic. My narrative in each section flows chronologically in order to reflect the dynamic, recursive nature/process of the evolution of these identities.

Personal Identities: From Person of Color to Emerging Scholar

I begin my article, "At the Intersections: A Postcolonialist Woman of Color Considers Western Feminism" (an invited contribution to a themed issue on teaching about the "Women of the World" of the journal *Social Education*) by discussing the emergence of my identity as a person of color as follows:

> "Do you speak Spanish?" "Do you speak English?" "But you speak perfect English!" "You have a British accent." *Huh?* I was bewildered when, as a newcomer to the United States, I first encountered such questions and comments. I do not speak Spanish, I had always spoken English (along with other Indian languages such as Kutchchi, Marathi, Hindi, and Gujarati) and my accent is *Indian* not British. Such encounters, over a decade ago, as I was a beginning doctoral student in New York City, created new layers of identity for me. I began recognizing that, here in the United States, based only on my appearance, I may be variously construed as a Latina, an immigrant, a non-English speaker. And so, in New York City, I began identifying myself as a "person of color" and a "South Asian woman," identities I had not needed in India. Thus, I began recognizing the context-specific negotiation of my own new identities. (Asher, 2003a, p. 47)

Such epiphanies about my evolving identity made me realize that I was in the thick of it. Yes, I was working toward a doctorate in education—and even there, as I discuss in the next section, I had to search to identify my niche. At the same time, I found myself beginning to relate to the larger Asian American community and various progressive South Asian community organizations in New York City in order to situate myself personally and culturally in my new location. For instance, for a while, I worked with Sakhi—a community organization for and run by South Asian women to address domestic violence in New York City. Many of the women who contacted the organization struggled with barriers of language, socioeconomic status, and immigration, among others. My awareness of issues of marginality became sharper, allowed me to situate more clearly and fully, my own experiences as a "foreign" student in relation to historical and extant power structures such as colonization and race relations.

At the same time, in my pursuit of my studies, I discovered critical theory—it offered me a language to help me make sense of the contradictions and struggles I was now consciously confronting. For instance, Homi Bhabha's (1994) *The Location of Culture* offered the constructs of hybridity and fluidity of identity and culture, which informed my own understanding of how individuals negotiate race, culture, and nation. Indeed, the next major step in my intertwined personal and professional journeys was to work on my first potential publication as a graduate student. On a trip to visit friends in Canada, I discovered the album *No Reservations* by Apache Indian (1993). Apache, né Steven Kapur, a British-born musician of Indian descent who blends North Indian folk music, rap, and reggae, became very popular among young South Asians in the mid-1990s. So taken was I with his catchy music and the themes to his songs, which spoke to such issues as colonization, marginalization, asserting new identities and cultures, and building alliances across racial minority groups, that I ended up writing an article (see Asher, 1997) theorizing the implications of such endeavors in resisting domination, and negotiating new forms of self-representation.

In addition to working in the community, reading, and writing, I found myself asserting my own identity in various ways. Friends of South Asian descent were progressive activists and scholars. The conservative segments of the Indian/South Asian community, I shunned. When doing research for my article on Apache, I had become more conscious of the differences in immigration patterns from India to the United Kingdom as compared to the United States. Here, South Asians are (stereo)typically portrayed as fitting the "model minority" image—educated, high achieving, and affluent. By contrast, South Asians in Britain have typically been working class, laborers, and often identified as Blacks along with Jamaicans and Trinidadians (again, witness Apache's hybrid music)—a reflection of the colonial relationship, of course. Well, I recall that, at one point during my time as a graduate student, I had my hair braided in cornrows, which, given the straightness of my hair, lasted for all of twenty-four hours! I realized, in retrospect, that I was exploring my own connection with "Blackness," my own experience of being a racial "minority" person. Kobena Mercer's (1990) analysis of the diversity in contemporary Black hair-styling as a cultural and political practice representing "an inventive, improvisational aesthetic" (p. 263) made sense to me. However, Mercer also points out that "there is another 'turn of the screw' in these modern relations of inter-culturation when these creolized cultural forms are made use of by other social groups" (p. 258). As I progressed in my personal and scholarly journeys, I recognized that in my own racial and ethnic identity quests, in braiding my hair (even if for a day), I, too, had participated in appropriating from "Black" culture. While such appropriation may be inevitable in negotiating identity and culture, particularly in contexts of diversity and difference, arriving at a consciousness of one's own struggles is ultimately critical.

Indeed as Minnie Bruce Pratt (1984) has written, with great clarity and insight, in her thought-provoking, self-reflexive essay "Identity: Skin, Blood, Heart":

> Sometimes we don't pretend to *be* the other, but we take something made by the other and use it for our own: as I did for years when I listened to Black folk singing church songs, hymns, gospels, and spirituals, the songs of suffering, enduring, and triumph. Always I would cry, baffled as to why I was so moved; I understood myself only after I read a passage in Mary Boykin Chesnutt's diary in which she described weeping bitterly at a slave prayer meeting where the Black driver shouted "like a trumpet": she said, "I would very much have liked to shout too." Then I understood that I was using Black people to weep for me, to express *my* sorrow at my responsibility. . . . Finally, I understood that I could feel sorrow during their music and yet not confuse their sorrow with mine, or use their resistance for mine. *I needed to do my own work*: express my sorrow and my responsibility myself, in my own words, by my own actions. (p. 41)

I recall that, years ago, when I first encountered bell hooks's (1990) powerful essay, "Homeplace: A Site of Resistance," I was moved and inspired by her narrative. hooks talks eloquently about the role the Black women in her family had in creating dignity, integrity, and safety in the home, even as they engaged in hard, manual labor for White folks during the day to earn their living. This narrative of resisting race and class oppression made me think of my own mother and her mother who suffered—and survived—the loss of their home when the British ruled India. I have realized since that, while engaging the narratives of other activists and scholars is helpful in developing my own consciousness and critique of oppressive structures, it is not enough. As a postcolonialist, feminist academic, I find that it is important also for me to understand how my particular narrative emerges from and is linked to the larger context of colonial oppression that has shaped the history of India and its relationship to the West.

Similarly, today, as an academic and an Asian American, I find it is essential to deconstruct the model minority stereotype for various reasons. As Lee (1996) has noted, the model minority stereotype depicts Asian Americans as the "good," uncomplaining, hardworking, and therefore successful minority community. In contrast other peoples of color, such as African Americans, are represented in the media and public discourses as troublemakers who do not assume responsibility for their own progress. Such fallacious representations contribute to the politics of "divide and rule," and, ultimately, serve to keep communities of color on the margins. Furthermore, the model minority stereotype is a seemingly benign, apparently flattering representation, created by those in power, which serves to circumscribe the participation of Asian Americans in the larger sociopolitical context. When Asian Americans—within and without the academy—conform to it, they limit their own voices as critics of such oppressive forces as racism and ethnocentrism and their participation as agents of transformation in the larger social context.

Thus, my evolution as a scholar has been intertwined with my personal identity quests. The recursive, rigorous process of working through layers of differences and contradictions, to arrive continually at a sense of integrity, allowed me to develop a *mestiza* consciousness (Anzaldúa, 1987), a consciousness of my own borderlands, and to be "on both shores at once" (p. 78): on the margins as a "person of color" and in the center as an "emerging scholar." Thus, my early struggles as a "foreign" student and a South Asian woman in New York City led me to "work the hyphens" (Fine, 1994) between self-and-other and "learn through conflict" (Kumashiro, 2000). These struggles to maintain integrity, combined with my engagement with scholarly critiques of oppressive structures such as colonization, patriarchy, and sexism enabled me to situate myself as "academic Self-woman of color Other" in the academy (Asher, 2001). Today, as a South Asian woman academic in the field of education, I find that I am *both* insider *and* outsider in terms of race, nation, culture, gender, and sexuality in the academy and in relation to the larger Indian/South Asian/Asian American communities.

Professional Identities: A Postcolonial Feminist Academic

Although it is now in the distance, I recall distinctly that, in the "early days" as a graduate student, I searched for a dissertation topic that felt meaningful to me. After writing a lengthy research paper on bilingual education, I decided to explore the area of Asian American education, particularly the dearth of representation of South Asians, for my study, coming one step closer to home, so to speak, in my interrogation of issues of marginality. My qualitative research project examined issues of identity and culture in the lives of ten Indian American high school students in New York City. The excitement of gathering and sifting through detailed interview data grew as the process of data analysis led me to relate my findings to the area of Asian American education, then multicultural education and postcolonial theory (see Asher, 1999). At the same time, several wonderful mentors at Teachers College—including two Asian American women academics, who became powerful role models—invited me to teach or present at conferences or write for publication with them. Finally, I began feeling connected to the field and, more important, able to speak to the larger curriculum questions (for instance, the relevance of the curriculum to the lives of students) that had haunted me and led me to embark on the doctorate. Thus, not only did my identity as a scholar begin taking shape, but also I benefited from and learned the value of collaboration and mentoring as an academic woman and a woman of color.

Today, I identify as a postcolonialist, feminist scholar. I also see my scholarship, mentoring, and teaching as "sites of resistance" (hooks, 1990) to the forces of "othering" in the larger field of education and, more particularly, in the academy. My areas of inquiry and teaching are postcolonialism and feminism, critical perspectives on multiculturalism, and Asian American education. As a scholar and a teacher, I emphasize the need to interrogate the dynamic, context-specific intersections of race-class-gender-culture-language-history-and-geography (see Asher & Crocco, 2001). At the heart of my work—and, I believe, any solid scholarship—are rigor and integrity, two principles that strengthen each other. Let me elaborate.

Years ago, at the annual meeting of the American Education Research Association (AERA), I attended a mentoring seminar for scholars of color. In responding to a question from someone in the audience about how much time and energy one should give to academic politics, one of the panelists—a woman of color, tenured at a major research university—responded saying that the most important thing was to "do good work." I have always remembered this and, at a subsequent conference, I told this colleague how much I have valued her advice. Certainly, I am conscious of and speak to issues of race, gender, marginality, and colonization in the academy. At the same time, I also know that, as a scholar, what matters to me most is that my work should stand on its own as a solid contribution to the field. I find that my efforts to maintain integrity—across the different areas of my scholarship and between my writing and my teaching—bring their own rigor to the development of my work. Again, let me elaborate with a couple of examples.

When I brought theoretical analyses of the intersections of race, class, and ethnicity to bear on how the Indian American participants in my study negotiated identities, I was able to unpack some of the contradictions that emerged in their narratives. For instance, an analysis of the career-related messages my participants got from those at home, revealed specific gendered expectations. While girls were encouraged to achieve well and pursue high-paying, science-related professions, they were also expected to fulfill traditional, social expectations regarding marriage and raising a family (see Asher, 2002). The exercise of writing this article allowed me to bring critical theory to inform the discourse on Asian American education and also relate my findings to the larger discourse of multiculturalism and marginality.

More recently, I have reflected on the complexities and contradictions I confront in the process of my own multicultural teacher education pedagogy in my current location, the Deep South. I have written:

> I, the well-meaning, "enlightened," teacher of multiculturalism, armed with a doctorate earned in that bastion of bewildering difference—New York City—came to the South to teach. How can I ensure that I do not other/colonize my students? I know that I want to be open to and engage my students' particular stories and contexts, and at the same time, avoid the pitfall of slipping into a seemingly benign cultural relativism. How can I work the hyphens between self-and-other and foster the emergence of a hybrid consciousness for each? How can I follow the recommendation that Margaret Crocco and I (2001) have offered—to create a multicultural teacher education pedagogy which offers curricular spaces for "students to present their own stories on their own terms"—even as I work with my Southern students to deconstruct histories and practices of racism and prejudice? (Asher, in press)

I found myself working on the above article as one way to make sense of/deal with my current situatedness as a South Asian woman academic, teaching at Louisiana State University, a historically and predominantly White university, located in Louisiana's conservative capital, and in a school district that has the dubious distinction of having the longest-running school desegregation case. Once again, such a self-reflexive exercise also helps me clarify for myself the relevance of the work I do—teaching and writing—in relation to the larger discourses of multiculturalism and postcolonial theory as well as the field of education.

Further, in this recent article, I have also discussed how, in some powerful ways, Louisiana evokes home—as in India—for me.

> When I first visited LSU, as a candidate, I fell in love with Louisiana. It was warm, beautiful, and lush green. The campus was lovely—with its majestic old live oaks and the azaleas in bloom. And the air smelled like home, sweet, rich, fragrant, reminding me of India. The spell Louisiana's beauty cast over me only got stronger during my house hunting trip that summer. The sugarcane, the lush foliage, the steaming warmth, the bungalows with their windows which could be left open allowing homes to breathe, the porches with their swing seats and ceiling fans, the buzz of insects, all so evoked home. (Asher, in press)

I have gone on to discuss how crossing borders has led me to new interstitial locations and pushed me to grow. On the one hand, I am drawn (in)to Louisiana's beauty. And yet, on the other, I find myself struggling not to exoticize "the South," and to find a balance in the interstices between openness to my southern students' narratives and perspectives and (en)gendering a critical multiculturalism in the classroom (Asher, in press).

As I noted in the previous section, I recognize that no one compelled me to come to Louisiana. My interest in developing my theoretical work was key in my applying for a job at LSU where the Department of Curriculum and Instruction houses the Curriculum Theory Project. Colleagues in my department, the College of Education, and Women's and Gender Studies have consistently supported and encouraged my academic work. I have also collaborated with graduate students on presentations and writing projects. And yet, my sense of outsiderness, as a South Asian, lesbian, non-Christian woman, in Louisiana remains present.

When a Black student said in class that, for her, I am sort of like bell hooks, I was deeply moved by the sense of connection and trust she felt. When another student wrote me a card, which had Winnie the Pooh peering into a pool on the cover, about how she found the reflective process in our classes so meaningful, I was thrilled. Joyous moments in teaching! However, when episodes such as the one I recounted at the outset occur or when I read students' accounts of racism or sexism or homophobia in my multicultural education classes, I experience anger, pain, sadness, and exhaustion.

For instance, as I have written elsewhere (Asher, 2003b, pp. 241–242), I was shocked, drained, and saddened when I read Jessica's (a pseudonym) reflections regarding a racist incident that occurred at her former high school. Jessica, a young, White, southern woman in my undergraduate class on multiculturalism, described in her autobiography assignment how a racial conflict erupted in her high school, when one of her male friends had hurled a racist epithet at a peer. Furthermore, Jessica struggled to reconcile her consciousness that racism is wrong with her desire to support her friend, who "stood up for his beliefs," and "continued coming to school after his suspension with his head high." She concluded these reflections by asserting, "This event taught me to stand up for what I believe in and be proud of who I am and my heritage. That was exactly what he had done and to this day he would do the same thing" (Asher, 2003b, p. 242). Even through the shock I experienced as I read Jessica's words, as her teacher, I reminded myself that, typically, most students, regardless of their racial/ethnic identification, are certainly more troubled by racism—at least overt racism—than this student was as she wrote her autobiography. Besides, the fact that she narrated this episode as she did indicated that she was not entirely at ease with this matter. And, once again, I reminded myself that "unpacking" such complex, difficult issues is part of a decolonizing multicultural education pedagogy (for a more in-depth discussion, see Asher, 2003b, in press).

However, the few instances when colleagues have exhibited ignorance and prejudice have been the hardest for me. For instance, I was shocked when, at one point, a couple of colleagues with whom I was teaching at that time proposed giving journals with quotes from the Bible to a cohort of graduating students. The shock was worsened when they explained that they wanted to run this by me, because they had thought I might disagree with this plan, given that I did not follow the Christian faith. Well, they were right and wrong. I did not agree with the plan. But, of course, it had nothing to do with my particular religious beliefs. I was shocked (I think I still am today) that faculty at a state university—even if it *is* in the Deep South, where religious sentiment runs strong—saw fit not only to select such a gift but also chose to position me as the outsider and, therefore, the "problem" in this case. Ultimately, we found other, more appropriate (from my perspective) gifts. However, I am aware that, although I mentioned my concern to them, my colleagues and I did not work through the larger issue of their having "othered" me. At other times, when I have identified myself as a "person of color," several colleagues have expressed surprise. I have wondered if this is because race relations in the South are construed mainly in terms of Black and White. Indeed, one even stated that the students would probably just see me as White! Once again, the implication is twofold: first, that I can gain acceptance by aligning myself with the dominant culture/ race, and second—a mistaken notion—that this is what I would want. Although such encounters are, thankfully, few and far between, within the larger climate of support, they contribute to the exhaustion, anger, and frustration of fighting against the various forms of prejudice that afflict us, individually and collectively, in today's global world.

Building Agency and Community: Embracing Difference

As a South Asian woman academic I address issues of identity, representation, oppression, and marginalization through my teaching and research. Ultimately, of course, as I noted in the previous section, my mantra is to continue to "do good work" and maintain integrity between theory and practice. Indeed, my efforts to deepen my work in context-specific ways and develop my own "engaged pedagogy" (hooks, 1994) push me further, keep me near the edge. As I have written recently about teaching multiculturalism in the Deep South:

> I recognize that our [my students' and my] distinct identities, emerging from our particular social, cultural, historical, and political contexts come together in the in-between space of the multicultural teacher education classroom. And that, in order for each of us to benefit from the pedagogical process and our dialogical exchange, each of us—student and teacher— needs to do her ongoing, self-reflexive border work. To that end, I strive to acknowledge and work through both my students' struggles with issues of race-class-gender and my own emotional responses to histories of racism and prejudice (see Asher, 2003b). I find that such "engaged theorizing" frees me, leading me to understand the roots of my own pain and desire for change in relation to the work I do *and* meet my students on their own journeys of conscientization and growth. (Asher, 2003b, p. 246).

Service to the field is also an important aspect of my work as an academic. (Perhaps, post-tenure, I may actually return to volunteering with a community organization . . .) For instance, I am involved in the activities of AERA's Special Interest Groups (SIGs) on Research on the Education of Asian and Pacific Americans—SIG/REAPA—and Postcolonial Studies and Education. I view my efforts as acts of intervention to rupture forces of marginalization and silencing. For instance, when I organize a panel that draws out and highlights the multiplicities of Asian Americans' educational experiences I believe that I am contributing in some small measure to deconstructing the model minority stereotype. Furthermore, such endeavors are necessary for developing and sustaining a critical community of scholars. Indeed, I have found that my critical dialogues and collaborations with diverse mentors, colleagues, and students have enhanced me personally and professionally.

At the systemic level, I believe that it is necessary for Asian American scholars and scholars in Asian American studies/ethnic studies in education to interrogate critically relations of power that shape interminority and minority-majority relations. We need to deconstruct vigorously essentialist notions of identity. For instance, when our fellow scholars present quantitative data about how well young Asian Americans are doing at school or in the workplace, we need to acknowledge this, *and* at the same time to bring to light the narratives of those Asian Americans who do not have adequate access to schooling, possibly because of barriers of language or class but also because of the operation of the model minority stereotype as a "hegemonic device" (Lee, 1996, p. 6) and the underlying "racist love" (Chin & Chan, 1972). In other words, it behooves us to resist and speak out against such marginalizing forces and scholarship that perpetuates/reifies them. Certainly, we may also do this work outside of the academy in dialogue with community organizations and parents/guardians of young Asian Americans. Indeed as Lisa Lowe (1996) has discussed:

> The articulation of an "Asian American identity" as an organizing tool has provided a concept of political unity that enables diverse Asian groups to understand unequal circumstances and histories as being related. . . . Yet to the extent that Asian American culture fixes Asian American identity and suppresses differences—of national origin, generation, gender, sexuality, class—it risks particular dangers: not only does it underestimate the differences and hybridities among Asians, but it may also inadvertently support the racist discourse that constructs Asians as a homogeneous group, that implies that Asians are "all alike" and conform to "types." (p. 71)

But the work of deconstructing essentialist notions does not end here. We need also to be conscious of the stereotypes we, Asian Americans, hold about diverse others. For instance, as Rey Chow (2002, p. 60) has noted, "racist rejection of Black people" occurs among Asians in the United States and elsewhere. Indeed, just as I was shocked when my colleagues bought journals with religious messages, so was I taken aback when, in a discussion at a national conference, a well-regarded Asian American scholar advised younger scholars that we need to be more "like the Blacks" and be assertive about our rights. Yes, those of us who are on the margins *do* need to assert ourselves and claim our rights. But, no, we cannot participate in stereotyping "Blacks" as a monolithic community of vocal, aggressive people. In so doing, we continue to participate in the politics of divide and rule. Rather, as Lowe (1996, p. 71) has advised, I believe that it is critical for us, Asian Americans, to build alliances with other groups on the margins and at the same time to engage in "internal critical dialogues" among ourselves to interrogate the multiplicities, hybridities, and contradictions we encounter in terms of culture, identity, and location within and without the academy. In other words, when we place ourselves in interstitial locations—the dynamic spaces between identifications and cultures—we are able to "diversify our practices to include a more heterogeneous group and to enable crucial alliances—with other groups of color, class-based struggles, feminist coalitions, and sexuality-based efforts—in the ongoing work of transforming hegemony" (p. 83).

References

Anzaldúa, G. (1987). *Borderlands/La frontera: The new mestiza.* San Francisco: Spinsters/Aunt Lute.

Apache Indian. (1993). *No reservations* [CD]. St. Laurent, Canada: Island Records.

Asher, N. (1997, Spring). Apache Indian's syncretic music and the representation of South Asian identities: A case study of a minority artist. *Taboo: The Journal of Culture and Education,* pp. 99–118.

Asher, N. (1999). *Margins, center, and the spaces in-between: Indian American high school students' lives at home and school.* Unpublished doctoral dissertation, Teachers College, Columbia University.

Asher, N. (2001). Beyond "cool" and "hip": Engaging the question of research and writing as academic Self-woman of color Other. *International Journal of Qualitative Studies in Education, 14,* 1–12.

Asher, N. (2002). Class acts: Indian American high school students negotiate professional and ethnic identities. *Urban Education, 37,* 267–295.

Asher, N. (2003a). At the intersections: A postcolonialist woman of color considers Western feminism. *Social Education, 67,* 47–50.

Asher, N. (2003b). Engaging difference: Towards a pedagogy of interbeing. *Teaching Education, 14,* 235–247.

Asher, N. (in press). At the interstices: Engaging postcolonial and feminist perspectives for a multicultural education pedagogy in "the South." *Teachers College Record.*

Asher, N., & Crocco, M. S. (2001). (En)gendering multicultural identities and representations in education. *Theory and Research in Social Education, 29,* 129–151.

Bhabha, H. K. (1994). *The location of culture.* New York: Routledge.

Chin, F., & Chan, J. P. (1972). Racist love. In R. Kostelanetz (Ed.), *Seeing through schuck* (pp. 65–79). New York: Ballantine.

Chow, R. (2002). *The protestant ethnic and the spirit of capitalism.* New York: Columbia University Press.

Fine, M. (1994). Working the hyphens: Reinventing self and other in qualitative research. In N. K. Denzin & Y. S. Lincoln (Eds.), *Handbook of qualitative research* (pp. 70–82). Thousand Oaks, CA: Sage.

hooks, b. (1990). *Yearning: Race, gender, and cultural politics.* Boston: South End Press.

hooks, b. (1994). *Teaching to transgress: Education as the practice of freedom.* New York: Routledge.

Kumashiro, K. K. (2000). Toward a theory of anti-oppressive education. *Review of Educational Research, 70,* 25–53.

Lee, S. J. (1996). Unraveling the "model minority" stereotype: Listening to Asian American youth. New York: Teachers College Press.

Lowe, L. (1996). *Immigrant acts: On Asian American cultural politics.* Durham, NC: Duke University Press.

McCarthy, C., & Crichlow, W. (1993). Introduction: Theories of identity, theories of representation, theories of race. In C. McCarthy & W. Crichlow (Eds.), *Race, identity, and representation in education* (pp. xiii–xxix). New York: Routledge.

Mercer, K. (1990). Black hair/style politics. In R. Ferguson, M. Gever, T. M. Trinh, & C. West (Eds.), *Out there: Marginalization and contemporary cultures* (pp. 247–64). Cambridge, MA: New Museum of Contemporary Art and MIT Press.

Pratt, M. B. (1984). Identity: Skin, blood, heart. In E. Bulkin, M. B. Pratt, & B. Smith (Eds.), *Yours in struggle: Three feminist perspectives on anti-semitism and racism.* Brooklyn, NY: Long Haul.

9

UNMASKING THE SELF

Struggling with the Model Minority Stereotype and Lotus Blossom Image

Eunai Kim Shrake

"I can't understand a word of her English."
  "You are a damn charming woman."
  "The instructor is too opinionated."
  "You are one of the most diplomatic professors I have ever experienced, and I thank you for showing me that aspect of teaching."

The above comments are from the narrative student evaluations of some of the courses I taught at various American public universities. I quote these comments here to illustrate my seven years' journey toward "(re)discovering my face." Here I use the term "face" to symbolize the "unmasked self" as opposed to the mask I have been hiding behind throughout my teaching experience in predominantly White, higher educational institutions.

Over the past three decades, American higher educational institutions have made great efforts to promote racial and gender diversity among their faculty, staff, and student bodies. As a result, university campuses have indeed become more diverse and there are now more faculty members whose racial and gender backgrounds are different from that of White males. Unfortunately, however, increased numbers are not necessarily translated into acceptance and respect for diversity (Johnsrud & Sadao, 1998). On many university campuses, female faculty members of minority racial backgrounds are still perceived as different, and these differences are often equated with intellectual and cultural deviation or deficiency by both colleagues and students.

In this uncompromising environment, it is not unusual to note that many minority female faculty confront structural as well as emotional challenges and difficulties within and outside their classrooms. Regrettably, preparing cognitively and emotionally to deal with a stressful teaching experience becomes a priority for the minority female, especially junior faculty (Vargas, 1999). To put it differently, it is essential for minority female faculty to acquire appropriate coping strategies to avoid costly emotional tolls that these challenges may bring about.

As a female faculty of color, I was not an exception to this rule. Throughout seven years of teaching at various universities in Southern California, I have had to develop coping strategies to deal with difficult situations that were imposed upon me, in large part, because of my race and gender. One strategy I developed in order to cope with difficulties prompted by my racial and gender status was to construct and maintain an elaborate "mask" to wear in public.

"Masking," or using a disguise in public, may be a common human behavior that shows our tendency to try to control how we present ourselves to others. In other words, how we project ourselves to others is in part a conscious and voluntary construction. However, if one is masking because of one's minority status in society, masking becomes an act of defense against racism and/or sexism. For example, for women of color, masking allows avoidance of unpleasant situations or challenges that are often directly related to their racial and gender minority status. As a double minority because of their race and gender, women of color lose the power to define others, and instead they become defined by them. It is in this context of disempowerment that women of color are forced to assume a mask in order to present a face that is "acceptable" to the dominant society. For women of color, masking is an act of subordination, that is, a psychological attempt to fit in to the prescribed images (stereotypes) of them held by the dominant group. In addition, it is also a resistance strategy to contend with the racism and sexism that are imbedded in the stereotypes. Here, the duality of the "mask" is revealed. The mask becomes the site of subordination on one hand, and the site of insubordination on the other. Likewise, masking became my strategy to submit myself to and to contend with stereotypes that resulted from my race and gender. In this context, the mask became the site of (re)negotiation for my racial and gender status.

As an Asian American female faculty member, I have encountered problems and challenges on multiple fronts. Besides the struggle with language, I have experienced that my power and authority as a teacher are often undermined by existing racial and gender stereotypes that are thrust upon me by both my colleagues and students. These racial and gender stereotypes have forced me to operate within certain boundaries that limit my freedom to assert myself as a unique individual with a complex identity and personality. Instead of freely defining my own personality and style, I was constrained to assume a mask that corresponded to the simplified, stereotypical images of the racial and gender groups to which I belong. I, as a unique individual, was buried behind the mask while I, as a token representative of my race and gender group, emerged with the mask. Lost to the mask was the multiplicity of my identity as a self-confident, expressive, and competent person that would have emerged but for the real and perceived need to disguise my self. Presenting an acceptable face and hiding my inner self, I moved between dualized selves and dualized worlds behind the mask. In other words, I was living a schizophrenic life. Inevitably, inner conflict and contradiction arose from this dual existence, and thus ensued my struggle to (re)negotiate my identity and reclaim my face.

It took me almost seven years of struggle to undo much of the psychological damage that the dual stereotypes inflicted on me and to finally reclaim my individuality. In this chapter, I will describe my teaching experience as a personal journey toward unmasking the self. In so doing, I will first outline the racial and gender stereotypes pertaining to my dual minority status that provided a context for constructing a mask. Then, I will explain how these two stereotypes converge in the professional experiences of an Asian American woman. What I hope to reveal in this chapter is how converging racial and gender stereotypes of Asian American women as model minority and lotus blossom penetrate the power dynamics between a teacher and students, and thus necessitate the struggle to reclaim selfhood for Asian American female faculty in American public universities.

Contours of Masking

Before I came to America for graduate studies, I finished my master's degree in education and taught sociology and education courses at a junior college in Seoul, Korea. During the two years of teaching in this college, my students often evaluated me as one of the most competent, understanding, and humorous teachers they had. In retrospect, I was a very confident and expressive teacher as well. This image of myself as a confident and expressive teacher became severely challenged when I started teaching in American public universities.

Like other nonnative, minority faculty, the initial challenge to my confident self-image arose from my anxieties regarding language difficulty and cultural differences. However, the biggest challenge turned out to be the mainstream perception of how an Asian American female should behave. Throughout my teaching experience in America, I realized that the way I think about myself might differ considerably from the way my students and colleagues perceive me. How I perceived myself didn't matter to others. To them, I was just a woman of color. I felt that my ability and talents were shortchanged because of my race and gender minority status.

Since receiving a doctorate degree in social sciences and comparative education at the University of California, Los Angeles, I have taught courses in Asian American studies, sociology, and education departments at four public universities in southern California. Except for a couple of general education courses, which tend to attract more White students, students in the Asian American studies courses I taught were predominantly Asian American. In these courses, students rarely posed any problems because with our shared ethnicity, there was a certain level of understanding between the students and myself. The students respected me as a professional and were patient with my accent. As a matter of fact, I had a couple of standing ovations from the whole class at the end of such courses.

Contrary to these positive experiences, courses in sociology and education with predominantly White students often caused challenges and problems that painfully reminded me of my double minority status as a woman of color. Aside from the not-so-positive student evaluations of my courses, I often encountered resentful and condescending remarks and attitudes from some (mostly White) students. It seems that, when they see a minority woman as their teacher, White students tend to expect this teacher to behave according to their own stereotypes. If the teacher deviates from what is expected of her, it incites their anger and hostility.

Students' negative attitudes toward the content of my courses and my teaching methods were very apparent in multicultural education and interracial relations courses, which explored issues of educational inequity, racial and economic inequality, and racial prejudice and stereotypes, and in which I attempted to instill critical thinking among the students. In those classes, I openly expressed my criticism and dissatisfaction with U.S. society as a way to elicit critical discussions from the students. I naively assumed that most students would be encouraged to share their viewpoints with me. However, some students seemed to construe my efforts to promote critical discussion as "White bashing." In extreme cases, students openly expressed their hostility, arguing that I, as an immigrant who made it in America, should be grateful instead of criticizing any aspect of U.S. society.

I was shocked when one White student indignantly blurted out, "It is easy to criticize if you are an outsider," in response to my comments on racial structure in American society. Though I noticed subtle racism in her remark, at first, I didn't know what to make of it. It was not until the end of the semester when I received the student evaluations that I fully comprehended what that student actually meant. In the narrative section of the evaluation form, a couple of students wrote that I was too opinionated and critical. Another student noted that my class was mostly about White bashing and he was often offended in the class. Reading those comments, I finally understood that I had set myself up for trouble by speaking my mind as if I were an insider, while the majority of students perceived me as an outsider. It was quite ironic to realize that while my main focus in those courses was on leveling the playing field for racial minorities and minority children, it was difficult to level the playing field for myself in the classrooms!

The students' negative responses and resistance motivated me to reassess my position as a minority female faculty member in a predominantly White academia. I had to rethink my personality and discourse style in order to cope more effectively with my racial and gender status. I began noticing that, being Asian American and a female, I was not expected to criticize or challenge the dominant society because Asians are supposed to be apolitical, reserved, and compliant. In other words, expectations of me were for uncomplaining perseverance and quiet accommodation, rather than questioning and challenging. It was clear that these expectations had much to do with stereotypes that resulted from my ethnicity and gender, which center on two existing stereotypes of Asian American women as model minority and lotus blossom. These two stereotypes put Asian American women like me at a particular risk of being racially and sexually harassed because of the synergy that results when they are combined (Cho, 1997). Being an Asian American who is supposed to be apolitical, and also an Asian woman who is supposed to be submissive, I was expected to comply with these stereotypes by being passive, uncritical, and nonthreatening.

Given that it is difficult for the disempowered individual to defy society's expectations (Vargas, 1999), and also that all stereotypes, whether positive or negative, serve as self-fulfilling prophecies that gradually lead to internalizing them (Chow, 1989), I slowly picked up on the stereotypes and began acting accordingly. In other words, to avoid harsh judgment and scrutiny, I assumed a mask to conform to the racial and gender stereotypes that were imposed on me. I fell victim to my race and gender by accommodating, and compromising with, the imposed stereotypes. As a female and a racial minority, it was hard just to be myself.

In the next section, I will outline the two prevalent and converging stereotypes of Asian American women, model minority and lotus blossom, that constitute the contours of my "mask."

Model Minority: Genderized Racial Stereotype

My mask was primarily associated with the image of Asian Americans as being a model minority. The idea that Asian Americans have been a successful minority that made it in America through hard work and perseverance emerged as a popular news media theme in the mid-1960s (Petersen, 1966a, 1966b). After a century of negative stereotypes as "unassimilable heathens" and "Yellow Peril," Asian Americans found themselves cast in an increasingly positive light by the popular media. The media portrayed Asian Americans as a model minority group that had overcome racial barriers to realize the American dream, as shown by their economic, educational, and professional success. The image quickly caught on and dominated the stage for decades (Chun, 1980; Petersen, 1970). While the 1980s would generate much research critical of unqualified accounts of Asian American success, the model minority stereotype not only survived into the 1990s with its fundamental thesis largely unchanged (Osajima, 2000) but was even extended to newly arrived immigrants from Southeast Asia. As a result, the model minority image of Asian Americans has been firmly implanted in the American public minds, and, despite much criticism and repudiation, it is still prevalent today.

The model minority stereotype is based on statistical data on the group-wide educational, economic, and social achievements of Asian Americans. While some Asian Americans accept the media's model minority portrayal of Asian Americans as a positive development that puts them on a pedestal, many others see it as a critical point of contest. The concept of the model minority has been criticized as simplistic, masking extreme inequalities within and between different Asian American groups, as well as diverting public attention from the existence of discrimination (Woo, 2000). It is also criticized as a politically divisive tool that pits Asian Americans against other minority groups (Hurh & Kim, 1989; Rohrlick, Alvarado, Zaruba, & Kallic, 1998).

Behind the image of a model minority, there is the notion that good minorities are supposed to be grateful for having been accepted by the dominant White culture, while feeling content to stay one level below Whites because they can never fully measure up to their standards. Accordingly, the model minority image produces a specific minority position within the hegemonic racial structure in American society; one level lower than Whites and one level higher than other minorities. In other words, the image of the model minority reinforces the dominant culture's idea of acceptable minorities and, by extension, the negative impression of those recalcitrant "other" minorities (Palumbo-Liu, 1999). As some Asian American writer-activists cynically phrase it, the idea of model minority is nothing but "racist love" from dominant Whites, and nothing more than self-contempt by the Asian Americans themselves (Chin & Chan, 1972).

In addition, a closer look at the image suggests competing or contradictory themes. One image is that Asian Americans exemplify a spirit of perseverance and ingenuity that enable them to overcome structural and racial barriers. On the other hand, they are also seen as compliant, politically passive, and content with their social lot (Woo, 1989). In other words, it assumes that good minorities know their place within the system and don't challenge it.

Therefore, at the center of the model minority stereotype, lie associated images of uncomplaining perseverance and submissiveness to authority. In other words, the model minority stereotype paints a misleading portrait of Asian Americans as a polite, docile, and nonthreatening people. It is at this point that the model minority stereotype becomes genderized (feminized). Asian Americans as a model minority are supposed to assume feminine qualities of passivity, submissiveness, self-effacement, and reticence to speak out. Hence, behind this seemingly positive stereotype lurks the danger of subordination because this stereotype may pressure Asian Americans to act in accordance with these associated feminine images. The model minority stereotype is particularly dangerous because it tells Asian Americans how to behave. It tells us to pose no threat to the White establishment, to take things quietly, not to complain, and not fight back.

This stereotyped expectation of model minority, though not overt, was clearly manifested in students' comments and questions in my classroom. As soon as I started teaching courses that explored issues of race relations and educational equity, I noticed some students had certain expectations of me.

For the most part, I was expected to be nonconfrontational and nonaggressive. I was not expected to criticize American society and its system because Asian Americans, being a model minority, are supposed to conform to and not challenge their model minority stereotype. When I deviated from this expectation, I encountered negative and sometimes even intimidating remarks and attitudes from some students. This was especially apparent in my multicultural education course, in which predominantly White students who were in the teaching credential program were enrolled. Among them were some extremely vocal students—White males who were often older than other students in the class. On many occasions, I confronted condescending attitudes and remarks that were pertinent to my model minority status.

"You are a model minority. You made it in America despite your accented English. Why do you complain for other minorities?" When I criticized White racism in the socioeconomic mobility structure in order to explain reasons for the low achievement of some racial minority groups in the educational system, one White student angrily responded, "If they don't like this country that much, why don't they move out?" Another student, a White female, snapped when I discussed the historical and structural backgrounds of African Americans' construction of oppositional culture and identity. When I threw her question on why didn't they leave back at her—asking, "Where to?"—she accused me of attempting to silence her.

On another occasion, a couple of students from working-class backgrounds expressed resentment toward my model minority status. "They made it in America. I am White, but I am from the working class. And I am still struggling to make ends meet. What are they complaining about?" One White male student retorted when I talked about the lowered socioeconomic status of some Asian American immigrants who are from high-class and high-educational backgrounds in their original country. "If they think they can be better off in your country, why don't they go back?" was another student's condescending remark. Even if they used a pronoun—"they"—in their comments, I clearly understood that the remarks were directed at me.

The negative reactions by students were also revealed in their course evaluations. In the narrative portion of the course evaluations, some students wrote angry and resentful comments. For example, one student wrote, "This course was too much of White bashing. I felt very offended because the instructor tried to put blame on me about all of the social ills." Another student commented, "For an Asian, the instructor is too aggressive and outspoken. She seems to believe she has the right to criticize White people just because she is not White."

I believe that my critical view of U.S. society, combined with my racial status as a model minority, incited some students' hostile attitudes. Whenever I expressed strong criticism of White racism, not only my teaching evaluations suffered but also I received complaints that had to do with my English proficiency. One student showed her aggression by writing on the course evaluation, "I can't understand a word of her English. The class was a waste of time."

Occasionally, unpleasant experiences also occurred in relationships with my colleagues. For instance, when I tried to reprimand a student who cheated during the final exam, the student became overtly hostile and started complaining about my teaching and my class content to the chair of the department. When I consulted with the chair and other colleagues (mostly Whites) to find out the way to punish him, they discouraged me from any further action other than just giving him a C. It was clear that they expected me to quietly accommodate the situation without making waves.

Of course, there were students who consistently supported me. They thanked me for opening their minds and providing new perspectives. However, some of these students unconsciously showed patronizing attitudes. On one occasion, eager to impress me with his multicultural attitudes, one student proudly pronounced in the class session, "Living in California all my life, I don't have any problems with different accents. I don't mind Arnold Schwarzenegger's accent or Dr. Shrake's accent." I was not sure if I should take this as indicating support!

When I conferred with more experienced colleagues for their advice, some suggested that I remove issues from the course content that were too controversial, and also trim down my critical comments. One White male colleague even suggested that I should act more Asian, revealing his belief in the quiet model minority stereotype. One Latina colleague suggested jokingly that I wear double-breasted jackets to look more formal and dignified. However, these talks with colleagues made me feel even more disempowered.

Pressed by these challenges from students and feeling disempowered, I couldn't help but become extremely sensitive to how I was perceived by my students. I became very apprehensive about stereotyped expectations of me and, as a result, I began to act accordingly. Gradually but recognizably, I changed my teaching and communication styles. I began changing the tone of my voice to sound confiding rather than intimidating. I also toned down my criticism of the "White" system. At the beginning of each semester, I asked my students not to take my course readings and my criticism of Whites as personal attacks, though I secretly wished otherwise.

In short, recognizing that conforming to acceptable stereotypes is the most convenient strategy to avoid unpleasant and stressful situations, I took on the model minority traits of compliance and quiet accommodation. Though I knew that it was selling out and accepting humiliation, it was the most expedient survival tactic. However, this strategy was really just a form of internalized colonialism, whereby minority individuals buy into their presumed inferiority and powerlessness and as a result, succumb to stereotypical expectations imposed on them by the dominant group (Ng, 1995). Instead of challenging the stereotype, I ended up surrendering myself to racial subordination. This was the way my first mask surfaced. I now turn to the second stereotype that is related to my mask.

Lotus Blossom Image: Racialized Gender Stereotype

Another stereotyped image that compounded my masking was related to my being an Asian woman. Although most female faculty experience challenges to their authority in the classroom because of their gender, for a racial minority female teacher, the devaluation of her authority and credibility is compounded by her race and ethnicity (Ng, 1995). The Asian American female faculty member is particularly susceptible to this "double trouble," because of the overlay of the racial (model minority) stereotype on the gender (lotus blossom) stereotype. The model minority traits of passivity and submissiveness are intensified and genderized through the image of obedient and servile Asian women in everyday campus life. As a matter of fact, the story of racialized sexual experience is not uncommon among Asian American women in academia.

Historically, Asian and Asian American women have been trivialized and exoticized by American mainstream popular culture and media. They are portrayed as exotic, erotic, mysterious, seductive, available, and willing to please and cater to every whim of White men. The most popular and widespread image of Asian and Asian American women in Hollywood movies, literature, and popular media is the "lotus blossom (aka China Doll or Oriental Flower)," an exotic, docile, delicate, and utterly feminine woman (Cho, 1997; Hagedorn, 2000; Rifkin, 1993). In this racialized sexual image, the intelligence of Asian American women is underestimated, their humanity is overlooked, and their diverse cultures are treated as interchangeable (Hagedorn, 2000). In other words, the "lotus blossom" image depersonalizes and objectifies Asian American women as mere sexual objects who can't be taken seriously by society.

The media portrayal of Asian women as lotus blossoms has its roots in the history of Western colonialism. It is based on western male sexual fantasy, a product of colonial and military domination interwoven with sexual domination (Cho, 1997). What is sexualized is not gender but power. In other words, it is the power relation between Asia and the West that has shaped sexual stereotypes of Asian women. For example, rehearsing the western male sexual fantasy, writers in the colonial era described Asian women as "Indian Chocolate Sweetmeats," "China Dolls," and "Malay Girls" (Wee, 1990). Such colonial images of Asian women have persisted to the present through Hollywood movies and other popular culture. In addition, these derogatory images have expanded to apply to Asian American women in an international transfer of stereotypes through mass media and popular culture.

For over eighty years, Hollywood movie and media industries have persisted in their stereotypical portrayal of Asian and Asian American women. In such movies as *Sayonara, Flower Drum Song,* and *The World of Suzy Wong,* Asian women have been consistently portrayed as the lotus blossom, a passive sexual-romantic object (Tajima, 1989). This Hollywood image of lotus blossom has spilled over into the mainstream image of Asian American women. As a result, Asian women are viewed for their hyperfeminine qualities such as passivity and servility. The repeated projection of compliant and superfeminine Asian American women feeds mainstream thinking, especially White males' belief of Asian American women as sexual objects par excellence. Not surprisingly, this objectification of Asian women has helped spawn the Asian sex tourism industry and thriving mail-order bride business.

Along with this colonial portrayal of Asian women, the image of Asian Americans in general as a passive and subservient model minority has contributed to the prevalence and stability of this overly sexualized image of Asian American women. In other words, the model minority characterization of passivity and submissiveness has reinforced and intensified the image of the quiet and catering Asian American woman. In conjunction with the model minority stereotype, the sexual stereotype of Asian American women becomes racialized. The lotus blossom image is a feminized version of model minority stereotype and the model minority stereotype is merely an extension of the lotus blossom image.

Given this cultural and racial backdrop to the gender stereotype, Asian American women are openly exposed to a double jeopardy situation, namely, racialized sexual harassment. Speaking from my own experiences, I have often been called "cute" and "exotic" by my students and occasionally by my colleagues. Some students even commented on my Asian accent as cute.

Many also commented on my being petite and thin as two Asian feminine qualities. Though these comments are generally harmless, from time to time I confronted sexually suggestive and patronizing remarks from my students and colleagues.

On one occasion, a White male student told me that he switched from another class because the White female instructor in that class was too strong and opinionated, suggesting that he expected me to be more feminine. On a particularly memorable occasion, one middle-aged White male student suggested that I should take him out for lunch or dinner to discuss how to improve my teaching. Later, the same student wrote in the course evaluation journal, "If I may be granted some informal and very direct writing, you are a damn charming woman."

However, the most obvious sexual advance came from a White male colleague. In one university where I taught as a lecturer, he approached me suggesting that he could help me get a permanent position. As our conversations proceeded, he repeatedly mentioned that his former girlfriend was Asian, and that Asian women are pretty, and so on. When he heard that I found a permanent position at another university, he became extremely enthusiastic about the news, and insisted on taking me out for lunch to congratulate me. During lunch, he asked me if I could consider him as my boyfriend. Even after I told him that I didn't want any relationship with him other than a professional one, he continued sexual advances toward me until I left that school.

As these experiences illustrate, Asian American female faculty become easy prey to patronizing and unwanted sexual advances by male students and colleagues because of the racialized gender stereotypes imposed on them. Similar to other Asian American female faculty's experiences, these sexualized racial stereotypes exposed me to sexual harassment. To make things worse, these stereotypes also held me back from overtly resisting those sexual advances. Being perceived persistently as exotic, subservient, passive, and nonassertive, I internalized these stereotypes and thus behaved in accordance with these stereotyped expectations.

Therefore, I dressed more conservatively: no low-cut blouses, no short skirts, and no no-sleeves. I also tried to look demure, feminine, pleasant, nice, and reserved. I spoke more softly and quietly. Rather than stating a clear "No" to sexually suggestive moves, I tried to avoid these students and colleagues. I was eagerly accommodating to students' needs and the campus environment. Again, I was trying to cope with racial and sexual challenges by masking myself.

Unmasking

A significant turning point that marked the beginning of my unmasking
came quite unexpectedly. It was during my fourth year of teaching when my
three teaching assistants walked out on me during my lecture. Interestingly,
it occurred in a class I taught in the Asian American studies department. It
was an introductory Asian American studies course with over 160 predominantly Asian American students. Because of the large class size, the department assigned three teaching assistants to the course. Most of the students
in the class were appreciative of my teaching style and personal style. With
my encouragement, many students visited my office to discuss academic as
well as personal matters. Many students even mentioned that it was their
first time to visit a professor's office in their three to four years of student
life. Owing to our shared ethnicity, many students felt comfortable visiting
and talking with me.

Sharing the same ethnicity worked well with my students. However,
sharing ethnicity and gender created a problem in the relationship between
my teaching assistants and myself as well. My teaching assistants, all of
whom were Asian American females, showed disrespectful attitudes toward
me from the beginning of the quarter. As Ng (1995) discussed, their attitudes
were probably a reflection of internalized colonialism whereby members of
minority groups internalize their own presumed inferiority and lack of authority and thus treat other members of the same group as less credible and
authoritative. In this volume, Li (2006) also discussed her unpleasant experiences with coethnic female graduate assistants, in the context of a White
male hegemony in academia. Students inadvertently accept White norms,
thereby participating in the denigration of minority female faculty members.

It may also have had to do with my nonassertive and nonconfrontational
personal styles that were related to my model minority and lotus blossom
mask. At the beginning of the quarter, when the teaching assistants and I
discussed how to lead class discussion and to grade assignments, I, as an advocate of critical pedagogy, tried to reduce the power differential between
myself and the teaching assistants by giving them freedom and autonomy as
much as possible, even though I provided them with clear guidance. However, they interpreted my liberal gesture as a sign of weakness and as a result,
they overempowered themselves in dealing with students.

In the middle of the quarter, I noticed that they had been abusing their
power over the students to the extent of torturing them. For instance, one
of the assistants told her students that she would selectively grade only five

weekly assignments out of ten without telling them beforehand which ones would be graded. Then, she didn't grade any of the first four consecutive weeks' assignments, making her students notice that they did all four assignments without getting any credit. As a result, her students felt frustrated and cheated. When I told her to recollect papers and grade at least two of them, she became hostile and accused me of minimizing her authority. In the next class, when I told students to return their papers to be graded, she walked out and the other two teaching assistants followed her.

This experience was both oppressive and liberating. It was oppressive because it was extremely painful and humiliating. It was liberating because it helped me reject my dualistic mask. However painful and humiliating it may have been, this experience forced me to reexamine my mask and its implications. It became clear to me that my mask, rather than precluding challenges, had compounded my vulnerability. Realizing that, I decided to search and re-search for my true and honest self, instead of shrinking behind a mask. Finally, the unmasking had begun.

First of all, the unmasking process involved decolonizing myself. Acknowledging that hypersensitivity to stereotyped expectations was a form of colonized mentality and self-defeat, I decided to resist students' stereotyped expectations pertaining to my race and gender. To do so, I had to change my personal and interpersonal styles. Instead of shying away from confrontation, I began acting more proactively by disposing of fear and anxiety about my otherness and outsiderness. Retrieving my former self that was self-confident and expressive, I became more assertive and straightforward, if not overly aggressive. I began making the tone of my voice loud and firm at times and buttering and confiding at others. In other words, I refused to be pushed to the margin. Instead, I claimed my right to be inside and in the center.

Second of all, the unmasking process entailed changes in my teaching strategy. As Kubota (2002) claimed her otherness as an asset, not a liability, I also decided to use my bicultural and bilingual identity as a vehicle to empower myself. I employed my biculturalism and bilingualism as part of multicultural strategies to encourage future teachers to embrace multiculturalism. Instead of being apologetic for my accent, from the first day of class, I began asking my students to appreciate my cultural and linguistic difference as part of a multicultural curriculum, and to take advantage of it to develop the skills, knowledge, and attitudes needed to work successfully with people from different cultures. I also declared that my dual perspective as both an insider and outsider (Asher, 2006) provided me with a better vantage point to critically view American society. Presenting myself as an example, I encouraged students to develop multiple perspectives. This strategy allowed me to affirmatively address racial and gender issues in the classroom. Whenever a student made egregiously racist or sexist comments, I encouraged the whole class to engage in critical dialogues to interrogate the multiplicities and contradictions of the statements by turning the issues in question into class debates. Also, I clearly demonstrated how and why I didn't agree with them. I was no longer afraid of disagreeing with others.

Last, but not least, I decided to disclose my complex personality to my students. I let students know that I am serious and playful, strong and weak, rational and emotional, and firm and flexible, all at the same time. I also used a healthy dose of self-depreciating humor in my lectures. Most important, I let students accept the fact that I am both an insider and outsider in terms of race and culture. All in all, I finally unveiled my honest self, my true face.

Currently, I am employed as an education specialist in the Asian American Studies Department at a state university in southern California. I teach courses that aim to prepare K–12 teachers. The students in my classes are still predominantly White, and still confront challenges that are often related to my race and gender. At times, I still feel uncertain and uneasy. However, I have prevailed with my unmasked self.

Last year, one of my students wrote in the student evaluation journal, "I learned a lot from this course about diversity and, most importantly, DIPLOMACY! You are one of the most diplomatic professors I have ever experienced, and I thank you for showing me that aspect of teaching." It was a great compliment for my personal style of teaching. Finally, I felt appreciated for just being myself.

My journey toward reclaiming myself as strong not weak, proactive not passive, expressive not reticent, and self-aware not self-conscious is far from over. However, what I have learned is that to be myself is the key and must continue to be the key. Now I believe all minority female faculty should understand that self-confidence and a strong sense of ourselves are needed to sustain us in the field.

Closing Remarks

In this chapter, I have tried to address issues of racial and gender subordination and insubordination by using my experience as a minority female faculty member at predominantly White institutions. It may seem strange to describe one's teaching experience this way, to choose to highlight a disguise (mask) as a centerpiece of a story. But more than any other image, masking/

unmasking truly captures my racial and gender (in)subordination as an Asian American woman.

What I have learned through the process of masking and unmasking is that minority female professionals should be conscious of the danger that we can unwittingly participate in our own subordination by taking on the dominant group's hegemonic devices of racial and gender stereotypes. In fact, I view my masking as a form of subordination (colonization), while my efforts to unmask were an act of insubordination (decolonization). By sharing my experience, I am trying to encourage minority female professionals within and outside academia to actively and continuously engage in a decolonization process by resisting forces that attempt to marginalize and silence them. Although my journey has been a solitary process, I believe that by sharing our stories, minority female faculty members can join in the collaborative journey toward a "counter-hegemonic" pedagogy (Kubota, 2002).

References

Asher, N. (2006). Brown in Black and White: On being a South Asian woman academic. In G. Li & G. H. Beckett (Eds.), *"Strangers" of the academy: Asian women scholars in higher education.* Sterling, VA: Stylus Publishing.

Chin, F., & Chan, J. P. (1972). Racist love. In R. Kostelanetz (Ed.), *Seeing through shuck* (pp. 65–79). New York: Ballantine.

Cho, S. K. (1997). Converging stereotypes in racialized sexual harassment: Where the model minority meets Suzie Wong. In A. K. K. Wing (Ed.), *Critical race feminism: A reader* (pp. 203–214). New York: New York University Press.

Chow, E. N. (1989). The feminist movement: Where are all the Asian American women? In Asian Women United of California (Eds.), *Making waves: An anthology of writings by and about Asian American women* (pp. 362–377). Boston: Beacon.

Chun, K. T. (1980). The myth of Asian American success and its educational ramifications. *IRCD Bulletin, 15,* 2.

Hagedorn, J. (2000). Asian women in film: No joy, no luck. In T. Fong & L. Shinagawa (Eds.), *Asian Americans: Experiences and perspectives* (pp. 264–269). Upper Saddle River, NJ: Prentice Hall.

Hurh, W. M., & Kim, K. C. (1989). The "success" image of Asian Americans: Its validity, and its practical and theoretical implications. *Ethnic and Racial Studies, 12,* 512–538.

Johnsrud, L. K., & Sadao, K. C. (1998). The common experience of "otherness": Ethnic and racial minority faculty. *Review of Higher Education, 21,* 315–342.

Kubota, R. (2002). Marginality as an asset: Toward a counter-hegemonic pedagogy for diversity. In L. Vargas (Ed.), *Women faculty of color in the white classroom: Narratives on the pedagogical implications of teacher diversity* (pp. 293–307). New York: Peter Lang.

Li, G. (2006). Navigating multiple roles and multiple discourses: A young Asian female scholar's reflection on within-race-and-gender interactions. In G. Li & G. H. Beckett (Eds.), *"Strangers" of the academy: Asian women scholars in higher education.* Sterling, VA: Stylus Publishing.

Ng, R. (1995). Teaching against the grain: Contradictions and possibilities. In R. Ng, P. Staton, & J. Scane (Eds.), *Anti-racism, feminism, and critical approaches to education* (pp. 129–155). Westport, CT: Bergin & Garvey.

Osajima, K. (2000). Asian Americans as the model minority: An analysis of the popular press image in the 1960s and 1980s. In M. Zhou & J. Gatewood (Eds.), *Contemporary Asian America* (pp. 449–458). New York: New York University Press.

Palumbo-Liu, D. (1999). *Asian/American: Historical crossings of a racial frontier.* Stanford, CA: Stanford University Press.

Petersen, W. (1966a, January 9). Success story, Japanese American style. *New York Times*, pp. 20–21, 33, 36, 38, 40–41, 43.

Petersen, W. (1966b, December 26). Success story of one minority in the U.S. *U.S. News and World Report*, pp. 73–78.

Petersen, W. (1970). Success story, Japanese American style. In M. Kurokawa (Ed.), *Minority responses* (pp. 169–178). New York: Random House.

Rifkin, A. (1993, September). Asian women L.A. men. *Buzz*, pp. 73–112.

Rohrlick, J., Alvarado, D., Zaruba, K., & Kallic, R. (1998, May). *From the model minority to the invisible minority: Asian & Pacific American students in higher education research.* Paper presented at the Annual Forum of the Association for Institutional Research, Minneapolis, MN.

Tajima, R. E. (1989). Lotus blossoms don't bleed: Images of Asian women. In Asian Women United of California (Eds.), *Making waves: An anthology of writings by and about Asian American women* (pp. 308–317). Boston: Beacon.

Vargas, L. (1999). When the "other" is the teacher: Implications of teacher diversity in higher education. *The Urban Review, 31*, 359–383.

Wee, V. (1990). *Body and self: The politics of sex and "race" in Singapore.* Paper presented at the International Workshop on the Construction of Gender and Sexuality in East and Southeast Asia, Los Angeles, CA.

Woo, D. (1989). The gap between striving and achieving: The case of Asian American women. In Asian Women United of California (Eds.), *Making waves: An anthology of writings by and about Asian American women* (pp. 185–194). Boston: Beacon.

Woo, D. (2000). The inventing and reinventing of model minorities: The cultural veil obscuring structural sources of inequality. In T. Fong & L. Shinagawa (Eds.), *Asian Americans: Experiences and perspectives* (pp. 193–212). Upper Saddle River, NJ: Prentice Hall.

WITHIN THE "SAFE HAVEN" OF WOMEN'S STUDIES

A Thai Female Faculty's Reflection on Identity and Scholarship

Piya Pangsapa

A s a young female scholar from a third world country, educated primarily in the United States, my experiences in the (Western) academy have been rather unique. By "unique," I am referring to my location in the interdisciplinary department of women's studies, a small department of only women professors. Being in the company of other minority female scholars, without the presence of men, has allowed me to freely pursue, explore, and share my research interests and my scholarship with my colleagues and predominantly female students, all the while being able to "circumvent" the usual gender barriers. Applying a grounded feminist approach in research and pedagogy, I am able to openly embrace and engage in multiple discourses while fulfilling the college's mission of interdisciplinarity across the social sciences and humanities. My fluency in both my native tongue and in English further shields me from the stigma of language and communication in the classroom. Not having to overcome linguistic and cultural barriers, I seem to embody two identities—the "foreigner" and the "native."

In this essay, I will talk about the contributions of Asian female scholars to women's studies, our approach to research and pedagogy as a truly transformative aspect of this interdisciplinary field, and I will reflect upon my own experiences as a third world feminist scholar situated within the marginal but "legitimate" space of "women's studies" in a Western academic institution. I conclude by discussing Asian feminist scholars' radical ability to transform traditional models of thinking and learning through their scholarship and teaching as made possible by their location in women's studies. Given the increasingly corporatized structure of higher education, third world women scholars are able to work against the grain of mainstream academia and uphold the integrity of critical research while resisting appropriation of her intellectual space. Thus our role as radical educators helps to shape and define this unique academic discipline. I posit that women's studies is an emerging academic discipline where Asian female scholars are engaged in the production of new knowledges and are committed to social change and transformation. Our quest to bridge the gap between theory and practice in a discipline that addresses the configurations of oppression, exploitation, and subordination further fortifies our status and visibility in higher education. As such, I argue that this interdisciplinary space allows Asian female scholars to attain their voice and visibility in the academy as demonstrated by the growing contributions of Asian female scholars. Removed from the rigid and circumscribed spaces of traditional disciplines, Asian female scholars benefit from an academic space that naturally allows for openness and inclusiveness of the "other."

We simply cannot ignore the considerable presence of Asian women throughout institutions of higher learning and the significant scholarly contributions made by them to their respective fields and to the discipline of women's studies. The diverse array of their scholarly contributions emanating from their positionality in women's studies further demonstrates how women's studies is a field that empowers women and allows minority female scholars to flourish and address the many critical issues they consider to be imperative. In this regard, women's studies is a place where Asian scholars are making a difference and making a safe haven for academic research and publication that may not have been possible within disciplinary boundaries and/or in male-dominated academic fields and spaces. The time has come for us to offer a telling of our own stories and it is only fitting that this collected volume intends to highlight and celebrate the struggles and achievements of Asian female scholars in higher education. By the same token, it is time for the disciplines to recognize our contributions and our potential as role models to Asian women everywhere, especially through our research and continuing activist commitments inside and outside the academy.

Asian Female Scholars and Their Scholarly Contributions

According to Mohanty (2003), women's studies evolved alongside other interdisciplinary programs such as Black and ethnic studies. The first women's studies program was set up at San Diego State University in 1969 (p. 198). Women's studies can therefore be traced to the tumultuous period of the sixties during the rise of the women's liberation, civil rights, and antiwar movements, and other oppositional struggles that drew in a large segment of ethnic minorities. The subversive nature of its past might explain why women's studies departments figure prominently at large, top-ranking, public research universities rather than at private, ivy league institutions. Currently, there are only a handful of universities in the United States that offer a doctorate degree in women's studies.[1]

Many prominent minority faculty members in women's studies are tenured professors who chair and direct programs or departments at large research institutions, sometimes in conjunction with other minority studies programs such as African, Asian, and Latino/Chicano studies. Women studies core and affiliate faculty are by and large feminist scholars who hold degrees in the social sciences or humanities with areas of specialization ranging from cultural and media studies to law and public policy. Other areas of specialization include labor studies; immigration; social policies; gay, lesbian and queer studies; literature; female sexuality; social movements; postcolonial studies; and legal theory. Additionally, several large women's studies departments benefit from the generous support and resources of affiliated gender institutes and centers devoted to feminist research such as the Center for Research on Women and Social Justice at the University of California, Santa Barbara; the Institute for Women's Leadership, the Center for American Women and Politics, and the Center for Women's and Gender Studies at the University of Texas–Austin; the Center for Women's Global Leadership, the Center for Women and Work, and the Institute for Research on Women at Rutgers University; the Center for the Study of Women at UCLA; the Center for Feminist Research at the University of Southern California; the Consortium on Race, Gender, and Ethnicity at the University of Maryland–College Park; the Center for Advanced Feminist Studies at the University of Minnesota; the Center for the Study of Women and Society at

---

[1] Numbering about ten: Claremont Graduate University, Clark Atlanta University, UCLA, Emory University, University of Iowa, University of Maryland–College Park, University of Minnesota–St. Paul, Rutgers University, Ohio State University–Columbus, and University of Washington–Seattle.

City University of New York; and the Institute on Research and Education on Women and Gender at the University at Buffalo. An overview of these centers and institutes and their proposed research areas demonstrates the discipline's pursuit of collaborative research.

More broadly, women's studies programs set out to deepen our understanding of the differences between the lived experiences of women along the intersections of race, ethnicity, class, and nationality, and to question how women's lives are changing in the context of the new global economy. Boxer (1998) indicates that "a major effort in broadening the scope of women's studies has come from 'a group of Third World' women including women born in the West with roots in Africa, Asia, and Latin America, indigenous North American women, and recent immigrants—who associate themselves with postcolonialism" (p. 109). Their impact on the discipline coalesced at an international conference at the University of Illinois in 1983 under the title, "Common Differences: Third World Women and Feminist Perspectives." Today, the discipline of women's studies embraces a broad spectrum of academic feminist scholars from a diverse array of nationalities, races, and ethnicities. Several well-established women's studies departments have in residence distinguished Asian female scholars as part of their core faculty (e.g., Professor Inderpal Grewal at the University of California–Irvine; Associate Professors Laura Hyun Yi Kang and Kavita Philip at the University of California–Irvine; Associate Professor Priti Ramamurthy at the University of Washington, Seattle; Associate Professor Seung-kyung Kim at the University of Maryland–College Park; Assistant Professor Grace Chang at the University of California–Berkeley; Assistant Professor Rhacel Parrenas at the University of Wisconsin–Madison; Assistant Professor Meena Khandelwal at the University of Iowa; and Assistant Professor Jigna Desai at the University of Minnesota).

The aforementioned scholars have made some very important contributions to the fields of sociology, anthropology, comparative literature, and gender, ethnic, and labor studies with publications that have been nationally and internationally recognized. Activist Miriam Ching Yoon Louie's book, *Sweatshop Warriors: Immigrant Women Workers Take on the Global Factory*, tells the stories of sweatshop workers struggling for better living and working conditions; writer and activist Grace Chang published her book on *Disposable Domestics: Immigrant Women Workers in the Global Economy*; Rhacel Parrenas's book, *Servants of Globalization: Women, Migration and Domestic Work*, examines the lives of Filipina domestic workers in Italy and the United States; Kamala Kempadoo, who teaches women's studies at the University of

Colorado, published an edited volume with activist and researcher, Jo Doezema, *Global Sex Workers: Rights Resistance, and Redefinition*, that presents the stories of sex workers from around the world; and Seung-Kyung Kim documents the lives of female factory workers in Korea in her book, *Class Struggle or Family Struggle? The Lives of Women Factory Workers in South Korea*. In the areas of postcolonial studies, cultural studies, and transnational feminism, several established South Asian female scholars have also made significant contributions to their respective fields. A list of recent publications include *Home and Harem Nation, Gender, Empire and the Cultures of Travel* by Inderpal Grewal; *Scattered Hegemonies: Postmodernity and Transnational Feminist Practices*, edited by Inderpal Grewal and Caren Kaplan; *Civilizing Natures: Race, Resources, and Modernity in Colonial South India* by Kavita Philip; *Women in Ochre Robes: Gendering Hindu Renunciation* by Meena Khandelwal; and *Beyond Bollywood: The Cultural Politics of South Asian Diasporic Film* by Jigna Desai.

Professor Inderpal Grewal's work encompasses areas of transnational feminist theories, cultural studies, British nineteenth-century studies, and South Asia and its diaspora. Professor Laura Hyun Yi Kang, who teaches women's studies and comparative literature, specializes in feminist epistemologies and theories and cultural and ethnic studies and has written about Asian/American women and writings of Korean Americans. Professor Kavita Philip's research centers on science and technology studies, race, gender, and postcolonialism. Professor Priti Ramamurthy is a member of the South Asia Center and her research interests include transnational feminisms and feminist critiques of international economic development, consumption, and commodity cultures. Professor Seung-Kyung Kim's research focuses on women and work, Asian and Asian American women, anthropology of gender, labor organizing, and the feminist movement in Korea. Professor Grace Chang's areas of study include women of color, immigrant women, globalization studies, and social justice movements. Professor Rhacel Parrenas teaches women's studies and Asian American studies. Professor Meena Khandelwal, also a faculty member in anthropology, teaches Introduction to the Study of Culture and Society, Gender and the Indian Diaspora, and Feminist Anthropological Theory. And Professor Jigna Desai's research interests include postcolonial, queer, and diasporic cultural studies, and the significance and function of popular Hindi cinema. In addition to their scholarly contributions, Asian women scholars have made a tremendous impact on learning in the classroom. In the following section, I will talk about some of my own experiences of teaching as it relates to being situated in women's studies and how Asian female scholars are able to uphold their activist commitments precisely through their unique positionality in the academy.

Our Approach to Pedagogy

"Women's Studies is a place where I can pursue my activist politics and my scholarly endeavors," states Seung-kyung Kim, a scholar from South Korea who is an associate professor of women's studies at the University of Maryland.[2] Two of her colleagues share similar views about being in a women's studies department: "The interdisciplinary character of the women's studies department has broadened my perspective and approach to teaching and research,"[3] says Professor and Chair Bonnie Thornton Dill. "At UM, our community of women of color scholars provides a setting where ideas are respected. This enables us to intellectually and spiritually engage in issues that have an impact on the lives of people,"[4] reflects Professor A. Lynn Bolles. My own feelings about being in women's studies echo exactly the sentiments expressed above. In many ways, I feel very much at home and at ease in a niche where I feel I can experiment with new research ideas and methods, and not have to doubt ethical and political commitments that include the commitment to present the plight of women from third world countries and to communicate their experiences as part of local and global struggles of women. Women's studies occupies a legitimate space where concerns and issues can be raised and debated with colleagues and students. Perhaps my contribution might have carried less weight had I been situated in a larger department where there were more male faculty members present, and where I would be only one among many young untenured scholars. At least in a small but growing department, I have the constant support of my senior colleagues, who are always willing to offer advice and guidance and who would like to see their junior colleagues secure tenure.

At State University of New York at Buffalo (UB), I have been able to coalesce my activism and scholarship through a variety of channels. As an Asian feminist scholar, my research focuses on poor, working-class women in developing Asian countries. In my undergraduate classes, for example, I introduce students to documentary films that look at the situation of work-

---

[2] www.womensstudies.umd.edu/people.htm.
[3] www.womensstudies.umd.edu/people.htm.
[4] www.womensstudies.umd.edu/people.htm.

ing women in Asia, and that examine the effects of international monetary institutions on local people and economies.[5] At the end of my second semester at UB, I organized a public screening with the "UB Students Against Sweatshops" group of an award-winning film, *Behind the Labels: Garment Workers on US Saipan* (2001), that reveals the situation of Chinese and Filipina women who work in garment factories on the Pacific island of Saipan. While carrying out fieldwork for my dissertation in Thailand, I worked in cooperation with local and regional workers unions and labor rights groups that were investigating labor violations at subcontracting factories. Here at UB, I find myself surrounded not only by a socially committed network of feminist educators, but also by a vocal group of students in women's studies who are actively involved in both campus politics and community activism.

Our approach to pedagogy is therefore one truly transformative aspect of this interdisciplinary field, and in this sense, I believe that Asian female scholars who are affiliated with women's studies at their institutions have made and continue to make a great impact in the classroom. In this regard, women's studies is a "safe haven" not only for Asian women but for other women of color whose work espouses principles of social equality and justice and who, as scholars and educators, can effect change and make their voices heard under this framework of interdisciplinarity. I feel that I am able to uphold my activist commitments through my work and scholarship without being perceived as a "threat," however accommodating. As Mohanty (2003) asserts, women's studies makes up precisely these "new analytic spaces that have been opened up in the academy, spaces that make possible thinking of knowledge as praxis, of knowledge as embodying the very seeds of transformation and change" (p. 195). That these spaces function within existing structures of knowledge and have been appropriated by the institution, only further strengthens its theoretical foundations and purported discourse. Women's studies therefore presents one major venue in which Asian feminist scholars can engage and pursue their goals while working against the grain of mainstream academia. Mohanty (2003) writes,

---

[5] *Dolls and Dust* (1998) documents the impact of industrial restructuring and globalization on women workers in Sri Lanka, Thailand, and South Korea with additional footage from Japan, Hong Kong, and China. *Life and Debt* (2001) looks at the stories of individual Jamaicans in the context of structural adjustment policies and free trade. *Working Women of the World* (2000) looks at relocation of garment production from Western countries to nations such as Indonesia, the Philippines, and Turkey. *Chain of Love* (2001) looks at Filipina domestic migrant workers and the effects of their migration on their families and the families they work for.

> By their very location in the academy, fields such as women's studies are grounded in definitions of difference, difference that attempts to resist incorporation and appropriation by providing a space for historically silenced peoples to construct knowledge. These knowledges have always been fundamentally oppositional, while running the risk of accommodation and assimilation and consequent depoliticization in the academy. (p. 195)

The strategic positioning of women's studies within the arts and sciences, based upon its epistemological approach to research and teaching, gives it a strong footing within the academy. It is in this sanctuary or "safe haven" that female minority scholars can indeed grow as they maintain their commitment to social activism while being able to combine theory with practice.

In her discussion of pedagogies of accommodation and dissent, Mohanty raises the important issue of how an educator from a non-Western part of the world should teach about the West in its relation to other countries. I feel that Asian female scholars, precisely because of their non-U.S./Western origins, are able to negotiate the ways in which they teach so as not to privilege one perspective over the other, but rather to encourage different ways of thinking about the world. For Mohanty, a feminist scholar from South Asia, education should be liberating for the student and the teacher. In my few years of teaching, I have found that students in my classes from other fields of study such as psychology, business, engineering, pre-law, medicine, and so forth, feel somewhat liberated from the more rigid structures of their majors that provide clear and straightforward guidelines for achieving success in their specializations. Students often tell me how they have truly benefited from women's studies courses that compel them to think about how things are and why they are approached in a certain way. In this regard, women's studies has the ability to radically transform the traditional models of thinking and learning within the academy. This pedagogical approach is part and parcel of the process of politicization and conscientization that transcends "the usual systematic forms of spreading knowledge" (Mohanty, 2003, p. 201).

Because women's studies is fundamentally multidisciplinary in its approach to teaching and learning, we help students understand that there are substantive relations, for instance, between political science and literature, economics and anthropology, and sociology and public policy. And even though some women's studies courses are taken to fulfill general education requirements, they should not be equated with the standardized curriculum of gen-ed courses offered at the undergraduate level. *What distinguishes women's studies courses lies in the discipline's unique approach to knowledge and learning, an approach that always considers the broader historical context along the intersections of gender, race, and class, and requires students to question and reflect upon any idea, concept, or definition that is introduced.*

As Mohanty (2003) points out, "feminist pedagogy has always recognized the importance of experience in the classroom" (p. 200). The courses I offer in women's studies cover a wide range of women's experiences in different localities. I also use in my classes a wide range of documentary films on women. Hence, the form and content of my courses fulfill and embody the mission of an interdisciplinary program of study in a department whose scholars are committed to social change and transformation. As Mohanty (2003) writes, "the academy and the classroom . . . are also political and cultural sites that represent accommodation and contestations over knowledge by differently empowered social constituencies" (p. 194).

My Experiences at UB

Given that the overall objective of my courses is to introduce students to problems facing women in developing countries, I try to look for other perspectives within which to introduce topics about women in my classes. Nevertheless, the texts I continue to use in the classroom are researched and written largely by third world feminist scholars (such as those mentioned previously) from the perspective of third world women. The opening to the "other" and different ways of looking at the world from dominant perspectives is an essential component of my approach. While some women's studies classes focus on U.S. history and issues, I focus on third world countries in order to introduce the "other" through third world issues. A constant challenge I find in teaching, especially at the undergraduate level, is how to make such topics (e.g., women and work, women's roles in social movements) "relevant" to and for American students in such a way that does not objectify the "other." Students should not leave the classroom feeling that what they are learning are "foreign," "far away," or "distant." Rather they should leave the classroom feeling that they have a better understanding of how their lives intersect with the lives of women in other parts of the world and this is achieved by bringing the "otherness" "home" through the linking of local and global struggles. And it is through the research contributions of Asian female scholars that allow students to make these interconnections. In this regard, women's studies may be one of the very few intellectual "spaces" within the academy where Asian women scholars can bring up challenging social issues and debate freely and fearlessly.

The women's studies department at the University at Buffalo offers courses in three clusters: cultures and identities, women and global citizenship, and gender and public policy, each of which recognizes developing trends in the studies of women in Asia, Africa, the Caribbean, Latin America, Europe, and the United States. Formerly a program in the Department of American Studies, it is fairly new as a free-standing academic department even though the program has been in existence at the university for over thirty years. I was instantly drawn to an interdisciplinary department because I knew I would be in the company of female educators who had different areas of specialization but who were devoted to interdisciplinary feminist scholarship. One of the most encouraging aspects of being in such a department was the free reign I was given to develop the kinds of courses I felt should be offered at both the undergraduate and graduate levels, thus allowing me to help strengthen and anchor the social sciences component in women's studies. Moreover, upon my arrival at UB, I was asked to join the Asian studies program as an affiliate faculty member.

I identify myself as a feminist researcher, activist, teacher, and scholar, and I would communicate these significations to my students through the content of my courses. On the first day of class, I would introduce myself as a Thai national who conducts research on Thai women. Students are initially surprised by my "American" accent and immediately inquire about my upbringing and educational background. In a way, I simultaneously embody both the non-Western "other" (foreigner) and perhaps also the "Asian American" (native), simply by virtue of being bilingual. Soon, my Americanness, as evidenced in my mannerisms and speech, seemingly overrides any Thai-ness I try to project as I teach about women workers in Thailand and in other developing countries. I usually find myself throwing in Thai expressions and colloquialisms from time to time as I feign forgetfulness of common English ones just to remind my students of my native tongue. Perhaps my proficiency in both languages lends a certain kind of currency to my authority and credibility in the classroom, especially when I initiate debates and criticisms of Western values and ideologies from "third world" perspectives. I have found that students, the overwhelming majority of them women, are immediately drawn to my own research work and are genuinely interested in learning more about women in other cultures. As the foreign, nonnative "outsider" located within the American academy, I have been able to import my native "insider" Thai experiences and expertise into my classrooms and into my scholarship. At the same time however, this very positioning of my self as the Thai female foreign teacher in the American classroom can also be problematic. As Boxer (1998) cautions, "experience is no longer a sufficient basis for assertion of authority when personal histories are deconstructed and ideological components in identity formation are exposed" (p. 123). This is a critical issue to think about especially from the perspective of a female minority scholar whereby the privileging of one's own personal histories and experiences is unavoidable. While I remind my students of my identity as a Thai female scholar, I do so to complement my rigorous methods of analyses and by conveying my rigorous methods of analysis and interest in scholarship. The "image" I try to project is not that of the "token" foreigner but as an "other" interested in conveying and adding to the realm of studying the "difference" and "otherness" in order to open up the curiosity of students. In effect, students come to the realization that they should not tokenize or exoticize the "other" but learn to accept the otherness and learn from it. And this is facilitated first by my "identity" and second, by the interdisciplinary aspect of such a field as an important conveyor of knowledge. Given the nature of our research and the content and structure of our courses, I discuss in the following section how Asian female scholars are constantly negotiating and challenging the contours and boundaries of what is perceived to be a marginal space in the institution of higher learning.

Asian Feminist Scholars and the Academy

In her essay "Situating Feminist Dilemmas in Fieldwork," Diane Wolf (1996) raises the issue of access and negotiation in situations where the feminist researcher is forced to accommodate, through deception, in order to gain access to her female subjects (e.g., lying about one's marital status or one's class background for social acceptance and entry into rigidly structured societies). I would draw an analogy here to the constant negotiation that the Asian female educator must engage in not only within the classroom but as a member of the larger academic community. Wolf further notes that "there is now a great deal of research about women by women, but there is not much academic feminist research 'with' and 'for' women" (p. 3). She attributes this dilemma to the difficulties a feminist scholar faces upon exit from her research field and upon her reentry to the university where she is forced to consider the presentation of her end product in a way that is not too confrontational to the structure of academia or of the discipline, since her work will inevitably be judged by the institution and by her peers. Similarly, Jayati Lal (1996) reflects upon the acquiescent nature of feminist research that tends

to suppress the voices of our subjects, especially for young, untenured scholars who owe allegiance to their institutions and the powers that be. She
writes,

> the conditions under which we produce and labor as intellectuals tend to
> push us into being more accountable to The Academy than to the commu-
> nities we study. . . . The politics of the academy also makes students more
> accountable in the legitimate appropriation of new writing genres than
> those with more power. (p. 206)

Fully aware of the power relations that are in play within the academy,
I nonetheless feel that educators have found ways to maintain their political
commitments through their research work and through the empowering nature of the discipline upon students who are about to embark on their own
research projects. Furthermore, by highlighting a kind of path for openness
and inclusiveness can the various impediments to knowledge ever really be
removed (Said, 1997, p. 135). In this regard, third world feminist scholars in
women's studies can mark the pedagogical space that prepares new generations for a more interdependent world and understanding of global interconnections by making sure that the "other" is close and not far, that is,
difference without eliminating that difference or otherness.

Mohanty's critical analyses of the institutional and pedagogical practices
in the U.S. academy points to the increasingly corporatized structure of
higher education and the resulting tendency for minority scholars to accommodate their research and teaching to a neoliberal model of efficiency and
effectiveness. Mohanty (2003) extends her discussion to women's studies
classrooms and university-sponsored diversity workshops as sites of co-optation and assimilation that have "long term effects on the definition of identity and agency of nonwhite people in the academy" (p. 196). The third
world/minority scholar should therefore take precautions in how learning
and education are practiced and expressed in her classroom in such a way
that upholds the integrity of critical research while resisting appropriation of
her intellectual space. Mohanty (2003) further contends that "teaching practices must also combat the pressures of professionalization, normalization,
and standardization" (p. 202) that come with the territory of higher education. This brings me back to the form and content of women's studies
courses and the discipline's unique areas of concentration that draw upon
the concepts of social inequality, racism, sexism, and classism. In this regard,
Asian female scholars have indeed been able to deliberately and effectively

voice and address their concerns as they recognize that universities have no choice but to respond to the demand for such programs. Co-optation and accommodation notwithstanding, one need only take a look at the undergraduate and graduate catalogs of courses offered in women's studies and at the vast proliferation of critical feminist publications in recent years to appreciate the discipline's rich and broadly multicultural and interdisciplinary character and its location as a site open for "otherness" and as a site that is also a "safe haven."

Moreover, we continue to see more and more evidence of collaborative efforts among and between Asian scholars from different areas of interest, not only in the co-teaching of certain courses but in shared research projects in line with the discipline's objectives. The notion of interdisciplinarity is part and parcel of women's studies' overarching mission to enrich feminist scholarship, and this is achieved by fostering links to other academic departments in a concerted effort to broaden the knowledge base of feminist research and activism. Hopefully, this dynamic and constantly challenging topography will have an impact on and provide a conduit for the next generation of Asian educators, scholars, and activists in particular, precisely because of the nature of their research and methods of inquiry where "otherness" and openness to difference allows for a safe haven for both academic research and feminist pedagogy.

Conclusions

Women's studies is increasingly being regarded as an academic discipline and an intellectual space where new methodologies are constantly being devised and applied to women's lived experiences and are thus contributing to knowledge production. I see more advantages than disadvantages for Asian female scholars situated within such a field of study, where they have indeed been able to gain acceptance, respect, and visibility. In sum, the contributions of Asian female scholars to women's studies are considerable and significant. From the perspective of the third world/minority scholar, our role as committed researchers and activists lies in our relentless search for new theories and conceptual frameworks within which to address our practical concerns, that is, the struggle against oppression in relation to women's lived realities. As researchers, we adopt the conceptual and methodological tools from our respective fields such as Marxist sociology, critical sociology, historical and comparative sociology, and labor studies, to apply to the study of third world women with the hope of improving women's lives, which leads to further critical reflection and debate. As teachers, our approach to pedagogy is truly an aspect of this interdisciplinary field as we study and present as broad a range as possible of women's experiences across time and place, and situate these experiences historically and assess them using the most appropriate methods. Darder (2002) raises the issue of empowerment in pedagogical practices that is firmly embedded in a "political understanding of schooling as a permanent terrain of struggle, resistance, and transformation" (p. 61). We extend our aim to the classroom where we seek to invoke consciousness in our students through teaching. As such, Asian feminist scholars demonstrate a radical ability to transform traditional models of thinking and learning through their scholarship and teaching as made possible by their location in women's studies.

I feel that Asian female scholars in women's studies programs and departments will continue to play a vital and integral role within the academy even as they are situated within "the boundaries of conservative or liberal white-male dominated institutions" and "face questions of cooptation and accommodation" (Mohanty, 2003, p. 197). As a woman from Thailand, the space offered to me by women's studies has been a welcoming one, and I believe that other Asian female scholars from their own multiple positionalities would feel the same empowering potential that women's studies offers as it invites us to bring our expertise into and beyond the classroom and the academy. Lastly, I would like to make a point raised by Darder (2002) regarding Paulo Freire's conviction in the "rebuilding of solidarity among educators" (p. 41). As mentioned earlier, the strategic positioning of women's studies as an interdisciplinary program allows the multiple voices of "strangers"/"others" to be heard and making the "other" (and differences) part and parcel of modes of understanding. Having firmly anchored itself within colleges of arts and sciences, women's studies occupies a legitimate space, due in large part to Asian women scholars who have brought themselves together to shape and define this unique academic discipline. We see that the discipline has been able to attract a dynamic array of female scholars from across the humanities and social sciences, and that it has, in the process, been able to carve out a space where women faculty of color (foreign and U.S.) can be at the forefront of radical education. Women studies is here to stay, and its practitioners will continue to push the boundaries of social research from within the norms of the academy as it gradually moves away from the ascribed margins into the foreground of knowledge production. What we are doing is creating alternative channels for social inquiry and reshaping the limits of knowledge and learning. Burawoy, Burton, Ferguson, and Fox (1991) stress that, "people can sometimes go beyond a negotiated order and carve out spheres of self-organization" (p. 287). Here, Asian women scholars share a collective commitment to a liberal arts education with broad historical and international dimensions, and thereby are constantly forced to "question the legitimacy of the boundaries set by the system" (Chow, Zhang, & Wang, 2004, p. 182). We need to look at struggles and forms of resistance that are taking place, and view forms of domination and authority as contested bodies that will constantly be challenged and negotiated. To a certain extent, we all want to become established scholars whose work is respected, and we all want to be reminded that what we do is important and worthwhile. And while achieving this may require acquiescence to certain norms of the academy, we can remind ourselves that there is always room to maneuver, and we can appropriate our own spaces and fulfill our intellectual aspirations.

References

Boxer, M. J. (1998). *When women ask the questions: Creating women's studies in America*. Baltimore: Johns Hopkins University Press.

Burawoy, M., Burton, A., Ferguson, A. A., & Fox, K. J. (1991). *Ethnography unbound: Power and resistance in the modern metropolis*. Berkeley: University of California Press.

Chang, G. (2000). *Disposable domestics: Immigrant women workers in the global economy*. Cambridge, MA: South End Press.

Chow, E. N., Zhang, N., & Wang, J. (2004). Promising and contested fields: Women's studies and sociology of women/gender in contemporary China. *Gender & Society, 18*, 161–188.

Darder, A. (2002). *Reinventing Paulo Freire: A pedagogy of love*. Boulder, CO: Westview Press.

Desai, J. (2004). *Beyond Bollywood: The cultural politics of South Asian diasporic film*. New York: Routledge.

Gerwal, I. (1996). *Home and harem nation, gender, empire and the cultures of travel*. Durham: NC: Duke University Press.

Gerwal, I., & Kaplan, C. (Eds.). (1994). *Scattered hegemonies: Postmodernity and transnational feminist practices*. Minneapolis: University of Minnesota Press.

Kempadoo, K., & Doezema, J. (Eds.). (1998). *Global sex workers: Rights resistance and redefinition*. New York: Routledge.

Khandelwal, M. (2003). *Women in ochre robes: Gendering Hindu renunciation*. Albany, NY: SUNY Press.

Kim, S. (1997). *Class struggle or family struggle? The lives of women factory workers in South Korea*. Cambridge, U.K.: Cambridge University Press.

Lal, J. (1996). Situating locations: The politics of self, identity, and "other" in living and writing the text. In D. L. Wolf (Ed.), *Feminist dilemmas in fieldwork* (pp. 185–214). Boulder, CO: Westview Press.

Lessin, T. (2001). *Behind the labels: Garment workers on U.S. Saipan.* New York: Witness.

Louie, M. C. (2001). *Sweatshop warriors: Immigrant women workers take on the global factory.* Cambridge, MA: South End Press.

Mohanty, C. T. (2003). *Feminism without borders: Decolonizing theory, practicing solidarity.* Durham, NC, and London: Duke University Press.

Parrenas, R. S. (2001). *Servants of gloalization: Women, migration and domestic work.* Stanford, CA: Stanford University Press.

Philip, K. (2003). *Civilizing natures: Race, resources, and modernity in colonial south India.* New Brunswick, NJ: Rutgers University Press.

Said, E. (1997). *Covering Islam: How the media and the experts determine how we see the rest of the world.* New York: Vintage Books.

Wolf, D. L. (1996). Situating feminist dilemmas in fieldwork. In D. L. Wolf (Ed.), *Feminist dilemmas in fieldwork* (pp. 1–55). Boulder, CO: Westview Press.

11

BETWEEN THE WORLDS

Searching for a Competent Voice

Yan Guo

I was born in a suburb of Dalian, a metropolitan city in northern China. My mother was a nurse in a military hospital and my father was a technician. My parents were strong believers of Marxism/Leninism/Mao Zedong (Mao Tse-Tung) thought, which, among many other things, promote the sacrifice of oneself to the interests of the Communist Party and the nation. I will return to Marxism's influence on me later. We moved to a small village, my mother's hometown, in Shandong province in northern China when I was five. My father, originally from Sichuan province in southern China, speaks Chinese with a strong Sichuan accent. Local people often laugh at his accent and he is always frustrated. When I was little, I asked my father: "Why can't you speak like the rest of us?" Today, I live in Calgary, Alberta, Canada. I speak English with a Chinese accent. My accent is derided, and my writing is questioned.

The primary purpose in writing this chapter is to help myself regain confidence in second language writing. I was trained to be an English teacher in China. I taught English majors in a Chinese university for about three years upon completion of my master's in English language and literature. I then went to pursue a second master's in English literature at the University of Regina, Canada. In 2002, I successfully completed my doctorate in Teaching

I would like to thank Gulbahar H. Beckett, Guofang Li, Ling Shi, Tammy Slater, Jérémie Séror, and Sandra Zappa-Hollman for their constructive comments for revision and their emotional support, without which this chapter would not have been published.

English as a Second Language (TESL) at the University of British Columbia (UBC). I am now working as an assistant professor at the University of Calgary, Canada. In this chapter, I explore my autobiographical self (Ivanič, 1998) by reflecting on my personal experience of learning to write in English. The chapter examines the process of how I, as a successful and confident writer in China, became an incompetent writer at the beginning of graduate school in Canada, of how I struggled to "appropriate voices" (Bakhtin, 1981), and eventually regained my confidence in English. Another purpose of this chapter is to explore and position myself, a nonnative TESL professional in an English-speaking environment. It describes how I struggled to create a hybrid identity in the process of learning to write in my second language. This process is guided by an underlying assumption that language can be seen as an act of identity and writing as giving voice to that identity (Ivanič, 1998). I take an antiessentialist view of identity, that is, identity is not a fixed personality trait that is independent of the social context, but is socially constructed (Hall, 1991; Norton Peirce, 1995; Papastergiadis, 2000; Toohey, 2000). Rather than locating identity in fixed binaries—the polarities of Chinese and Canadian in my case—identity may be conceived as "an ongoing process of hybridity, in which one's sense of self is continuously made and re-made" (Pryer, 2003). This recognition permits me to actively construct, negotiate, and transform the sense of self on an ongoing basis by means of language, my second language (Duff & Uchida, 1997). This chapter is also written to fill a gap that Braine (2002) identified as lacking in second language writing research: the authentic voices of nonnative graduate students.

Liu (2001) argues that "writing is a skill: the more you practice it, the better your writing is" (p. 130). To me, writing is not only a skill, but also a social practice. According to Cumming (1998), the word "writing" refers not only to text in written script but also to the acts of thinking, composing, and encoding language into such text; these acts also necessarily entail discourse interactions within a sociocultural context. Therefore, learning to write academically is not only a matter of mastering writing skills, it is also a process of becoming socialized into the academic discourse community (Casanave, 1992; Spack, 1997). This belief about writing derives from the social constructionist approach, best represented by Vygotsky's theories, especially his emphasis on the dialogic and intertextual nature of literacy (see Johns, 1990, for details).

To me, writing is also a process of self-construction. Learning to write in a second language is related to identity—how I see myself and am seen by others as a graduate student, as a writer, and as an English as a Second Language (ESL) teacher educator (e.g., Harklau, 2000). For a graduate student, learning to write in English is a long process of creating a second language writer's identity in the academic community. Ivanič (1998) maintains that:

> Writing is an act of identity in which people align themselves with socio-culturally shaped possibilities for self-hood, playing their part in reproducing or challenging dominant practices and discourses, and the values, beliefs and interests which they embody. (p. 32)

Ivanič suggests there are three ways of thinking about a writer's identity. They are, first, the autobiographical self: What aspects of people's lives might have led them to write in the way that they do? Second, the discoursal self: What are the discourse characteristics of particular pieces of writing? Third, the self as author: How do people establish authority for the content of their writing? The autobiographical self captures the idea that "it is not only the events in people's lives, but also the way of representing these experiences to themselves which constitutes their current way of being" (p. 24). Furthermore, from a post-structuralist perspective, identity is not an individualized practice; it is "multiple, a site of struggle and subject to change" (Norton Peirce, 1995, p. 9). From this stance, second language writing is seen as a social practice. The sense of self I present in this chapter is influenced by how institutions position second language writers like me and how we resist, accommodate, and reshape those positionings (Benesch, in press; Matsuda, Canagarajah, Harklau, Hyland, & Warschauer, 2003). In this chapter, I chose to explore events and people that have affected my second language writing. I also chose to use narrative to construct my self because I am the authority for the content of my writing: my journey of second language writing.

I also write for both native English speakers and nonnative speakers. As is apparent throughout the chapter, I stretch the genre of literacy autobiography (Connor, 1999) and take more creative risks than I have normally in academic writing. As Dias, Freedman, Medway, and Paré (1999) argue, genres can often be constraining and limiting, but they can also be potential spaces for identity transformation and learning:

> We need to argue also for the potentialities of genres for creating spaces for forming and realizing new versions of self as one discovers new motives and transforms the self in response to the new communicative needs and opportunities. (p. 21)

I use the "opportunity space" (a phrase Dias et al. [1999, p. 21] attribute to Bazerman) available to me to experiment by blending literacy autobiography and my readings in second language education. Although what I will describe is based on personal experience, many international graduate students I talked to said that some of the things that I had to go through resonated with them. Given the fact that more than 17 percent of graduate students in Canada were international students (Canadian Bureau for International Education, 2002), educators of these students need to take into account cultural, linguistic, and social factors in teaching and learning in response to student diversity. I hope my autobiographical reflections will help educators to better address the sociocultural, rhetorical, and linguistic differences (Silva, 1993) of international graduate students in their second language writing on the one hand and inspire international graduate students to value their multiplicity of languages and cultures on the other.

Confident Chinese Self

I started to learn English when I was thirteen in China in the late '70s. This was a period when the ten-year Cultural Revolution was over and China started to open its doors to new and foreign things and ideas. One example of this was the introduction of English as a compulsory subject in middle school (grades seven to nine). I was motivated to learn English because at that time I wanted to be an ambassador and to travel around the world. I still remember how our school principal walked into our classroom on the first day of our English class and said: "By now you already know how well you will do in subjects such as math, chemistry, and Chinese. Today you will start a new subject, English. It is a blank page. You can do whatever you want with it. You can fly!" I took his metaphor of flying literally and fell in love with English on my first day. I wanted to learn English so that I could fly to many countries in the world.

Writing was the last skill I learned after listening, reading, and speaking. Honestly, I cannot remember if I was taught how to write in English in high school. The purpose of writing was to get high marks on exams and eventually become successful on the national university entrance exam. As an English major at the university, I was introduced to the five-paragraph essay format in my composition course, including different types such as narration, description, classification, cause-effect, and argumentation. I loved writing in English. My essays were often considered the best in my class. My English composition teacher would comment in class on the strength of my writing and would ask my fellow students to reflect on and improve their own writing using my essays as models. My classmates also borrowed my essays to read and told me how much they enjoyed my writing. As such, I was a confident writer.

I did very well when I wrote my master's thesis in China. My topic was the quest for self in three novels by Doris Lessing. I had two Chinese professors as cosupervisors of my thesis, and one American professor on my committee. The two Chinese professors had studied at the Beijing Foreign Language Institute, the most prestigious foreign language university in the country. They also worked as visiting scholars in the United States and Canada. They were all well-respected scholars. One of my cosupervisors, Professor Zixiu Li, who had edited several books, edited my thesis carefully, from vocabulary, to grammar, and on to content. My American professor had a doctorate in American literature. He and I had many heated discussions about the concept of self. He strongly argued for a Western sense of an independent self in contrast with others. He also showed a great interest in learning the historical and cultural meanings of the relational self in Chinese philosophy. Chinese self is always embedded within social and cultural networks (Tung, 2000; Wang, 2004). I felt that I could augment my supervisor's understanding of self despite the fact that I was a student. In the process of writing my thesis, I learned the importance of highlighting my own interpretations of the literary texts and supporting my arguments with examples from the texts and from other literary critics. My analytical and writing abilities had earned me a position in the university where I completed my master's.

In the university, I taught a variety of courses such as intensive reading, extensive reading, listening, speaking, grammar, British literature, and American literature. I also taught composition. In that course, I taught the rules of English composition. For instance, I taught my students that a good English essay normally includes a topic sentence, a thesis statement, at least three supporting ideas, and a conclusion. I was well loved by my students. I also wrote for publication. One of my articles, "Cynthia Ozik's View on Writing," was published by *Trends of Foreign Literature*, a journal of the Foreign Literature Institute, Academy of Social Sciences of China (Guo, 1987). It is the most prestigious journal in foreign language and literature in China.

At that time identity was not an issue for me. Unlike Lu (1987) who struggled between two discourses, a mainstream Marxist discourse at school and a Western humanistic discourse at home that her parents wanted her to learn in China, I was brought up on only one discourse—the Mao Zedong/Marxist discourse (e.g., Shen, 1989). This means that I analyzed English literature from a class perspective, often from the struggle between the proletariat and the bourgeoisie, like the one I did with Charlotte Brontë's *Jane Eyre* in the example in the next section. In my English writing I used "we" instead of "I" (Shen, 1989) because I believed that collectivism is better than individualism. I came to English writing with a strong Chinese identity. I took pride in being a Marxist, a successful learner, a competent teacher, and Chinese.

Chinese Self Repels English Self: Crash Landing in Canada

Everything changed after I came to study as an international student at the University of Regina in Canada. I was somebody in China, and now suddenly I had become a nobody. Like many other well-established Chinese professors, I had to start all over again (e.g., Hirvela & Belcher, 2001). I was accepted into a master's program in English on the condition that I would take several undergraduate courses. I had to get at least 80 percent in each course I took before I was officially allowed to take graduate courses.

My confidence as a writer was totally destroyed by my first professor, Dr. Smith (pseudonym) in Canada. I was taking eighteenth-century English literature, one of my favorites in China. I ran into conflicts with Dr. Smith in every essay I submitted. My essays were said to be "strange," "illogical," and "socialist." Every time my essay was returned, I went to see Dr. Smith during his office hours. I tried to explain how my essay was normal, logical, and valid. For example, in one essay, I cited a famous Chinese writer, Mao Dun, to argue for the preconditions of creative writing. I wrote: "Only when you are as humble as bamboo, as perseverant as cattlehide, as passionate as fire, then you will be able to create a true art." Dr. Smith commented that there was no connection between humbleness and bamboo. I tried to explain to him that in Chinese culture there is a connection. Bamboo is always a beautiful image in Chinese paintings, and a beautiful metaphor in Chinese writing, because it usually supports other flowers and plants. It does not want to dominate the picture. Moreover, it stands strong to face the cold wind. Sometimes it is forced to bend, but it never gives up. In a sense bamboo represents the humbleness and perseverance of good Chinese character. Dr. Smith dismissed my explanation and asked me to write a metaphor that an English reader would understand. In another essay I passionately praised Jane Eyre's challenge to the injustice of the bourgeoisie. At the same time I felt sorry for her because she invariably found her fulfillment in being married to a dominant man of wealth and/or of social position, thus revealing the impossibility for women to achieve genuine freedom or independence in the capitalist society. Dr. Smith regarded it as "poor writing," and writing from a "Communist perspective." Unaware of the social stigma attached to Communism in Western society, I argued there was nothing wrong with a Communist perspective, the one I was brought up with. I remember I was angry before our meetings and furious afterward. He was not convinced and I refused to give in.

Consequently I got a very low mark for the course, the lowest in my entire schooling history. I was traumatized with embarrassment. At that time I was not able to articulate what had gone wrong, and I wanted to quit the program. Casanave (1992) reports that a Hispanic woman, Virginia, withdrew from her Ph.D. program in sociology because she refused to participate in a process that required the use of the kind of academic discourse that was adopted by the powerful and prestigious White male group. Unlike Virginia, I blamed myself for my incompetence. I felt I was excluded from class discussion not because I was a shy Chinese but because of the alien topics covered in the course. I used to be an active speaker, but now, most of the time I could not understand my professor's and classmates' jokes, and could not tell when Dr. Smith was talking about content and when he was digressing. I was silent in most of the classroom discussions because silence protected me from humiliation. I thought, if I spoke it would confirm my differences and othernesses (Duff, 2002; Losey, 1997; Morita, 2002). Occasionally I had the courage to speak in class, but my professor and classmates ignored my comments. I felt that my knowledge, my history, and my accent were being devalued (Kumar, 2002) because when I did speak, my classmates and my professor only showed their impatience. After I spoke, there was usually dead silence, and then the others quickly moved on to topics with which they felt more comfortable. However, in my writing, even though my unique ideological and sociopolitical stance "made no sense to or would not be accepted" (Hamp-Lyons & Zhang, 2001) by Dr. Smith, I refused to be silenced. Behind my oral silence in public, I actively negotiated my positioning in my writing.

Looking back, I still blame Dr. Smith for his insensitivity toward and ignorance of the Chinese ways of thought and expression. Watkins and Biggs (1996) note the negative aspects of uncritically applying Western concepts and methods to a non-Western learner: "When Confucian-heritage culture people are viewed through the lenses of familiar western polarities, the focus becomes blurred and even distorted" (p. 270). Fortunately, not all the professors were as narrow-minded as Dr. Smith. In the third course I took, Professor Dobson (pseudonym) was a caring teacher and mentor. He suggested that I read background information to broaden my understanding of the short stories on his reading list. He also offered feedback on both the content and form of my writing, and allowed me to write multiple drafts before my assignments were due. I was very happy that he corrected my writing and explained why his rewrites were better than mine. More important, he was willing to accept my ideological positioning in my essays. Meanwhile I was also learning from examples by reading my classmates' A papers as well as actively participating in social activities that contributed to my oral fluency and confidence. In the end, one of my essays was selected as a model essay for class analysis. That was a moment of pride for me, given the fact that I was the only nonnative speaker in the class.

Nonetheless, I realize that my cultural background shaped—and shapes—my approaches to writing in English. Recently I was introduced to the article "The Classroom and the Wider Culture: Identity as a Key to Learning English Composition" by Fan Shen (1989). In this fascinating article, the author discusses how he struggled between his Chinese identity and English identity in the process of learning to write in English. His paper echoes many experiences that I have gone through in the past ten years. Writing in English, to borrow Shen's (1989) words, "redefined—and redefines—my ideological and logical identities" (p. 459). By "ideological identity" he means the system of values that he acquired from his social and cultural background. And by "logical identity" he means the Chinese way he organized his thoughts in writing. He explains how Chinese "pictorial logic," such as the bamboo metaphor I used in my essay, sounds illogical to western "verbal logic," and how the relational Chinese self (Wang, 2004) sounds strange to the independent western self (Hall & Ames, 1987). The process of "learning to write in English is in fact a process of creating and defining a new identity and balancing it with the old identity" (Shen, 1989, p. 466). While I kept nodding my head when I read Shen's article, I was disappointed by his idea that "to be truly 'myself,' which I knew was a key to my success in learning English composition, meant *not be my Chinese self* [emphasis in original] at all" (Shen, 1989, p. 461). I pondered: Do I need to erase my Chinese self in my English writing? Do I need to hide my Chinese self in order to be successful in an English-speaking society? Is it possible to draw strengths from both cultures and languages?

Validating Chinese Self with English Self: Claiming the Right to Speak

I took about ten undergraduate and graduate courses in English literature, but none of them were quite related to my personal experience. I did my assignments and sometimes got good marks. I was awarded with a university graduate scholarship, but the learning experiences were no longer exciting. I had always enjoyed reading and learning, but unlike my learning in China, the course work in my master's studies in Canada did not bring me happiness (Noddings, 2003). What was wrong?

By the time I had to decide on a topic for my master's thesis, I was searching for one that I could feel excited about, that I could speak about as an authority, and that could validate my Chinese identity. At the time I was staying at an education professor's house and therefore had opportunities to talk to her about my struggle. The professor recommended that I read Maxine Hong Kingston and Amy Tan, two Chinese American female writers. I did, and their writing fascinated me. In fact, I was so fascinated that I decided to write about mother/daughter relationships in three novels by Maxine Hong Kingston and Amy Tan. However, I encountered two challenges. One was that I had difficulty finding a professor who would be willing to supervise me on this topic. Some professors told me that the novels I chose were not considered literature, thus it was not a scholarly topic. Fortunately Dr. Nicolas Ruddick, who had emigrated from the United Kingdom, took me on.

Another challenge was that the library lacked the resources I needed. Most of the books and journal articles I requested came from the United States through interlibrary loan. Maxine Hong Kingston and Amy Tan were not on any course reading list, either, so my supervisor and I started to order, in his name, new resources for the library. Even at my oral defense, there were people who questioned the validity of my topic. I had to argue for its "legitimacy" (Bourdieu, 1977). Some people asked: "Is this English literature?" With a smile I replied: "Well, I believe it is high time for us to expand the notion of English literature to include literature written by minority authors, given the fact that North America is becoming more and more multicultural and multilingual." Secretly, I felt lucky to get this question because my supervisor and I discussed the issue before my oral defense.

Despite the difficulties, my master's thesis, "Heritages: Mother/Daughter Relationships in Three Novels by Chinese American Women" (Guo, 1995)—a seventy-nine-page literary analysis, was finished in a year's time. In the thesis I analyzed the conflicts and reconciliations between Chinese immigrant mothers and their daughters, and explored the factors that contributed to these conflicts and reconciliations. The following opening paragraph from chapter 2 provides an example of such an analysis:

> Amy Tan's first novel, *The Joy Luck Club* (1989) starts with a Chinese mother's beautiful dream for her American daughter. Ironically, though

> the American-born daughter does speak "only perfect American English" (p. 3), mother and daughter cannot communicate with each other, since they both literally and figuratively speak different languages. When one of the four daughters in the novel observes that "mother and I spoke two different languages . . . I talked to her in English, she answered back in Chinese" (p. 23), she speaks for all the Chinese mothers and their American-born daughters in the novel. In addition to the language barrier, the cultural chasm is a major cause of conflict between mother and daughter. While the mother holds fast to her traditional Chinese culture, her American-born daughter rejects it as she grows to adulthood. (Guo, 1995, p. 29)

The above example suggests a confident writer. But it was my mentor, Dr. Ruddick, who helped me convey such a confident voice (see Connor, 1999, for a similar experience). I selected the research topic and wrote many drafts. Dr. Ruddick read and reread all the chapters and commented on all the drafts. We spent many hours discussing his comments after he read each chapter. Perhaps because he was willing to listen to my opinions about the Chinese mothers in these novels, I was more willing to accept his suggestions about the content, organization, and mechanics of the thesis, more willing than I was with my first professor, Dr. Smith. Even though I was a novice in second language writing, I felt I was able to contribute to my mentor's understanding of the Chinese women in the novels in particular and of Chinese culture in general. There was a feeling of being respected.

I think one of the reasons I chose this topic was that I wanted to take a critical look at Chinese traditional culture and its impact on Chinese women. While discussing the conventional devaluation of women in traditional Chinese culture, I wanted to highlight an important message. That is, even though the Chinese mothers in the novels could not speak perfect English, like some immigrant parents, they struggled to pass on their *chi*, "a fundamental self-respect, a desire to excel, a willingness to stand up for one's self and one's family" (Shear, 1993, p. 197), to their American-born daughters. The Chinese heritage helped these daughters make peace with their ethnic identity: It is possible to have the best combination of American circumstances and Chinese character. Another reason I chose this topic could be that I missed my precious son, who was still with my parents in China at that time. The thesis was an expression of guilt on the part of a mother. I could not find a novel that explores the Chinese mother–son relationship, therefore I chose to explore the mother–daughter relationship. Deep down, I also wanted to challenge the canon of mainstream literature (Smith, 1996) and give Asian American literature a legitimate place in the department, informing Western educators with an insider's view of Chinese culture. At the same time I started to actively participate in classroom discussions, no longer afraid of my differences and othernesses. Like other adult immigrants, I wanted to claim my right to speak (Norton Peirce, 1995; Sharkey, Shi, Thompson, & Norton, 2003) and validate my Chinese self with my English self.

Hybridity of Chinese Self and English Self

After three years' struggle, I went to another prestigious Canadian university to pursue my Ph.D. I switched from the English department to the faculty of education because I was interested in research about the educational experience of immigrant children. In the past six years, I have learned the rules of the game, from doing literature reviews, to conducting educational research, writing research proposals, presenting at provincial, national, and international professional conferences, and writing a doctoral dissertation. For every single assignment, I had to consider the basic differences of writing conventions between a faculty of arts and a faculty of education. I have learned that an analysis of narrative technique, valued in the faculty of arts where I studied for my master's degree, is not valued as much in the faculty of education where I was pursuing my doctorate in the field of second language acquisition (SLA) research in general and Teaching English to Speakers of Other Languages (TESOL) in particular. I am pleased to see that recently many scholars in education have challenged such a notion (Blanton, 2003; Casanave, 2003; Connelly & Clandinin, 1990; Pavlenko, 2003; Sharkey et al., 2003). I remember that the first time I read articles published in *TESOL Quarterly*, I became suspicious of the long list of citations given in brackets in the literature reviews; I wondered if the author really read all these research papers/books. Eventually, I was socialized into the academic discourse of second language acquisition, and over the years learned to accept the conventions of TESOL in order to get good grades in my courses and to publish. As a result, I was no longer a timid peripheral participant. With the help of supportive peers and professors, I transformed myself into a legitimate participant in academia (Lave & Wenger, 1991). Writing in English is always a site of struggle. But struggle is not necessarily a bad thing. In the following sections I illustrate some of the struggles I have been through and how I used these struggles as sites of creativity.

One of the most painful struggles was that my credibility as a TESOL professional who is not a native English speaker has been challenged by my colleagues, classmates, and by my native and nonnative English-speaking students. For example, in her evaluation of a content-based ESL course I taught, one of my Japanese students wrote: "Yan is a good teacher. But she is a Chinese. We want to learn English from a native speaker." I was hurt by such a comment. Some Japanese ideologies legitimate the superiority of native speakers of English (Kubota, 1998). It is possible that, to this student, a Chinese woman appeared less legitimate as an English instructor than would an English native speaker. In another course I taught for a preservice teacher education program, four students dropped out of the course within the first two weeks. These students may have had other reasons for dropping the course, but since all four had Asian surnames such as Huang and Yamaguchi, I took their decision personally. I thought they dropped the course because it was being taught by an English-speaking Asian. Similar instances happened to other English-speaking Asian scholars whom I talked to. I felt these students never gave me a chance to show that I could teach what they needed to learn in the course.

My credibility as a language educator has also been challenged in hiring practices. Since I completed my doctorate in TESL at a prestigious Canadian university, I had been looking for a tenure-track position in a North American university. I have received numerous rejection letters. Even though I am not supposed to take these personally, I still blame myself for my inability to secure permanent employment (Mysyk, 2001). Meanwhile, as I was searching for temporary employment in language schools and colleges, this is one of the rejection messages I got:

> Using words like "terrific" and "fabulous," our Head Teachers told me you have an excellent knowledge of teaching and that they believe you are highly skilled. They also mentioned that your English is not quite perfect and gave me a number of examples.
>
> The model we present in our classrooms must be flawless. This is because we expect our students to form and test their hypotheses about the way English works against the authority of their teachers' use, and to otherwise base their acquisition on our faculty's precise model. I expect that your English is better than many native speakers, though as yet, it's not quite at the particularly high level we require of our teachers. We are proud of the few non-native teachers we do have and encourage you to contact us again once you've achieved that last step in your English.

I was angry when I received this message. My English "is not quite perfect." I wish I could ask the person who wrote the e-mail message, "Is your

English perfect?" Native speakers' communicative competence differs one from another and the language of a speech community is perceived as a standard not because the language is the most perfect, but because the community has power (Davies, 2003). I think there is an unwritten policy in these language schools: Nonnative speakers need not apply. My own experience and my Chinese friends' experiences in the past six years confirm the existence of such a discriminatory policy. One Chinese friend who takes her husband's English last name and has an atypical Chinese first name told me that interviewers were shocked to find out she is Chinese, given the fact that she has such an impressive curriculum vitae for jobs advertised in the TESOL field. These examples seemed to imply that to these employers, a Chinese speaking English as a second language should have no connection with an impressive curriculum vitae in TESOL.

On second thought, I asked myself: "Can my English ever be perfect?" I need to spend my entire life learning English (see Li, 1999; Tsai, 2001, for a similar point). Do I always have to look at my nonnativeness as a deficit? Do I see myself as an incompetent ventriloquist, or as a competent bilingual educator and scholar (Nieto, 2002)? How should I position myself? Kramsch (1997) asserts that native speakership is neither a privilege of birth nor of education, but "acceptance by the group that created the distinction between native and nonnative speakers" (p. 363). Similarly, Thomas (1999) challenges the "birthright mentality" that gives in to "the fallacy that anyone who speaks a certain variety of English as a native language can teach it" (p. 6). An Indian-born medical doctor, Abraham Verghese (1997), puts it nicely: We are "like a transplanted organ—lifesaving and desperately needed, but rejected because we are foreign tissue" (as cited in Braine, 1999, p. xiii). Li (1999) notes that many people think teaching English is the exclusive right of native speakers. She continues:

> Although our credibility and competence as English educators are put to the test every day and occasionally challenged by our colleagues and students, we are compensated with a larger and richer repertoire of pedagogical, linguistic, and cultural knowledge that only between-the-worlds residents are privy to. (p. 44)

Both Li's academic writing and her personal experience speak to me at this point in my life. I need to rise from the shadow of self-doubt. I have begun to see myself in a new light. My otherness is an asset, not a liability (Kubota, 2002). English is not my birthright, but it is *my* language, too, now.

Li (1999) states that "as a non-native speaker, I could not claim authority over the language" (p. 53), but I can claim ownership of it. As an owner of two languages and cultures, English and Chinese, I can take advantage of "the vantage point of an insider/outsider" (p. 43). I have started seeing writing with a combination of my Chinese self and English self, as an attempt to absorb the best from both and as a site of creativity. Now, I see that my in-between experience—something that Bakhtin called "outsideness" or "trans-gredience" (Holquist, 1990, p. 26), and Kramsch (1993) refers to as "a third place"—is a condition of creativity.

Nonnative Speaker as a Privilege

How do I take advantage of being a nonnative speaker? First of all, I should be proud to be a nonnative English speaker as it can be a privilege. One such privilege I have is the ability to develop a unique teaching style from my teaching experiences in China and Canada. Matsuda (p. 15) puts it nicely: "the assumption that *native* is somehow more positive than *nonnative* needs to be challenged" (2003). In examining the idealization of the native speaker, Widdowson states, "when the emphasis is moved from the contexts of use to contexts of learning, the advantage that native speaker teachers have disappears. In essence, the native speaker teacher is better aware of the appropriate contexts of language use, not the contexts of language learning" (as cited in Braine, 1999, pp. xv–xvi). Having learned English as a foreign, and then a second language myself, I can share firsthand experience with my ESL students that a native speaker that has not gone through the same process of learning a second language just does not have. I can be sensitive to the ideological and logical differences that my students experience (Kim, 2004; Shen, 1989). Recently one of my ESL students, who came from mainland China and has lived in Vancouver for two years, said to me: "Yan, your teaching style is different from my Chinese teachers. Yet it is not the same as my Canadian teachers. I don't know what to call your style." I smiled and took it as a compliment. In my teaching I have created a unique style that is based upon both my Chinese and Canadian educational experiences.

Another privilege of my nonnative background is "the insider perspective on the immigrant experience, second language (L2) socialization, and bilingualism that allows me to walk back and forth across the divide in the field of Second Language Acquisition (SLA) often separates 'us' (academics) from 'them' (L2 learners and users)" (Pavlenko, 2003, p. 182). In my doctoral research, I explored the differences between ESL teachers' and Chinese immigrant parents' views on the education of immigrant students, and how they negotiate their differences (Guo, 2002). I have an in-depth knowledge of education, especially language education in China, and I have acquired an in-depth knowledge of language education in Canada. I am myself an immigrant parent with a son in the Canadian public school system. I am active in my son's education, learning with him to become confident in Canadian schools and society. My language learning/teaching, cultural background, and parenting experience allow me to explore ESL programs from the multiple perspectives of student, parent, teacher, and researcher. In addition, my personal experience of communicating with schools over the past six years may enable me to understand better the immigrant parents who go through a similar process. Furthermore, the fact that I shared a similar linguistic and cultural background with the parent participants in my doctoral research may have allowed me to obtain more and even different kinds of information than a researcher from another linguistic and cultural background could (see Beckett, 1999, for a similar point).

I always remember what my father taught me: "Be humble." I continue to learn English and Chinese on a daily basis. I continue to write in English and Chinese. Writing excites me. After ten years of relentless struggle, I can finally say that I am a proud Chinese Canadian, a successful learner, and a competent teacher. My journey ahead will be challenging but colorful because I know that, as a young minority woman scholar, I need to continue to argue for the legitimacy of my topic, my nonnativeness, and my participation (e.g., Amin, 1999; Vargas, 2002). With ambition, determination, and perseverance, I can achieve my life goal—to become a fine scholar and passionate teacher.

Green and Winfrey (1997) convinced me that if you live in the past and let the past define what you are doing, you'll stop growing. That's why I have gone back to take a further course after finishing my Ph.D. As an unclassified student, I am categorized as an undergraduate student. I remember the day when I picked up my new library card. I looked at my new identity, an undergraduate student, and I smiled. It did not matter how other people categorize me. What mattered was how I see myself.

Ang, Thomas, and Goldman (2001) produced a documentary film about a diverse group of Lebanese Australian teenagers at a shopping center in Parramatta, a suburb of Sydney. The film is called *Parra: It's Not Where You're From, It's Where You're At*. I had been a sessional lecturer at two universities, which means I teach in different temporary positions, with last-minute notice, little pay, no job security, no benefits, and no say in how my department, let alone the university, is run. Where I was at, as a sessional lecturer or "invisible faculty" (Mysyk, 2001, p. 82), was not where I wanted to be; therefore, I think we need to modify the second part of Ang, Thomas, and Goldman's title of the movie: *It Is Where You Want to Be.*

Unlike young ESL learners who tagged along after their parents (Yasuko, 2002), I chose to come to Canada to pursue a higher degree, initially hoping to return to China to teach at a university. Instead, I chose to stay in Canada after completing my doctorate. Among many reasons for making such a decision, I want to highlight two of the major ones. One was that I wanted to be an ambassador. For example, after hearing my presentation in my L2 writing class, one Chinese visiting scholar who had taken a one-year leave from her Chinese university, told me: "Go back to China." I think she meant to say I do not need to suffer here. I can go back to China and get the respect I want from my students. However, according to Green and Winfrey (1997), you cannot run away from your problems. You have to face them. I started learning English wanting to be an ambassador. After more than two decades, I have become one. I see myself as an ambassador for Chinese people and non-Chinese people. I see myself as an ambassador for my students who come from diverse cultural and linguistic backgrounds. I am enjoying living in more than one culture (Yasuko, 2002). Another reason that I chose to seek employment in North America instead of returning to China was that my son started his kindergarten in Canada and he has now reached a point where his schooling cannot be interrupted by moving to China (Beckett, 2004).

I was asked by one of my friends after I got my Canadian citizenship: "Yan, are you a Chinese or are you a Canadian?" I found that the dominant dichotomies of either/or, like native versus nonnative, are oversimplified and unhelpful. I decided to take more complex positions, considering "alternative possibilities of both/and" (Akindes, 2002, p. 168). With a smile, I replied: "I am Yan." By the way, my name, Yan, means swallow. In English it is just a bird, but in Chinese it represents a beautiful image. It could be a bird flying, a symbol of youth, and a sign of spring. I have now realized that I do not have to painstakingly attempt to resolve the cultural, linguistic, and ideological conflicts between China and Canada. I can embrace the differences and enjoy being myself (Freire, 1970). China is always my beloved home country and Canada is now my new home.

Implications

I agree with Li's (1999) suggestion that everyone can write and the gift is there inside if only one is willing to reach for it. The question is, as teachers, how can we provide conditions that help second language learners reach for that gift? How should educators address the sociocultural, rhetorical, and linguistic differences (Silva, 1993) of students like me? Scholars also suggest writing with authority (Braine, 1999; Li, 1999). But, do educators encourage second language learners to write with authority? Is it possible for teachers to accept the student's authority if it does not support the teachers' own position and writing style?

Existing literature seems to suggest that learning to write in a second language is a one-way socialization into the western academic community for international graduate students. My experiences demonstrate that there is a need for mutual accommodation (Nieto, 1999, 2000). That is, international graduate students need to learn the conventions and genres of academic writing in English in order to succeed in North American academia. At the same time, North American educators need to value the cultural and linguistic capital (Bourdieu, 1986) that international graduate students bring with them. This is important because the social, political, and cultural forces that they bring with them have shaped their linguistic choices. It is important that these forces are acknowledged and students' prior knowledge and expertise are built upon so that international graduate students can contribute to and help enrich the North American academic community. Educators need to acknowledge that many international graduate students are well-respected scholars in their home countries and are capable of making contributions to their respective fields. Their credentials and expertise need to be valued and their expertise needs to be nurtured.

Learning to write in a second language is also a lifelong journey of searching for self. International graduate students must first value their own cultural and linguistic capital and communicate its value to their peers and their professors (Kubota, 2002) in their second language writing. As they go through the process of learning, they experience an identity change (Hyland, 2002; Norton, 2000). In my particular case, with or without support, I developed a strong bilingual and bicultural identity. At the same time, my experiences demonstrate that international graduate students cannot do this alone. They need help from educators and administrators in the academic community. For instance, one thing that educators can do to help is to celebrate, not devalue, the hybridity and heterogeneity evident in the multilingual and multicultural community of academia. On that note, I would like to end the chapter with a quote from Canagarajah (as cited in Matsuda et al., 2003, p. 157) that inspired me:

> As multilingual writers shuttle between different communities and literate discourses—between Chinese and English, for example—we realize that

they can bring the strengths from alternate backgrounds to enrich their writing in English.

That is what I am aiming to achieve in my writing—searching for a unique voice to continue to construct my between-the-worlds identities.

References

Akindes, F. Y. (2002). The Pacific Asianized other: Teaching unlearning among midwestern students. In L. Vargas (Ed.), *Women faculty of color in the white classroom: Narratives on the pedagogical implications of teacher diversity* (pp. 163–181). New York: Peter Lang.

Amin, N. (1999). Minority women teachers in ESL: Negotiating white English. In G. Braine (Ed.), *Non-native educators in English language teaching* (pp. 93–104). Mahwah, NJ: Erlbaum.

Ang, I., Thomas, M., Goldman, M., & Mukhtar, E. (Writers), & Goldman, M. (Director). (2001). *Parra: It's not where you're from, it's where you're at* [Television series episode]. In M. McMurchy (Producer), *Hybrid life*. Australia: Special Broadcasting Service.

Bakhtin, M. (1981). *The dialogic imagination: Four essays*. Austin: University of Texas Press.

Beckett, G. H. (1999). *Project-based instruction in a Canadian secondary school's ESL classes: Goals and evaluation*. Unpublished doctoral dissertation, University of British Columbia, Vancouver, Canada.

Beckett, G. H. (2004). Foreword. In V. Gonzalez, *Second language learning and cultural adaptation processes in graduate international students in the U.S. universities*. New York: University Press of America.

Benesch, S. (in press). What about the students? English language learners in postsecondary settings. In J. Cummins & C. Davison (Eds.), *Handbook of English language teaching*. New York: Kluwer Academic.

Blanton, L. L. (2003). Narrating one's self: Public-personal dichotomies and a (public) writing life. In C. P. Casanave & S. Vandrick (Eds.), *Writing for scholarly publication: Behind the scenes in language education* (pp. 147–157). Mahwah, NJ: Erlbaum.

Bourdieu, P. (1977). The economics of linguistic exchanges. *Social Science Information, 16*(6), 645–668.

Bourdieu, P. (1986). The forms of capital. In J. G. Richardson (Ed.), *Handbook of theory and research for the sociology of education* (pp. 241–258). New York: Greenwood Press.

Braine, G. (Ed.). (1999). *Non-native educators in English language teaching*. Mahwah, NJ: Erlbaum.

Braine, G. (2002). Academic literacy and the non-native speaker graduate student. *Journal of English for Academic Purposes, 1*, 59–68.

Canadian Bureau for International Education (CBIE, 2002). *The National report on international students in Canada 2000/01.* Ottawa, Ontario, Canada: Author.

Casanave, C. P. (1992). Cultural diversity and socialization: A case study of a Hispanic woman in a doctoral program. In D. E. Murray (Ed.), *Diversity as resource: Redefining cultural literacy* (pp. 148–182). Alexandria, VA: TESOL International.

Casanave, C. P. (2003). Narrative braiding: Constructing a multistrand portrayal of self as writer. In C. P. Casanave & S. Vandrick (Eds.), *Writing for scholarly publication: Behind the scenes in language education* (pp. 131–145). Mahwah, NJ: Erlbaum.

Connelly, F. M., & Clandinin, J. (1990). Stories of experience and narrative inquiry. *Educational Researcher, 19*(5), 2–14.

Connor, U. (1999). Learning to write academic prose in a second language: A literacy autobiography. In G. Braine (Ed.), *Non-native educators in English language teaching* (pp. 29–42). Mahwah, NJ: Erlbaum.

Cumming, A. (1998). Theoretical perspectives on writing. *Annual Review of Applied Linguistics, 18*, 61–78.

Davies, A. (2003). *The native speaker: Myth and reality.* Clevedon, UK: Multilingual Matters.

Dias, P., Freedman, A., Medway, P., & Paré, A. (1999). *Worlds apart: Acting and writing in academic and workplace contexts.* Mahwah, NJ: Erlbaum.

Duff, P. A. (2002). The discursive co-construction of knowledge, identity, and difference: An ethnography of communication in the high school mainstream. *Applied Linguistics, 23*(3), 289–322.

Duff, P. A., & Uchida, Y. (1997). The negotiation of teachers' sociocultural identities and practices in postsecondary EFL classrooms. *TESOL Quarterly, 31*(3), 451–486.

Freire, P. (1970). *Pedagogy of the oppressed.* New York: Seabury Press.

Green, B., & Winfrey, O. (Producers). (1997). *Oprah: Make the connection . . . It's about changing your life* [Video]. California: Buena Vista House Video.

Guo, Y. (1987). Cynthia Ozik's view on writing. *Trends of Foreign Literature, 10*, 8–15.

Guo, Y. (1995). *Heritages: Mother/daughter relationships in three novels by Chinese American Women.* Unpublished master's thesis, University of Regina, Saskatchewan, Canada.

Guo, Y. (2002). *Chinese parents and ESL teachers: Understanding and negotiating their differences.* Unpublished doctoral dissertation, University of British Columbia, Vancouver, Canada.

Hall, D., & Ames, R. (1987). *Thinking through Confucius.* Albany, NY: SUNY Press.

Hall, S. (1991). The local and the global: Globalisation and ethnicity. In A. King

(Ed.), *Culture, globalisation and the world-system: Contemporary conditions for the representation of identity* (pp. 19–39). London: Macmillan.

Hamp-Lyons, L., & Zhang, B. W. (2001). World Englishes: Issues in and from academic writing assessment. In J. Flowerdew & M. Peacock (Eds.), *Research perspectives on English for academic purposes* (pp. 101–116). Cambridge, UK: Cambridge University Press.

Harklau, L. (2000). From the "good kids" to the "worst": Representations of English language learners across educational settings. *TESOL Quarterly, 34*(1), 35–67.

Hirvela, A., & Belcher, D. (2001). Coming back to voice: The multiple voices and identities of mature multilingual writers. *Journal of Second Language Writing, 10* (1–2, special double issue on "voice" guest-edited by Belcher & Hirvela), 83–106.

Holquist, M. (1990). *Dialogism: Bakhtin and his world.* London: Routledge.

Hyland, K. (2002). Options of identity in academic writing. *ELT Journal, 56*, 351–358.

Ivanič, R. (1998). *Writing and identity: The discoursal construction of identity in academic writing.* Amsterdam, Netherlands: John Benjamin.

Johns, A. M. (1990). L1 composition theories: Implications for developing theories of L2 composition. In B. Kroll (Ed.), *Second language writing* (pp. 24–36). Cambridge, UK: Cambridge University Press.

Kim, J. (2004, April). *Creating their own identity: A story of NNS ESL professionals.* Paper presented at the American Association for Applied Linguistics, Portland, OR.

Kramsch, C. (1993). *Context and culture in language teaching.* Oxford, UK: Oxford University Press.

Kramsch, C. (1997). The privilege of the nonnative speaker. *PMLA, 112*, 359–369.

Kubota, R. (1998). Ideologies of English in Japan. *World Englishes, 17*, 295–306.

Kubota, R. (2002). Marginality as an asset: Toward a counter-hegemonic pedagogy for diversity. In L. Vargas (Ed.), *Women faculty of color in the white classroom: Narratives on the pedagogical implications of teacher diversity* (pp. 293–307). New York: Peter Lang.

Kumar, P. (2002). Yellow lotus in white lily pond: An Asian American woman teaching in Utah. In L. Vargas (Ed.), *Women faculty of color in the white classroom: Narratives on the pedagogical implications of teacher diversity* (pp. 277–291). New York: Peter Lang.

Lave, J., & Wenger, E. (1991). *Situated learning: Legitimate peripheral participation.* Cambridge, UK: Cambridge University Press.

Li, X. (1999). Writing from the vantage point of an outsider/insider. In G. Braine (Ed.), *Non-native educators in English language teaching* (pp. 43–55). Mahwah, NJ: Erlbaum.

Liu, J. (2001). Writing from Chinese to English: My cultural transformation. In

D. Belcher & U. Connor (Eds.), *Reflections on multiliterate lives* (pp. 121–131). Clevedon, UK: Multilingual Matters.

Losey, K. M. (1997). *Listen to the silences: Mexican American interaction in the composition classroom and community.* Norwood, NJ: Ablex.

Lu, M. (1987). From silence to words: Writing as struggle. *College English, 49,* 437–448.

Matsuda, P. K. (2003). Proud to be a nonnative English speaker. *TESOL Matters, 13*(4), 15.

Matsuda, P. K., Canagarajah, A. S., Harklau, L., Hyland, K., & Warschauer, M. (2003). Changing currents in second language writing research: A colloquium. *Journal of Second Language Writing, 12*(2), 151–179.

Morita, N. (2002). *Negotiating participation in second language academic communities: A study of identity, agency, and transformation.* Unpublished doctoral dissertation, University of British Columbia, Vancouver, Canada.

Mysyk, A. (2001). The sessional lecturer as migrant labourer. *The Canadian Journal of Higher Education, 31*(3), 73–92.

Nieto, S. (1999). *The light in their eyes: Creating multicultural learning communities.* New York: Teachers College Press.

Nieto, S. (2000). *Affirming diversity: The sociopolitical context of multicultural education.* New York: Longman.

Nieto, S. (2002). *Language, culture, and teaching: Critical perspectives for a new century.* Mahwah, NJ: Erlbaum.

Noddings, N. (2003). *Happiness and education.* New York: Cambridge University Press.

Norton, B. (2000). *Identity and language learning: Gender, ethnicity, and educational change.* London: Longman/Pearson Education.

Norton Peirce, B. (1995). Social identity, investment, and language learning. *TESOL Quarterly, 29*(1), 9–31.

Papastergiadis, N. (2000). *The turbulence of migration: Globalizing, deterritorialization, and hybridity.* Cambridge, UK: Polity.

Pavlenko, A. (2003). The privilege of writing as an immigrant woman. In C. P. Casanave & S. Vandrick (Eds.), *Writing for scholarly publication: Behind the scenes in language education* (pp. 177–193). Mahwah, NJ: Erlbaum.

Pryer, A. (2003). Orphans: On hybrid identities and absent narratives. *Educational Insights, 8*(2). Vancouver, British Columbia, Canada: Centre for the Study of Curriculum and Instruction, University of British Columbia. Retrieved July 28, 2004, from www.ccfi.educ.ubc.ca/publication/insights/v08n02/aoki/guo.html

Sharkey, J., Shi, L., Thompson, B., & Norton, B. (2003). Dialogues around "Social identity, investment, and language learning," by Norton Pierce (1995). In J. Sharkey & K. E. Johnson (Eds.), *TESOL Quarterly dialogues: Rethinking issues of language, culture, and power* (pp. 55–74). Alexandria, VA: TESOL.

Shear, W. (1993). Generational differences and the diaspora in *The Joy Luck Club. Critique: Studies in Contemporary Fiction, 34,* 193–199.

Shen, F. (1989). The classroom and the wider culture: Identity as a key to learning English composition. *College Composition and Communication, 40,* 459–466.

Silva, T. (1993). Toward an understanding of the distinct nature of L2 writing: The ESL research and its implications. *TESOL Quarterly, 27*(4), 657–671.

Smith, D. (1996). Identity, self, and other in the conduct of pedagogical action: An east/west inquiry. In W. Pinar (Eds.), *Contemporary curriculum discourses: Twenty years of JCT* (pp. 458–473). New York: Peter Lang.

Spack, R. (1997). The acquisition of academic literacy in a second language. *Written Communication, 14,* 3–62.

Tan, A. (1989). *The joy luck club.* New York: Ivy Books.

Thomas, J. (1999). Voices from the periphery: Non-native teachers and issues of credibility. In G. Braine (Ed.), *Non-native educators in English language teaching* (pp. 5–13). Mahwah, NJ: Erlbaum.

Toohey, K. (2000). *Learning English at school: Identity, social relations and classroom practice.* Clevedon, UK: Multilingual Matters.

Tsai, M. (2001). Learning is lifelong process. In D. Belcher & U. Connor (Eds.), *Reflections on multiliterate lives* (pp. 135–140). Clevedon, UK: Multilingual Matters.

Tung, M. (2000). *Chinese Americans and their immigrant parents: Conflict, identity, and values.* New York: Haworth Clinical Practice Press.

Vargas, L. (2002). Introduction. In L. Vargas (Eds.), *Women faculty of color in the white classroom: Narratives on the pedagogical implications of teacher diversity* (pp. 1–22). New York: Peter Lang.

Wang, H. (2004). *The call from the stranger on a journey home: Curriculum in a third space.* New York: Peter Lang.

Watkins, D., & Biggs, J. (1996). *The Chinese learner: Cultural, psychological and contextual influences.* Hong Kong: Comparative Education Research Center, University of Hong Kong.

Yasuko, K. (2002). The development of bicultural identities: Japanese returnees' experiences. *The Language Teacher, 26*(6), 12–16.

12

MODERATION, MODESTY, CREATIVITY, AND CRITICALNESS

A Chinese American Medical Professor Speaks

Gulbahar H. Beckett and Jianhua Zhang

T he number of minority scholars in North American universities and colleges has increased steadily since the 1980s (Harvey, 2003; U.S. Department of Education, 2002). This has resulted in some publications that explore various issues encountered by minority scholars in general (e.g., Belcher & Conner, 2001; Braine, 1999; Kingston-Mann & Sieber, 2001) and female faculty in particular (Li, 2005; Liang, 2005; Lin et al., 2004; Vargas, 2002). This body of work shows that minority faculty encounter various challenges in their work. For example, Braine (1999) describes being underappreciated as an English as a Second Language (ESL) instructor in the United States, as some of his students dropped out of his classes based on the native speaker fallacy (Phillipson, 1992) that assumes only native speakers are good language teachers. That is, despite his near-native proficiency in the English language and expertise in English language teaching, he felt his students dropped out of his courses with an assumption that, as a nonnative speaker of English, he would not be able to do a good job of teaching ESL. Similar findings are presented and discussed in Liang (2005), a study that investigates three Asian female professors' ongoing battles with linguistic, gender, racial, and cultural issues. According to the participants in this study, their students questioned their credibility as course instructors and challenged their authority because of their accented English.

Loo and Ho (2005) provide a detailed account of their experiences with merit pay increases, promotion, and tenure. They feel their universities treated them unfairly by concealing crucial departmental policies, being overly critical of their work, and denying them the promotion and tenure they deserved because of racism. According to them, their White male colleagues with lesser qualifications were promoted and given tenure because of their race. The narrative study by Lin and colleagues (2004) includes a discussion of similar issues from different angles such as the participants' feelings of being victimized by the same gender politics and colonial ideologies. For example, one of the participants in this study felt she was regarded as a second-class citizen by her White female colleagues who took on the role of speaking for her. She writes about feeling disempowered when her dean told her that her research on her own ethnic community was not considered serious research. A second participant in this study reports being deprived of opportunities to teach higher-level graduate courses and working with good doctoral students. Another participant in the same study narrates and discusses her experience of being underappreciated by colleagues from her own ethnic and cultural background. The authors explain their experiences as legacies of race and gender politics as well as colonialism. According to them, their White female colleagues might have seen themselves as the second-best group of people (next to White men) allowed to discriminate against and speak for other people including minority women because of their colonial belief in White superiority. That is, they may have believed that, although they are women, they are still superior because they are White. Though they criticize White men for discriminating against them and others, they act as if they should also be in a superior position to judge and speak for other people.

Along a similar line, Li (2005) discusses her experiences of being a young Asian female graduate advisor at a U.S. university where she encountered disrespect and disobedience from her Asian female graduate students. According to Li, her Korean and Chinese graduate assistants did not show her the same respect they showed her White male colleagues. Specifically, her graduate assistants did not complete assigned tasks on time, talked back, entered her office without knocking, canceled meetings, and scheduled holidays on the days that they were supposed to work without consulting her as their supervisor. In contrast, one of the Korean graduate assistants showed so much respect to one of Li's White male colleagues that he said it embarrassed him that the student always walked out of his office backward. Like

Lin and colleagues (2004), Li explains these experiences as legacies of race and gender politics as well as colonialism. According to Li, her experience with graduate assistants could have something to do with the fact that women, particularly minority women, have always been marginalized in higher education. She cites U.S. Department of Education statistics showing that in 1995, 75 percent of full professors, 63.5 percent of associate professors, and 47.5 percent of assistant professors in American universities are White males. The same data source reveals that in 1999, 50 percent of college faculty were White males, 35 percent were White females, and only 5 percent were Asian/Pacific Islanders. Li speculates that such demographics can contribute to the perpetuation of White male superiority in the academe, an argument that seems to be supported by people from various ethnic and racial groups (Bassett, 1992).

The above literature review represents some of the emerging discussion of issues related to minority faculty in North American colleges and universities. However, what is noticeably missing from this body of work is an examination of issues faced by natural science faculty of Asian origin. Studying this particular population is important because it represents a significant percentage of minority faculty. For example, a National Study of Postsecondary Faculty (1998–1999) survey of 960 institutions show that Asian Pacific Islanders consist of 5.1 percent of science, mathematics, and engineering professors compared to 5.0 percent non-Hispanic Blacks and 3.5 percent Hispanics, the rest being White and other ethnic groups. This chapter bridges these gaps through excerpts from a Chinese American medical professor's narrative of her journey from being a Chinese student in China to a Chinese American professor in the United States. Furthermore, the interpretation of issues faced by minority faculty has largely been from critical perspectives such as racism, feminism, and colonialism. This may have resulted from autoethnographic studies that have been conducted mostly with social science faculty who themselves work with these theories. Interpreting lived experience of a natural science professor from other theoretical perspectives such as the Eastern Confucian and the Western Deweyan educational cultural perspectives could add to our understanding of the issues encountered by minority faculty. The focal points we discuss in the chapter include how the Confucian theory of modesty and moderation was useful in preparing Mei, the participant, to be an extremely successful student and person in China, but became a hindrance to quick success in American society.

Specifically, we illustrate and discuss how Mei aced all of her examinations in China, entered a top university at age fifteen, and came to the United States as one of a chosen elite; but also how a Confucian upbringing that socialized her to be modest and moderate became an obstacle to passionately pursuing her studies and career with creativity. We do this using Mei's narratives as a legitimate data source (Bakhtin, 1981; Clandinin & Connolly, 1994; Mirriam, 1998). This approach was chosen because, according to Mirriam, "meaning is embedded in people's experiences" (p. 6), and data analysis depends on the subjective interpretation of the lived experiences of the participant (van Manen, 1990). Data interpretation was structured within Clandinin and Connolly's (1994) typology of internal and existential conditions. The former refers to the participant's voices and the latter to broad questions beyond participant experience. Emergent patterns (Spradley, 1980), narrative threads, and surprises were identified, and then triangulated with the participant (Clandinin & Connolly, 1994).

We apply Confucianist Eastern educational and Deweyan Western educational views (Gardner, 1989) to interpret the issues identified in the chapter. We also make useful suggestions for existing and aspiring Asian female faculty as well as for the North American universities and colleges that employ them. We believe this chapter contributes to our understanding of the trials and tribulations some Asian female faculty undergo during their journey from student to faculty. Such understanding can benefit other scholars of similar origin in their transition from their home culture to their host cultures. Universities and colleges in the United States can benefit from it in their efforts to help scholars of similar origin make a smoother transition to their new institutional cultures.

Growing Up in China and Becoming a Graduate Student, Postdoctoral Fellow, and Faculty Member in the United States

Who am I, where did I come from (physically and literally), where am I going: These are some of the questions that Mei asks herself when she is in search of her identity. In this section of the chapter, we will present some of Mei's answers to these questions. Although these are uniquely Mei's answers, we believe this sharing of her experience will spark further discussion of issues faced by Asian female science faculty in North America.

Growing Up in China

I grew up in the Beijing suburb where the Chinese Academy of Sciences is located. The residential areas in this suburb are intermingled with a dozen different research institutes, and my parents and most of my childhood friends' parents were scientists. So when I was little, I thought that everybody would grow up to become a scientist. Of course after entering school, we were told that we ought to be reeducated by humble people—workers, peasants, and soldiers—to become one of them. The Communist propaganda then was that humble people are the smartest and the most noble while intellectuals are the stupidest. When I was growing up, China had one billion people, only a small fraction of whom were intellectuals. Nonetheless, my elementary school years were arguably the best time of my life. As kids, my friends and I were allowed to spend after-school hours without adult supervision. We were latch-key children who ran around with home keys tied to chains that hung on our necks.

Not much critical and creative work was asked of my friends and me, as rote learning memorization was the prevalent teaching and learning approach then. Children were asked to read and reread the same story a million times till everyone could recite it before they could move on to another story. The rationale was that "books read a hundred times can make themselves clear and obvious." Also, "if you remember all the three hundred Tang poems, you yourself will become a poet."

Nevertheless, my friends and I did visit each other's homes and we read our parents' books. A friend of mine had the most amazing books on heavenly objects. I was particularly amazed by the pictures of galaxies and stars. We also read about how to make sophisticated calculations in our heads and competed on who could calculate the results the fastest. We read about why ink bottles can freeze and break in the winter, why one's mirror image is upside down on the back of a spoon, and why a kid can run with the wolves and become a werewolf. At the same time, I personally liked to read novels and poetry. In my preschool years, I was locked up in our twelve-square-meter apartment whenever I was sick and was not allowed to go to kindergarten. I had nothing else to do but read newspapers, poetry, and novels. But, my thirst for natural science was never dominated by my thirst for social science.

I aced my middle school entrance exam and classes. One day, my teacher asked me to ask my mother to visit him. I was nervous about what he would tell my mother. It turned out that he recommended me to take college entrance exams without going through high school. After a crash course studying high school subjects such as chemistry, political sciences, and Chinese literature for a week, I took the university entrance exam with three boys from my school. I was the only one who passed the exam, and this resulted in my spending the rest of my teenage years at the University of Science and

Technology of China. As I did not learn high school math and science, it took me a few months to catch up with my classmates. Soon, I started excelling in physics, although by then I was more interested in the biology-related courses. However, because of the nature of university course work in China, I gained very little empirical research experience. In addition, the scientific, especially biomedical, research of the time was significantly behind that in America and Europe.

My school teachers and university advisors were all very attentive, fatherly, and gave detailed instructions about what to read and what to learn. They took pride in being responsible for their students and maintained very close guidance. My university strongly discouraged our social life, especially dating, so that we could focus on our studies. I was able to focus on my science subjects and this enabled me to graduate a year early from the university and to pass the China-U.S. Physics Examination and Application Program to come to the United States.

Becoming a Graduate Student and a Postdoctoral Fellow in the United States

I grew up in a country whose Communist propaganda was that capitalists exploit people and used Andersen's (1846) *The Little Match-Seller* as an example of how poor people die outside of rich people's houses on Christmas Eve. As a result, I grew up hating the Western world and wanting to liberate all the miserable people slaving away for capitalists. The irony was that, after all this propaganda, China suddenly opened her doors and sent students abroad to study. I was one of sixty biology students who passed a national competition and came to America in 1985 at age twenty.

I discovered that graduate school life in the United States was not something I was prepared for, as it resembled nothing I had experienced in China. For the entire first semester, I could not understand much of what the professors said in class. They seemed to speak very fast with heavy accents. The English they spoke was nothing like the BBC or Voice of America English we listened to and emulated in China. Still I did reasonably well with my exams as I could make use of most of the subjects I had learned in China. I also enjoyed my laboratory experiences. I chose one particular lab for my Ph.D. thesis, primarily because everything worked the first time during my rotation. My positive experiences gave me an optimistic view of graduate school life. However, once I joined the laboratory, things were not as rosy as I imagined. Many people told me that graduate school is like swimming in the ocean, you either learn to swim or you sink.

Specifically, I found graduate school in the United States to be very much an independent endeavor. For example, my Ph.D. advisor told me that he had studied with someone who took a three-year sabbatical during his study. His advisor told him that he could do anything he wanted in terms of biomedical research. So my advisor hit the library and found something to work on. When his advisor came back, he asked my advisor to write up what he had found and defend his thesis. My advisor was one of the most brilliant people in the Western world in biomedical research. I felt that I could become at least one of the best in my class, but only if a topic was assigned and everybody studied the same thing. I discovered that higher learning in the United States means choosing one's own area of study, which can determine one's success or failure. Although this way of pursing knowledge was what I had wanted since my childhood, what I needed to do in U.S. graduate school still came as a surprise, because I was not prepared for it by my studies in China.

My advisor was from Great Britain. He was brilliant, charming, and kindhearted, but he was also hot-tempered. He was so straightforward that he even cursed and yelled. I could not develop a rapport with him for the longest period of time. One day, we had a conversation that totally changed me. He came to me and said: "Why are you always so bloody quiet? I don't see fire in your belly. Where is the passion?" "What? Passion?" I thought. Confucius said that noble people do everything in moderation. In my usual way, I bit my tongue and said nothing. He continued: "You've got to do everything in excess, work excessively hard, and play excessively hard. You've got to laugh out loud, don't hold it all in." I said, after gathering all the courage I had, "Then I may die sooner." He said, "You may die happier." "Happier?" I thought. Being happy was a sin, at least that was how I was taught as a kid. We should carry the whole world on our shoulders and make it better before we should allow ourselves to experience happiness. Well, I did not say anything to him that day. But the thought of allowing myself to be passionate and happy kept growing in me.

I was also very shy and humble when I first came to the United States, but I was eager to learn. I always sat in the front row taking notes in classes and in seminars. I took notes every time my advisor said anything to me. But I never asked any questions. I always went back and diligently studied what I was taught. One day, my advisor got really tired of hearing echoes of his own voice without any back-channeling from me. He said: "You have to ask questions. From now on, you have to ask at least one question in every one of our conversations, in every class, and every seminar." I was shocked.

Me? Posing questions to an authority, especially during seminars when the topics are something that I am not entirely familiar with? But I did it since my advisor told me to and I discovered that asking questions can be fun and empowering. I found out that asking questions forces one to think critically and creatively and that professors actually appreciate students asking questions.

My postdoctoral years were also quite interesting. I thought that I had finally got this Ph.D. and could walk on air and be confident among students, but I was humbled by the experience. Most of the fellows in my post-doc institute were brilliant. They had their own fellowships and they were independent and creative. They claimed that they published better papers than I did. Everybody was eager to do the ultimate experiment that would lead to a Nobel Prize–winning discovery. My advisor was also brilliant and outgoing. He had parties for us in his house, took the entire lab on white-water rafting and skiing trips, and held volleyball matches in his backyard. I was still my old quiet self, participated in the volleyball games, but skipped the skiing trips and the white-water rafting. In retrospect, I could have been more active and interactive, which would have allowed me to discuss new ideas with my colleagues and my advisor and to make faster and better progress in my research. I was very hard on myself during my postdoc years. I worked diligently seven days a week and almost twenty-four hours a day, thinking and dreaming about, conducting, and writing up my research. At the end of my postdoc period, I helped identify components of a large complex in terms of gene regulation and my work was part of a very significant paper. But somehow, I still did not have the feeling that I had done something really important.

Being an Asian Female Faculty: An Even More Challenging Experience

I have been a research assistant professor for the past eight and a half years. During this period, I faced many more new challenges as well as some exciting moments, which I share in this section. One of the questions I keep asking myself is, what does it mean to work in the natural sciences field? My work as a natural science faculty reminds me of a quotation from my teenage years: "There is no royal road in science. Only those who do not dread the fatiguing climb along the steep path have the chance of gaining the luminous summit." I loved the saying then, but failed to fully understand the meaning of it. As a natural science professor now, I think this quotation really means that natural science involves research into the unknown. Our hypotheses sometimes work, but they also fail at times because of limitations in technical skill or in funding and other resources. As such, I realize that natural science is hard work that requires imagination, creativity, and a 24/7 commitment even from professors.

Another question I often ask myself is, what does it mean to be an Asian female professor of natural science? As I mentioned before, people of Asian heritage grow up with Confucian doctrines: "Be moderate, be modest, be swift in action and inert in words." However, I have learned over the years that such an upbringing can become an impediment to quicker and larger success in American academia. Here, let me provide some examples, beginning with the difficulty I have with self-promotion. I worked very hard for years and waited to be discovered only to realize that, in this country, people have to promote themselves to get the opportunities they want. "Seek and thou shall find" seems to be the way of thinking in this country. I have been promoted three times during the past eight and a half years, but all three times I had to ask for it. The first promotion was after my first National Institute of Health (NIH) grant, which I was very proud of. However, I did not get any promotion because of the grant alone. A senior faculty in the department had to ask for it on my behalf. I was too embarrassed to ask for it myself as I was taught to be modest, and "to ask what you can do for your institution, not what your institution can do for you." The other two times, I gathered up a lot of courage and asked for promotions myself. Once I got another big grant from the Department of Defense, and another time I published a high-impact article in a top journal. I asked for a promotion after finding out that other people with similar experience got promoted. I also found that some colleagues had asked for and were given extra equipment by the department. I tried to follow suit by identifying a real need and by providing a convincing argument based on the likelihood of productivity, and I actually got some equipment for my laboratory, too.

A second example of the impediments of my upbringing concerns voicing my opinion. This has been a special challenge for me as an Asian female faculty. Asian females are good listeners and we tend to think that other people have better things to say. However, I learned that I also have important things to say and people actually value my opinion if I express it and if it is worthwhile. If I do not, issues that are important to me get overlooked. For example, I suggested that we organize a national meeting at the university to stimulate collaboration and to increase the national visibility of our university. My suggestion was accepted by our program director. I remained on the committee and I suggested speakers. During one meeting, I suggested the names of two Chinese scientists. One committee member asked: "Why do you always have to recommend Chinese?" Being my usual self, I did not say anything immediately. I did not know whether the question was meant to be humorous or something else. But clearly if I were not Chinese, the question would not have been asked. After a few more scientists were nominated and discussed, and when we still had not found an appropriate speaker, I came back to one of the Chinese scientists I had recommended. I asked "What about so-and-so? Is there anything wrong with him besides being a Chinese?" The committee agreed that he was a good scientist and strongly supported my recommendation.

A third example relating to my Asian femaleness has to do with my never wanting to say I am ambitious. At one job interview, my interviewer asked me how I was going to win my Nobel Prize. I said honestly that I did not think I could win a Nobel Prize. Another faculty later told me that I was seen as "lacking ambition." I had always thought that I should hide my "sharp edges" and achieve before making noise about it. But my only reward was not getting the job I applied for.

A fourth example has to do with teaching, which I am always nervous about. I often feel limited in how much I can do to inspire students and postdocs who are not Asian. I found my American colleagues often use humor and put a positive spin on things. Students seem to be more productive and happier in their laboratories. But I do not feel I have the kind of language skills and cultural knowledge to do what my colleagues do with their students. I feel I should try to memorize all the facts to be confident in answering questions without consulting books.

What Now?

Now that I have identified at least some of the issues that I have faced as an Asian female natural science faculty, what do I do with them? What do I do with all the missed opportunities of exchanging ideas with and learning from brilliant colleagues during my postdoc years and missed opportunities as a result of not getting critical and constructive feedback on my research and grant proposals during the first few years of my faculty career? I am now making conscious efforts to be more interactive. For example, I volunteered to play a major role in a collaborative project involving about twenty researchers, and after a lot of hard work a paper based on this work got published in a good journal. I will continue to search for improvement, and hope the experience I share here will help others like me find ways in their journey to make unique contributions to science and society, to live more fulfilling lives, and to become better scientists and better people in general.

Issues and Possible Explanations

Several themes from the above have emerged (Spradley, 1980) from Mei's narrative (Bakhtin, 1981; Clandinin & Connolly, 1994; Mirriam, 1998). One, Mei is a bright and successful person, but she would have been even more successful had there not been something in her holding her back. Two, Mei aced it all in China by listening closely to her teachers and professors as they lectured and advised, reading what they told her to read, taking notes with modesty, making it to a top university at age fifteen, and coming to America as one of a chosen elite. However, her narrative seems to suggest that those strategies became an impediment to success in American graduate schools. Three, unlike her previous experience in China, Mei found that to succeed in the United States she needed to passionately and independently pursue a field of study with creativity and criticalness as well as self-confidence and even self-promotion as a graduate student, postdoctoral fellow, and as a professor. She found that she could not just learn from authority (i.e., professors and texts) with humility and moderation. Instead, she needed to be creative, to question critically what she read and heard, and that she needed to interact and work with her colleagues to maximize her achievement. Four, Mei found that resources are something one needs to request. If there is a legitimate reason for it, the request is usually granted. Five, Mei discovered opinions must be voiced to be heard, and that suggestions put forward may be adopted. Six, ambitions must be expressed when the circumstance calls for it. Finally, Mei felt that her pedagogical resources (e.g., teaching skills as well as linguistic cultural resources) needed to be expanded.

Why did Mei encounter these issues? Specifically, why was Mei doing all the listening and reading but not questioning what she read and heard? Why did Mei not know that she could ask for resources, voice her opinion, and make suggestions? Why did she not answer her interviewer's question confidently by saying that, as a bright scholar, she hopes to win a Nobel Prize one day? And why did Mei not use humor in her class as she wished she could? As Mei mentioned briefly in her narrative, these issues may have something to do with Mei's Chinese Confucian upbringing that clashes with the Deweyan Western educational view that is prevalent in the United States. We will discuss this in the next section of the chapter.

Moderation, Modesty, Creativity, and Criticalness: Confucian Eastern and Deweyan Western Educational Views

Chinese social and educational cultures are heavily influenced by doctrines of Confucius (551–479 BC), who is believed to be the first great Chinese philosopher and educator. The aim of Confucianism is to bring harmony to society, thus the theory of Zhong Yong (The Doctrine of the Mean). Zhong Yong dictates that it is a virtue to be able to live in obscurity and be submerged in the mass. In fact, only people possessing lots of strength and ability can be totally fair, tolerant, and judicious and harmonious with the universe. These ideas lead to prudence, caution, and, most important, modesty and moderation. Self-promotion goes against the Zhong Yong ideas. As a result, Chinese people grow up believing that "noble people are swift in action, but inert in words," which is also translated as "The superior man is modest in his speech but exceeds in his actions" (see www.crystalinks.com/confucius.html). Such beliefs are so prevalent that Mao Zedong even named his two daughters after the doctrine that "noble people are swift in action (Li Min), but inert in words (Li Na)." Such an influence on Mei's upbringing may explain how Mei was modest and moderate in showing her passion for her work during class, meetings, and seminars.

Chinese educational views based on Confucius's doctrines are significantly different from the Western view of education evolved from Rousseau, Dewey, and Piaget (Beckett, 1999). Gardner (1989) and Hsu (1981) argue that Chinese and Western cultures "embrace two radically different solutions to the dilemma of creativity" (p. 7). According to Gardner (1989), the United States "has defined itself in opposition to the past and tradition. It has looked to its frontier and to its youth to forge new and unanticipated ways of living" (p. 280). In this context, independence, critical thinking, distinctiveness, and communication skills come to be seen as fundamentally important. Chinese society, on the other hand, has been historically oriented toward tradition, and it honors individuals who have mastered proven knowledge. The Chinese believe that acquiring huge amounts of basic knowledge and skills is more important than creativity. From a Confucian perspective, acquiring historical knowledge is highly regarded because, according to this perspective, the present cannot be understood without knowledge of the past. As such, student interpretation and independent thought are not regarded as valuable. Therefore, learning from authoritative sources such as professors and texts without much emphasis on creativity and critical questioning are common in Chinese educational culture (Beckett, 1999).

Such contrasting views between the Chinese educational culture Mei grew up in and the American educational culture she adopted may account for Mei's experience regarding reading and listening without questioning the texts and her professors, and her advisor's frustration that Mei did not say much in class or during meetings. That is, because of her Confucian upbringing, Mei may have been quiet and unquestioning because she thought that her professors and advisors are the authority figures whom she needs to admire (Ho, 1996) and whose job it is to transmit knowledge to her. At the same time, she needs to listen quietly and receive and consume external knowledge, as a student's role is not that of a creator of knowledge (Pratt, 1992).

A third issue we would like to explore is that of access to information, resources, and promotion. As discussed earlier, other works have reported and discussed these issues from a racial discrimination point of view (e.g., Lin et al., 2004; Loo & Ho, 2005). However, Mei's narrative seems to suggest that this could also be a cultural issue. That is, some Asian faculty may feel that information, resources, and promotions are not so much withheld as simply waiting to be discovered when Asian faculty cease equating asking for things with challenging authority (Ho, 1996). A fourth issue is that of voicing opinion. In her narrative, Mei says she was simply shy in voicing her opinion, indicating that it is a personal trait. While that may be the case, there could be another explanation for this. That is, Mei may have been hesitant in expressing her opinion because of her Chinese Confucian socialization that encouraged face-saving, group solidarity, and the inappropriateness of shining in front of one's peers (Flowerdew & Miller, 1995).

The point about Mei feeling she had limited resources to do a better job with her teaching and advising postdoctoral students is an interesting one. As discussed earlier, the issue of teaching and advising has been examined in other work (Braine, 1999; Li, 2005; Liang, 2005). As we will recall, Braine reports experiencing disrespect from his students because of his nonnative speaker status, which he discusses from a critical linguistics perspective. Li reports experiencing disrespect from her Asian female graduate students, perhaps because of her ethnicity, age, and gender, which she discusses from a colonial perspective. Mei's narrative does not mention disrespect from her students, but her desire to expand her linguistic and cultural resources is an interesting one. A similar point is made by Liang (2005) who reports similar issues and expresses a similar desire. Further exploration of this issue from a cultural point of view would be interesting. That is, it would be interesting to know how Chinese female professors feel about having to increase their resources in order to teach and advise students from other racial and gender backgrounds.

Conclusion

In this chapter, we discussed a natural science professor's lived experience in China and the United States. Although the discussion is of one person's experience, we know that it contributes to the emerging work on issues encountered by minority faculty in general and Asian female faculty in particular. It bridges the gap on the paucity of similar work on natural science faculty of Asian origin. This chapter can be a useful source of knowledge for aspiring Asian female graduate students, postdoctoral fellows, and existing faculty as it helps them understand that it is great to have grown up with good virtues such as diligence, respect, moderation, and modesty. But, in order to continue their success in North America, they must also understand that, while keeping those good virtues, they need to learn the virtues, demands, and expectations of the North American societal and educational cultures.

This chapter should also be an informative source for North American university and college professors as well as administrators in their understanding of international minority students, colleagues, and their employees. After reading this chapter, those professors and administrators should understand that their Asian students and colleagues may appear modest and uncritical, but that does not mean that they are less knowledgeable and that they lack important opinions to voice. It means that they are exercising their good virtues by being respectful and modest. When circumstances call for it, they can be critical and voice their opinions that are worthwhile just as their North American counterparts do.

This chapter should also help various parties to understand that Asian female faculty have good virtues that need to be nurtured, but they may also need assistance and resources in their pursuit of the virtues, expectations, and demands required of them in North American institutions of higher education. The discussion in this chapter should empower these parties for their development of strategies for a more successful career in studying, professing, and administering.

References

Andersen, H. C. (1846). *The little match-seller*. Retrieved on November 8, 2004, from http://hca.gilead.org.il/li_match.html

Bakhtin, M. (1981). *The dialogic imagination: Four essays.* (M. Holoquist, Ed. & Trans.). Austin: University of Texas Press.

Bassett, P. (1992). Resolving pink and brown conflicts resulting from the white male system. In L. B. Welch (Ed.), *Perspectives on minority women in higher education* (pp. 13–22). New York: Praeger.

Beckett, G. H. (1999). *Project-based instruction in a Canadian secondary school's ESL classes: Goals and evaluations.* Unpublished doctoral dissertation, Vancouver, Canada.

Belcher, D., & Conner, U. (Eds.). (2001). *Reflections on multiliterate lives.* Clevedon, UK: Multilingual Matters.

Braine, G. (Ed.). (1999). *Non-native educators in English language teaching.* Mahwah, NJ: Erlbaum.

Clandinin, D. J., & Connolly, F. M. (1994). *Personal experience methods.* In N. Denzin & Y. Lincoln (Eds.). *Handbook of qualitative research* (pp. 413–427). London: Sage.

Confucious. Retrieved November 11, 2004, from www.crystalinks.com/confucius.html

Flowerdew, J., & Miller, L. (1995). On the notion of culture in L2 lectures. *TESOL Quarterly, 2*(29), 345–371.

Gardner, H. (1989). *To open minds: Chinese clues to dilemma of contemporary education.* New York: Basic Books.

Harvey, W. (2003). *Minorities in higher education 20th annual status report.* Washington, DC: American Council of Education.

Ho, D. Y. F. (1996). *Filial piety and its psychological consequences.* In M. H. Bond (Ed.), *The handbook of Chinese psychology* (pp. 155–165). Hong Kong: Oxford University Press.

Hsu, F. L. K. (1981). *Americans and Chinese: Passage to differences* (3rd ed.). Honolulu: University of Hawai'i Press.

Kingston-Mann, E., & Sieber, T. (2001). *Achieving against the odds: How academics become teachers of diverse students.* Philadelphia: Temple University Press.

Li, G. (2006). Navigating multiple roles and multiple discourses: A young Asian female scholar's reflection on within-race-and-gender interactions. In G. Li & G. H. Beckett (Eds.), *"Strangers" of the academy: Asian women scholars in higher education.* Sterling, VA: Stylus Publishing.

Liang, X. (2006). Professing in a nonnative tongue: Narrative construction of realities and opportunities. In G. Li & G. Beckett (Eds.), *"Strangers" of the academy: Asian women scholars in higher education.* Sterling, VA: Stylus Publishing.

Lin, A., Grant, R., Kubota, R., Motha, S., Sachs, G. T., Vandrick, S., et al. (2004). Women faculty of color in TESOL: Theorizing our experiences. *TESOL Quarterly, 38*(3), 487–504.

Loo, C., & Ho, H. (2006). Asian American women in the academy: Overcoming stress and overturning denials in advancement. In G. Li & G. H. Beckett

(Eds.), *"Strangers" of the academy: Asian women scholars in higher education.* Sterling, VA: Stylus Publishing.

Mirriam, S. (1998). *Qualitative research and case study applications in education.* San Francisco: Jossey-Bass.

National Study of Postsecondary Faculty. (1998–1999). Retrieved November 13, 2004, from http://nces.ed.gov/surveys/nsopf/

Phillipson, R. (1992). *Linguistic imperialism.* Oxford, UK: Oxford University Press.

Pratt, D. (1992). Chinese conceptions of learning and teaching: A Westerner's attempt at understanding. *International Journal of Lifelong Learning, 11*(4), 301–319.

Spradley, J. P. (1980). *Participant observation.* Fort Worth, TX: Harcourt.

U.S. Department of Education. (2002). *Digest of education statistics.* Washington, DC: Office of Educational Research and Improvement.

van Manen, M. (1990). *Researching lived experience: Human science for an action sensitive pedagogy.* New York: SUNY Press.

Vargas, L. (Ed.). (2002). *Women faculty of color in the white classroom: Narratives on the pedagogical implications of teacher diversity.* New York: Peter Lang.

PART FOUR

BUILDING BRIDGES, BUILDING THE FUTURE

13

THE ROAD LESS TRAVELED

An Asian Woman Immigrant Faculty's Experience Practicing Global Pedagogy in Teacher Education

Guichun Zong

We live in a world of increasing complexity, interconnectedness and volatility; a world in which
the lives and livelihoods of every one of us are
bound up with processes operating at a global
scale.

Peter Dicken

A s a first-generation Chinese immigrant woman faculty having taught in two Research 1 universities in the United States, I have crossed many borders, built bridges, and negotiated cultural differences. In this chapter I trace my experiences from my childhood during the Mao era of China to my professional journey in the United States in order to address issues of the impact of lived experiences on pedagogy, especially in the context of an immigrant woman faculty member working at a Research 1 university in the southeastern region of the United States. By talking and writing about my own trajectory and by reflecting on my adjustments, challenges, struggles, and rewards, in this descriptive and interpretative essay, I explore the following questions: How have my lived experiences shaped my teaching pedagogy today? How have I reconciled my duality and marginality and used them as assets to advance teaching from a global perspective? To respond to these interrelated questions, I hope this analysis of my own experiences will shed light on questions of a much wider scope, such as "why aren't teachers being prepared to teach for diversity, equity, and global interconnectedness?"

(Merryfield, 2002, p. 429). Or, how can our entry as immigrant professors contribute to making colleges and universities institutions of global learning?

Writing this essay is guided by the theory and research related to understanding lived experience (van Manen, 1990), the influence of teachers' stories and narratives (Connelly & Clandinin, 1999), and the contribution of cross-cultural experiences to the development of multicultural and global educators (Merryfield, 2002; Wilson, 1982, 1998). Relying on the power of interpretive autobiography and reflective inquiry to investigate social interaction and lived experiences (Angrosino, 1989; Denzin, 1997; Ellis & Bochner, 2003; van Manen, 1990), I use my personal experience and autobiographic voice (Creswell, 1998; Davies, 1999) to guide and frame my writing. The account is based on my own recollections of and reflections on classroom events, and a close reading of documents and archival materials such as student evaluations, syllabi, discussion notes, and samples of students' work. In addition, I have drawn upon published autobiographical research of other women faculty of immigrant background.

What constitutes lived experiences? How do people make sense of their lived experiences? In searching the literature on understanding lived experiences, I found van Manen's (1990) comments on the temporal nature of lived experiences particularly germane to my inquiry:

> Various thinkers have noted that lived experience first of all has a temporal structure: it can never be grasped in its immediate manifestation but only reflectively as past presence. . . . Lived experience is the breathing of meaning. . . . Thus a lived experience has a certain essence, a "quality" that we gain in retrospect. (p. 36)

Van Manen (1990) also points out how reflective writing interacts with experience to "teach us what we know, and in what way we know what we know" (p. 127). I also agree with Britzman's (1994) and McCarthy's (1998) post-structuralist perspective on the dynamic influence of one's identity and the contexts of power on how experiences are seen and interpreted over time. They argue that power undergirds the construction of identities and interpretations of experiences. This interaction across identity, power, and experience is central to understanding how lived experiences create meaning in people's lives. It is in the telling of experiences, in creating narratives of one's experience, that who a person is and what the person has experienced become important and meaningful. Because of the interconnectedness of identity, power, lived experience, writing, and reflection, learning from lived experiences may differ considerably among those who differ in race, class, gender, language, and national origin.

In this interpretative and self-reflective essay and by recounting my journey from a girl growing up during the Mao era of China to an immigrant faculty in the United States, I try to explore how to understand my past experiences in relation to the time and place where I am today, and how these experiences have shaped my work in and commitment to multicultural and global education.

Personal History: Growing Up during the Mao Era in China

Like many first-generation immigrants to this country, my story is also one of crossing borders—cultural as well as physical. My childhood, my travels, and my cultural resilience (Montero-Sieburth, 2000) have a lot to do with who I am and what I have decided to pursue in my academic career today. I was born in a small town located in the northeastern part of China in 1966, the year when the Chinese Cultural Revolution began. My childhood and early education were significantly influenced by the rhetoric of that historic era. However, contrary to the all-too-familiar themes of political persecution, victimization, and sexual repression presented in existing memoirs written in English by Chinese and about the authors' experiences during the Cultural Revolution, such as *Wild Swans, Red Azalea,* and *Spider Eater,* my memories are related more to the Mao era's gender equality policies, which were rather liberating to those of us who grew up female (Zheng, 2001). As many Chinese women who grew up during those years, I was deeply influenced by slogans such as "women were holding up half of the sky," "equal pay for equal work," and "girls can do everything boys can do" (Rong, 2002, p. 132). I had always enjoyed participating in sports and studying math and science. During three years of high school, my academic achievement was always in the top 5 percent among two hundred students in the science track. My childhood dream was to become a scientist to build a strong and prosperous China, as well as to serve people around the world.

At the age of eighteen, I took the national college entrance exam and was admitted to Beijing Normal University (BNU). As one of the leading national universities in China, BNU's prestige lies not only in its academic rigor and excellence, but also in its long history of students' active participation in the nation's social and political movements, including the famous May Fourth movement in the 1920s (BNU, 2004). The students at the university were selected from every province, autonomous region, and municipality in China, and represented many of the fifty-six official ethnic groups or nationalities. During my seven-year stay at BNU working on my bachelor's and master's degrees, I studied and worked with students from many ethnic groups across China, such as Mongolians, Tibetans, Uighurs from the northwest, Koreans from the northeast, and Miao, Yi, and Zhaung people from the southwest part of China. This provided me with my first cross-cultural learning experiences.

During the same time that I was studying at BNU (1984–1991), China was going through many profound and rapid changes, economically, ideologically, and socially. One of the major changes was that China gradually opened up to the international community after decades of isolation during the Mao era. Fascinated by the dynamic changes taking place in the society and the social science courses that I was taking at the university, I decided to switch my major from math and science education to social studies education. After graduating from Beijing Normal University, I worked in China's National Research Institute for Curriculum and Instruction for five years, where I participated in several national projects in K–12 curriculum development, teacher professional training, and school-based research activities, before I came to the United States in 1995 to pursue a doctorate degree in social studies education.

This restructuring of my experience in China is important. In retrospect, it has had a great impact on who I am and how I perceive myself today. Because I am a Han Chinese, the largest ethnic group in China both culturally and numerically, making up over 92 percent of nation's population (Zou, 2000), and also because I was from a region in which standard Chinese is spoken, I had always been part of the majority culturally as well as linguistically, even if I didn't realize it at the time. Because I did not grow up as a member of a domestic minority in the United States, the development of my self-identity has not been significantly affected by either internal colonization or misconceptions and media stereotypes of Asians in general and of Chinese in particular. I do not see myself falling into any of the categories of Asian women portrayed in Deborah Gee's documentary *Slaying the Dragon*: the sinister dragon lady, the sexually submissive geisha girl, or "Connie Chung," the token minority news anchor (*Slaying the Dragon*, 1988). When confronted with shameful injustice and unfair treatment, instead of being "quiet and compliant," or simply walking away (Akindes, 2002; Nakanishi, 1993), I stand up and fiercely fight back.

In fact, it has taken me a very long time to realize at all that my accent, my color, my national origin, and my ethnicity may be attached to me as a scholar in the academy and that this could associate me with marginality in some way. In contrast to my awareness of minority status and marginalized experience, which developed much later after I came to the United States, my experiences from China have provided me with a solid self-confidence and a strong desire to challenge the deeply rooted stereotype of "oriental feminine passiveness and permissiveness," to resist the imposition of an identity as "invisible and outsider," and to promote understanding among world cultures and its people. These experiences, along with a later experiential understanding of discrimination and outsider status encountered in the United States, have significantly shaped my consciousness of nationality, class, culture, race, gender, and ethnicity. It is this consciousness that has transformed how I perceive myself—my identity—and how I teach—my pedagogy—and it is also this consciousness that prompts me to make global and multicultural awareness and action the centerpiece of my teaching and research.

Situating Myself

In the summer of 1995 I left Beijing and came to the United States to pursue my doctoral degree in social studies and global education with the late Professor Jan Tucker, an internationally known social studies educator and one of the earliest advocates for global education in the nation. I was deeply influenced by his vision of teacher education in a global age. He challenged the prevailing conception of teacher education as only content plus pedagogy and called for teacher-educators in the universities to be at the vanguard of the change process in global education (Tucker, 1982, 1991). Most of my coursework was centered on understanding globalization and its implications for education. I was actively engaged in inquiries about the historical and contemporary connections among nations. Also during this time, I visited the USS *Arizona* Memorial in Pearl Harbor and the Holocaust Museum in Washington, D.C. I also went to Japan with a group of social studies teachers from Miami on a two-week study trip, where we visited Hiroshima Peace Park. Throughout my doctoral program, I worked closely with teachers from the multicultural greater Miami area in various teacher professional-development activities in global education. Immediately after graduation in the fall of 1999, I joined the faculty of a comprehensive Research 1 university in Kentucky as an assistant professor in the college of education. My major teaching responsibility was to prepare preservice and practicing teachers to teach social studies.

At the time I joined the university, out of ninety-four faculty members in the college of education, only three of us were immigrant faculty. One was from Germany. One was from New Zealand. I was the only one from Asia and from a developing country. The student population in the college was predominantly White with 7.1 percent from minority backgrounds, which was consistent with the general population of the state. In my social studies methods class, each semester I had about fifty-five to sixty college seniors who majored in elementary education. Among them, there were two or three African American students, the only ethnic minority in the group. Most of the students were White females from middle-class backgrounds from the state of Kentucky. They were not generally accustomed to being taught by faculty with an immigrant background, particularly in their education courses. At the time the students were in my social studies class they were also taking three other methods courses in what the program called the professional block: language arts, mathematics, and science. During my first year at this university, I was the only female, foreign, and junior faculty member among the four professors who taught in the block.

After teaching in this Kentucky university for four years, in August of 2003, I moved to my current university, also a Research 1 university but located in a multicultural urban setting. The teaching experiences I describe in this chapter mostly took place in the first university where I worked.

Teaching Globally

My philosophy of teaching has been informed by the tenets of global pedagogy, which posits that teaching social studies from a global perspective differs from traditional approaches to the study of communities, cultures, geography, and history both substantively and perceptually (Case, 1993; Hanvey, 1976; Kniep, 1989; Merryfield, 2001; Wilson, 1997). My earlier work had been influenced by Hanvey's five dimensions of global perspectives: (a) perspective consciousness, an awareness of and appreciation for other images of the world; (b) state-of-the-planet awareness, an in-depth understanding of prevailing global issues, events, and conditions; (c) cross-cultural awareness, a general understanding of the main characteristics of world cultures with an emphasis on understanding differences and similarities; (d) knowledge of global dynamics, a familiarity with the nature of systems and an introduction to the complex international system in which state and nonstate actors are linked in patterns of interdependence and dependence in a variety of issue areas, and a consciousness of global change; and (e) awareness of human choices, a review of strategies for action on issues in local, national, and international settings. More recently I have found Merryfield's (2001, 2002) writing in global education particularly illuminating. She argues that in order for global education to be truly global or world centered, it is critical to examine how the educational legacy of imperialism has shaped mainstream academic knowledge; to incorporate the experiences, ideas, and knowledge of people who are usually omitted, marginalized or misrepresented in mainstream academic knowledge; and to engage in cross-cultural experiential learning (2001, p. 182).

These principles guide my curricular and instructional decisions, which are student centered and world oriented. The central aim in all my classes is to help students understand various global connections and to tap into their sense of themselves as global citizens, as intercultural beings (Luthra, 2002). I have organized various teaching-learning experiences in pursuit of these goals. These have included inquiry-based community study projects to explore real-life connections between the local community and people and places around the world, Internet-based multinational discussion forums to practice cross-cultural experiential learning, and contrapuntal readings (Said, 1993, p. 51; Wilson, 1998, p. 421) to broaden students' worldviews.

Community study and state history are two major components of most states' required elementary and middle school social studies curriculums. In order to help preservice teachers explore and analyze various local and global connections within the mandated curriculum, one activity that I developed for a social studies methods class is an inquiry-based project titled, "The World in Our Community/Our Community in the World." The preservice teachers are expected to choose one aspect of their community, such as arts, economy, government, recreation, or values and beliefs and examine how the chosen aspect has changed in the past several decades. They are encouraged to use various historical inquiries such as analyzing primary sources and conducting interviews to reconstruct the development of the community. Their examinations and analyses are guided by two central questions: What evidence is there that this aspect of the community has changed over time? What evidence is there that this aspect of the community has been internationalized? Most students find this a very challenging but rewarding assignment, and realize that their community is connected with the world in multiple ways, economically, politically, and culturally. Some students find representations of global issues at the local level. For example, one student explored the history of Kentucky's coal mining industry. She unexpectedly "discovered" the history of child labor, an issue she had always thought as a problem in developing countries. In reflecting her experience with the project, this student wrote:

> In our class project of the community study, my group selected coal mining in Kentucky. As we were looking for information about mining, we discovered that children were used frequently in the small, dangerous mine areas. Children were also used to sort the coal pieces in machinery, leading to the frequent loss of fingers. I had always thought child labor as an issue of poor countries and had never realized the prominent history of child labor in our country. This is something that American children can easily relate to, since children their own age all over the world are suffering in deplorable conditions. When I have my own classroom, I will definitely teach the issue of child labor. I will begin by teaching coal mining as a part of our state history. I will organize a unit on child labor all around the world. I think this will give students a local perspective on the world issue and help them feel empowered to change things.

Another strength that I bring to teaching as an immigrant faculty member is that I firmly believe in cross-cultural experiential learning. As suggested by Merryfield (2001) and Wilson (1982, 1997), cross-cultural experiential learning goes beyond the academic study of differences to place people in real-life situations in which they experience the complexities of deep culture. It requires students to demonstrate their ability to use cultural knowledge and skills in actual cross-cultural communication and conflict management. We are not just Black, White, Asian, or Latino—we are also world citizens, inhabitants of planet Earth, and as such we are obligated to try to learn about others on the international scene, seek to understand multiple lives and experiences, and examine the issues that confront human beings as a whole. This learning has become particularly important after the events of September 11, 2001. The terrorist attacks and their aftermath have posed both new challenges and provide new opportunities for educators to rethink what Americans should know and understand about the world.

Since it has been so important in my own professional development, I actively create learning activities that encourage students to participate in cross-cultural experiential learning in all my classes. I have adopted Angene Wilson's (1997) "Hierarchy of Intercultural Experiences" model to guide and assess students' progress in cross-cultural learning. Starting in the fall semester of 2001, I have integrated an Internet-based multinational communication project, International Education and Resource Network (iEARN) into my teaching at both undergraduate and graduate levels. With iEARN online discussion forums, my students are able to talk with students and teachers from nearly thirty countries around the world on a range of topics, from local culture/history in Baku, Azerbaijan, to child labor practices in Pakistan; from child soldiers in Sierra Leone to hunger in Zimbabwe; from women's roles in Iran to the U.S-led wars in Afghanistan and Iraq. Through these online discussion forums, students not only learn about various issues facing the world today, but also get different perspectives on these issues. Most students appreciate their exposure to the authentic voices of ordinary teachers and students from other countries, the voices that are generally left out or marginalized in the mainstream media and official textbooks. At the end of one class, an undergraduate student wrote:

> I would like to begin by thanking you, Dr. Zong, for giving us the opportunity to participate in this communication project. My experience over the course of the semester with the iEARN interactive forums proved to be highly educational and enlightening. Through the project, I gained insight into various global perspectives and happenings throughout the world. I interacted with people from the United States, Bulgaria, China, Lithuania, Mexico, and Pakistan. I don't feel that I have had much experience with global education in my life. I don't know if it was a trend when I was in elementary school that we didn't study a whole lot about other countries. The only experience I can remember of learning about countries other than the United States was when I was in high school and took Spanish as my foreign language. We learned about Spanish and Mexican cultural elements. Otherwise, I don't know much about other countries. I don't want this to be the case for the children that I will teach someday. It is important to have a global view and to see other countries' perspectives on issues.

Another student commented:

> I have really learned a lot through my experiences of using iEARN message board. I was amazed to learn and read about life in other countries. Although I have learned about other countries and know that the life is different, it is still sometimes easy to forget until you are able to hear from those people *themselves*. I thought it was especially interesting to hear people's opinions on some of the major issues, especially the war (in Iraq), which was very pertinent at the time. I really enjoyed reading the thoughts of people in various countries concerning United States' involvement in the war.

In various iEARN discussion forums, the most heated discussions have been centered on the perceptions of the United States held by people from other countries. In reading several online messages posted by high school students from Asian countries harshly criticizing U.S. involvement in the Middle East, most students in my class were shocked and quite a few of them were very upset and defensive. They blamed those who wrote the messages for being ignorant or being manipulated by foreign media or their governments. Only one or two students each semester felt that there was some truth to the messages and that it was time for us to carefully examine U.S. foreign policies. This is often a very tense experience for students, since they don't want to be labeled or thought of as either unpatriotic or uncritical. I am very careful to explain to the students that we all are ethnocentric to some extent and have both positive and negative stereotypes ingrained in our psyches, and that my classroom is a place to explore and address how we have come to some of these opinions and visions of others and ourselves. It is also very important to separate facts from opinions when we judge people, government, and policies.

Rewards and Resistance

Many immigrant and U.S.-born women faculty of color strive to engage their students in learning about societies and cultures other than their own and to make global perspective a defining element of their teaching (Davis, 2002; Luthra, 2002). Like them, I have learned that global pedagogy brings remarkable teaching-learning opportunities to the classroom, even while it presents both professors and students with a new challenge.

Over the years, I have received many positive responses from students who appreciate my practice of global pedagogy. One graduate student wrote in her course evaluation, "This course has changed the way I think about the world we live in. It made me realize that for so many reasons, our world is a much smaller place. It is no longer possible to remain isolated Americans. I am much more interested in the news and have found myself watching CNN a lot more often!" Some of my students took the ideas and learning from my classes further in their practica, student-teaching placements, and later on, their own classrooms. Quite a few of my former students have invited me to their classrooms as a guest speaker when they organize units on East Asia, particularly on China. My memories of driving along the winding roads of east and central Kentucky to visit my students' classes and to talk about the world with their students still provides the strongest source of encouragement for what I am doing today.

Other students have appreciated the way I address diversity issues and the inclusive learning environment I have created in my classroom. Many of my students from Appalachian areas have found ways of making their identities and histories visible in my class in a way that they cannot do in most other courses. Some of them have been vocal for the first time, saying they find it difficult to join discussions in other courses because of their "mountain accent."

Like many educators who practice progressive pedagogy, I have also met some resistance to my teaching from a global perspective, even though the resistance is subtle most of the time. Some of the resistance was related to the nature of the courses that I was teaching; other kinds were directly related to my position as an immigrant faculty. Since my students were undergraduates who majored in elementary education, and the state curriculum at elementary level only requires teaching about Canada and Mexico besides the content on the United States, many students' understanding of and motivation in learning about global events and issues was limited. They were also deeply concerned about being politically safe, and reluctant to teach anything that might be controversial. Although I never had any students write negative comments about my efforts to bring a global perspective into teaching, I can tell some students were not very comfortable with some of the ideas discussed in the class, particularly the ones critical of the U.S. government and its policies. As hooks (1994) reminds us, engaging in progressive pedagogies is not easy and not without discomfort and uncertainty. Like hooks (1994), I have found that "in the transformed classroom, there is often a much greater need to explain philosophy, strategy, intent than in the 'norm' setting" (p. 42).

Conclusion

The journey of a Chinese girl who grew up in the Mao Era of China and who became an immigrant woman faculty practicing global pedagogy in American universities required constant identity adjustments, border crossings, and cultural negotiations. It has been an ongoing, ever-present transformation, both on a personal level and a professional level. I have learned to negotiate unfamiliar situations, carved my own reality for myself, and developed an inner self-reliance to survive in different circumstances and live in multiple cultures. I have also been able to draw upon the experiential learning gained from these experiences to advance my teaching.

My pedagogy today emanates from my lived experiences in a small town of northeastern China, in cosmopolitan Beijing, in multicultural and multiethnic Miami, and in seemingly homogeneous yet increasingly diverse central Kentucky. It is a pedagogy that draws upon learning from my trips to the USS *Arizona* Memorial in Pearl Harbor, the Holocaust Museum in Washington, the Nanjing Massacre Memorial in Nanjing, China, and the Hiroshima Peace Park in Japan. My lived experiences shape my consciousness as a teacher committed to global education and enable me to translate theoretical concepts into everyday practice. They also inform my understanding of teaching and learning and explain why much of my teaching is grounded in an experiential orientation.

Connelly and Clandinin (1999) argue that studying teachers' lives provides valuable insights and assists educational reform and restructuring. This reflection on and analysis of my experiences has helped me to put my teaching experiences as an immigrant woman faculty in a new perspective. It has allowed me to bring my collective teaching experiences into a clearer focus. Although the experiences and the perceptions are my own, I hope this work will provide some insight into the unique contributions that faculty with immigrant backgrounds can bring to our colleges and universities.

As American culture, demography, economics, politics, and technology become increasingly globalized, colleges and universities in the United States have been called upon to be at the vanguard of the change process in global education (Stromquist, 2002; Tucker, 1982). With the many strengths that we bring to the institution, such as our cultural and linguistic background, knowledge of our nations of origin, and diverse cultural perspectives, we immigrant professors have the potential to make significant contributions to this change process in global education. The very presence of immigrant faculty on campus provides experiential learning opportunities for cross-cultural communication and understanding, which is an essential skill to thrive in our increasingly diverse society, a society where cross-cultural and cross-linguistic contacts in communities, schools, and the workplace are increasingly becoming the norm rather than the exception, where the future lies with those who are able to accommodate, communicate, and collaborate across racial, ethnic, cultural, and linguistic lines (Kubota, 2002). Wilson (1998) suggests that because of the impact of experiences, a cross-culturally experienced person often becomes a cultural mediator or a bridge between cultures. Obviously, an immigrant faculty is in a good position to play that role.

References

Akindes, F. Y. (2002). The pacific Asianized other: Teaching unlearning among midwestern students. In L. Vargas (Ed.), *Women faculty of color in the white classroom: Narratives on the pedagogical implications of teacher diversity* (pp. 163–181). New York: Peter Lang.

Angrosino, M. V. (1989). *Documents of interaction: Biography, autobiography, and life history in social sciences perspective.* Gainesville: University of Florida Press.

Beijing Normal University. (2004). *Brief history of Beijing Normal University.* Retrieved June 10, 2004, from www.bnu.edu.cn/focus/survey/history.htm

Britzman, D. P. (1994). Is there a problem with knowing thyself? Towards a poststructuralist view of teacher identity. In T. Shanahan (Ed.), *Teachers thinking, teachers knowing: Reflections on literacy and language education* (pp. 53–75). Urbana, IL: National Conference on Research in English/National Council of Teachers of English.

Case, R. (1993). Key elements of a global perspective. *Social Education, 57*, 318–325.

Connelly, F. M., & Clandinin, D. J. (1999). *Shaping professional Identity: Stories of educational practice.* New York: Teachers College Press.

Creswell, J. W. (1998). *Qualitative inquiry and research design.* Thousand Oaks, CA: Sage.

Davies, C. A. (1999). *Reflective ethnography.* London: Association of Social Anthropologists.

Davis, Z. I. (2002). Pushing beyond the stereotypes and fostering collaboration: One student's approach to teaching media production. In L. Vargas (Ed.), *Women faculty of color in the white classroom: Narratives on the pedagogical implications of teacher diversity* (pp. 201–217). New York: Peter Lang.

Denzin, N. K. (1997). *Interpretive biography.* Newbury Park, CA: Sage.

Dicken, P. (2003). *Global shift.* New York: Guilford Press.

Ellis, C., & Bochner, A. P. (2003). Autoethnography, personal narrative, reflexivity. In N. K. Denzin & Y. S. Lincoln (Eds.), *Collecting and interpreting qualitative materials.* Thousand Oaks, CA: Sage.

Gee, D. (Director). (1988). *Slaying the dragon* [Videocassette]. San Francisco: National Asian American Telecommunication Association.

Hanvey, R. G. (1976). *An attainable global perspective.* New York: Center for Global Perspectives in Education.

hooks, b. (1994). Eros, eroticism, and pedagogical process. In H. Giroux & P. McLaren (Eds.), *Between borders: Pedagogy and the politics of cultural studies.* New York: Routledge.

Kniep, W. M. (1989). Social studies within global education. *Social Education, 53,* 399–403.

Kubota, R. (2002). Marginality as an asset: Toward a counter-hegemonic pedagogy for diversity. In L. Vargas (Ed.), *Women faculty of color in the white classroom: Narratives on the pedagogical implications of teacher diversity* (pp. 293–307). New York: Peter Lang.

Luthra, R. (2002). Negotiating the minefield: Practicing transformative pedagogy as a teacher of color in a classroom climate of suspicion. In L. Vargas (Ed.), *Women faculty of color in the white classroom: Narratives on the pedagogical implications of teacher diversity* (pp. 109–123). New York: Peter Lang.

McCarthy, C. (1998). *The use of culture.* New York: Routledge.

Merryfield, M. M. (2001). Moving the center of global education: From imperial worldviews that divide the world to double consciousness, contrapuntal pedagogy, hybridity, and cross-cultural competence. In W. Stanley (Ed.), *Critical issues in social studies research for the 21st century* (pp. 179–208). Greenwich, CT: Information Age Publishing.

Merryfield, M. (2002). Why aren't teachers being prepared to teach for diversity, equity, and global interconnectedness? A study of lived experiences in the making of multicultural and global educators. *Teaching and Teaching Education, 16,* 429–443.

Montero-Sieburth, M. (2000). The use of cultural resilience in overcoming contradictory encounters in academia: A personal narrative. In H. Trueba & L. Bartolome (Eds.), *Immigrant voices: In search of educational equity* (pp. 219–246). Lanham, MD: Rowman & Littlefield.

Nakanishi, D. T. (1993). Asian Pacific Americans in higher education: Faculty and administrative representation and tenure. *New Directions for Teaching and Learning, 53,* 51–55.

Rong, X. L. (2002). Teaching with differences and for differences: Reflections of a Chinese American teacher educator. In L. Vargas (Ed.), *Women faculty of color in the white classroom: Narratives on the pedagogical implications of teacher diversity* (125–144). New York: Peter Lang.

Said, E. W. (1993). *Culture and imperialism.* New York: Knopf.

Stromquist, N. P. (2002). *Education in a globalized world.* Lanham, MD: Rowman & Littlefield.

Tucker, J. L. (1982). Developing a global dimension in teacher education: The Florida International University experience. *Theory into Practice, 21,* 212–217.

Tucker, J. L. (1991). Global perspectives for teachers: An urgent priority. *Journal of Teacher Education, 42,* 3–10.

van Manen, M. (1990). *Researching lived experiences: Human science for an action sensitive pedagogy.* Albany, NY: SUNY Press.

Wilson, A. (1982). Cross-cultural experiential learning for teachers. *Theory into Practice, 21,* 184–192.

Wilson, A. (1997). Infusing global perspectives throughout a secondary social studies program. In M. Merryfield, E. Jarchow, & S. Pickert (Eds.), *Preparing teachers to teach global perspectives: A handbook for teacher education* (pp. 1–24). Thousand Oaks, CA: Corwin Press.

Wilson, A. (1998). Oburoni outside the whale: Reflections on an experience in Ghana. *Theory and Research in Social Education, 26,* 410–429.

Zheng, W. (2001). Call me "QINGNIAN" but not "FUNU": A Maoist youth in retrospect. In X. Zhong, Z. Wang, & D. Bai (Eds.), *Some of us: Chinese women growing up in the Mao era.* New Brunswick, NJ: Rutgers University Press.

Zou, Y. (2000). The voice of a Chinese immigrant in America: Reflections on research and self-identity. In H. Trueba & L. Bartolome (Eds.), *Immigrant voices: In search of educational equity* (pp. 187–202). Lanham, MD: Rowman & Littlefield.

14

FROM MENTORSHIP TO FRIENDSHIP, COLLABORATION, AND COLLEGIALITY

Xue Lan Rong and Judith Preissle

I n the 1980s because of internal and external pressures to comply with affirmative action goals or to fulfill diversity expectations, U.S. higher education institutions launched efforts to recruit women and members of minority groups. As a result a record number of minority women have been brought into U.S. colleges and universities, including a considerable number of Asian American women (e.g., Kolodny, 2000). The climate in the United States has since changed as affirmative action programs have come under legal challenge. This is a propitious time to consider the career progress and advancement of minorities and women: the interplay of class, race, gender, and ethnicity in these situations; the consequences of institutional and collegiate efforts for the lives of academics in graduate school and beyond; and the influence of a diversified academic workforce on scholarship and teaching. The academic preparation of Asian graduate students who aspire to become researchers and teachers in higher education has received little attention in the research literature, and the professional advancement of Asian American faculty members through the academic pipeline remains largely unstudied.

This chapter is based on the paper, "An Ethnographer, a Demographer, and the 'Graphy,'" presented at the annual meeting of the American Educational Research Association, April 11, 2001, Seattle, Washington. We are grateful for the critical reviews of our colleague Linda Grant and our editors Guofang Li and Gulbahar H. Beckett.

In this chapter we offer an autoethnography of the experiences of an Asian American scholar, Xue Lan Rong, and her European American colleague, Judith Preissle. We draw from a contextual-developmental theory defining mentoring as a dynamic, reciprocal association between an advanced career incumbent (the mentor) and a less experienced protégé (a mentee) aimed at promoting career development and qualitative identity transformation for both scholars (Frierson, 1997). These experiences illustrate patterns in mentoring that compare and contrast with the literature. Our experiences may also have implications for academic practice and academic induction. We speculate about the influences of mentoring across differences on research collaboration, multiple methods research, and what has come to be called interdisciplinarity.

Mentoring has been claimed as important in the career advancement of academics across stages, from studying in graduate programs to working for tenure (e.g., Fort, 1993). However, it may be essential in higher educational institutions for minority members and women, who were seen as "unconventional" scholars and professors by their students and colleagues in the 1980s and early 1990s (e.g., Rong, 2002).

Mentoring, advocated by Bramen (2000) as crucial to socialization in academic environments, facilitates collegiality and positive social contact, intellectual exchanges, and other valuable opportunities. Requiring constant effort, these functions are critical for getting novices into "the loop." The literature on mentoring indicates it has a common developmental function in individuals' personal, professional, and psychological lives. These functions include such activities as providing mentees with interpersonal networks, counseling, guidance, instruction, modeling, and sponsorship.

In considering the extensiveness of the relationship and its positive effects on the mentee's academic career, Holland (1995) used a grounded theory approach to identify five types of relationships that African American doctoral students have with their major advisors: formal academic advisement relationships, academic guidance relationships, quasi-apprenticeship relationships, academic mentoring relationships, and career mentoring relationships. The latter two relationships are the most extensive and may produce ultimate positive results and a constructive long-term relationship for both mentor and mentee. As described by Welch (1997), in these developmental relationships the mentors take a personal interest in the mentees, become developmental role models who share with mentees their own successful or less than successful experiences, and work closely with mentees to enhance their academic preparation and career success.

Many questions remain about mentoring, however. Merriam (1983) emphasizes the limitations on what we know about it because mentoring research lacks common conceptualizations of what mentoring is. Holland (1995), as we note, suggests it can be advising, guiding, apprenticing, academic directing, or career counseling. Weil (2001), however, cautions that the intensity, intimacy, and commitment of long-term mentoring ought not be confused with such institutionally mandated roles as advisor or thesis director. She emphasizes that the former is voluntary and can occur only with the devoted contributions of both mentor and mentee. Mirandé (1988) discusses the experience of becoming a successful academic without a mentor, and Collins (1983) speculates about the limitations of mentoring, especially its fostering of conventionality. Mentoring may ensure individuals' career success at the cost of discouraging the innovative, the creative, and the daring. Mentors may seek clones, copies of themselves, rather than encourage difference. Collins advocates peer networking as an alternative to mentoring, but Menges and Exum (1983) comment that the same forces that limit the availability of mentors also limit the range of peers in most fields.

Another topic missing in the already scant higher educational literature is cross-cultural mentorship. Added to this is a lack of research on collaborations between scholars different from each other in academic discipline and research methodology as well as in professional stage, race and ethnicity, nativity, and mother tongue. Collaborative research is certainly valued and advocated in academia (e.g., Macrina, 1995), but inquiry about the development of mentorship into collaborative efforts is rare.

In this study, we focus our narratives and analyses on the transformation of our mentor-mentee relationship, emphasizing knowledge inquiry through mutual cultural exploration and interdisciplinary research collaboration. This informal mentorship, not part of any institutional requirement, has been a spontaneous relationship from the beginning. We characterize our ongoing and evolving relationship as reciprocal, dynamic, and rejuvenating. This relationship started as an Asian international student eagerly looking for guidance from a European American professor in a graduate program. It has developed into an ongoing journey of mutual cultural exploration, cross-disciplinary writing, and multiple methodological inquiries.

Our Stories

How do researchers move from the information that they designate as data to the claims and interpretations that once were taken as representations of how the world works and now are regarded as privileged explanations of that world? How does the writing of these representations and explanations get done, and what happens as the scholars are doing it? If the privileged explanation is a perspective, how do people work together to devise a common perspective? How does that happen when the people are different from one another in many ways? Furthermore, how does collaboration evolve and how is the value of joint writing substantiated when the contributors begin as unequal in academic rank, research sophistication, and publication experience?

We are a professional demographer and a professional ethnographer whose collaboration is nearly twenty-five years old. Ethnography and demography—what we study and how—are central to our experiences together. "Graphy" has a Greek root and means "writing." Both "demo" and "ethno" refer to people, although in modern times demo-graphy means writing about distributional patterns of population characteristics and ethno-graphy means writing about people's lived experiences. So we both write, and we both write about people, but about different aspects of humans and their societies.

Our research and writing collaboration has developed along three contrasting and complementary relationships:

1. An immigrant-host relationship that grew into a relationship of mutual cultural exploration
2. A student-teacher relationship that grew into a collaborative and collegial relationship
3. A demographer-ethnographer and macrosociologist-anthropologist relationship that grew into an interactive search for how to connect the universal and the particular and how to represent the connection.

In the following pages we discuss our work together as it developed over time through the frameworks of these three relationships. Although we discuss them separately, they actually overlapped and intertwined, the way the strands of a rope wind together to make a strong connection. The growth and transformation of each relationship enhanced the other relationships, and together they have strengthened the ties between us.

We classify the approach we take in this chapter as autobiographic and autoethnographic. This is an unconventional, but increasingly recognized research design for studying groups and individuals who "differ" from the "mainstream cultural norms" and for offering for analysis the lived experiences of even so-called ordinary people (Ellis & Bochner, 2000). Autoethnography links the self (auto) to the culture (ethno) through analysis of experience against patterns of social life and through examination of shared beliefs and behaviors through the prism of experience (Reed-Danahay, 1997). This design allows researchers to share very personal experiences with other academics. The writing of our stories combines personal, practical, and theoretical positions that link narrative, interpretation, application, and theory through analyzing interactions of the multiple aspects of our professional lives as teachers, scholars, community servers, administrators, and institutional citizens in higher education (Davies, 1999).

We also see the ongoing relationship, including our collaborative writing, as a process of intercultural communication (Y. Y. Kim, 2001). We are seeking what M.-S. Kim (2002) calls bicultural communication competence, a self-conscious and mutual selection of communication patterns that respects our cultural identities but recognizes these as fluid and dynamic. Collier (2003) emphasizes that writing interculturally requires recognizing the power of context and attending to how relationships and alliances are both enabled and constrained by institutions, ideologies, and histories. Successes and failures in bridgework and cultural translation should be acknowledged because all relationships involve both.

The narratives that follow are our testimony, jointly and separately. Sometimes we talked to each other, and other times we listened to each other without comment. We have written in a common voice in the narrative and analysis sections, but speak in our individual voices in italicized format where we are reconstructing individual experiences of events. This is intended to show how the texture of "our" voice is woven from the interaction of "my" voice and "my" voice. Despite our long association, like all people, we see things with different lenses and from different perspectives. Also like others, our memories are selective, and hence we each remember some events better or differently than other events. Even on those occasions when we seem to talk past each other, the accounts reveal crossroads and highlight intersections.

We have worked together in one capacity or another since 1982. During this period we have also written alone and in collaboration with other authors. This collaboration has exerted substantial impact on our research together and separately. The facile notion of research traditions as representing competing, mutually exclusive paradigms is challenged by our experience. Collaborative research and writing demand that individuals articulate their own various and often conflicting assumptions about knowledge: what it is, how it is generated, how it is represented, and what it means. This reflexivity can demystify research thought, illuminate the kaleidoscope of values informing research, and permit researchers to represent the richness, complexity, and downright ambiguity of social inquiry.

First, what we are claiming in this article is that writing is itself a relationship that develops between writer and presumed reader. When the writing is collaborative, the relationships are multiple. We write initially to each other to find out what we mean and whether our meanings are similar, different, or even incommensurable. We suspect that, when the meanings are irreconcilable, the process becomes turn writing; collaborators each take turns writing with no integration of text.

In our case what began as a collaboration in binaries, as represented by the left-hand side of our three relationships presented earlier, transformed into a collaboration that opened us each to multiplicities—to both/and perspectives of the world rather than either/or views. We represent this on the right-hand side of the aforementioned three relationships. Our beginning challenge was to work from an I-You relationship to an I-Thou relationship with each other, a more respectful, trusting, and open stance (Buber, 1970). Our present challenge is to move our writing from I-You with our audience to what we consider to be an I-Thou standpoint.

Second, our collaboration affects not only our research, but also our pedagogy and our participation in our communities—lay groups as well as professional associations. Our collaboration embodies the new social fabric of U.S. higher institutions of learning in the twenty-first century. United States society has further diversified in the past three decades, as have U.S. schools. Trends at the university level—especially the increase in women and minority students translating into an increase in the recruitment of women and minority faculty—have reflected national trends in diversity and have represented a partial answer to new challenges. By examining and reexamining our relationship and its development, from student-mentor, to colleagues, to coauthors (what the relationship was, is, and will be), we provide one path for the many dimensions of the transition and transformation of higher education institutions—the intergenerational adaptation patterns of networking, collegiality, and socialization of university faculty, how each faculty cohort adapts the way it was taught and prepared to teach to prepare succeeding cohorts.

Using autoethnography, we offer two voices: Xue Lan Rong, a Chinese American immigrant whose English is her second language, and Judith Preissle, or Jude, a native-born European American. When we two first met, Xue

Lan was an M.A. student and Jude was a newly tenured and promoted associate professor. Xue Lan received her doctoral degree in 1988, became an assistant professor in 1991, and earned tenure and promotion to associate professor in 1999 (cf. Okoli, 2001, for the experience of newcomers to organizations). We narrate our experiences individually, responsively, and consensually within a social constructivist framework and address these three questions:

1. How has this relationship helped Xue Lan bridge linguistic, cultural, social, and institutional differences between China and the United States and enabled her to play the multiple roles of an Asian female scholar within and between multiple cultural and value systems? How has the relationship helped Jude, born in 1943, bridge her own past understandings and enabled her to contribute to an expanding and diversifying world in a new century?

2. How has this relationship helped Xue Lan meet the challenges an Asian female scholar may face at each professional stage and how do each of us view these challenges? How has this relationship fostered an insider/outsider and self/other transformation for both Xue Lan and Jude?

3. How has the collaboration between a macrosociologist-demographer and anthropologist-ethnographer fostered a better understanding of the complexity of the school-related sociocultural issues we have studied and generated more innovative and creative approaches to new questions? How has this collaboration allowed us to do the kind of research neither of us is able to do alone? How has this collaboration channeled us into interdisciplinary and cross-disciplinary research and research using methods different from the ones we were trained to use?

Immigrant-Host Relationship

Jude: In 1982 Xue Lan took an independent study course from me in cultural anthropology. We met weekly to discuss material I assigned, and Xue Lan tape-recorded these conversations to assist her in developing facility in English. We talked about the concepts from cultural anthropology through the examples of the cultural learning she was experiencing week to week the first year in the United States. Working with Xue Lan in this independent study class brought me for the first time into the life of a young

Chinese woman scholar. The questions she asked taught me about the urban Chinese intellectual experiences of the Cultural Revolution and furthermore led me to see elements of my own U.S. and academic cultures hitherto invisible to me. I still recall my shock when Xue Lan told me about the proselytization to which many immigrants to the United States are subjected. Young people viewed as "foreigners" are often approached by strangers in the United States who seek to convert them from their "heathen" beliefs. Having experienced many conversion pressures myself, growing up in the United States, I was nevertheless horrified that people who should be regarded as guests were sometimes subjected to such rudeness and even harassed by these efforts.

Much of our conversation in that initial tutorial focused on the differences between Chinese culture and U.S. culture that required Xue Lan to change her behaviors, perceptions, and expectations of others for friendship and collegiality, teacher-student relationships, and gender relationships. Xue Lan came to realize that language transition was not only about language, but also about assumptions connected to language use. For example, we discussed why Xue Lan's advisor sent her to his wife for certain information about dress and demeanor rather than inform her himself. He had this information, of course, but in the United States at that time discussing makeup and hairstyles with a female student might have suggested a sexualized relationship that this advisor sought to avoid. Our conversations also provided Xue Lan her first face-to-face opportunity for intellectual cultural interaction and gave her a taste of the unique pedagogical approach U.S. graduate studies can provide for its students. The tutorial situation was a new experience for Xue Lan, who had previously had only large-group instruction—the more formal, hierarchical instruction traditional in China.

What the tutorial meant for me was an immersion in a comparative experience. As an anthropologist whose field experiences were limited to the rural United States, I found myself learning the culture of my own society through the questions raised by someone from elsewhere. I realized how invasive and offending, for example, proselytization is—an activity I had learned to tolerate early in my life. I also saw how vulnerable young women had become in the climate of open sexuality that had developed in the United States. The increasing freedom I had myself enjoyed, growing up at midcentury, seemed, through the issues that Xue Lan was raising, to threaten as much as to free us.

Xue Lan: While I immersed myself in a new learning experience in the format of conversation and discussion in a relatively equal relationship, this initial contact with Jude became an opportunity for me to have in-depth observations of and discussions with a woman, a female scholar, and an instructor in a completely different cultural frame and instructional circumstance. It provided a window for me to view cultural explanations of many social phenomena in China from an American scholar's point of view. The intellectual contact led me to reflect culturally on myself: who I was, what I was, how my perceptions of myself were changing during my stay in the United States, and how many more changes might be on the way. Would I find the changes desirable or even acceptable, and how might these changes conflict with my already firmly established Chinese identity, so deeply rooted in China's culture? For all these reasons there were many emotional moments for me during my meetings with Jude. As a student in an unfamiliar situation I felt both the excitement and ambivalence that accompany a process of many adjustments. The experience elevated my anxiety level: I was so uncertain about the outcome of these transformations. But I also realized, to my surprise, that my own expectations of myself had risen. I now perceived the enormous opportunities I had for personal and professional growth on this journey of knowledge inquiry. I recall going through graduate school as both an intellectual and emotional journey. Every step toward my degrees was a new challenge. Fortunately key people shepherded me early in my graduate career, eventually becoming my friends and coauthors during the long and still ongoing journey.

Xue Lan and Jude: This relationship navigates the insider/outsider and I/You situation. Jude initially served as a cultural broker for Xue Lan, enabling her to function in a U.S. graduate school, and Xue Lan served as a cultural bridge for Jude, exploring Chinese culture and working closely with an immigrant student in a mutually trusting and interested relationship. Over the years, we both have gone through multiple identity (social, racial, cultural, and professional) transformations: Xue Lan, from an international student, became an Asian American faculty member; Jude, from an associate professor, became a professor who served as a department chair, living, working, and providing leadership in a world of increasing diversity. Along with the role changes, our mutual cultural exploration has gone beyond the immigrant-host relationship, more profoundly and deeply into the socialization affecting us. Xue Lan recalled a relatively warm and diverse human environment in her graduate program quite different from the homogeneous and competitive human environment of the institution where she became a faculty member. We talked about incidents with racial or gender implications in our professional lives. We worried together about decisions that seemed unfair to us, speculating on whether some of our colleagues were conflating race and gender expectations with assessments of competence. We also discussed how we understood and interpreted such decisions "subjectively," "objectively," and interactively. Because the pattern for our mutual cultural exploration was set in the early years of our relationship, we have learned to recognize some of the cultural differences surrounding our perceptions and have become more sensitive to our differences in beliefs and worldviews as well as in communication and conflict management styles (Singh & Stoloff, 2003). We both tend to examine our own and other people's lives critically within their cultural context, but without judging the values of the cultures themselves (Welch, 1997). We believe we have been able to maintain openness and honesty when our conversations have dealt with controversial issues, such as the workplace treatment of junior faculty members and racial, gender, and cultural stereotypes. We believe we have been transformed in our journey of mutual cultural exploration while we also have been able to maintain the integrity of our individual cultural identities.

Student-Teacher Relationships

Xue Lan: I finished a bachelor's degree in Chinese language and literature in Beijing and came to the United States to study for a master's degree in social science education in 1982. I met Jude my first semester when I took the independent study course with her. I then took her two qualitative research methods courses during doctoral study several years later. I worked for Jude as a research assistant, and Jude served on both my thesis and dissertation committees. In the later 1970s student-teacher relationships in Chinese universities were significantly different from those in the United States and may well be different from those in today's Chinese universities. The framework of the Chinese relationship was formality, morality, and meritocracy, and the student-teacher relationship occurred in large-group instruction. This framework didn't leave much room for student-teacher interaction, and it didn't allow for the development of the more personal relationship of mentor-mentee that can promote apprenticeships, reciprocal learning, and scholarly collaboration.

In the early 1980s Jude was a recently tenured young professor who showed no anxiety to establish her authority in working with me. Rather, I always felt Jude was too friendly, too curious, and too nonjudgmental to be a "professor." Taking the independent study course with her was the beginning of an emotional journey for me—an unfamiliar style of learning, in an unfamiliar environment, in a strange land. Our earliest meetings made me uneasy (role confusion) because the line between the roles of teacher and student seemed to blur. This professor's passion for cultural inquiry confused and sometimes embarrassed me, but eventually became that which most charmed and disarmed me. During our independent study, Jude frequently asked me questions from genuine cultural curiosity. She showed me that she was learning things too, and it implied to me that a good class should offer learning opportunities for both teacher and students. I have kept this belief as one of the cornerstones for my teaching philosophy until today. The experience also laid a foundation that later enabled me to develop more mature, confident, and equitable collegial collaborations with other people in the academic community. I have to laugh when I realize that my acculturation to the U.S. university started right in Jude's office. However, even then neither of us anticipated this relationship would blossom into one of mutual nurturing and empowerment, trust, and lifetime guidance.

Jude: Despite these early satisfactions our journey together sometimes faltered. From my point of view the crisis in our teacher-student relationship occurred at Xue Lan's doctoral defense. As she says, we had worked together in what I had considered to be a trusting and creative pedagogical relationship for several years. Her master's thesis was a revealing glimpse into the lives of rural Chinese elementary schoolteachers and students in the third quarter of the twentieth century. Her doctoral dissertation would be a ground-breaking demographic analysis of the educational attainment of U.S. immigrants, their children, and grandchildren since 1890. What one of my colleagues from sociology and I found in the initial draft of the document, however, were some ideas that reflected opinions of Xue Lan's demographic advisor, rather than her own, and an organization that needed substantial attention. My sociology colleague and I would not have sent the draft to the committee. The five members of the dissertation committee talked this through for nearly two hours while Xue Lan waited outside to be called in to defend the document. The committee finally agreed to delay the defense to permit a revision of the dissertation. Xue Lan's composure and grace at this unexpected news were remarkable. To this day I feel the pain of that disappointing, yet necessary, decision. Although concerned with a loss of face among her fellow students, Xue Lan expected her committee to provide constructive, broadening, and doable recommendations. Meeting her expectations forged a scholarly bond that continues to this day.

Xue Lan: Initially, this was a heavy blow when I found out I would not be allowed to defend my dissertation on that day. However, since the message from the committee was constructive with many useful and interesting suggestions, I felt I was able to make the kind of changes the committee desired in a short period of time. Looking back to that incident, I see several factors that contributed to the later smooth revision of my dissertation. First, all members of my committee had won my trust. I knew them well and had good relationships with all of them. Therefore, I believed they had acted in my best interest. Second, they provided me with sound and concrete ideas for the revision and their commitment for any help I might need. Jude later spent long hours each week working with me on my writing and conceptualization. In addition, I had very little idea about what the "normal" dissertation defense process should be at that time. Therefore, I easily put that incident behind me and moved on. However, recollection of this incident made me more sensitive and cautious later on when serving myself on many dissertation committees. I learned that, in the best interest of the student, committee members should voice their evaluative opinions regardless. However, committee members also have the responsibility to give students more guidance during their writing rather than dropping a bomb at their defense. I don't expect every student to take it as well as I did because of different histories with the committee and different dynamics within the committee.

The process of revising my dissertation significantly deepened and broadened my inquiry; it especially gave me opportunities to work with two ethnographers, a micro/macrosociologist and an anthropologist. After hours and hours of discussion on the revision plan, I learned to look at my data in different ways and with different research questions. I thought more about the meanings of my data and how to express what I thought. Therefore, I also rethought the theoretical and practical meanings of various methodologies, compared and contrasted their rationales and possible outcomes, and reframed my inquiry with theories from multiple fields. Moreover, Jude worked very diligently with me on revising my dissertation. As an English as a Second Language (ESL) graduate student, I had ample opportunities to observe how a sophisticated ethnographer chose what words to use, and how a tiny change in wording may strengthen or weaken an argument or partially transform the implications of a sentence. This revision process offered me valuable opportunities to work closely with Jude and her colleague in sociology on my own research project—my dissertation. This closeness not only helped me get to know them well as academics and people (aware of and understanding the different academic journeys they had taken to become who they were and what they were), it also inspired me to write with them collaboratively on projects that fit my research interests in the future.

Xue Lan and Jude: On Xue Lan's graduation this student-teacher relationship grew into what we call a mentoring collegial relationship. We had worked many hours on the computer together in Xue Lan's office on her dissertation revisions in the spring of 1988, which may have portended our mentoring collegial relationship. We began writing together as colleagues soon after Xue Lan successfully defended her study. Although Jude continues to provide the mentoring a senior faculty member can offer to a junior colleague, the relationship has become balanced over time. It is a relationship of mutual critique and self-conscious reflection. The mutual obligations are those of respecting one another, inspiring one another, and sharing leadership and nurturing responsibilities. Jude expects Xue Lan to persevere through processes that may sometimes appear bizarre and unpredictable, such as difficult dissertation defenses and arduous tenure and promotion ordeals. Xue Lan expects Jude to show how challenges can be faced and to reveal honestly Jude's own struggles in balancing roles as a conscientious teacher, a sincere researcher, and a woman in academia. The reciprocity in our mentorship is embodied in the openness in Jude's self-disclosure, revealing her own anxieties, feelings of inadequacy, and vulnerabilities in her academic and personal life. This equal-tending reciprocity may imply to a mentee that the mentor can be trusted for navigating difficult situations, such as guiding a doctoral dissertation through to completion as well as facing other challenges. The openness in the relationship may also give a mentee a sense of equality and validate the mentee's self-concept and self-perceived adequacy (Hood & Boyce, 1997; Wilson, 1997). The risk, of course, is that such openness may become exploitative; we have both witnessed faculty members who use their students and younger colleagues as emotional crutches. Such relationships always seem to end badly for everyone involved. We believe we have avoided this by maintaining multiple collaborations with others and by accepting each other's individual priorities as part of balancing our collaborative priorities.

Looking back, we both recognize how Xue Lan was marginalized in her U.S. higher educational institution as a foreigner, an international student from a developing country, a non-English speaker, and a racial minority. Despite support from Jude and several other professors, Xue Lan was vulnerable to a variety of negative effects from the larger social context on her self-identification and self-expectations, social life, and academic networking. Dismissive students, suspicious peers, and unwelcoming members of local communities were some of her challenges. Our stories may demonstrate that, if mentoring is important for all graduate students, it is vital for a minority foreign student. Jude could not prevent many of the negative experiences Xue Lan had, but she could help Xue Lan interpret them and make her aware of her sources of support and aid.

Demographer-Ethnographer Relationship

Jude and Xue Lan: Our collaboration may have more meaning that mere methodological and disciplinary complement. Jude entered the higher education labor force in 1975, one of the few women hired by Research 1 universities at a time when ethnographic research in education was scarcely acknowledged. Xue Lan was recruited in 1991, during the peak of diversity recruitment in higher education. She had completed an undergraduate degree in Beijing and done her major precollegiate teaching at a rural school in China. Her research interests and topics were novel in 1991, but her quantitative research methods were more traditional and mainstream. To study race, culture, and education with quantitative methods required innovative thinking, creative approaches, and asking new and different questions. Addressing these new research questions required a different kind of collaboration and methodological merging.

Our first experience working together in the demographer-ethnographer relationship occurred when Xue Lan, still a graduate student, located census data for use as background material for an ethnographic study Jude had conducted on a rural elementary school. What Xue Lan was able to generate in this situation was a historical profile of the community and its composition from the late eighteenth century to the present, providing context and interpretive clues for the experiences of European American and African American children in the local public schools (Goetz & Breneman, 1988). Without this contextual view across time, interpretation of the immediate, day-to-day experiences of the children in the study would have lacked adequate perspective.

Xue Lan: Although I had majored in Chinese literature, like many international students from East Asia, I also had a solid background in high school mathematics, and my quantitative research skills had been further enhanced by the eight graduate research courses I took for my degrees, many of them in the Department of Statistics. I also had two years' experience as the senior coordinator in a large educational research lab, consulting on faculty and doctoral students' research projects. As a writer and Chinese literature teacher I was curious about narrative writing and about the life experiences of real people. However, this interest was hindered initially in the United States by the barrier of the English language and the concept of what constitutes "real" research. I began my scholarly writing in a thesis, an atypical ethnographic study of a Chinese elementary school. However, my subsequent writing—the dissertation and several research papers—used quantitative methods. In my eyes one of the many contributions Jude made to my scholarly life was when she demonstrated how skillfully an ethnographer could study cultural phenomena and how powerfully these studies could bridge cultural perceptions. I have worked in three universities and observed some opinionated dichotomizing of qualitative research versus quantitative research among the faculties. However, I believe that research inquiry needs both, and that genuine researchers can and should appreciate and complement each other's methodologies. This belief from my early academic life has resulted in three ethnographic articles and one historical publication in recent years, though my other publications have been mainly quantitative.

Jude and Xue Lan: Our research collaboration was further developed when Xue Lan, who had collected census data on Asian American teachers in U.S. schools, asked Jude to assist with identifying theoretical and conceptual frameworks for use in interpreting the patterns revealed in the census material. Because demographic studies describe population characteristics with numbers, censuses or surveys contain items addressing only what is considered to be factual information. Items representing attitudes, opinions, or other expressions of behavior, as well as items difficult to measure through the use of one or two self-administered questions, are excluded

(Rives & Serow, 1984). To study the causes and effects of the shortage of Asian American teachers, however, we had to combine data from sources other than the census, to imbue the study with social and cultural theories and to equip it with historical information about the American teaching workforce and its subgroups by gender, nativity, race and ethnicity, and other traits. We also had to answer the question of why our study was important and in what context.

Jude: Until recently I had forgotten that one of the excluded chapters from Xue Lan's dissertation was the same chapter that we eventually worked together on so long to publish. Candidly, this material stretched my styles of thinking and interpreting. For nearly my whole career I had studied face-to-face social and cultural behavior. Trying to interpret highly aggregated and abstracted patterns of relationships was a challenge. What helped me move beyond what felt like the hubris of overinterpretation was the familiar act of comparing and contrasting. What I was comparing and contrasting demographically was far different from the ethnographic analyses I'd been accustomed to, but the thinking processes and argumentation patterns were similar.

Jude and Xue Lan: The Asian American teacher project took eight years to complete. Through the use of census data and a demographic approach we found remarkable patterns in the shortage of Asian American teachers and compared them to patterns in the employment of other teachers. Because of the breadth of scholarship we came to use, we were able to present our study in a richer, more meaningful way. We struggled with this and came to realize we were working on a paper that not only required combining data from several sources, but also depended on a mixed research method that combined the insights of a demographer and an ethnographer as well as a macrosociologist and an anthropologist. Xue Lan collected, organized, and analyzed all the census data; Jude then used her skills in detailed reading to check the sums and frequencies to assure their match with the claims we were making. Xue Lan took the lead in identifying and synthesizing the literature on immigration, and Jude took the lead on the literature in teacher education. Jude worked through the theoretical implications of the literature and the findings to assure consistency in conceptualization.

Jude: When we received yet another revise and resubmit decision in 1995 of our manuscript on the shortage of Asian American teachers in the United

States, Xue Lan and I were both frustrated and disheartened. We had started the piece in 1988, and it seemed doomed to circulate in manuscript form forever. The reviewer's comments were generally positive, but the three reviewers offered conflicting recommendations, and the expectations for revision seemed impossible to us. Most challenging was one reviewer's question, "If Asian children generally are performing well in school, why is this [the continuing decline in Asian American teachers] a problem?"

Jude and Xue Lan: Our solution was to stop thinking about the work as a sociological examination of macrosocial patterns and to start thinking about framing this work as an anthropological case study of microcultural patterns. We reformulated the research as a historical case study of diversity in the U.S. teaching workforce during the twentieth century. We examined the representation of Asian Americans in this workforce as an example of the varying pattern of diversity among U.S. teachers and compared the experiences of Asian Americans with various other groups across time (Rong & Preissle, 1997).

Demographers and some sociologists find macrosocial patterns interesting in and of themselves. They are often more concerned with explaining the origin of a pattern than in specifying why the pattern is worth examining. Mainstream macrosociologists of the 1990s had traditionally been concerned with universal patterns of social life, and their research tended to focus on comparisons among large population groups, rather than on differences within groups. Ethnographers and anthropologists, on the other hand, are fascinated by the complexity of the everyday microsocial world and are more accustomed to justifying focus on a particular aspect of it and explaining why the uniqueness of individuals is important. Anthropologists generally have focused on particular patterns of social life. Arguing the value of cases and what they reveal about ranges is an anthropological necessity. Following this thinking, we subsequently applied the Asian American teachers' case to examine diverse perspectives in recruitment, training, and experiences of all U.S. teachers. We opened with this statement: "In this article we examine the increasing disparity between the population of minority youth in schools and the proportion of minority adults in teaching by using as a case example one of these groups, Asian Americans" (Rong & Preissle, 1997, p. 268). We opened our policy recommendations in the article with a similar statement: "The case we have presented thus far is that because the pattern of shortage is different for each minority group, different approaches must be tailored to different supernationalities" (p. 283).

What we have found is that our different perspectives bring different ideas on how to explain social phenomena. Xue Lan, as a demographer and an Asian American, thought about the comparison of occupational patterns across race and gender groups and about the sensitivity among Asian youths and their parents to long-standing biases and discrimination toward Asian Americans in specific occupations. Jude, as an ethnographer and a European American former schoolteacher, thought about how U.S. classrooms may provide international students with common challenges, but they rarely afford students from different cultures instruction tailored to meet their particular difficulties. Both the universal and the particular are ever-present in these views. The issue is what is background and what is foreground. Sometimes the universal is the background for the particular. Such was the case for Jude's study of the rural school, where the census data Xue Lan located provided context. For the Asian American teacher shortage study we had to redefine what we saw as a universal pattern into the particular patterns others saw. Having formulated this as a case study, we then were able to establish its significance against a background of the broader patterns of U.S. variation in the teaching workforce.

We have learned to use our evidence more comprehensively than either of us does alone. The collaboration has enlarged the scope of our knowledge and our understanding. We ask broader and deeper questions about what patterns mean, where they come from, and where they might be going. This combination of knowledge and assumptions from different disciplines has been advocated in recent decades in the development of interdisciplinarity (Finkenthal, 2001; Klein, 1990; Moran, 2002). Interdisciplinarity results when people from different disciplines work on common problems and issues, such as we have done together, or when people seek education across their initial disciplines, such as Jude's 2001–2002 study in philosophy.

Conclusion

In concluding our stories, we would like to show our understanding of how our three relationships—immigrant-host, student-teacher, and demographer-ethnographer and macrosociologist-anthropologist—are tied together. We argue that, without a strong desire to know about each other and to take risks to build a trusting and trusted relationship between two academics with different cultural backgrounds and history, no mentor relationship would have emerged. However, this relationship has been deepened and substantiated with mutual cultural exploration, which not only has strengthened and enriched the relationship, but also has given it rationale and moral grounding. Finally, such relationships may not grow into long-term professional alliances unless the collaboration is mutually beneficial and enriches research experiences of both.

Mentors awaken mentees to their potential and aid their transformation of potential to express creativity by providing mentees with insights into both the overt activities of human productivity and the more inner processes of thought (John-Steiner, 1985). As recommended by Welch (1997), mentoring minority mentees must foster equity, validating both mentor's and mentee's experiences, histories, backgrounds, and critical perspectives. In fostering equality in the relationship, Welch also indicates that the collaboration of two academics with a strong commitment to their work but from different backgrounds may be enhanced if they can use their different lenses and perspectives to improve how they frame and address problems when researching contemporary topics. Finally, cross-cultural mentorship is necessary because most minority students still find themselves in situations where there are few, if any, faculty who are of the same culture or ethnicity in widely recognized graduate programs in major research universities. Cross-cultural mentorship may also broaden the opportunity of students, enabling them to interact closely and frequently with mentors from backgrounds different from themselves.

Our collaboration has brought us renewed energy (a new and different research agenda, a lasting desire for inquiry, and intellectual growth through conflicting and complementary philosophies), renewed power (inspiration, excitement, and provocation), renewed resources (expertise in various methods, experience with educational institutions at various levels and in various geographic regions, and language and cultural skills), and a revitalized understanding of the complexity of the issues we research, precisely because of our different backgrounds. This collaboration opens the door to the possibility of doing the kind of research neither of us is able to do alone. And it might well answer an urgent call from inside academic institutions on the long-term effects of faculty diversification. After years of recruitment for diversity, a large cohort of diverse faculty now exists in the higher education pipeline. How does the sort of intergenerational mentor-collegial relationship we have described here develop, and what might it mean for higher education in transdisciplinary, transethnic, transcultural, and transnational integration of research and teaching? Can this sort of relationship change not only our scholarship, but also the very social fabric of our institutions of higher learning and, eventually, all individuals connected to higher education in the United States? We hope our relationship will be seen as a response to the challenges of diversity and that this paper may serve as a testimonial to its potential.

Finally, in sharing our collaborative experiences in this paper, we invite others to consider several more general issues for future research in this area. For instance, how are research design and construction (the selection and formulation of research questions and data selection, collection, analysis, and interpretation) affected when they are informed by multiple perspectives (e.g., Tashakkori & Teddlie, 1998)? What are the benefits and the limitations of these influences on the inquiry, on the inquirers, and on those inquired about (Ragin, 1987)? How does ethnography inform demography and demography contextualize ethnography (Davies, 1999; Wolcott, 1999)? How is the process of writing reports and representing the work influenced by approaches that are contrasting, complementary, or sometimes incommensurable (e.g., Bloom, 1998)? What do such collaborations—those that bring together varying research designs and researchers with different orientations—mean for understanding and illuminating complex social and educational issues (Brizuela, Stewart, Carrillo, & Berger, 2000)? How do they affect the researchers as teachers and learners as well as inquirers (Coffey, 1999; Trifonas, 2000)? These are concerns we hope to pursue in years to come, independently and collaboratively, together and with other colleagues.

Writing these stories has helped us better understand the nature of our relationship; it has empowered us and helped us envision the future. It has been therapeutic to us; and if making good sense of our experiences helps others develop new human resources and more constructive educational climates, then we will be doubly rewarded. By presenting to others complexities and paradoxes in the mentoring process and its outcomes, our stories may offer valuable information to administrators and policy makers who are interested in such mentoring-related issues as retention and attrition and career advancement of Asian American faculty members, other minority and women faculty members, international scholars, and all academic newcomers.

References

Bloom, L. R. (1998). *Under the sign of hope: Feminist methodology and narrative interpretation*. Albany, NY: SUNY Press.

Bramen, C. T. (2000). Minority hiring in the age of downsizing. In S. Lim & M. Herrera-Sobek (Eds.), *Power, race, and gender in academe* (pp. 1–7). New York: Modern Language Association.

Brizuela, B. M., Stewart, J. P., Carrillo, R. G., & Berger, J. G. (Eds.). (2000). *Acts of inquiry in qualitative research* (Harvard Educational Review Reprint Series No. 34). Cambridge, MA: Harvard Educational Review.

Buber, M. (1970). *I and thou* (W. Kaufman, Trans.). New York: Scribner's. (Original work published 1923)

Coffey, A. (1999). *The ethnographic self: Fieldwork and the representation of identity.* London: Sage.

Collier, M. N. (2003). Negotiating intercultural alliance relationships: Toward transformation. In M. N. Collier (Ed.), *Intercultural alliances* (pp. 1–16). Thousand Oaks, CA: Sage.

Collins, R. L. (1983). Colonialism on campus: A critique of mentoring to achieve equity in higher education. *Journal of Educational Equity and Leadership, 3,* 277–287.

Davies, C. A. (1999). *Reflexive ethnography: A guide to researching selves and others.* London: Routledge.

Ellis, C., & Bochner, A. (2000). Autoethnography, personal narrative, reflexivity: Researcher as subject. In N. K. Denzin & Y. S. Lincoln (Eds.), *Handbook of qualitative research* (2nd ed., pp. 733–768). Thousand Oaks, CA: Sage.

Finkenthal, M. (2001). *Interdisciplinarity: Toward the definition of a metadiscipline?* New York: Peter Lang.

Fort, D. C. (1993). *A hand up: Women mentoring women in science.* Washington, DC: Association for Women in Science.

Frierson, H. R., Jr. (1997). Introduction. In H. T. Frierson, Jr. (Ed.), *Diversity in higher education* (pp. 1–8). Greenwich, CT: JAI Press.

Goetz, J. P., & Breneman, E. A. R. (1988). Desegregation and Black students' experiences in two rural southern elementary schools. *Elementary School Journal, 88,* 489–502.

Holland, J. (1995, April). *Paths to the academy: The faculty development of African American doctoral students.* Paper presented at the Annual Meeting of the American Educational Research Association, San Francisco.

Hood. S. L., & Boyce, J. (1997). Refining and expanding the role of professional associations to increase the pool of faculty researchers of color. In H. T. Frierson, Jr. (Ed.), *Diversity in higher education* (pp. 141–160). Greenwich, CT: JAI Press.

John-Steiner, V. (1985). *Notebooks of the mind: Explorations of thinking.* Albuquerque: University of New Mexico Press.

Kim, M.-S. (2002). *Non-western perspectives on human communication: Implications for theory and practice.* Thousand Oaks, CA: Sage.

Kim, Y. Y. (2001). *Becoming intercultural: An integrative theory of communication and cross-cultural adaptation.* Thousand Oaks, CA: Sage.

Klein, J. T. (1990). *Interdisciplinarity: History, theory, practice.* Detroit, MI: Wayne State University Press.

Kolodny, R. (2000). Raising standards while lowering anxieties: Rethinking the promotion and tenure process. In S. Lim & M. Herrera-Sobek (Eds.), *Power, race, and gender in academe* (pp. 83–111). New York: Modern Language Association.

Macrina, F. L. (1995). Collaborative research. In F. L. Macrina (Ed.), *Scientific integrity: An introductory text with cases* (pp. 157–178). Washington, DC: American Society for Microbiology Press.

Menges, R. J., & Exum, W. H. (1983). Barriers to the progress of women and minority faculty. *Journal of Higher Education, 54,* 123–144.

Merriam, S. (1983). Mentors and protégés: A critical review of the literature. *Adult Education Quarterly, 33,* 161–173.

Mirandé, A. (1988). I never had a mentor: Reflections of a Chicano sociologist. *American Sociologist, 19,* 355–362.

Moran, J. (2002). *Interdisciplinarity.* London: Routledge.

Okoli, E. J. (2001). The impact of cultural dynamics on the newcomer to the organizational environment. In V. H. Milhouse, M. K. Asante, & P. O. Nwosu (Eds.), *Transcultural realities: Interdisciplinary perspectives on cross-cultural relations* (pp. 251–265). Thousand Oaks, CA: Sage.

Ragin, C. C. (1987). *The comparative method: Moving beyond qualitative and quantitative strategies.* Berkeley: University of California Press.

Reed-Danahay, D. (1997). *Auto/Ethnography: Rewriting the self and the social.* New York: Berg.

Rives, N. W., & Serow, W. J. (1984). *Introduction to applied demography: Data sources and estimation techniques.* Newbury Park, CA: Sage.

Rong, X. L. (2002). Teaching with differences and for differences: Reflections of a Chinese American teacher educator. In L. Vargas (Ed.), *Women faculty of color in the White classroom: Narratives on the pedagogical implications of teacher diversity* (pp. 125–145). New York: Peter Lang.

Rong, X. L., & Preissle, J. P. (1997). The continuing decline in Asian American teachers. *American Educational Research Journal, 34,* 267–293.

Singh, D. K., & Stoloff, D. L. (2003, January). *Mentoring faculty of color.* Paper presented at the Annual Meeting of the American Association of Colleges for Teacher Education, New Orleans, LA.

Tashakkori, A., & Teddlie, C. (1998). *Mixed methodology: Combining qualitative and quantitative approaches.* Thousand Oaks, CA: Sage.

Trifonas, P. P. (2000). *The ethics of writing: Derrida, deconstruction, and pedagogy.* Lanham, MD: Rowman & Littlefield.

Weil, V. (2001). Mentoring: Some ethical considerations. *Science and Engineering Ethics, 7,* 471–482.

Welch, O. M. (1997). An examination of effective mentoring models in academe. In H. T. Frierson, Jr. (Ed.), *Diversity in higher education* (pp. 41–62). Greenwich, CT: JAI Press.

Wilson, R. (1997). Negative mentoring: An examination of the phenomenon as it affects minority students. In H. T. Frierson, Jr. (Ed.), *Diversity in higher education* (pp. 177–186). Greenwich, CT: JAI Press.

Wolcott, H. F. (1999). *Ethnography: A way of seeing*. Walnut Creek, CA: AltaMira Press.

15

BUILDING BRIDGES, WORKING FOR A BETTER WORLD

Jing Lin

Our identity is necessarily connected with our gender, ethnicity, race, social class, and cultural background. However, we are not bound by these definitions, rather we can transcend them to seek out our universal qualities with others and to build cultural bridges rising above our differences and to work together for a better world. It is based on these commonalities that we can understand each other as complex cultural beings, and work toward building true respect and understanding as equal human beings regardless of our differences (Lin, 2005).

As a Chinese American scholar working in a research university, I am constantly reminded of my identity based on my external definitions. For example, my university's provost office recently sent me a letter to include me as a "woman of color" in their activity on promoting diversity. This letter reminds me again how often we are put into certain categories by institutions and individuals. Asian female faculty, like other groups, need to struggle with "other's definition" and their own definition of who they are all the time.

In my professional career, while I recognize the part of me as an Asian woman, and am proud of the rich cultural background I come from, I have always maintained the fact that I am a human being first and foremost, and that I am a global citizen, an element in the universe who has an interconnected relationship with all existences, or using a Buddhist term, with all sentient and nonsentient existences. The recognition of my own distinct background allows me to recognize the cultural lenses with which I understand the world, while maintaining my fundamental quality as a human being empowers me to see that we can overcome our differences and reach out to each other and build bridges for understanding and respect.

In this chapter, I first attempt a reflection of the Asian American experience in the United States, tracing the struggles and triumphs of Asian Americans, and noting the general characteristics of those who come from mainland China. Next, I reflect on my experience living in China, characterized by switching my identity as a majority and a minority, as a privileged person as well as a disadvantaged person because of changes of context. I then recall my experience in the United States and Canada, from being a stranger to finding a community of friends, from dismissing my own culture, to reclaiming my own heritage. In particular, I share my transformation from seeing myself as an Asian woman to regarding myself as a global citizen, my path to realizing our commonality as human beings and the power of respect and love to build cultural bridges. My transformation has come from role models in my life, from learning about the common core values of world religions and cultures, and from experiencing and embracing the interconnectedness of all human beings and existence in the world through a heightened spiritual awareness. Finally, I conclude that we can all be builders of cultural bridges and work for the common good if we embrace a global ethic of love based on our universal humanness.

Asian Americans' Struggle

Much research has been conducted to examine the experience of Asian Americans. Asian Americans have suffered horrible discrimination in the United States, through the exclusion laws and humiliation and unfair treatment in daily life (Espiritu, 1997). In the early stage, Chinese Americans were discriminated against and deprived of their rights to be citizens by the Chinese Exclusion Act in 1882. They were treated as third-class citizens facing discrimination in jobs, being forced to work mainly as gold miners, railroad workers, and laundry workers (Weinberg, 1997). They were not allowed to bring their families to join them until 1960. Prejudices and stereotypes abounded against the Chinese immigrants (Moyers, 2003). To survive, many Chinese Americans found home away from home working within the context of Chinatown (Moyers, 2003).

Asian Americans have experienced an intense struggle to maintain their own culture and fit into the mainstream. Although they tried hard to be like Americans, they never felt fully accepted, living at the margin of the dominant culture (Hahn, 2000). Immigrant parents feared for the loss of their culture in their children and thus sent their children to weekend Chinese schools and insisted on their children speaking Chinese at home. Carrying the tradition of seeing education as the gateway to opportunities and family glory, Asian parents held high expectations for their children's learning (Braxton, 1999; Takaki, 1998).

This has led to Asian Americans becoming a "model minority" since the 1980s, when the stereotype developed that Asian American students would achieve high scores in standardized tests. And they have been the most rapidly growing new students on university campuses, also registering the most impressive graduation rate (Escueta & O'Brien, 1995). In 1980, 33 percent of Asian Americans aged twenty-five and above had at least four years of college. By 1990, the proportion rose to 40 percent, almost double the figure for Whites (23 percent) (Escueta & O'Brien, 1995, p. 259).

The Asian American population in the United States reached almost 7.3 million in the 1990 census, representing 3 percent of the total U.S. population. In academic positions in higher education, the proportion of Asian Americans employed is equal to the overall population proportion. However, Asian American women have not reached parity with the overall population. Of the full-time faculty in U.S. colleges and universities, between 4 and 5 percent are Asian Americans, of whom 78 percent were male and 22 percent were female (Escueta & O'Brien, 1995, p. 267).

Chinese Americans from mainland China share similar experiences with early immigrants. Many have felt rejected, excluded, stereotyped. They have to struggle long and hard to find their footing. China and the United States severed relations for nearly three decades, from 1950 up to 1977. When China reconnected with the United States and the first groups of mainland Chinese students arrived, they had little support. Some came with $20 in their pocket. The luckier ones had a research or teaching assistantship to cover their basic living costs, while others had to work in restaurants or clean campus apartments or engage in some other labor-intensive job. Having gone through the tumultuous decade of the Cultural Revolution (1966–1976) in China when the economy was at a near breakdown, they had no savings and their family members in China could not help them in any way financially. To survive, many lived in cheap housing and counted pennies. Many had language difficulties, on top of which cultural barriers forced them to adjust their thinking style, writing style, and to stare blankly while people laughed when a joke was told. It was a painful process for many.

However, gradually they got to know Americans as colleagues and friends, and established their support networks as they got to know more of the Chinese students who were coming in greater numbers as years passed by. They also made friends with Chinese people from Taiwan and Hong Kong. The ideological differences between China, the United States, and other places at times presented a struggle between groups and within the self. The language barrier shut many doors, and cultural differences led to misunderstandings and discrimination, yet as time went on, most Chinese Americans adjusted to their environment. They tried to strike a balance between keeping their Chinese culture and identity and learning as much as they could to fit into the new environment. Eventually, a large number of them got their degrees and found employment in companies and universities. Some opened up their own businesses.

Of those working in universities, most are in science and technology, and those in education are rare among the mainland Chinese immigrants. For the small number of them who eventually built their career in a higher education institution, they have had to go the extra mile to make up their cultural differences to construct their professional niche and win colleagues' and students' support. The low representation of Asian Americans in academia has made them feel isolated, lonely, unsupported, and sometimes even shortchanged. In the two colleges I have worked in, I was one of only two Asian faculty members. In order to fit in and be accepted, Asian faculty found themselves alienated from their own culture and torn by the question of who they are. Yet, the intellectual environment, where there is autonomy to explore scholarship and where collegiality is desired and pursued, also allows them to create space to connect and find mutual support with people in the same environment. They find being Asian American in an American university is not their only identity. In the day-to-day interaction with people as human beings, they start to define who they are recognizing the multi-dimentionality of their own identity. They may lose themselves, find themselves again, and unite their differences to form a new self.

In my own experience, I have traveled the same path as most Chinese Americans from mainland China. I have worked hard to carve a place for myself in society. I have gone from an intense dislike of my own culture in the first stage of my stay in North America to reclaiming my own culture; I have gone from learning about the beauty of our world's rich cultures to understanding the common core values that penetrate all cultures. While I developed critical perspectives to analyze social problems as a scholar, I also formed a constructive outlook on how we should work as human beings to facilitate positive changes through the work of the heart in my daily life as well as my professional life. As I expand my understanding about life and the interconnectedness of all beings in the world, I embrace the fact that regardless of our origin, gender, race, class, language, ethnicity, we are all human beings in search of joy and wisdom. By working together we can turn our world into a better, friendlier, and more understanding world.

My Background

I grew up in China in a province where 39 percent of the population are minorities: the Zhuang, Miao, and Muo Lao people. Together they form the largest minority in the nation. Yet in my childhood, I seldom encountered anyone from the minority groups. My home county and adjacent counties were inhabited by the Han, the majority group. Overall in the country, minorities usually reside in the western part of the country, in the mountains, or in deserts and plateaus, while the Hans reside in the eastern part, living on the plains and the arable land. When I came to the provincial capital city to study in a university in the late 1970s, I still did not have opportunities to see many minority students, for almost all of them attended minority higher learning institutions, rather than a comprehensive university such as the one where I studied.

After I became a teacher in the same university, I began to teach groups of students from the minority regions. They impressed me as being very eager to learn, but overall they had low self-esteem in the overwhelming Han cultural environment. This was my first experience of encountering people "different" from me. I looked similar to them, but the classification of them as "minority" and myself as "majority" transmitted a message about who I was and who they were. Thinking back, I realize the political and economic dependence of the minority groups on the Han government, and cultural and social discrimination in contemporary China have generated stereotypes against minorities, and caused them to have doubts about themselves and even a strong sense of shame (Lin, 1993).

What is paradoxical about this experience is that while I was in the province, I was seen and treated as a member of the Han majority with much pride and privileges. I, like my fellow students and colleagues, saw the minority people as others, having exotic cultural traditions but also moving "backward" in values and customs. Yet, when I traveled outside the province, in the eyes of others, my coming from a minority province instantly lumped me with a minority group (the Zhuangs) which in China is still stigmatized as less "civilized" than the Han majority. I had not changed a bit, yet a change in location rendered a different judgment of who I am. The fluidity of our identity, and the quick change in definition of who we are in different contexts caused me to think about the fact that the nature of our identity is highly subjective and circumstantial. This revelation formed the initial grounding for me to see myself first and foremost as a human being regardless of other's definitions and regardless of changes in my environment.

I grew up in a rural setting, but my parents were state salaried workers, and in the extremely difficult time of the 1960s and 1970s, this meant that although we never had any excesses, we never went hungry either. Thus my class background was between the rural peasants and the "proud" urban residents who looked down upon rural people and treated them like third-class citizens. Urban workers from the 1950s to the early 1980s in China used to have more privileges than rural peasants had, such as government housing, a regular salary, health care, a retirement pension, a rich urban cultural life, and so forth. This unequal treatment had given urban residents a sense of superiority. I witnessed on many occasions how urban residents humiliated rural peasants and I felt this was very unfair. I also grew up in a time when people were all classified in certain "class categories." One category was the proletariat class comprising workers, government cadres, and rural poor peasants, while the other category was the "enemy" class comprising capitalists, rich landlords, rich farmers, so named because of their ownership of property before 1949, and also called "traitors, leftists," and a host of other names because of their political acts and affiliations. The "enemy" class was discriminated against in educational and employment opportunities, while the proletariats were trumpeted as "advanced," and treated favorably (Lin, 1991). When Deng Xiaoping came to power in 1978, he started rehabilitating the people who were considered enemies, and since the 1980s, the once "suspected" "untrustworthy" intellectuals have become the main force the government relies on for the modernization of China. Again, this experience has convinced me that we are fundamentally human beings, but political forces place all kinds of labels on us and treat us accordingly. Over time, people forget who we truly are and we forget about it also.

I also grew up in a time when women were encouraged to forget about their gender and do all that men can do. "Women holding up half of the sky" was a powerful slogan then that gave women a lot of confidence. Although many scholars today criticize the neglect of women's gender difference and the suppression of women's femininity during the Mao Zedong era, the spirit of living at that that time did convey to women a persuasive message: Women can achieve and should achieve what men can do. The changes in different generations of women's life in China were astounding indeed. At the beginning of the twentieth century my grandmother was thrust into a carriage to marry my grandfather without having met him once, yet in the 1950s my mother met my father on her own and married him based on their mutual agreement. In mid-1980, I met my husband and we have since established an equal relationship sharing household work and supporting each other. This transgenerational change demonstrates to me that time changes and our role and our perception of what we can do also change with time. As women living in an era where we have a much higher social status in general, we need to play a positive role in facilitating social changes.

Becoming a "Stranger" and Finding Home

When I first landed in the United States in 1985, I had the unforgettable experience of becoming a "stranger." It felt as if my cultural roots were suddenly taken from under my feet and I was hanging in the air. I watched TV hosts cracking jokes but understood none of them. Three days of McDonald's food would create cramps in my stomach.

What's more, it seemed that overnight my identity changed. I was no longer someone from a certain province or a rural urban background; rather I was someone representing a whole country—I was a Chinese representing China's 1.3 billion people. It was assumed that if I came from China I must like and be able to make egg rolls although I had never seen one before I came to the United States. And for the first time I was defined by my race. I was asked to fill out forms that indicated my race, namely, the color of my skin, which I have never thought to be anything significant or to have anything to do with my character and identity. Self-doubts were created in my mind. However, having lived in China for more than twenty-three years before I moved to the United States, my sense of self was rather solid and consistent. In this new environment I identified myself as a Chinese and someone who needed to understand why people were categorized this way and to adjust to and work with the environment.

Many studies have pointed out the difficulty of straddling two cultures, the insecurity of not being accepted in either one, and the need to give up much of one's own identity in order to be accepted as mainstream (Hahn, 2000; Wong, 1989). I would say at times I felt and experienced these difficulties, insecurity, and loss of self. But as I interacted more and more with American people and people from around the world, I quickly found that we have so much in common as human beings that our differences seem shallow. Just as Chinese people are similar but also different, the American people are also similar and different among themselves. We may have greater similarity as individuals across nations, gender, race, and such. In China I had been helped by many people, and in the United States I have also been supported by many Americans and people from all over the world not because I am a Chinese but because I am a human being. I have been powerfully influenced by my mentor, Dr. Terrence Tice, who never fails to care for and respect anyone from all backgrounds. Dr. Tice enabled me to see that we can transcend our differences and embark on the search for universal respect and love among all human beings. The support and enlightenment I received from Dr. Tice makes me want to reciprocate what I had been given when I became a professor. I see being a professor as a privilege and I want to return the favor I have been bestowed.

I also experienced great friendship from my fellow graduate students. The memories of arguing about a new book, of giving each other surprise parties, of walking the streets with weird hats on just to attract curious stares, are still very heartwarming. With these experiences, my self-doubt was washed away, and my confidence grew with our ever-deeper engagement in knowing each other as human beings.

In summary, cultural barriers can be broken down when intellectuals consciously and unconsciously work on building a "beloved community" in which people of different backgrounds learn from each other and treat one another with respect (Ayres, 1993). Our "humanness" can be brought out and nurtured, above and beyond our labeling and categorizations.

Losing and Reclaiming My Own Culture

When I first arrived in the United States, I was only twenty-three. Full of curiosity to learn new things, and with a strong desire to learn "advanced" Western knowledge and culture and to find an ideal theory for social reform, I spent all of my time absorbing theories about education by such philosophers as Plato and John Dewey. I also read works by radical critics of Chinese culture, and started to dismiss Chinese culture as too collective, too authoritarian, too moralistic—in a word "too backward," although I knew little about its essence. As a person growing up during the Cultural Revolution when many traditional Chinese cultural traditions and classical texts were denounced and burned, Confucius was labeled as a "reactionary figure," and all religions were banned. I did not have opportunities to become acquainted with the culture and philosophies of traditional China. With this emptiness I "drank" in Western culture like a thirsty person.

I was very fortunate that after I graduated with my doctoral degree, I landed a job in a top-ranked university in Canada. After working there for more than eight years, I moved to a research university in the United States and have worked here since 2000. In my faculty positions, I continued to learn new Western theories in education, sociology, philosophy, and psychology, basing my teaching and research on these frameworks. In 1998 I embarked on learning Yan Xin Qigong, a traditional Chinese cultivation system, that greatly and profoundly changed my views on Chinese culture and my views about life, nature, and the universe. This cultivation system is related to the traditional philosophies of Taoism, Confucianism, and Buddhism, but it goes beyond them by helping people to cultivate their bio-energy and open themselves up to connect with the universe's vast network of energies through practicing virtues such as respect, care, forgiveness, and understanding. These virtues are treated not only as beliefs or values. They are also taken as techniques and a mechanism to align oneself with the energy of the universe that works in great harmony guided by the principles of virtue. As my body opened up to the life force, *qi*, which is in everything and permeates the universe, I started to feel the divinity in all existences, and I experienced the interconnections of all lives, feeling their joy, pain, and love. This cultivation system gave me a powerful new lens to look at the teaching of reciprocal responsibilities in Chinese culture, and its emphasis on virtues as the foundation of a functioning society. With great interest, I returned to my roots and spent a huge amount of time making up the lost lessons on Chinese culture, reading not only about Chinese philosophy and religion, but also medicine, literature, history, and many other fields. I felt I was filling up the other half of the glass with this kind of intensive learning. I discovered that great wisdom has no national border, and no time limitations. Reading thoughtfully the great works passed down from five thousand years of the history of Chinese civilization, such as the *Book of Change, The Analects, Tao Te Ching, Zhuang Zi, Great Learning, Li Ji* (*Book of Rituals*), *Shiji* (*Book of History*), I reclaimed my Chinese culture.

Expanding into the Richness of World Culture

The great virtue of being a professor in a Canadian and an American university is that one has the autonomy to teach courses she enjoys. My career teaching courses on culture has given me excellent opportunities to force myself to constantly learn from books, colleagues, and my students. In my teaching and research, I have been learning about the American and Chinese cultures. I am also getting more and more into understanding other cultures such as Buddhism, Hinduism, Judaism, Christianity, Islam, African American cultures, and Native American cultures. I have also studied the Mayan and the Egyptian civilizations. I realize that each culture has a wealth of knowledge and wisdom to offer. The rich wisdom of various cultures reveals different paths to understanding about our life and the world. The more I learn, the more I realize that no culture is essentially in opposition to any other culture. If we adopt an understanding and a humble-learning attitude, we can learn from the vast reservoir of wisdom from all cultures anytime we come into contact with them.

In Search of Common Core Values in the World's Traditions and Great Teachings

The search for wisdom in different cultures helps me understand that we can find common core values among all world traditions and cultures. I realize that all world religions teach us to love, to have compassion and forgiveness, to serve without thinking of reward, and to treat others as one's own family members. I draw this understanding from religious texts, as well as from books for spiritual cultivation (Walsh, 1999). I realize that barriers established by social hierarchies and distortions of cultural messages have complicated our views and blinded us to a very simple truth: We need to have a loving world in order to live in peace and joy. I feel incredibly empowered by this understanding, and seek to transform myself so that I can love and forgive unconditionally, so that I can see the divine light in all human beings and in all existences. With this realization I am embarking on a journey to promote global peace through teaching peace education courses and writing in this area. I set it as my goal to transform my students one at a time to help them treat their students as divine souls, and give hope and joy to students and those around me through unconditional love. I am convinced that only love can transcend hatred and our education must teach students to love in order to have a peaceful world.

Cultural Diversity as Beauty and Great Learning Opportunities

Teaching courses, doing research, mentoring students, and participating in professional conferences are all incredible opportunities for a professor to learn more. I see different cultures as autumn leaves: Their different colors are all essential for the beauty of the season and the world. In all of my students I see great beauty, and I give them opportunities to display their creativity and distinctive personal characteristics. Looking back on my path through life, I find that it is essential that we break down the notion of deficit (in gender, race, nationality, etc.) and see our own and others' unique background and experience as assets. It is important to draw on and continue to learn about our own cultural wisdom to ground ourselves in the world, while it is equally critical for our growth to maintain our enthusiasm and openness to learn more about world cultures.

Developing a Critical and Constructive Perspective

While I am critically aware of inequalities based on gender, race, social class, and other factors in all sectors of our society, I refuse to allow bitterness to build up in my heart. I believe constructive thinking is the key to creating a positive environment, transforming ourselves while also transforming others for the better. The education I received and the teaching and research I conducted later on as a faculty member equipped me with a critical eye to examine social inequality and injustice. Feminist theories give me a lens to critically examine the deprivation of women's opportunities, and delve deeply into the roots of subordination of women by a patriarchal culture and system (Tong, 1998). Critical theories advanced by Paulo Freire (2000), Henry Giroux (1989, 1992, 2000) and Peter McLaren (1991) enable me to see power struggles in the arena of culture and education, and become acutely aware of "subtle" and yet powerful imbalances in power in education. Multicultural and postmodern theory opens me to new perspectives on knowledge (Banks, 1993; Greene, 1993a, 1993b; Nava, 2001) and gives me the lenses to see problems in a society that upholds rationalistic and mechanistic perspectives. The scholarly environment I work in is grounded in a passion for social justice and equality through a critical intellectual framework, one in which I find my work to be important and meaningful.

I have also powerfully benefited by theories on holistic education (Nava, 2001), and from traditional philosophy on our innate potential to be good and kind. Over the years of research and teaching—or I might say my search for truth in life—I am convinced we need to have a constructive mind-set in order to effect changes in society. Making changes in our daily life has little to do with the fact that we are Asian, African American, Caucasian, Latin American, and so on, as long as we are ready to give love and are willing to forgive and embrace others as family. Love transcends and connects. Thus, daily we transform our classrooms into positive learning environments, and our communities into positive and constructive places for cultural sharing and understanding.

Teaching across Cultures

When I first arrived at Michigan State University and enrolled in a course with Professor Howard Hickey, he announced to the class: "Call me 'Howard' or I will not respond." Though this was a joke, I seriously felt it an act of disrespect to call a professor by his first name. Growing up in the Chinese tradition I had been expected to look up to my teacher and calling him by his first name was not a way to be respectful. A second dilemma was that in classroom discussions and in doing assignments we were required to exercise critical thinking on educational theories and schooling practices. Accustomed as I was to "absorbing" knowledge rather than questioning it, I remember sitting at my desk flipping the pages of textbooks, almost hoping someone would tell me how to criticize an authoritative source. But soon I adjusted and felt a strong sense of liberation. I unlocked my inquiring potentials and started to look at myself as an equal to the "authority." My Chinese training started to benefit me in a positive way. My ability to acquire a large amount of information, to structure knowledge, and particularly my quality of perseverance, so emphasized in Asian education, helped me to flourish intellectually. I wrote a critical dissertation in two and a half years, which later was published as a book.

In my teaching in North American universities, I have started to try to blend my Western and Eastern training on teaching. Following the Chinese tradition of emphasizing structure, which I benefited a lot from in my own education, I structure the curriculum very carefully, so that the students can gain a good foundation in the field. A traditional teaching mantra in China is: "For a teacher to give a student, she needs to have a bucket of water." Lecturing is seen as an act of the teacher giving her students the "glass of water" after much refinement of her knowledge. Hence, instead of rejecting lecturing as "banking" students, I carefully prepare my notes and I spend about one-third of my time on lecturing, summarizing the main ideas and findings in the field to give students the foundational knowledge, "to have a ground to stand on before they jump," which is widely believed to be important by Chinese educators. However, I also see a profound advantage in a class that stimulates students' thoughts and connects to their knowledge and experience. Thus I posit myself most of the time as a facilitator, a "midwife" who helps students to find their own way and give birth to their own under-standing. Crossing cultural boundaries and drawing from strengths of both my Chinese educational experience and my Western changes has shaped my teaching approach.

Consistent with my conviction for social equality, I have integrated criti-cal perspectives into all of my teaching. I underscore the importance of stu-dents knowing how to identify and analyze inequalities based on gender, race, social class, and other factors, and feel justifiably angry about inequali-ties deeply ingrained in our economic, political, and social structures. How-ever, I have persisted in that my students go beyond critiquing our world's problems and engage the power of love to connect, transcend, heal, nurture, and reconstruct. I ventured into teaching courses on peace education and spirituality education in which all cultures are brought into the classroom for mutual learning and understanding, while stereotypes are being de-bunked and prejudices deconstructed. Transforming oneself always happens before transforming others. I have striven over the years to forgive no matter how hard it is, to love by focusing on the divine spark in all beings. Living the example of love has had an impact on my students. One example of this is evident in what a student who was in the military for two decades said when nominating me for the 1,000 Women for Nobel Peace Prize 2005: She said she has been transformed by me from working for war to working for peace. Another student writes:

> Dr. Lin's teaching on peace is not restricted to classrooms. As a person, she is a mentor with sincere love and deep respect for others. Her uncondi-tioned loving heart has always supported and encouraged me throughout these years. Her openness and forgiveness have accompanied me during difficult times. I would not hesitate to say that Dr. Lin is a peaceful person with love, integrity and character. Simply being around with her would make me feel refreshed and enlightened.

Support and Challenges

We cannot accomplish many things without support from a large number of people. This is true in the academic arena. I cannot forget the encourage-ment I received from colleagues and students. The staff members in all my workplaces demonstrated deep caring and selfless service. Reflecting on my career working as a professor for a dozen years, many warm faces come to mind.

Are there challenges especially for Asian women working in higher education in the United States? I would say there are challenges for anyone, and perhaps one special challenge for Asian women is that their cultural upbringing has encouraged them to be quiet and accommodating rather than aggressive and outspoken. The definition of what constitutes a "good woman" in an Asian culture may consciously and subconsciously affect our behavior so that we do not confront discrimination directly. But overall, it is not helpful—it is even harmful—to stereotype and generalize, as Asian women, like any group of people, are different with their own unique personalities. As an Asian woman, I grew up with numerous female role models who were strong and intelligent. This was very different from the traditional feudal context in China. I feel for myself the greatest challenges come from expanding and transcending my own understanding of the meaning of life and my role in helping to bring light and hope to our world. What can we do in education? How can we transform our world through education? These are the questions that are constantly in my mind.

Building Bridges and Working for the Common Good

In this chapter, I have discussed my change of identity as defined by others and myself as a minority and a majority in different times and contexts; I have examined the development of my conviction that despite our differences, we are all human beings who can transcend culture, gender, and other kinds of differences. Being Asian and a woman, and having crossed two cultures, in fact gives me a unique angle to see the nature of identity construction and change it into positive experiences to build cultural bridges and work for the common good.

Overall, a great focus on goals, building supportive relationships with colleagues, finding mentors, learning from all people, searching for knowledge and spiritual wisdom—these have been key elements in my growth as a person and as a professional. Many Asian female faculty have experienced exclusion and discrimination, but over time, obstacles can be removed through persistent efforts to build understanding. Love can move mountains. Love can dissolve misunderstanding and bond our hearts no matter who we are.

My experience points to the possibility that we can assemble a new perspective on identity construction and politics. We all have differences, yet our different culture and backgrounds may provide us with a different vantage point to see issues that we may not ordinarily see. For many people, the experience of having been labeled and marginalized could be used constructively by refraining from treating others in a similar manner. My experience also points to the fact that we all have multiple dimensions in our identity. We may be a minority in one context but a majority in another context. We may have advantages and disadvantages at the same time. These experiences inform us that identity is a social construction, and it takes conscious awareness and wide-awakeness (Greene, 1978, p. 162) to see through biases and prejudices, and we can act as social transformers to change the situation for the better. In all contexts, we can resort to respect and understanding as the tool for effecting changes in others and making a difference in the world.

There is no fundamental conflict in that Asian American female faculty are Asian as well as global citizens. Personal, reflective, cross-cultural living and working experiences inform us that regardless of their nationality, parents of different countries all deeply care for their children, and people around the world long for peace and respect. These daily experiences enable us to transcend labeling and categorization to see humaneness in all people although they come from very different backgrounds.

We are living in a world in which distance is greatly shortened by airplanes, ships, and cyberspace. Quick communication needs to be accompanied by a greater sense of global community. It takes respect, understanding, and compassion to cross cultural boundaries and reach the hearts and souls of people. We need to use rational thinking to analyze and differentiate, but more important we need to rely on our love and compassion to share and connect.

Women or men, Asian or other ethnicity, minority or majority, we need to find our own voices, build our niches professionally, and incorporate these into searching for a path that leads to a larger community that allows diverse possibilities. Looking back, I find myself consciously and unconsciously carving a life path that is underpinned by the pursuit of human equality and social justice. As I journey down my intellectual and professional path, my life and work center more and more on the belief that all we should contribute to the common good. The common good could mean working for social justice and equality, promoting multicultural respect, advocating environmental protection, or taking action to promote lasting peace. In this effort, we are not only a certain ethnic group or race or gender, we are human beings needing to come together to construct a new world based on love and understanding.

References

Ayres, A. (Ed.). (1993). *The wisdom of Martin Luther King, Jr.* New York: Meridian.

Banks, J. A. (1993). Multicultural education: Characteristics and goals. In J. Banks & C. Banks (Eds.), *Multicultural education: Issues and perspectives* (pp. 385–407). Boston: Allyn and Bacon.

Braxton, R. (1999). Culture, family and Chinese and Korean American student achievement: An examination of student factors that affect student outcomes. *College Student Journal, 33,* 250–256.

Escueta, E., & O'Brien, E. (1995). Asian Americans in higher education: Trends and issues. In D. T. Nakanishi & T. Y. Nishida (Eds.), *The Asian American educational experience* (pp. 259–272). New York: Routledge.

Espiritu, Y. L. (1997). *Asian American women and men: Labor, laws and love.* Thousand Oaks, CA: Sage.

Freire, P. (2000). *Pedagogy of the oppressed.* New York: Continuum.

Giroux, H. A. (1989). *Critical pedagogy, the state, and cultural struggle.* Albany, NY: SUNY Press.

Giroux, H. A. (1992). *Border crossings: Cultural workers and the politics of education.* New York: Routledge.

Giroux, H. A. (2000). The war against cultural politics: Beyond conservative and neo-enlightenment left "oppositions": A critique. In C. J. Ovando & P. McLaren (Eds.), *The politics of multiculturalism and bilingual education: Students and teachers caught in the crossfire.* Boston: McGraw-Hill.

Greene, M. (1978). *Landscape of learning.* New York: Teachers College Press.

Greene, M. (1993a). The passions of pluralism: Multiculturalism and the expanding community. *Educational Researcher, 22*(1), 13–18.

Greene, M. (1993b). Diversity and inclusion: Toward a curriculum for human beings. *Teachers College Record, 95*(2), 211–221.

Hahn, S. (2000, May). Identity and growth. *The ICAS (Institute for Corean-American Studies) Lectures* (No. 2000-0818-SHH). Blue Bell, PA: Institute for Corean-American Studies.

Lin, J. (1991). *The Red Guards' path to violence: Political, educational, and psychological factors.* New York: Praeger.

Lin, J. (1993). Ethnic relationship and minority education in Guangxi, China: A case study. *Canadian and International Education, 22,* 5–21.

Lin, J. (2005). *School for love: Education in the 21st century.* Lanham, MD: Scarecrow.

McLaren, P. (1991). *Current perspectives on the culture of schools.* Cambridge. MA: Brookline Books.

Moyers, B. (2003). *Becoming American: The Chinese experience* [Television special series]. Washington, DC: Public Broadcasting Service.

Nava, R. G. (2001). *Holistic education: Pedagogy of universal love.* Brandon, VT: Foundation for Educational Renewal.

Takaki, R. (1998). *A history of Asian Americans: Strangers from a different shore.* Boston: Little, Brown.

Tong, R. P. (1998). *Feminist thought* (2nd ed.). Boulder, Co: Westview Press.

Walsh, R. (1999). *Essential spirituality.* New York: John Wiley.

Weinberg, M. (1997). *Asian-American education: Historical background and current realities.* Mahwah, NJ: Erlbaum.

Wong, J. S. (1989). *Fifth Chinese daughter.* Seattle: University of Washington Press.

EDITORS AND CONTRIBUTORS

Nina Asher is an assistant professor in Curriculum and Instruction and Women's and Gender Studies at Louisiana State University. She has published in the areas of postcolonial and feminist theory in education, Asian American education, and critical perspectives on multiculturalism.

Gulbahar H. Beckett is an assistant professor of Sociolinguistics at the University of Cincinnati. She earned her Ph.D. from the University of British Columbia, Vancouver, Canada. Gulbahar has published in such journals as *TESOL Quarterly, Modern Language Journal,* the *Canadian Modern Language Review, TESL Canada Journal, English Language Teaching Journal,* and *Journal of Asian Pacific Communication.* Her second book (coedited with Paul Chamness Miller), titled *Project-Based Learning in Second Language Education: Past, Present, and Future,* will be published by Information Age Publishing in 2006.

Yan Guo received her Ph.D. from the University of British Columbia, Vancouver, Canada, and is an assistant professor in the Teaching English as a Second Language (TESL) program in the Faculty of Education at the University of Calgary, Canada. She teaches courses in second language learning and English as a Second Language (ESL) special topics. Her research interests include intercultural communication, second language acquisition and identity, second language writing, minority parent involvement, content-based ESL teaching, discourse analysis, diversity in teaching and learning, and cultural differences in acquiring essential skills.

Hsiu-Zu Ho is professor of Education and Psychology in the Gevirtz Graduate School of Education at the University of California, Santa Barbara. Her earlier work focused on developmental behavioral genetic research in the areas of reading disability, spatial cognition, and gender-related issues in cognitive development. Her current research focuses on individual differences in academic achievement with particular consideration of cultural and gender variations in a range of educational settings both locally and internationally.

Shirley Hune currently serves as associate dean in the Graduate Division at the University of California, Los Angeles. She is also professor of Urban Planning in the School of Public Affairs, and she is a faculty affiliate of the Asian American Studies Department and the Center for the Study of Women at UCLA. Among her recent publications is *Asian/Pacific Islander American Women: A Historical Anthology*, edited with Gail M. Nomura (New York University Press, 2003).

Ryuko Kubota is associate professor in the School of Education and the Department of Asian Studies at the University of North Carolina at Chapel Hill. She is involved in foreign language teaching and second language teacher education. Her research interests include culture and politics in second language education and critical pedagogies. Her publications have appeared in journals such as *Canadian Modern Language Review, Foreign Language Annals, Journal of Second Language Writing, TESOL Quarterly*, and *World Englishes*.

Jaekyung Lee is assistant professor of Education at the University at Buffalo. Lee is a former National Academy of Education postdoctoral fellow, and his research also has been supported by the National Science Foundation and the U.S. Department of Education. His current research focuses on the issues of educational equity, particularly closing the achievement gaps among different racial and social groups. He is the author of many publications, including an influential article in *Educational Researcher* on racial achievement gaps.

Guofang Li is an assistant professor of Education at the University at Buffalo. Her research interests include home and community literacy practices of immigrant and minority groups, the interrelationship between minority literacy practices and mainstream schooling, and second language and literacy education. Her recent publications include two books: *East Is East, West Is West? Home Literacy, Culture, and Schooling* (Peter Lang, 2002), and *Culturally Contested Pedagogy: Battles of Literacy and Schooling between Mainstream Teachers and Asian Immigrant Parents* (SUNY Press, 2005).

Xiaoping Liang received her Ph.D. from the University of British Columbia, Vancouver, Canada, and is an assistant professor in the Department of Linguistics at California State University, Long Beach. She teaches courses in Teaching English as a Second Language (TESL) methodology, TESL practicum, second language curriculum development, language acquisition, and research methodology. Her research interests include second language classroom discourse and socialization, academic discourse development in the first and second languages, bilingual classroom code-switching, and language attitudes and cultural identities.

Angel Lin is an associate professor in the Department of English and Communication, City University of Hong Kong. She works in the areas of critical discourse analysis, urban and school ethnography, feminist cultural studies, and postcolonial studies. Her research articles have appeared in *TESOL Quarterly*; *Linguistics and Education*; the *International Journal of the Sociology of Language*; *Journal of Pragmatics*; *Curriculum Inquiry*; *Language, Culture and Curriculum*; and *Journal of Language, Identity and Education*.

Jing Lin is an associate professor at University of Maryland, College Park. She has done extensive research on Chinese education, culture, and society. She is the author of four books: *The Red Guards' Path to Violence* (1991), *Education in Post-Mao China* (1993), *The Opening of the Chinese Mind* (1994), and *Social Transformation and Private Education in China* (1999). Her fifth book, *School for Love: Education in the 21st Century*, will be published in 2005.

Chalsa M. Loo is a clinical psychologist in private practice in Hawaii and a clinical research psychologist at the National Center for Post-Traumatic Stress Disorder with the U.S. Department of Veterans Affairs, Pacific Islands Health Care System in Honolulu. She is the author of *Chinatown* (Praeger/Greenwood, 1991) and *Chinese America* (Sage, 1998) and is the 1991 recipient of the Asian American Psychological Association Distinguished Contribution award. She serves as an expert witness on civil and criminal cases involving sexual harassment/assault and worker compensation.

Suhanthie Motha is a Sri Lankan–born Australian who currently practices in the United States. Her research explores the complexity of identity, power, language, and pedagogy in second language learning. She teaches in the graduate programs in Teaching English as a Second Language (TESL) and Teacher Education at the University of Maryland, College Park.

Piyasuda Pangsapa is an assistant professor in the Department of Women's Studies at the University at Buffalo. She is director of the Global Citizenship

Concentration in Women's Studies and an affiliated faculty member of the Asian Studies Program. Her areas of specialization include gender and development, women and work, globalization and social movements. Fluent in both Thai and English, she spent one year conducting ethnographic fieldwork on women textile factory workers in Bangkok, Thailand.

Judith Preissle is the 2001 Distinguished Aderhold Professor in the qualitative research program at the College of Education, University of Georgia (UGA), and an affiliated faculty member of UGA's Institute for Women's Studies. She teaches, researches, and writes in educational anthropology, qualitative research, and ethics. She shares two miniature schnauzers and two Chinese pugs with a computer network manager at UGA. All five share her interest in philosophical quandaries.

Xue Lan Rong is an associate professor at the University of North Carolina at Chapel Hill. Her areas of research include education, immigration, cultures and race/ethnicity, and international education focusing on China. Her publications include "The Continuing Decline in Asian American Teachers" in *American Educational Research Journal* (with Preissle, 1997), "Educating Immigrant Students" (with Preissle, 1998), and "The Effects of Immigrant Generation and Ethnicity of Educational Attainment among Young African and Caribbean Blacks in the United States" in *Harvard Educational Review* (with Brown, 2001).

Keiko Komiya Samimy is associate professor in foreign- and second-language education at Ohio State University where she coordinates the master's, the master's of education, and the doctoral programs. Her research interests include empowerment of nonnative English-speaking professionals, World Englishes, and effective variables and the willingness to communicate.

Eunai Kim Shrake is an assistant professor in the Department of Asian American Studies at California State University at Northridge, where she teaches courses on multicultural education with a special emphasis on Asian American students and their culture. She has a Ph.D. in social sciences and comparative education from the University of California at Los Angeles. Her research focuses on cross-cultural studies in the areas of parenting styles, ethnic identity, and adolescent problems.

Wendy Wang is an associate professor of English as a Second Language/ Teaching English to Speakers of Other Languages (ESL/TESOL) at Eastern

Michigan University. She has taught English as a Foreign Language (EFL), ESL, and English for Speakers of Other Languages (ESOL) teacher education courses in China, Canada, and New York state. Her current research interests are pre- and in-service teacher learning in second language teacher education, and issues related to nonnative English-speaking TESOL professionals.

Shelley Wong is a fifth-generation Chinese American from California. She is an associate professor at George Mason University in Fairfax, Virginia, in bilingual/multicultural/English as a Second Language (ESL) education. She has taught in secondary schools, adult schools, colleges, universities, and teacher education programs in Hong Kong, Los Angeles, New York, the Washington, D.C., area, and Columbus, Ohio. Her research interests are dialogic approaches to Teaching English as a Second Language (TESL)/ Bilingual Education, sociocultural approaches to literacy, and critical multiculturalism.

Jianhua Zhang received her bachelor of science degree from the University of Science and Technology of China and came to the United States in 1985. She got her Ph.D. degree in 1991 at the University of Texas Southwestern Medical Center at Dallas. She worked in the Whitehead Institute for Biomedical Research from 1991 to 1995 as a postdoctoral associate. She joined the faculty in the Department of Cell Biology, Neurobiology, and Anatomy at the University of Cincinnati College of Medicine in 1996.

Guichun Zong is an assistant professor of social studies education at Georgia State University. Deeply influenced by her trips to the USS *Arizona* Memorial in Pearl Harbor; the Holocaust Museum in Washington, D.C.; the Nanjing Massacre Memorial in Nanjing, China; and the Hiroshima Peace Park of Japan, Guichun centers her scholarly interest on developing pedagogies that enhance global awareness and cross-cultural understanding. Her writings have appeared in such journals as *Social Education, Trends and Issues*, and *Theory and Research in Social Education*. She is currently completing her manuscript titled "Which Half of the Sky? Women in Chinese Middle School History Textbooks."

INDEX

Qi, 297

Race. *See also* Racial discrimination; Racial
    stereotype
    discourses of in higher education, 125–127
    discussion of as dangerous, 69–70
    as social construction, 17–18, 58
      "model minority", 18–20
Racial discrimination. *See also* Racial
    stereotype; Racism
    affecting APAs, 26
    experiences of, 58–60, 140, 145–146,
      156–160, 172–173, 245
    between minorities, 175–176
Racial stereotype. *See also* Ethnic stereotype;
    Racism; Sexual stereotype
    competency expectations and, 27, 32, 33,
      52–53, 91–92, 127–128, 154–155
    model minority stereotype as, 183–187, 254
    pressure to perform as, 26, 65, 173–174,
      182–183, 191
    "unpacking", 173
    women of color as "angry" and "sulky",
      74–75
Racial theory, 17–18
Racism, 179, 182. *See also* Racial
    discrimination
    confronting in classroom, 192
    "dysconscious racism", 126–127
    "racist love", 175
Ramamurthy, Priti, 198, 199
Red Azalea, 253
Religion, 173–174, 273, 298
Research. *See also* Grants; Publication;
    Research and scholarship
    Asian female scholarly contributions,
      197–200
    collaboration in, 268–272
    collaboration in
      demographer-ethnographer
      relationship, 279–283
    in general, 268–272
    mentoring and support for, 107–109
    on minority female scholars, 118–119,
      205–207
    natural science research, 240–242

non-acceptance of
    classroom research, 62, 73–74
    effect on promotion, 137, 138, 157, 159
    women's studies, 31, 78
    as "site of resistance", 170
Research and scholarship. *See also*
    Promotion; Tenure
    committee review of, 62
Resources, 241, 243
Respect, 77, 122, 181, 220, 234, 289
Risk, ethic of risk, 76–77
Rogers, Carl, 108
Role. *See also* Identity; Role model;
    Stereotype
    gender role, dual references to, 129–130
    managing multiple roles, 106–107, 112–114
    "role overload", 112
    multiple discourses, 118–131
      dual references to gender roles, 129–130
      native/nonnative English skills, 127–129
      race and gender, 125–127
    "role continuance", 107
    role reversal, 123–125
Role model, 33, 40. *See also* Mentor
    effect on career choice, 48
    husband as, 109–110
    lack of role models, 53
    mentor as, 107–109, 170, 267
    teacher as role model, 98

Safe haven, 196, 201, 202, 207. *See also*
    Women's studies
Safety, 70, 77
    political safety, 261
    "safely uncomfortable", 76–77
Sakhi, 166–167
San Diego State University, 197
Sayonara, 188
Scattered Hegemonics (Grewal), 199
Schizophrenia, 180. *See also* Marginalization;
    Masking
"Scholar on the periphery, A" (Sasaki), 114
Science major. *See also* Science, math,
    engineering
    GPA by race and gender, 46f
    men's choice for, 43, 44, 47–48